W9-CTW-402

CONSTITUTIONAL LAW
Cases and Commentary

ISBN 0-8273-7187-X

90000

9 780827 371873

Paralegal Titles from Delmar Publishers

Legal Writing, 2nd ed., Steve Barber, 1997
Administration of Wills, Trusts, and Estates, 2nd ed., Gordon W. Brown, 1997
Basics of Legal Document Preparation, Robert R. Cummins, 1997
Constitutional Law: Cases and Commentary, Daniel E. Hall, 1997
Criminal Procedure and the Constitution, Daniel E. Hall, 1997
Survey of Criminal Law, 2nd ed., Daniel E. Hall, 1997
California Estate Administration, Zella Mack, 1997
Torts and Personal Injury Law, 2nd ed., Cathy J. Okrent, William R. Buckley, 1997
California Criminal Law and Procedure, William D. Raymond, Jr., Daniel E. Hall, 1997
The Law of Corporations, Partnerships, and Sole Proprietorships, 2nd ed.,
    Angela Schneeman, 1997
Texas Legal Research, 2nd ed., Pamela R. Tepper, Peggy N. Kerley, 1997

Legal Research, Steve Barber, Mark A. McCormick, 1996
Wills, Estates, and Trusts, Jay H. Gingrich, 1996
Criminal Law and Procedure, 2nd ed., Daniel E. Hall, 1996
Introduction to Environmental Law, Harold Hickok, 1996
Civil Litigation, 2nd ed., Peggy N. Kerley, Joanne Banker Hames, Paul A. Sukys, 1996
Client Accounting for the Law Office, Elaine M. Langston, 1996
Law Office Management, 2nd ed., Jonathan S. Lynton, Terry Mick Lyndall,
    Donna Masinter, 1996
Foundations of Law: Cases, Commentary, and Ethics, 2nd ed., Ransford C. Pyle, 1996
Administrative Law and Procedure, Elizabeth C. Richardson, 1996
Legal Research and Writing, David J. Smith, 1996

Legal Research and Writing, Carol M. Bast, 1995
Federal Taxation, Susan G. Covins, 1995
Everything You Need to Know About Being a Legal Assistant, Chere B. Estrin, 1995
Paralegals in New York Law, Eric M. Gansberg, 1995
Ballentine's Legal Dictionary and Thesaurus, Jonathan S. Lynton, 1995
Legal Terminology with Flashcards, Cathy J. Okrent, 1995
Wills, Trusts, and Estate Administration for Paralegals, Mark A. Stewart, 1995
The Law of Contracts and the Uniform Commercial Code, Pamela R. Tepper, 1995
Life Outside the Law Firm: Non-Traditional Careers for Paralegals, Karen Treffinger, 1995

An Introduction to Paralegal Studies, David G. Cooper, Michael J. Gibson, 1994
Administrative Law, Daniel E. Hall, 1994
Ballentine's Law Dictionary: Legal Assistant Edition, Jack G. Handler, 1994
The Law of Real Property, Michael P. Kearns, 1994
Ballentine's Thesaurus for Legal Research and Writing, Jonathan S. Lynton, 1994
Legal Ethics and Professional Responsibility, Jonathan S. Lynton, Terri Mick Lyndall, 1994
Criminal Law for Paralegals, Daniel J. Markey, Jr., Mary Queen Donnelly, 1994
Family Law, Ransford C. Pyle, 1994
Paralegals in American Law: Introduction to Paralegalism, Angela Schneeman, 1994
Intellectual Property, Richard Stim, 1994

CONSTITUTIONAL LAW
Cases and Commentary

Daniel E. Hall

Delmar Publishers

an International Thomson Publishing company I T P®

Albany · Bonn · Boston · Cincinnati · Detroit · London · Madrid
Melbourne · Mexico City · New York · Pacific Grove · Paris · San Francisco
Singapore · Tokyo · Toronto · Washington

NOTICE TO THE READER

the products described herein or perform any independent analysis in con-
ntained herein. Publisher does not assume, and expressly disclaims, any obli-
than that provided to it by the manufacturer.

The reader is expressly warned to consider and adopt all safety precautions that might be indicated by the activities herein and to avoid all potential hazards. By following the instructions contained herein, the reader willingly assumes all risks in connection with such instructions.

The publisher makes no representations or warranties of any kind, including but not limited to, the warranties of fitness for particular purpose or merchantability, nor are any such representations implied with respect to the material set forth herein, and the publisher takes no responsibility with respect to such material. The publisher shall not be liable for any special, consequential, or exemplary damages resulting, in whole or in part, from the reader's use of, or reliance upon, this material.

Cover Design: Douglas J. Hyldelund
Delmar Staff:
Acquisitions Editor: Christopher Anzalone
Developmental Editor: Jeffrey D. Litton
Project Editor: Eugenia L. Orlandi
Production Coordinator: Jennifer Gaines
Art & Design Coordinator: Douglas J. Hyldelund

COPYRIGHT © 1997
By Delmar Publishers
a division of International Thomson Publishing
The ITP logo is a trademark under license.
Printed in the United States of America

For more information, contact:

Delmar Publishers
3 Columbia Circle, Box 15015
Albany, New York 12212-5015

International Thomson Publishing–Europe
Berkshire House
168-173 High Holborn
London WC1V 7AA
England

Thomas Nelson Australia
102 Dodds Street
South Melbourne, 3205
Victoria, Australia

Nelson Canada
1120 Birchmount Road
Scarborough, Ontario
Canada M1K 5G4

International Thomson Editores
Campos Eliseos 385, Piso 7
Col Polanco
11560 Mexico D F Mexico

International Thomson Publishing GmbH
Königswinterer Strasse 418
53227 Bonn
Germany

International Thomson Publishing Asia
221 Henderson Road
#05 - 10 Henderson Building
Singapore 0315

International Thomson Publishing–Japan
Hirakawacho Kyowa Building, 3F
2-2-1 Hirakawacho
Chiyoda-ku, Tokyo 102
Japan

1 2 3 4 5 6 7 8 9 10 XXX 01 00 99 98 97 96

Library of Congress Cataloging-in-Publication Data

Hall, Daniel (Daniel E.)
    Constitutional law : cases and commentary / Daniel E. Hall.
      p. cm.
    Includes bibliographical references and index.
    ISBN 0-8273-7187-X
    1. United States—Constitution law—Cases. I. Title.
KF4549.H278 1997
342.73—dc20
                                   96-16180
                                   CIP

CONTENTS

IIII CHAPTER 4:   The Judiciary: Jurisdiction 115

IIII CHAPTER 5:   Congress 185

IIII CHAPTER 6:   The Presidency 237

IIII CHAPTER 7:   Administrative Agencies in the Constitutional Scheme 283

IIII CHAPTER 8:   Contemporary Federalism: The State and Federal Relationship 315

IIII Appendices

DELMAR PUBLISHERS INC.

 AND

LAWYERS COOPERATIVE PUBLISHING

ARE PLEASED TO ANNOUNCE THEIR PARTNERSHIP TO CO-PUBLISH COLLEGE TEXTBOOKS FOR PARALEGAL EDUCATION.

DELMAR, WITH OFFICES AT ALBANY, NEW YORK, IS A PROFESSIONAL EDUCATION PUBLISHER. DELMAR PUBLISHES QUALITY EDUCATIONAL TEXTBOOKS TO PREPARE AND SUPPORT INDIVIDUALS FOR LIFE SKILLS AND SPECIFIC OCCUPATIONS.

LAWYERS COOPERATIVE PUBLISHING (LCP), WITH OFFICES AT ROCHESTER, NEW YORK, HAS BEEN THE LEADING PUBLISHER OF ANALYTICAL LEGAL INFORMATION FOR OVER 100 YEARS. IT IS THE PUBLISHER OF SUCH REKNOWNED LEGAL ENCYCLOPEDIAS AS **AMERICAN LAW REPORTS, AMERICAN JURISPRUDENCE, UNITED STATES CODE SERVICE, LAWYERS EDITION,** AS WELL AS OTHER MATERIAL, AND FEDERAL- AND STATE-SPECIFIC PUBLICATIONS. THESE PUBLICATIONS HAVE BEEN DESIGNED TO WORK TOGETHER IN THE DAY-TO-DAY PRACTICE OF LAW AS AN INTEGRATED SYSTEM IN WHAT IS CALLED THE ''TOTAL CLIENT-SERVICE LIBRARY®'' (TCSL®). EACH LCP PUBLICATION IS COMPLETE WITHIN ITSELF AS TO SUBJECT COVERAGE, YET ALL HAVE COMMON FEATURES AND EXTENSIVE CROSS-REFERENCING TO PROVIDE LINKAGE FOR HIGHLY EFFICIENT LEGAL RESEARCH INTO VIRTUALLY ANY MATTER AN ATTORNEY MIGHT BE CALLED UPON TO HANDLE.

INFORMATION IN ALL PUBLICATIONS IS CAREFULLY AND CONSTANTLY MONITORED TO KEEP PACE WITH AND REFLECT EVENTS IN THE LAW AND IN SOCIETY. UPDATING AND SUPPLEMENTAL INFORMATION IS TIMELY AND PROVIDED CONVENIENTLY.

FOR FURTHER REFERENCE, SEE:

AMERICAN JURISPRUDENCE 2D: AN ENCYCLOPEDIC TEXT COVERAGE OF THE COMPLETE BODY OF STATE AND FEDERAL LAW.

AM JUR LEGAL FORMS 2D: A COMPILATION OF BUSINESS AND LEGAL FORMS DEALING WITH A VARIETY OF SUBJECT MATTERS.

AM JUR PLEADING AND PRACTICE FORMS, REV: MODEL PRACTICE FORMS FOR EVERY STAGE OF A LEGAL PROCEEDING.

AM JUR PROOF OF FACTS: A SERIES OF ARTICLES THAT GUIDE THE READER IN DETERMINING WHICH FACTS ARE ESSENTIAL TO A CASE AND HOW TO PROVE THEM.

AM JUR TRIALS: A SERIES OF ARTICLES DISCUSSING EVERY ASPECT OF PARTICULAR SETTLEMENTS AND TRIALS WRITTEN BY 180 CONSULTING SPECIALISTS.

UNITED STATES CODE SERVICE: A COMPLETE AND AUTHORITATIVE ANNOTATED FEDERAL CODE THAT FOLLOWS THE EXACT LANGUAGE OF THE STATUTES AT LARGE AND DIRECTS YOU TO THE COURT AND AGENCY DECISIONS CONSTRUING EACH PROVISION.

ALR AND ALR FEDERAL: SERIES OF ANNOTATIONS PROVIDING IN-DEPTH ANALYSES OF ALL THE CASE LAW ON PARTICULAR LEGAL ISSUES.

U.S. SUPREME COURT REPORTS, L ED 2D: EVERY REPORTED U.S. SUPREME COURT DECISION PLUS IN-DEPTH DISCUSSIONS OF LEADING ISSUES.

FEDERAL PROCEDURE, L ED: A COMPREHENSIVE, A-Z TREATISE ON FEDERAL PROCEDURE—CIVIL, CRIMINAL, AND ADMINISTRATIVE.

FEDERAL PROCEDURAL FORMS, L ED: STEP-BY-STEP GUIDANCE FOR DRAFTING FORMS FOR FEDERAL COURT OR FEDERAL AGENCY PROCEEDINGS.

FEDERAL RULES SERVICE, 2D AND 3D: REPORTS DECISIONS FROM ALL LEVELS OF THE FEDERAL SYSTEM INTERPRETING THE FEDERAL RULES OF CIVIL PROCEDURE AND THE FEDERAL RULES OF APPELLATE PROCEDURE.

FEDERAL RULES DIGEST, 3D: ORGANIZES HEADNOTES FOR THE DECISIONS REPORTED IN FEDERAL RULES SERVICE ACCORDING TO THE NUMBERING SYSTEMS OF THE FEDERAL RULES OF CIVIL PROCEDURE AND THE FEDERAL RULES OF APPELLATE PROCEDURE.

FEDERAL RULES OF EVIDENCE SERVICE: REPORTS DECISIONS FROM ALL LEVELS OF THE FEDERAL SYSTEM INTERPRETING THE FEDERAL RULES OF EVIDENCE.

FEDERAL RULES OF EVIDENCE NEWS

FEDERAL PROCEDURE RULES SERVICE

FEDERAL TRIAL HANDBOOK, 2D

FORM DRAFTING CHECKLISTS: AM JUR PRACTICE GUIDE

GOVERNMENT CONTRACTS: PROCEDURES AND FORMS

HOW TO GO DIRECTLY INTO YOUR OWN COMPUTERIZED SOLO PRACTICE WITHOUT MISSING A MEAL (OR A BYTE)

JONES ON EVIDENCE, CIVIL AND CRIMINAL, 7TH

LITIGATION CHECKLISTS: AM JUR PRACTICE GUIDE

MEDICAL LIBRARY, LAWYERS EDITION

MEDICAL MALPRACTICE—ALR CASES AND ANNOTATIONS

MODERN APPELLATE PRACTICE: FEDERAL AND STATE CIVIL APPEALS

MODERN CONSTITUTIONAL LAW

NEGOTIATION AND SETTLEMENT

PATTERN DEPOSITION CHECKLISTS, 2D

QUALITY OF LIFE DAMAGES: CRITICAL ISSUES AND PROOFS

SHEPARD'S CITATIONS FOR ALR

SUCCESSFUL TECHNIQUES FOR CIVIL TRIALS, 2D

STORIES ET CETERA—A COUNTRY LAWYER LOOKS AT LIFE AND THE LAW

SUMMARY OF AMERICAN LAW

THE TRIAL LAWYER'S BOOK: PREPARING AND WINNING CASES

TRIAL PRACTICE CHECKLISTS

2000 CLASSIC LEGAL QUOTATIONS

WILLISTON ON CONTRACTS, 3D AND 4TH

FEDERAL RULES OF EVIDENCE DIGEST: ORGANIZES HEAD-NOTES FOR THE DECISIONS REPORTED IN FEDERAL RULES OF EVIDENCE SERVICE ACCORDING TO THE NUMBERING SYSTEM OF THE FEDERAL RULES OF EVIDENCE.

ADMINISTRATIVE LAW: PRACTICE AND PROCEDURE

AGE DISCRIMINATION: CRITICAL ISSUES AND PROOFS

ALR CRITICAL ISSUES: DRUNK DRIVING PROSECUTIONS

ALR CRITICAL ISSUES: FREEDOM OF INFORMATION ACTS

ALR CRITICAL ISSUES: TRADEMARKS

ALR CRITICAL ISSUES: WRONGFUL DEATH

AMERICANS WITH DISABILITIES: PRACTICE AND COMPLIANCE MANUAL

ATTORNEYS' FEES

BALLENTINE'S LAW DICTIONARY

CONSTITUTIONAL LAW DESKBOOK

CONSUMER AND BORROWER PROTECTION: AM JUR PRACTICE GUIDE

CONSUMER CREDIT: ALR ANNOTATIONS

DAMAGES: ALR ANNOTATIONS

EMPLOYEE DISMISSAL: CRITICAL ISSUES AND PROOFS

ENVIRONMENTAL LAW: ALR ANNOTATIONS

EXPERT WITNESS CHECKLISTS

EXPERT WITNESSES IN CIVIL TRIALS

FORFEITURES: ALR ANNOTATIONS

FEDERAL LOCAL COURT RULES

FEDERAL LOCAL COURT FORMS

FEDERAL CRIMINAL LAW AND PROCEDURE: ALR ANNOTATIONS

FEDERAL EVIDENCE

FEDERAL LITIGATION DESK SET: FORMS AND ANALYSIS

PREFACE

When the prospect of authoring a constitutional law text was first proposed to me, I experienced both excitement and trepidation. I was excited because I believe this subject to be of great importance. It is, in my opinion, particularly important to the undergraduate student. I continue to be surprised that undergraduate legal studies and political science programs teach many subjects of law and government without first providing an education in the fundamental law of the United States. I have found it difficult, for example, to teach federal and state jurisdiction in civil and criminal procedure classes to students who are not familiar with federalism. In the end, I must admit, I relished the project because I love the subject. This project is a milestone, a culmination, to my previous publications in this series, *Survey of Criminal Law, Criminal Law and Procedure, Administrative Law,* and *Criminal Procedure and The Constitution,* all of which have constitutional foundations.

I experienced trepidation because it was the most daunting project proposed to me. The subject can be dense, abstract, and theoretical. My challenge was to write a text that is understandable to the undergraduate student without oversimplifying the subject.

The text is organized into eight chapters. The first chapter provides the student with a brief historical framework from which to understand our Constitution. The Articles of Confederation, the Philadelphia Convention, and the ratification debates are featured in this chapter.

From the historical chapter the text moves to a discussion of basic governmental structures. Federalism, separation of powers, and checks and balances are introduced. The precise relationship between the federal and state governments (i.e., intergovernmental immunities) is explored in a later chapter.

Chapters 3, 4, 5, and 6 are devoted to detailed discussions of the three branches of government. Because of the importance of the judiciary to legal studies students, two chapters examine that branch. Chapter 3 discusses the structure of federal courts, their role in our nation, and the power of judicial review. The fourth chapter covers the jurisdiction of federal courts. Included in these chapters are discussions of how these principles apply to real cases with which the student may have contact. For example, the constitutional aspects of removal jurisdiction are examined.

The powers of Congress are the topic of Chapter 5 and presidential powers are discussed in Chapter 6. Election, impeachment, and duties are all discussed in these chapters.

Because of the importance of administrative agencies in the United States, Chapter 7 examines the creation of agencies, delegation of powers to agencies, and presidential and congressional control of agencies, as well as other contemporary topics.

Finally, Chapter 8 covers contemporary federalism. This chapter builds on the basic principles set out in Chapter 2 by examining specific issues, such as intergovernmental immunity and preemption. In addition, a complete discussion of the revival in state constitutional law is included.

The pedagogical features of my previous books have garnered favorable responses. Accordingly, I have included them herein. Legal terms are bolded and a glossary of those terms are included. Terms marked with a dagger are from *Ballentine's Legal Dictionary and Thesaurus;* these provide standard, general definitions to give students a grounding in typical legal terminology. More subject-specific definitions, tailored by the author for the context of this book, also help students in particular areas. Sidebars that discuss interesting related events or subjects appear throughout the book. The writing style is geared to the undergraduate student and illustrations are used to summarize and distill complex subjects. A new feature is the chapter introduction, *Amicus*. For lack of a better descriptive term, *Amicus* can be characterized as constitutional trivia; it is intended to provide a touch of constitutional history or political philosophy to the readings. Case questions that require a short answer or list of elements appear at the end of every chapter. Case problems that require greater analysis and critical thinking also appear at the close of every chapter. For the convenience of instructors, a test bank is also provided in the Instructor's Guide.

As is true of my other books in this series, the text can stand alone. That is, the instructor can remove the cases from the students' reading assignments without losing any blackletter law. Because of importance of case analysis to constitutional law, however, the case excerpts are bit longer than in other texts. Also, I provide the instructor with case briefs in the Instructor's Guide. The case law is current through early 1996.

This text is written for instructors and students. I value suggestions for additions, deletions, or changes from both groups. If you have such a suggestion for the next edition, please share it with me or a representative of Delmar Publishers.

ACKNOWLEDGMENTS

Several people assisted in the completion of this project. Carol Bast, colleague, friend, and scholar, wrote Appendix C on researching constitutional law. Two of my students, James Kirkpatrick and Martha Desjardins, provided valuable research assistance on a variety of topics. Both are now attending law school and will be honorable additions to the legal profession after graduation.

I also thank the reviewers who provided insightful comments and suggestions:

Clark Wheeler
    Santa Fe Community College
    Gainesville, FL

C. Suzanne Bailey
    Auburn University
    Montgomery, AL

Kathleen Jones
    Portland State University
    Lake Oswego, OR

Kathleen Urban
    Laramie Community College
    Cheyenne, WY

J.E. Barbee
    International Business College
    Lubbock, TX

Donald Lavanty
    Marymount University
    Arlington, VA

Michael Yates
    Missouri Southern State College
    Joplin, MO

Thomas Jackson
    Marywood College
    Scranton, PA

Finally, I express my gratitude to the Delmar and Graphics West personnel who worked on this project.

TABLE OF CASES

Note: **Boldface italics** indicate that the subject case is excerpted on the referenced pages.

CHAPTER 1

HISTORY OF
THE CONSTITUTION

§ 1.1 Constitutions and Rule of Law

This book is concerned with constitutional law. But what exactly is a constitution? *Ballentine's Legal Dictionary* defines *constitution* as "[t]he system of fundamental principles by which a nation ... is governed. A nation's constitution may be written or unwritten." In short, a constitution is fundamental law. In terms of a hierarchy, a constitution sits at the apex and all forms of law below it (statutes, ordinances, regulations, executive orders) must conform to it. Constitutional law is the foundation upon which government is built and other laws are created. Hence, an understanding of constitutional law is imperative in any law-related endeavor.

The influence of the United States Constitution is much broader than commonly realized. For example, the daily actions of police officers are guided by many constitutional provisions, such as the Fourth Amendment (prohibition of unreasonable searches and seizures). Attorneys, process servers, and legal assistants must contend with constitutional law in nearly every case. As examples, the due process guarantees of the Fifth and Fourteenth Amendments regulate service of process (especially on out-of-state defendants), the full faith and credit clause provides the law for enforcing foreign judgments, and many clients present cases that arise directly under the Constitution.

A constitution may be written or unwritten. The United States has a written constitution, whereas England has an unwritten one. In England, the rights of citizens are secured through the common law, customs, and several Acts of Parliament. There is no single constitutional document. Some commentators argue that England does not have a constitution, because Parliament is free to abolish all the rights enjoyed by the people. Others contend that these rights are so much a part of English society that they are secure against parliamentary intrusion. Today, most nations have written constitutions. The Constitution of the United States is the oldest written constitution in the world.

This book examines the law of the United States Constitution. Important historical and social influences are discussed, as are institutions (e.g., the United States Supreme Court), constitutional methodology, and case law. American constitutional law is commonly divided into two fields of study: one focusing on governmental powers and structures and another examining civil liberties. This text deals with the former.

In terms of development, legal systems and nations are often characterized as either adhering to rule of law or not. Rule of law is achieved in a legal system if the following elements are present:

1. There is fundamental law
2. that limits the power of government and
3. is enforceable by citizens.

The United States operates under rule of law because there is fundamental law (federal and state constitutions) that is enforceable by citizens in the courts through judicial review.

To fully appreciate why the framers of the United States Constitution selected the provisions they did, a brief historical foundation must be laid.

§ 1.2 Articles of Confederation

After the colonists arrived in what is now known as the United States, they established colonies. The original thirteen states were established from the geographical boundaries of these colonies. Although the states were largely autonomous and self-governing, they remained, ultimately, governed by England. Each state's governmental structure and relationship with England varied, but all shared common grievances with their mother country that led to the war for independence. Their declaration of independence was issued in 1776. Independence was won in 1781.

Even before independence was declared, the states had established a body to meet and address issues of national concern, the Continental Congress. The Continental Congress first met in Philadelphia on September 5, 1774. It operated from this date until 1781. This organization, though national in representation, did not have the authority to make binding laws. Its authority was primarily limited to raising an army and conducting diplomacy.

By the time the Declaration of Independence was adopted, there had been discussions in the Continental Congress concerning the adoption of a constitution to formally recognize a confederacy of the thirteen colonies. On June 7, 1776, Richard Henry Lee, a delegate to the Congress from Virginia, introduced a resolution that declared the "United

Colonies" to be "free and independent states, that they are absolved from all allegiance to the British Crown, and that all political connection between them and the State of Great Britain is, and ought to be, totally dissolved." Additionally, the resolution called for the development of a plan of confederation to be submitted to the states.[1] This resolution was not adopted, but the Congress adopted the Declaration of Independence, which was largely drafted by Thomas Jefferson, on July 4, 1776.

It was not until 1781 that the colonies adopted the Articles of Confederation and Perpetual Union, the first constitution of the United States. Under the Articles, the Continental Congress was disbanded and replaced by the Confederation Congress. Although the new Congress had more authority than its predecessor, the states continued to be the most powerful political entities. It was proclaimed in the Articles that "[e]ach state retains its sovereignty, freedom and independence, and every power, jurisdiction and right, which is not expressly delegated to the united states, in Congress assembled." Politically, the United States was a loose union of independent and sovereign states and members of the Congress were little more than ambassadors representing their respective states. As expressly stated in the Articles, the states entered into a "firm league of friendship."[2]

It was not many years before this league proved unworkable. The states were distant from one another. In an age without modern travel and technological means to disseminate information, this was critical. But they were distant in more ways than miles; they differed in history, culture, and politics. The result was parochialism, localism, and an interest in empowering the states rather than the national government. In the end, the states proved to be too independent and powerful; the national government too dependent and powerless.

Under the Articles of Confederation, the national government was responsible for negotiating treaties with foreign governments. That authority, however, was thwarted by the authority of the states to tax imports and exports, regardless of any treaties negotiated by the national government. Although the national government had the authority to declare war, it had no authority to establish a standing army. If it declared war, it could enlist volunteers, but lacked the power of conscription. It could request the assistance of state militias, but the states could refuse. Even more, funding for war efforts came from the states.[3]

Also, each state could prohibit the export and import of goods. The consequence was inconsistent and often competing commercial laws between the states. For the same reasons, foreign governments and merchants were discouraged from trading with the United States.

Jealousies between the states led to factionalism. Nine of the thirteen states had their own navies. Territorial disputes, as well as disputes over the authority to control the nation's waterways, plagued the nation.[4] Many of the states were engaged in economic war with one another and there were concerns that actual war would destroy the union.

The national government was clearly subservient to the states financially. Specifically, it did not have the authority to raise revenues directly from its citizens. The Articles provided that the states were to make contributions to the national treasury. However, the contributions were to be raised by action of each state and the national government lacked the authority to compel a state to contribute. As a result, the national government suffered financial difficulties because many of the states were regularly in arrears in their payments. As a result, the national government itself could not pay debts it owed to foreigners and citizens.

Governmental structure under the Articles was also confused. There was no independent executive. The President of the Congress served as the nation's highest executive officer, but the role of the president was not clearly understood and confusion between legislative and executive authority resulted. Many executive responsibilities were performed by legislative committees rather than the president—a practice that proved to be ineffective.

There was no national judiciary, except that the Congress selected four judges to hear cases in the Territory northwest of the Ohio River and a Court of Capture heard appeals from the state courts in admiralty cases.[5] Otherwise, there was no national court to bring the national perspective to litigation or to develop a uniform national jurisprudence.

The private sector was also affected. Inflation was high and the laws governing commerce differed from state to state. Inconsistent and often competing laws regulating interstate commerce impeded economic development. Again, the national government was virtually powerless to remedy the nation's ills. Lack of confidence in the future of the nation resulted in little investment and a significant decrease in the value of land.

In 1786, the nation's economic problems provoked a group of radical farmers in Massachusetts, led by Daniel Shays, to rebel against local government. The rebels, angered by the poor state of the economy, the imprisonment of small farmers who could not pay their debts, and court-ordered land forfeitures, took control of a number of courts and prevented them from operating. There was no national authority to defeat the rebellion and initially many local authorities were reluctant to become involved. Eventually, **Shays' Rebellion** was quelled by a

---

TERMS

Shays' Rebellion   Daniel Shays, a veteran of the American Revolutionary War, and a group of fellow farmers rebelled in protest of economic conditions. This incident was cited by many as justification for abandoning the

Amicus

The First President of the United States and the First Constitution of the United States

Who was the first President of the United States? Most people would say that George Washington was the first President. However, this is a matter of perspective.

The first national government maintained by the colonists was that under the Continental Congress. On September 5, 1774, Peyton Randolph was the first man elected president of that body; thus, he could be considered the first President of the United States.

John Hanson is another possible first President. He was the first President elected under the Articles of Confederation, although he had little authority in this position.

Finally, the third possible first President is George Washington, the first person elected President under the current Constitution of the United States.

The current Constitution is not this nation's first. The Articles of Confederation and Perpetual Union, commonly known as the Articles, were adopted in 1781. In most people's eyes, this was the nation's first constitution. However, the colonists operated under British rule prior to winning independence. Although the British do not have a single document expounding their fundamental law, they do have a body of law that, when taken together, constitutes the British "Constitution." During this period, the colonists were subject to and received the benefits of the British Constitution. Arguably, then, the nation's first fundamental law was that of England.

Finally, it has been asserted that the fundamental laws of the several Native American nations represent the true first constitutions of this land.   ▥

---

privately financed (merchants and creditors), state-legislature-authorized militia, but it was further proof that the nation's problems needed to be addressed.

The inadequacies of the Articles became critical. James Madison stated that the "insufficiency of present confederation [threatened the] preservation of the union." He continued, "we may indeed with propriety be said to have reached almost the last stage of national humiliation. There is scarcely anything that can wound the pride or degrade the character of an independent nation which we do not experience."[6] Madison was speaking for many. The mood of the nation

TERMS

Articles of Confederation, the theory being that a stronger national government could provide better economic conditions and that a national military would be most effective in defeating rebellions.

was one for change in order to save the union. The proponents of change recognized the problem to be the weakness of the national government. However, the colonists had also learned a lesson about unchecked centralized power while under British rule: it can be unfair and arbitrary.

These two experiences—first, the excesses of British power; and second, the inadequacies of the Confederation—resulted in a reserved and cautious attitude in favor of strengthening the national government. Some people, notably George Washington, Alexander Hamilton, James Madison, John Marshall, and John Hancock, favored a strong national government and thus are known as **federalists**. There were also people who opposed the creation of a strong national government. This group, known as the **antifederalists**, had among its ranks Thomas Jefferson, Luther Martin, George Mason, and Patrick Henry.

§ 1.3   Philadelphia Convention

The prevailing attitude was that a stronger national government could provide economic and political stability for the young nation. For several years the Congress had called for an increase in national authority to cure the nation's ills. James Madison zealously fought for a constitutional convention. The highly respected George Washington bitterly complained of the impotence of the national government. But the states were reluctant to give up any power, and this caused delay. Finally, there came a chance to mend the nation's problems.

The Delegates and Their Mandate

In 1786, a group of prominent Americans met in Annapolis, Maryland, to discuss interstate commerce issues. The meeting had been urged by the Virginia state legislature and was supported by many politicians

---

TERMS

federalist   1. A person who supports a strong, centralized government. 2. A political party that advocates a strong, centralized government.
antifederalist   1. A person who opposes establishment of a strong, centralized government in favor of local control. 2. A party that opposes establishment of a strong, centralized government in favor of local control.

from other states. However, little occurred, as only five states were represented. One important product did result from this meeting, however. Alexander Hamilton submitted, and the body approved, a recommendation to the Continental Congress that a convention be held to examine the problems of the nation and its constitution. The Continental Congress did approve such a meeting.

The congressional resolution approving of the convention read, in part, "Resolved that ... on the second Monday in May next a Convention of delegates who shall have been appointed by the several states be held at Philadelphia for the sole and express purpose of revising the Articles of Confederation." There was no mandate to the delegates to create a new constitution. Even more, they were representatives of the states and, arguably, not the people. In spite of this, they chose to act as representatives of the people. Therefore, they chose to begin the new constitution with "We the People," rather than the suggested "We the States."

Philadelphia was an appropriate location for such an auspicious gathering. Philadelphia was where the first Continental Congress met, where George Washington was appointed Commander of the Continental Army by the Second Continental Congress, and where two important documents (the Declaration of Independence and the Articles of Confederation) had been signed. Philadelphia would add the new constitution to its impressive list.

In total, seventy-four delegates were selected to attend the convention (see Figure 1-1), although only fifty-five actually attended. The reasons for not attending varied; some personal, others political. Patrick Henry rejected his appointment because he "smelt a rat."[7] He correctly foresaw what the convention would produce: not a revision of the Articles, but a whole new constitution, creating a whole new government. Later, during the ratification debates in the states, he would prove to be a vocal and vehement opponent of the new constitution.

The delegates who attended were the who's-who of colonial life. They were among the most respected men of politics, law, and business. It is said that Thomas Jefferson, who was in Paris during the convention, remarked that it was "an assembly of demi-gods," when he learned who the delegates were.

Of the attending delegates, one-half were college graduates, most were attorneys, and all were part of America's political or economic aristocracy.[8] Eight were foreign-born and eighteen had worked or studied abroad. Some were obviously influenced by what they had learned from the political experiences of other peoples in other nations. A few delegates were clergymen, but this did not affect the secular atmosphere of the convention.[9]

Connecticut	Nathaniel Gorham	**Pennsylvania**
Oliver Ellsworth	Rufus King	Benjamin Franklin
Roger Sherman	Caleb Strong	George Clymer
William Samuel Johnson		Thomas Fitzsimons
	New Hampshire	Jared Ingersoll
Delaware	John Langdon	Thomas Mifflin
Richard Bassett	Nicholas Gilman	Gouverneur Morris
Jacob Broom		Robert Morris
John Dickinson	**New Jersey**	James Wilson
George Read	David Brearley	
Gunning Bedford, Jr.	Jonathan Dayton	**Rhode Island**
	William Churchill	None
Georgia	Houston	
Abraham Baldwin	William Livingston	**South Carolina**
William Houston	William Paterson	Charles Pinckney
William Pierce		Charles Cotesworth
William Few	**New York**	Pinckney
	Alexander Hamilton	Pierce Butler
Maryland	John Lansing, Jr.	John Rutledge
Daniel Carroll	Robert Yates	
Daniel of St. Thomas		**Virginia**
Jenifer	**North Carolina**	George Washington
James McHenry	William Blount	James Madison
Luther Martin	William Richardson Davie	George Mason
John Francis Mercer	Alexander Martin	Edmund Randolph
	Richard Dobbs Spaight	John Blair
Massachusetts	Hugh Williamson	James McClurg
Elbridge Gerry		George Wythe

FIGURE 1-1 The States' Delegates to the Constitutional Convention of 1787

SIDEBAR

Where Was Thomas Jefferson?

Although it is commonly believed that Thomas Jefferson attended the Constitutional Convention, he did not. Where was the author of the Declaration of Independence and future President during such an important gathering? He was in France serving in the nation's diplomatic corps. Mr. Jefferson had great respect for the delegates, however. When he learned the identities of the membership, he commented that it was "[a]n assembly of demi-gods."

The convention was scheduled to open on May 14, 1787. Because of the absence of a quorum, though, the proceedings did not begin until May 25. They continued until September 17 with only two breaks, two days to celebrate Independence Day and another work-related, ten-day recess.

Of the thirteen states, all but one were represented at the convention. Rhode Island refused to send delegates. Two matters were immediately considered and agreed upon. First, with little discussion, George Washington was selected to chair the convention. Second, the delegates decided that what was to transpire was to remain secret until the final document was completed. Although there were small leaks during the convention, the rule was generally complied with by the members.

The absence of information from the delegates led to speculation and rumor about what was transpiring inside the hall. So wild was one rumor, to the effect that the delegates were considering a monarchy, that they issued a statement on August 15 to the contrary. Interestingly, there were a few delegates who supported the establishment of some form of monarchy. Alexander Hamilton, for example, proposed an "elective monarchy." Under this system, the President would have been elected for life, as would the Senate. Hamilton believed in the English way, equating the House of Representatives to England's House of Commons, the Senate to the House of Lords, and the President to the Crown. Edmund Randolph admitted to preferring the English system, but he also recognized that the people of the United States would never accept such a government.[10] Hamilton and Randolph's feelings did not represent those of most of the delegates. As a whole, they were faithful to republican (representative democratic, if you will) principles and were mindful not to place too much authority in any one person's or group's hands.

The Debates

Details of what transpired at the convention are not known. An official journal was kept and provides some insights. More thorough than the convention journal are the notes of James Madison, who was so diligent in his record keeping that he never left the convention for more than an hour. In total, his notes occupy three volumes. These items, as well as the personal notes and correspondence of all the delegates, give us an idea of what the delegates debated during that hot summer of 1787.

On the second day of the convention, Edmund Randolph, Governor of Virginia, presented the Virginia Plan, which was in large measure the work of James Madison. Although the Virginia Plan was not the only proposal presented to the convention,[11] it was to be the most influential. The Virginia Plan, or Virginia Resolves, set the tone for the convention and controlled the issues that would be considered. Many of the Plan's initial concepts were made a part of the Constitution, in whole or in part. Although the Plan claimed to be a revision of the Articles of Confederation, it was clear to the delegates that it was more:

it was a proposal to replace the existing confederation with a strong, centralized, and supreme national government. The convention took up the plan resolve by resolve. Some of the issues debated at the convention are discussed here.

The nature of the national legislature, Congress, was of particular importance to the delegates. What would be each state's representation in the new Congress? How would its members be selected? What powers would it possess? These are all issues that were considered, debated, and resolved by the delegates.

General Pinckney objected at this point and reminded the delegates that they were only authorized to revise the Articles of Confederation, not to replace them. Later, Edmund Randolph commented, "when the salvation of the Republic is at stake ... it would be treason to our trust not to propose what we find necessary."

The Virginia Plan called for a separation of powers: legislative, executive, and judicial. Madison, Hamilton, and other delegates were influenced by the theories of John Locke and Charles de Montesquieu, who had written extensively about the importance of dividing the functions and powers of government to preserve liberty. As stated by Madison, "The accumulation of all powers, legislative, executive, and judiciary, in the same hands may justly be pronounced the very definition of tyranny."[12] There was little discussion about the concept, as it was generally accepted. Additionally, all agreed, as evidenced by the final product, that few decisions should be made by one branch alone. The branches should check one another to maintain a balance of power.

As for a national legislature, the Virginia Plan provided for a bicameral Congress. There appears to have been little disagreement with this idea. However, the remaining questions were not so easily accepted. Concerning each state's representation, the Plan called for state representation to be based upon each state's number of free people or, in the alternative, based upon each state's contribution to the national treasury. The small states opposed the proposal, as they were accustomed to being treated as equals under the Articles of Confederation. The smaller states were convinced that the larger would always have their will, unless all were equals in Congress. They particularly feared the west, which represented potentially large and wealthy states in the future. Roger Sherman commented, "The smaller states will never agree to the plan on any other principle than an equality of suffrage in this branch." The larger states objected to equal representation, contending that this would devalue the franchise of their citizens.

Ultimately, an agreement known as the "Great Compromise" was reached. Representation in the lower house, the House of Representatives, would be based on population (the number of free persons, excluding Indians that were not taxed, and three-fifths of others);

representation in the upper house, the Senate, was to be equal. Initially, the delegates agreed that each state would be entitled to one representative to the Senate, but later this was changed, with no debate, to two. Included in this compromise was the resolution of another troubling issue: whether slaves were to be part of the equation for deciding representation. Because the delegates had decided, after debate, that the national government's taxes were to be based upon the same equation, the issue was doubly important.

This issue divided the delegates. Philosophically, the division was generally north/south over whether slavery should be permitted, but the delegates did not seriously debate this issue. However, the division over whether to count slaves for the purpose of representation and taxation transcended the north/south distinction. The south would pay more in taxes if slaves were counted. At the same time, the added numbers could increase its representation. Some of the southern delegates contended that southern white citizens would never accept being placed on a one-to-one basis with slaves.

Northern delegates were also split. Some contended that because slaves were property, they should not be included. Others insisted that all people should be included in the census. The two sides compromised and allowed three-fifths of slaves to be counted in determining both taxation and representation. The drafters of the Constitution were careful not to use the term *slave,* referring to "other persons" instead.

The number of representatives was thus set, but how were they to be selected? This proved to be another hotly debated issue. Delegates such as Elbridge Gerry and Roger Sherman believed that the people could not be trusted to choose their own representatives. To them, the people were an uninformed mass, subject to being "duped" by unscrupulous, charismatic politicians. They proposed that the state legislatures be empowered to appoint the representatives.

George Mason wanted the power to rest with the states, not because he distrusted the people, but because he was a states' rights advocate. "Whatever power may be necessary for the national government, a certain portion must necessarily be left in the states ... . The state legislatures also sought to have some means of defending themselves against encroachments of the national government ... . And what better means can we provide than to make them a constituent part of the national establishment." John Dickinson felt similarly. He contended that direct election would result in the total annihilation of the states as political entities.

Others believed that the people should elect their representatives (direct election). This issue was central to the convention. Were they creating a government of the states, or of the people? George Mason and James Madison were proponents of the direct election of at least one chamber of Congress. Mason pointed out that under the Articles of

Confederation, the national government represented the states, which then represented the people. He contended that the states should not stand between the people and the national government, as the states' interests are sometimes at odds with the people's. Oliver Ellsworth warned that the "people will not readily subscribe to the national constitution if it should subject them to be disfranchised." The decision went to the heart of how to define this new democracy.

The delegates were influenced by writings of John Locke, Charles de Montesquieu, and Thomas Hobbes. Natural-law theory was a part of the delegates' collective political ideology. If the authority to create a constitution emanates from the people, some delegates wondered how the people could be disenfranchised. Again, a compromise was reached. The members of the House of Representatives would be elected directly; senators were to be selected by the state legislatures. This method for selecting senators remained until the adoption of the Seventeenth Amendment in 1913, which provided for direct election.

The delegates also tackled the issue of qualifications to vote. There was discussion of limiting the right to vote to landowners. There were concerns that the less wealthy would sell their votes. This idea was defeated and the franchise was extended to all free men.

There was little debate over the powers that should be possessed by Congress. These were spelled out in the first article of the Constitution. The framers intended for the national government to be a limited government. Said another way, the national government possesses no authority that is not specifically granted through the Constitution. However, in the enumeration of its powers, Congress was granted the authority to regulate interstate commerce and to make all laws "necessary and proper" for enforcing its other enumerated powers. These clauses, matched with social, political, and technological changes, have proven instrumental to the growth of the national government and are concomitantly responsible for decreasing the authority of the states.

Another thorny issue for the delegates was the Virginia Plan's resolve that provided the national congress with veto power over state laws. The original proposal allowed the legislative veto of state laws that were in conflict with the national constitution. Later in the convention, this was extended to all laws that Congress found improper. Madison supported the idea, as did Pinckney. They contended that it was an effective and necessary means of keeping the states from encroaching upon the national sphere. There were strong objections. Elbridge Gerry argued that through such power, the national government could "enslave the states." It was suggested that the new constitution could enumerate the instances when Congress could exercise the power, but that idea was rejected, as was the entire proposal. The legislative veto was dead. Madison was not happy, but was consoled by the

COMPARING THE ARTICLES OF CONFEDERATION TO THE CONSTITUTION OF THE UNITED STATES

Articles	*Constitution*
States are supreme	National Government is supreme
Source of authority was states	Source of authority is people
Unicameral legislature	Bicameral legislature
No judiciary	Supreme Court and lower courts as Congress may establish
No independent executive	Independent executive
Limited authority to regulate interstate commerce	Broad authority to regulate interstate commerce
No authority to draft soldiers	Conscription
No authority to issue paper money	May issue paper money
No authority to tax directly	May tax directly
Could not compel states to respect treaties	Authority to make treaties that are binding upon states

fact that the judiciary would apparently have the authority to protect the national government from the excesses of the states.

What were the framers' thoughts on the executive branch? Under the Virginia Plan, the executive power would have rested in one person, who was to be limited to one term and selected by Congress. George Mason thought there should be three coequal executives. It was decided, with little debate, that executive authority should reside with one person. Nevertheless, the framers feared a monarchy and were careful not to create one. The title *President* was chosen over other more regal titles, such as *His Highness,* to avoid the appearance of monarchy.

One of the hardest decisions for the delegates to reach was the method of selecting the President. For the same reasons discussed earlier in regard to selecting members of Congress, direct election was not seriously considered. It was proposed that Congress make the selection. However, there was general agreement that this would place too much authority with the legislature and create too much executive dependence on the legislature. Others wanted greater state involvement in the process. Perhaps the state legislatures should select the highest executive? Most agreed that this process would be too political and too regional, likely resulting in each state supporting one of its own. There was intense debate over the issue. The result was the Electoral College. Under the electoral college system, each state has a number of electors equal to the total number of national congress members (members of the house and senate) it possesses. These persons constitute the Electoral College. The President is selected by this Electoral College. Alexander Hamilton said of this system:

> It was desirable that the sense of the people should operate in the choice of the person to whom so important a trust was to be confided. This end will be answered by committing the right of making it, not to any preestablished body, but to men chosen by the people for the special purpose, and at the particular conjuncture.
>
> It was equally desirable that the immediate election should be made by men most capable of analyzing the qualities adapted to the station and acting under circumstances favorable to deliberation, and to a judicious combination of all the reasons and inducements which were proper to govern their choice. A small number of persons, selected by their fellow citizens from the general mass, will be most likely to possess the information and discernment requisite to so complicated an investigation.[13]

The delegates agreed that, in the event of a tie in the Electoral College, the House of Representatives would choose between the candidates. The Senate was originally considered, but the delegates felt that they had already significantly empowered the Senate and that, in the interest of balance, this responsibility should be placed with the House of Representatives.

In regard to presidential responsibilities, the delegates agreed that the President should be the commander-in-chief of the military, negotiate and make treaties, and nominate the Cabinet members, members of the national judiciary, and other government officials, with the advice and consent of the Senate. They also decided to give the President the power to veto legislation, but checked that power by providing that Congress could override the veto with a two-thirds vote. Edmund Randolph believed that the total grant of authority to the President was excessive and characterized it as the "fetus of monarchy."

The final issue to be discussed concerning the executive also concerns the judiciary. It was proposed that a council be established comprising the President and a number of the Justices of the Supreme Court to review acts of Congress for constitutionality. Under the proposal, acts contrary to the Constitution could be declared void or revised by the council. Gerry opposed the measure because he believed it superfluous, as the judiciary has the power to nullify laws contrary to the Constitution. James Madison agreed, "A law violating a constitution established by the people themselves ... would be considered by judges as null and void." Rufus King also opposed the council. He contended that because it was the responsibility of the courts to review laws before them, and nullify those repugnant to the Constitution, it would be an improper mixing of functions to have judges participate in revising or voiding laws with the executive. Still another voice was heard in this vein. Luther Martin stated, "[A]s to the Constitutionality of laws, that point will come before the judges in their proper official character. In this character they have a negative on the laws." The measure was defeated, but the President was given the veto power, subject to override.

Interestingly, the delegates did not specifically mention, in the Constitution, the power of the judiciary to declare the acts of its coordinate branches or the states unconstitutional. However, the Supreme Court has determined that such a power is implicit in the judicial function. (This issue is discussed again in Chapter 3.)

Another issue the delegates debated was the role the national judiciary should play in the new United States. Some contended that they should create a system of national courts through the new constitution. Others feared, however, that if they created national courts, state courts would be displaced and divested of their authority. The compromise agreement was that the Supreme Court of the United States would be created by the new constitution along with "inferior Courts as the Congress may from time to time ordain and establish." Without a system of lower national courts, many delegates feared that national laws would go unenforced. To remedy this problem, the delegates included a provision in the new constitution requiring state courts to enforce national laws. This is embodied in Article VI, and reads, in relevant part:

> This Constitution, and the Laws of the United States which shall be made in Pursuance thereof: and all Treaties made, or which shall be made, under the Authority of the United States, shall be the supreme Law of the Land; and the Judges in every State shall be bound thereby, any Thing in the Constitution of any State to the Contrary notwithstanding.

This compromise satisfied the delegates who wanted to control the size of the national government and also assured that national laws would be enforced. Congress exercised its power to create inferior national courts when it enacted the Judiciary Act of 1798, which established thirteen district and three circuit courts.

There was little debate concerning the jurisdiction of the national judiciary by the delegates. This issue is examined more closely in Chapters 3 and 4.

Individual Rights and Slavery

To many people, there were two glaring problems with the Constitution. First, it did not explicitly set out individual rights. Second, it did not address slavery.

First, it must be pointed out that the delegates did not totally ignore issues of individual liberty. The Constitution does contain a number of provisions intended to protect civil rights. For example, Article I, § 9 provides for writs of **habeas corpus**. Section 10 prohibits Congress from passing any **bills of attainder** or **ex post facto laws**. Article III, § 3, provides that no person shall be convicted of treason except upon the testimony of two witnesses to the same act or upon a confession in open court.

In spite of this, the first ten amendments, commonly known as the Bill of Rights, were added to assure that the government would not encroach upon civil liberties. At the Constitutional Convention, George Mason argued for the inclusion of a bill of rights. Elbridge Gerry moved for such a bill to be included in the constitution. Alexander Hamilton saw no need to include a bill of rights, because the government lacked the authority to encroach upon an individual's liberty: "Why declare that things shall not be done, which there is no power to do."

Hamilton did not foresee the significant change that would come to the United States. Industrialization, a huge growth in population, and a specialization of functions have led to increased interdependence among people. Today, few persons live in such remote places that their activities do not affect others, and few supply their own food, clothes, and other necessities. American culture today involves continuous and frequent contact with other people. As human contact increases, so

---

TERMS

habeas corpus [Latin for] "you have the body." A writ whose purpose is to obtain immediate relief from illegal imprisonment by having the "body" (that is, the prisoner) delivered from custody and brought before the court. A writ of habeas corpus is a means for attacking the constitutionality of the statute under which, or the proceedings in which, the original conviction was obtained. There are numerous writs of habeas corpus, each applicable in different procedural circumstances. The full name of the ordinary writ of habeas corpus is *habeas corpus ad subjiciendum*.

bill of attainder A legislative act that inflicts capital punishment upon named persons without a judicial trial. Congress and the state legislatures are prohibited from issuing bills of attainder by the Constitution.

ex post facto law A law making a person criminally liable for an act that was not criminal at the time it was committed. The Constitution prohibits both Congress and the states from enacting such laws.

do conflicts and, accordingly, rules to regulate conduct. We look to government to establish and enforce most of these rules. To protect ourselves from an overzealous government, which we have entrusted with an ever-increasing amount of authority, we need a Bill of Rights.

Hamilton's view prevailed. The delegates decided not to include a bill of rights in the original document because they simply did not believe the government had the authority to legislate in the areas a bill of rights would cover. After the convention voted ten to zero to exclude it, Gerry moved that the freedom of the press should at least be included. For the same reason—that the delegates did not believe the government had the authority to regulate the press—this motion was also defeated. There was no bill of rights in the original Constitution.

Nevertheless, the absence of a bill of rights was troubling to the nation. A few states, such as New York and Virginia, attached to their resolutions of approval of the Constitution proposals to amend the new Constitution to add a bill of rights. In total, over 200 amendments to the Constitution were discussed in the state ratifying conventions dealing with individual rights.[14] It was a popular idea, and only three years after the Constitution was ratified, the Bill of Rights was ratified.

Slavery was a divisive issue. The issue arose in the context discussed previously: taxation and representation. It was at that juncture that many delegates voiced their objections to slavery. Luther Martin asserted that the slave trade was "inconsistent with the principles of the revolution and dishonorable to the American character to have such a feature in the Constitution."

The issue of slavery also arose in the context of the importation of slaves. Under the new constitution, this was an area under national jurisdiction, but many delegates representing the southern states did not want the national government to interfere with the importation of slaves. Again, some delegates who were opposed to slavery believed that the document should include a provision prohibiting the importation of slaves into the United States. George Mason, himself a slave owner, opposed slavery and wanted to include such a provision in the new constitution.

There were also delegates who opposed slave traffic but believed that the constitution should not prohibit it. Roger Sherman was in this group. He thought the states were moving toward abolition and that this movement should be permitted to run its course. Charles Pinckney warned that South Carolina would not accept any constitution that forbade the importation of slaves. He voiced what all the delegates feared: factionalism. They did not want to include a provision so repugnant to any particular region that ratification would be jeopardized. Benjamin Franklin, president of the Pennsylvania Society for the Abolition of Slavery, refused to present a petition from the group to the convention, fearing that it would drive an irreparable wedge between the states.

A compromise was reached. First, as discussed earlier, three-fifths of slaves were included in the initial determination of representation and taxation. As to the importation of slaves, the delegates agreed that Congress could not prohibit the importation of slaves until 1808 and capped the tax on each slave at $10. On January 1, 1808, Congress prohibited the importation of slaves. This did not, however, end slavery. It took a civil war to accomplish that goal.

Women and the Franchise

Women were not extended the right to vote by the new Constitution. In fact, it appears that there was no discussion of the issue at the Constitutional Convention. Women were not excluded entirely from political processes during this period, however. For example, the New Jersey Constitution of 1776 extended the vote to women who owned property (African-Americans were also allowed to vote). This was changed, however, in 1807 when the constitution was amended to restrict suffrage to "men."[15]

The women's suffrage movement can be traced back to Abigail Adams, wife of President John Adams. Later, feminists such as Elizabeth Cady Stanton and Susan B. Anthony led the women's suffrage movement that resulted in the Nineteenth Amendment (1920), which extended the right to vote to women.

§ 1.4 Ratification

James Madison, Alexander Hamilton, Gouverneur Morris, and Rufus King were responsible for drafting the Constitution. A local clerk was hired to actually pen the document. It took him forty hours to write the 4,400 words on a four-page parchment made of either calf or lamb skin. He was paid $30 for this task.

The signing occurred on September 17, 1787. Thirty-nine delegates signed. Three delegates, George Mason, Edmund Randolph, and Elbridge Gerry, refused to sign. Edmund Randolph was the delegate who introduced the Virginia Plan from which the Constitution was constructed. He, like Mason and Gerry, was concerned that too much power had been vested in the national government. Later, however, during the Virginia Ratification Convention, Randolph supported the Constitution to avoid dividing the nation.[16] Mason and Gerry, in contrast, later opposed the Constitution in their state conventions. Mason commented that he would rather cut off his hand than see the Constitution ratified.

The delegates transmitted a copy to the Congress, where it was received on September 20, 1787. Richard Henry Lee opposed sending the Constitution on to the states for ratification, and there was discussion of sending it on with objections. The Congress decided to do neither. Instead, it was transmitted to the states without any comment whatsoever.

The delegates had debated the method of ratification. Special conventions won out over state legislatures. Further, they decided that it should take only nine states to ratify the document, rather than the total of thirteen, and that ratification would be effective only among the ratifying states. All thirteen states would have at least one ratification convention. The state conventions were limited to ratifying or rejecting the document; no revisions or conditional ratifications were allowed. The conventions began in November 1787 and ended in May 1790.

During this period, numerous articles were published in magazines and newspapers, pamphlets were distributed, and speeches were made, arguing the pros and cons of the new Constitution. The most influential writings were those of James Madison, Alexander Hamilton, and John Jay, who published a series of eighty-five articles under the pseudonym *Publius*. Today, we know these as the *Federalist Papers*. Through these articles, these men made forceful arguments in support of the Constitution. The antifederalists had their outlet as well. Another series of articles, entitled the *Federal Farmer*, was published in opposition to ratification.

During the debates in the state conventions, three common objections were made to the Constitution. First, it was missing a bill of rights. Second, it emasculated the sovereignty of the states. Third, the delegates had exceeded their authority in replacing the Articles of Confederation. Delegates Luther Martin, Elbridge Gerry, and George Mason passionately opposed ratification.

Delaware was the first state to approve the Constitution, doing so on December 7, 1787. New Hampshire approved on June 21, 1788. It was the critical ninth state to approve, so the Constitution was then ratified and the Articles of Confederation superseded, and a new government could be formed. During the formation of the new government, the state conventions continued. By February 4, 1789, every state but Rhode Island had joined the union, and the nation's first Electoral College had selected George Washington the first President under the new Constitution. In April of that year, Congress had its first meeting. John Jay was selected as the nation's first Chief Justice during 1789.

SIDEBAR

Ratification of the Constitution

Article VII of the Constitution of the United States reads, in part, "The Ratification of the Conventions of nine States, shall be sufficient for the Establishment of this Constitution between the States so ratifying the Same." The delegates had decided that ratification would occur through conventions to be conducted in each state. Further, it took nine states' approval before the Constitution could be ratified, and then only among the ratifying states. It took two and one-half years, but eventually all thirteen states accepted the Constitution. The order of state approval was as follows:

1. December 7, 1787 — Delaware
2. December 15, 1787 — Pennsylvania
3. December 18, 1787 — New Jersey
4. January 2, 1788 — Georgia
5. January 4, 1788 — Connecticut
6. February 6, 1788 — Massachusetts
7. April 26, 1788 — Maryland
8. May 23, 1788 — South Carolina
9. June 21, 1788 — New Hampshire
10. June 25, 1788 — Virginia
11. July 26, 1788 — New York
12. November 21, 1789 — North Carolina
13. May 29, 1790 — Rhode Island

Rhode Island remained obstinate. Congress voted to sever the new nation's commercial relations with Rhode Island, which helped push that state to approval. Finally, on May 29, 1790, Rhode Island gave its approval. The nation was united under a new Constitution.

§ 1.5 Amendments

The framers of the Constitution lived in an era when changes to government came either by edicts of kings or by revolution. They desired to have a more fair and civil method. At the same time, they did not want to empower Congress to amend the Constitution. After all, the Constitution is fundamental law, intended to restrict the power of government in many instances.

The framers devised two methods to amend the Constitution. They are found in Article V. The first method is initiated by Congress. With a two-thirds vote in both houses, Congress may propose an amendment to the states. In the alternative, two-thirds of the state legislatures may call for a convention to make proposals. Congressional initiation is the only method of proposal that has been used to date.

A proposal is then ratified either by the legislatures of three-fourths of the states or conventions in three-fourths of the states. Congress designates the ratification method. Thomas Jefferson believed that this process realized the dream of providing for bloodless change by the people. He said

> [h]appily for us, that when we find our constitutions defective and insufficient to secure the happiness of our people, we can assemble with all the coolness of philosophers, and set them to rights, while every other nation on earth must have recourse to arms to amend or to restore their constitutions.[17]

Although the states were only given two alternatives in regard to the new Constitution (adoption or rejection), many states attached lists of proposed amendments to their adoption resolutions anyway. A few states, such as Virginia and New York, called for a bill of rights. Eight states called for an amendment protecting the sovereignty of the states. To satisfy these concerns, it was agreed that a bill would be added immediately after the original Constitution was ratified. The Bill of Rights, added on November 3, 1791, includes protections of individual rights and liberties and a provision intended to preserve the integrity of state sovereignty.

Today, there are a total of twenty-seven amendments. The twenty-seventh was ratified in 1992 and provides that compensation changes for members of Congress shall not be effective until after the next election of representatives. This amendment was one of the original twelve amendments proposed by James Madison in 1790.[18] It was not ratified with the original ten amendments and appeared to be dead for many years. However, in 1978, ratification restarted and the required thirty-eighth state ratified in 1992. Interestingly, the ratifying state, Michigan, did not exist at the time the amendment was proposed. Although the number of amendments is relatively small, the number of proposals to amend the Constitution that have been submitted is staggering. By 1993 the number of proposals introduced in Congress to amend the Constitution exceeded 10,000.[19]

§ 1.6   Politics and Constitutional Law

The remainder of this book examines how the Constitution has been applied and interpreted. Examining the decisions of the courts of the United States, particularly of the Supreme Court of the United

States, is the most common method of learning this subject. Be aware, however, that the judiciary does not exist in a vacuum. Its coequal branches (President and Congress) must interpret the Constitution, apply its principles, and, in certain ways, influence the judiciary's interaction with, and interpretation of, the Constitution.

For example, administrative agencies are largely responsible for the administration of government in this nation. They are the front line of government. To function, administrative agencies must interpret the law, often before any court has had an opportunity to address objections to that law. In some cases, a party may obtain pre-enforcement judicial review of a law, and in such instances the agency's role is diminished. When pre-enforcement review is not sought or is unavailable, the agency's role becomes more significant. In instances when a law is valid as written, but the agency's method of enforcement is questionable, the agency's role is again emphasized.

The perceived constitutionality of a bill may also affect legislative decision making. A bill that is seen as unconstitutional may not make it out of committee. Individual legislators may oppose proposed legislation that seems unconstitutional. This is not always the case, however. For political reasons, legislators may support a bill known to be unconstitutional. For example, the Supreme Court invalidated a Texas statute that protected the United States flag from desecration by a political protester in the 1989 case of *Texas v. Johnson*.[20] The Court reasoned that the protester's right to political expression under the First Amendment outweighed Texas' interest in protecting the integrity of the flag. One year later, the United States Congress enacted similar legislation, even though it clearly contradicted the Supreme Court's ruling in *Texas v. Johnson*. For that reason, the new law was quickly invalidated as well.

Also, Congress possesses considerable authority over the jurisdiction of the federal courts. Political concerns could, therefore, cause legislators to limit the jurisdiction of the judiciary over certain issues.

Many of the petitions filed with the Supreme Court are filed by the United States, by the Solicitor General of the United States. Such filings are examined with special care by the Court when it determines whether to hear the appeals. The executive branch therefore influences the Court by its partial control over the issues presented to the Court.

Although the Court is generally insulated from politics, it is generally believed that politics and public opinion play at least a minor role in influencing the Court's decision making. Because the Court has no method of enforcing its orders, it relies on the executive branch. This unenforceability, some contend, keeps the Court's decisions within the bounds of reason; that is, within a range the public will tolerate and the executive will enforce.

Politics also play a role in the selection of Article III judges. Supreme Court justices and judges of federal district and appellate courts are selected by the political branches of government; the President nominates and the Senate must confirm. In recent years, the process has been criticized as being too political, focusing on the political and ideological beliefs of nominees rather than on other qualifications, such as education, employment experience, prior judicial experience, intellectual ability, and the like. The confirmation hearings of Robert Bork (nominated by President Reagan and rejected by the Senate) and Clarence Thomas (nominated by President Bush and confirmed by the Senate) are used to illustrate this point.

Once appointed, an Article III judge maintains his or her position until one of three occurrences: retirement, death, or impeachment. The power to impeach a judge rests with Congress. Congress may impeach for high crimes and misdemeanors. This is, therefore, another limitation upon the judiciary by an external force. Congress has been true to the purpose of impeachment and has not used the power to achieve political objectives.

When possible, this book recognizes and refers to political or social influences, as well as to other actors that influence constitutional law. In any event, however, it is the judiciary that is charged with interpreting the law; the Supreme Court of the United States has the final word on what the Constitution means. For that reason, this book focuses on the decisions of that Court. To fully understand a decision of the Court, one must grasp the following: the history and facts that gave rise to the case; the law itself, including any policy considerations, as expressed in the Court's decisions; the political and social atmosphere surrounding the opinion; and the composition of the Court.

§ 1.7 Judicial Eras

There have been several significant "eras" in the history of the Supreme Court. These eras are marked by particular ideologies that were dominant on the Court. The respective powers of the national and state governments are the point of reference for the periods discussed in the rest of this chapter.

Marshall Court

John Marshall was Chief Justice of the United States from 1801 to 1836. John Marshall was a strong nationalist (federalist) and was appointed Chief Justice by President John Adams. Marshall had been Adams's Secretary of State. Adams lost his re-election bid to an antifederalist, Thomas Jefferson. In an effort to continue to influence government, Adams, with the support of a lame-duck federalist Congress, made a number of appointments of federalists to vacant judicial positions. Marshall was one of these appointees.

The Marshall Court is known for establishing the supremacy of the national government over the state governments. A number of important decisions were handed down by the Marshall Court, including *Marbury v. Madison,* 5 U.S. (1 Cranch) 137 (1803); *McCulloch v. Maryland,* 17 U.S. (4 Wheat) 316 (1819); and *Martin v. Hunter's Lessee,* 14 U.S. (1 Wheat) 304 (1816). (These decisions are discussed in Chapter 3.) In *McCulloch,* Marshall addressed the power of Congress; this decision is discussed further in Chapter 4. *Hunter's Lessee* concerned the division of authority between the national government and state governments and is the subject of more thorough examination in Chapter 7. The theme of *Marbury v. Madison* was different. In that case, the power of **judicial review** was established. Judicial review is the authority of the judiciary, as the final interpreters of the law, to declare the acts of the other coordinate branches unconstitutional. *Marbury v. Madison* and judicial review are discussed fully in Chapter 3.

Taney Court

Roger Taney replaced John Marshall as Chief Justice of the United States in 1836. Between 1836 and 1843, four other justices were appointed: Philip Barbour, John Catron, John McKinley, and Peter Daniel. McKinley and Daniel filled two new seats, expanding the number of justices on the Court to nine. Eight other justices would join the Court during Taney's tenure as Chief Justice, which did not end until 1865.

During this era, the Court's philosophy changed from strongly nationalist to one favoring states' rights. The Taney Court was not activist, that is, it was not aggressive in reversing the decisions of the Marshall Court. The Court did favor states' rights, however, when new issues were raised concerning the balance of power between the national and state governments.

The Taney Court is best known for *Dred Scott v. Sandford,* 60 U.S. (19 How.) 393 (1856). In that decision, the Supreme Court held that slaves

─────────────── TERMS ───────────────

judicial review   The power of the judiciary, as the final interpreter of the law, to declare an act of a coordinate governmental branch or state unconstitutional. The power is not expressly stated in the Constitution, but the Supreme Court announced that the judiciary possesses this power in *Marbury v. Madison,* 5 U.S. (1 Cranch) 137 (1803).

were property and possessed no rights or privileges under the Constitution. Further, for the second time in history, the first being *Marbury v. Madison,* the Court relied upon judicial review to invalidate a statute. In *Dred Scott,* the Court held a federal statute that conferred rights upon slaves unconstitutional. In short, the Court concluded that slavery was an issue of local, not national, concern.

Reconstruction Era

Salmon P. Chase became Chief Justice in 1865 and remained in that position until 1874. The Civil War had ended and the nation was rebuilding. The South had been defeated and slavery abolished. Most significantly, the war proved that the states were not independent members of a league, but parts of a larger, more powerful nation. The nation's political identity changed as a result of the war. People began to identify more closely with their national citizenship and less with their state affiliations. The consequence was a strengthening of the national government and a concomitant weakening of the state governments.

During this period, the so-called reconstruction amendments were adopted. The Thirteenth Amendment, ratified in 1865, forbids slavery. The Fourteenth Amendment, ratified in 1868, has four sections, but the first is the most significant, as it provides that every state shall extend to all persons due process and equal protection of the law. The Fourteenth Amendment extends to Congress the power to enact legislation to enforce its mandates. Congress did that through the Civil Rights Acts, found at 42 U.S.C. §§ 1981, 1982, and 1983. The Fifteenth Amendment, ratified in 1870, assures the franchise to persons of all color and race.

The Thirteenth and Fourteenth Amendments were not ratified under the most favorable of circumstances. The southern states were coerced into ratification. In fact, most of the southern states initially rejected the Fourteenth Amendment and acquiesced only after Congress enacted a reconstruction act that denied each state representation in Congress until it ratified the amendment. Such coercion would not be acceptable today, but the methods used by the national government in coercing the states into ratifying the reconstruction amendments have to be considered in light of the circumstances of the day.

It would be decades before the full force of these amendments would be realized. However, the reconstruction period marks an important point in constitutional history. Today, the reconstruction amendments and statutes are applied often and with significant effect on state actions. For example, the Fourteenth Amendment and federal discrimination statutes forbid state governments from discriminating against individuals on the account of race, religion, or gender when hiring employees or providing benefits to citizens.

Pre-New Deal Era

Salmon Chase was followed by Morrison Waite (1874–1888), Melville Fuller (1888–1910), Edward White (1910–1921), and William Taft (1921–1930) as Chief Justices. Again, the Court's philosophy changed during the tenure of these men, at least regarding federalism issues. During this period, the Fourteenth Amendment was used to limit the power of the states to regulate intrastate commerce. For example, in *Lochner v. New York*, 198 U.S. 45 (1905), the Court invalidated a state statute that set maximum working hours for bakers. The Court found the statute to be an unwarranted burden upon the right to contract, a liberty interest protected by the Fourteenth Amendment.

The authority of the federal government to regulate interstate commerce was also limited during this period, often for Tenth Amendment reasons (the federal government was encroaching upon the domain of the states).

Ironically, while the Court was using the Fourteenth Amendment to protect economic interests, it did not concomitantly protect the rights of black citizens, the primary goal of the amendment. The case that established the "separate but equal" doctrine, *Plessy v. Ferguson*, 163 U.S. 537 (1896), was rendered during this period. Not until 1954, when *Brown v. Board of Education*, 381 U.S. 479 (1954) was decided, was the separate but equal doctrine overturned as violative of the Fourteenth Amendment.

New Deal Era

The next significant judicial era occurred during the Great Depression. President Franklin D. Roosevelt was elected with a popular mandate to correct the nation's serious economic crisis. Roosevelt's New Deal plan included significant federal government involvement in economic matters. A number of programs were created with the intention of stimulating the economy. Additionally, national governmental regulation of commercial activities increased during the New Deal.

Early in Roosevelt's administration, the Court rendered a number of unpopular decisions invalidating some of the New Deal legislation. In 1935, the Court held the National Industrial Recovery Act unconstitutional in *Panama Refining Co. v. Ryan*, 293 U.S. 388 (1935), as it found that Congress had made an unlawful delegation of legislative authority to the President (violating separation of powers principles). There were other decisions unfavorable to the President: *Schechter Poultry Corp. v. United States,* 295 U.S. 495 (1935); *Railroad Retirement Board v. Alton Railroad,* 295 U.S. 330 (1935); and *United States v. Butler,* 297 U.S. 1 (1936). (This line of cases is more fully discussed in Chapters 5 and 7.) In short, they stood for the principle of a limited national government, one whose authority to regulate interstate commerce is limited by the right of individual contract and by federalism principles. These cases asserted the importance of separation of powers, substantive due process, and limitations on the authority that may be delegated by Congress to administrative agencies.

These decisions angered the President, who reacted with the famous "court-packing" plan. In an effort to "pack" the Court with justices sympathetic to his objectives, President Roosevelt proposed that for every justice over 70 years of age, an additional justice be appointed. At the time the suggestion was made, there were six justices over 70 on the Court. He contended that the additional justices were needed to meet the Court's heavy burden. Congress saw the proposal for what it was—an attempt to control the Court by the President—and ultimately it was defeated. Also contributing to the defeat were two decisions issued by the Court upholding New Deal legislation. The decisions were issued in early 1937 and the court-packing measure was defeated later that year. Roosevelt's court-packing scheme presented one of the most serious threats to the integrity and independence of the Court in its history.

As it turned out, Roosevelt did not need the court-packing scheme to gain the ideological sympathy of the Court. Recall that six justices were over the age of 70 when he made his proposal. As might be expected, a number left the Court during the New Deal era. By 1941, Roosevelt had nominated seven new justices, all of whom were confirmed.

The new membership on the Court transformed its attitude and approach to substantive due process and federalism. Beginning in 1938, and continuing thereafter, the Court consistently upheld New Deal legislation.

Warren Court

In 1953, Earl Warren, a nominee of President Eisenhower, became the new Chief Justice. Warren presided over a Court that is best known for its decisions protecting individual rights (civil liberties). Three other justices were prominent during this time for their "liberal" philosophies: William Douglas, William Brennan, and Hugo Black. In 1967, two years before the end of Warren's tenure, another liberal justice, Thurgood Marshall, was added to the Court.

Much constitutional law was established during the Warren Court era. Included in this Court's decisions are: the invalidation of the separate but equal doctrine of *Plessy,* in *Brown v. Board of Education;* the finding that privacy is protected by the Constitution, in *Griswold v. Connecticut,* 381 U.S. 479 (1965); the establishment of much of the First Amendment free speech law used today; and enhanced protection of the rights of persons accused of crimes, including *Katz v. United States,* 389 U.S. 347 (1967) (Fourth Amendment protects reasonable expectations of privacy), *United States v. Wade,* 338 U.S. 218 (1967) (right to counsel at pretrial (postarrest or charge) identifications), and *Miranda v. Arizona,* 384 U.S. 436 (1966) (right to counsel during interrogations), to name only a few.

Burger Court

Warren Burger was nominated by President Richard M. Nixon to follow Earl Warren as Chief Justice in 1969. President Nixon appointed three other justices, Harry Blackmun, Lewis Powell, and William Rehnquist, who were either conservative or moderate, to replace three more liberal members of the Warren Court, Earl Warren, Abe Fortas, and Hugo Black.

Although the Burger Court was more conservative than the Warren Court, it was not activist in its approach. Few decisions of the Warren Court were reversed; in fact, the early years of the Burger Court continued in the Warren Court tradition, emphasizing the preservation of civil liberties. However, just as the Burger Court did not proactively pursue a conservative agenda, it did not continue the liberal activism of the Warren Court. Rather, on the whole, the Court maintained the status quo, neither disturbing precedent nor engaging in social engineering.

This is not to say that the Burger Court did not issue important decisions. Important precedents concerning the freedom of speech, the rights of racial minorities, and the rights of women were established during the Burger era. For example, the Burger Court decided *Roe v. Wade,* 410 U.S. 113 (1973), wherein the Court determined that the right to privacy protects a woman's right to elect abortion in some situations. The Burger Court was also responsible for ordering President Nixon to hand over tape recordings of Oval Office conversations that related to the Watergate affair, in *Nixon v. United States,* 418 U.S. 683 (1974), *reh'g denied,* 433 U.S. 916 (1977). It was during the Burger era that the first woman joined the Court. Justice Sandra Day O'Connor was nominated by President Reagan and confirmed by the Senate in 1981.

Rehnquist Court

William Rehnquist succeeded Warren Burger in 1986. Between 1988 and 1991, Associate Justices Lewis Powell, Jr., William Brennan, Jr., and Thurgood Marshall retired. Their replacements, Justices Anthony Kennedy, David Souter, and Clarence Thomas, have been on the Court too short a time for precise assessment of their ideological positions, and there is always the possibility that a justice's ideology may change over time. It is nonetheless safe to say that they, and the Court as a whole, are more conservative than during the Warren and Burger eras, at least in regard to civil liberties. However, the Court appears to regard economic interests highly and may prove to be activist in this regard.

Some of the important cases decided during Rehnquist's term are *United States v. Lopez,* 115 S. Ct. 1624 (1995), which established a limit to Congress's power over interstate commerce. In *United States Term Limits v. Thornton,* 115 S. Ct. 1842 (1996), the Court invalidated state-imposed term limits on United States Congress members. Another important decision was *Casey v. Planned Parenthood,* 112 S. Ct. 2791 (1992), wherein the Court reaffirmed the basic holding of the Burger Court decision in *Roe v. Wade;* namely, that women have a privacy right to elect abortions in some situations. However, the Rehnquist Court invalidated the trimester analysis established in *Roe* in favor of another test.

Only time will show whether there will be a sufficient coalition among the justices and the Chief Justice for the Court to be known as the Rehnquist Court and, if so, what its impact on constitutional law will be. Some of the most significant cases of recent years are discussed throughout this book, and from those cases certain common themes may be discovered. See Appendix E for a chronological chart of the members of the Supreme Court.

Summary

Under the Articles of Confederation, the nation was fragmented and the national government too weak to solve its problems. The framers gathered in Philadelphia to revise the Articles of Confederation, to make the changes necessary to remedy the country's problems. Knowing that their task was greater than this, the delegates chose to abolish the Articles of Confederation and to write a new constitution. They knew that drafting a new constitution would be controversial. To preserve the integrity of the process, they agreed to keep their proceedings secret until the final document was completed.

They created a governmental structure in the new constitution. The national government would be stronger, but it was limited to the powers directly given by the Constitution. All others belonged to the states, the unit most framers wanted to continue to possess the bulk of governmental powers. Thus, powers that appeared inherently national were delegated to the national government, such as foreign relations and war. In addition, control over interstate, foreign, and Indian commerce was assigned to Congress. Everyday matters, such as intrastate commerce, crime, and social concerns, were left to the states.

The first state to accept the new Constitution was Delaware. The delegates decided that ratification would occur when the ninth state signed on. This happened in New Hampshire on June 21, 1788. The last of the thirteen states to ratify was Rhode Island, which did so on May 29, 1790. The Bill of Rights was added one year later.

The framers were successful in establishing a stronger national government and are credited with saving the union from economic disaster and civil war. The federal government has continued to grow in size and power under this Constitution. Whether the federal government has become too large and powerful is a controversial issue today. Federalism, or the division of governmental powers among the federal and state governments, is the subject of Chapter 2.

Review Questions

1. What were the names of the national legislative bodies before and during the period of the Articles of Confederation and Perpetual Union?

2. Distinguish federalists from antifederalists. State the basic philosophical differences between the two.

3. Identify two of the weaknesses of the Articles of Confederation that contributed to the need for a new constitution.

4. What was the mandate of the delegates to the Philadelphia convention?

5. Name the only one of the original thirteen colonies that was not represented at the Philadelphia convention.

6. Edmund Randolph introduced a plan, largely written by James Madison, that became the working document at the Philadelphia convention. What is the common name of this plan?

7. The delegates considered empowering the Congress with the authority to invalidate state laws. The idea was rejected. Madison, a proponent of the idea, was disappointed, but consoled by what fact?

8. The delegates agreed to strengthen the national (federal) government but maintain considerable state powers. Describe the relationship between the federal government and state governments as envisioned by the framers.

9. What were the terms of the Great Compromise?

10. Why did Alexander Hamilton oppose including a bill of rights in the original Constitution?

Review Problems

1. Do you believe that a bicameral legislature is necessary today? Explain your answer.

2. Amending the Constitution is a difficult process, at least when compared to creating legislation. The framers intended this. Why?

Notes

[1] A. McLaughlin, *A Constitutional History of the United States* 99–100 (D. Appleton-Century 1935).

[2] Articles of Confederation of Perpetual Union, art. III.

[3] Thomas & Thomas, *The War-Making Powers of the President* 3–4 (SMU Press 1982).

[4] Catherine Bowen, *Miracle at Philadelphia* 9 (Little, Brown, & Co. 1966).

[5] *Judges of the United States* (2d ed., Bicentennial Committee of the Judicial Conference of the United States 1983).

[6] *The Federalist* No. 15.

[7] George Anastaplo, *The Constitution of 1787* (Johns Hopkins University Press 1989).

[8] For a comprehensive discussion of the delegates' respective wealth and how their personal economic interests may have been a factor in their decision making at the convention, *see* Charles Beard's *Economic Interpretation of the Constitution* (1913) and Forrest McDonald's *We The People: The Economic Origins of the Constitution* (Transaction Publishers 1992).

[9] William Peters, *A More Perfect Union* 25 (Crown Publishers 1982).

[10] Neil MacNeil, "The First Congress, A Republic if You Can Keep It," 1 *Constitution* 5–6 (No. 3 1989).

[11] The other significant proposal was introduced by William Paterson. His plan became known as the New Jersey Plan and was in most respects the antithesis of the Virginia Plan. It called for continuing the Articles of

Confederation with revision. Notable differences between the two plans include: the Virginia Plan saw the Constitution's authority emanating from the people, whereas the New Jersey Plan continued to view the national government as representing the states; the Virginia Plan provided for a bicameral Congress, the New Jersey Plan for a unicameral Congress; the Virginia Plan gave the national government wide-sweeping jurisdiction, whereas the New Jersey Plan severely limited the jurisdiction of the national government.

[12] *The Federalist* No. 47.

[13] *The Federalist* No. 68.

[14] "The Fourth Amendment," *The Bill of Rights and Beyond.* Bicentennial Calendar (Commission on the Bicentennial of the Constitution 1991).

[15] Sara M. Shumer, *New Jersey,* "Ratifying the Constitution." In *New Jersey,* Gillespie et al., eds. (1989), 76–77.

[16] *The Creation of the Constitution* 58. Opposing Viewpoints Series (Greenhaven Press 1995).

[17] Letter to C.W.F. Dumas, September 1787, cited in Richard Bernstein, Amending America 222 (Random House 1993).

[18] It was originally the second amendment. The other unenacted amendment provided for an increase in the membership of the House of Representatives as the nation's population increased. It has never been enacted.

[19] Richard B. Bernstein, *Amending America: If We Love The Constitution So Much, Why Do We Keep on Trying to Change It?* xii (Random House 1993).

[20] 491 U.S. 397 (1989).

CHAPTER 2

DIVIDING GOVERNMENTAL POWER

§ 2.1 Federalism

The men who met in Philadelphia during that hot summer of 1787 knew that a new government would have to be formed to solve the nation's many problems. Under the Articles of Confederation, the nation's first constitution, the nation floundered. Economic and political instability were generally attributed to the weakness of the national government. Therefore, a new, stronger, national government was established.

The framers were concerned, however, with the centralization of power. Too much power residing in any one person or group could lead to tyranny. The belief that absolute power corrupts absolutely predominated the political philosophy of the framers.

Also, the framers were protective of state sovereignty. They wanted a stronger national government, but not to the point of obliterating the states. Three important concepts were included in the Constitution to prevent both the centralization of power and the death of state sovereignty: federalism, separation of powers, and checks and balances. This chapter introduces those concepts. Chapters 3 through 6 expand the discussion to include particular cases in which the concepts have been raised and applied.

The Constitution recognizes two forms of government: the national (federal) government and the government of the states. The division of governmental power between the federal and state governments is called **federalism**. Federalism represents a vertical division of power.

TERMS

federalism [†] 1. Pertaining to a system of government that is federal in nature. 2. The system by which the states of the United States relate to each other and to the federal government.

federalism A governmental structure in which two or more levels of government operate concurrently with jurisdiction over the same citizens, and in which each governmental entity has some autonomy over specific policy areas. This is opposed to a *unitary system*, where there is one centralized

The Constitution specifically enumerates the powers of the national government. Articles I, II, and III set forth the powers of the national Congress, President, and judiciary. The powers of the states are not specifically enumerated, for the most part. The absence of an enumeration of state powers concerned state rights advocates. The Tenth Amendment was included in the Bill of Rights to appease these concerns. That amendment reads, "The powers not delegated to the United States by the Constitution, nor prohibited by it to the States, are reserved to the States respectively, or to the people."

James Madison said, of the balance of powers between the national government and the states, that:

> The powers delegated by the proposed Constitution to the federal government are few and defined. Those which are to remain in the State governments are numerous and indefinite. The former will be exercised principally on external objects, such as war, peace, negotiation, and foreign commerce; with which last the power of taxation will, for the most part, be connected. The powers reserved to the several States will extend to all the objects which, in the ordinary course of affairs, concern the lives, liberties, and properties of people, and the internal order, improvement, and prosperity of the State.[2]

Several other clauses of the Constitution are critical to understanding federalism in the United States. First, Articles I, II, and III enumerate the powers of the national government by defining its three branches. Article I, § 8, for instance, lists the various powers of Congress. There are many, including, for example, the power to coin and borrow money, establish a post office, establish and maintain military forces, promote the arts and sciences, and create immigration laws. Article I, § 8, clause 18 is known as the **"necessary and proper" clause**. That clause provides that Congress shall have the power to "make all Laws which shall be necessary and proper for carrying into execution the foregoing Powers, and all other Powers vested by this Constitution in the Government of the United States, or in any Department or Officer thereof." The "foregoing Powers" referred to in the clause

---

TERMS

government; and a *confederation,* where two or more governments combine to create a confederation government that has no direct authority over the citizens of each of its members.

necessary and proper clause[†] Article I of the Constitution grants to Congress the power to make all laws "necessary and proper" for carrying out its constitutional responsibilities. The Supreme Court has long interpreted this provision to mean that Congress has the right not only to enact laws that are absolutely indispensable, but any laws that are reasonably related to effectuating the powers expressly granted to it by the Constitution.

are the enumerated powers of Congress, the President, and the judiciary. This clause, as discussed in Chapter 5, has been used to increase federal jurisdiction.

The **"commerce" clause**, also found in Article I, § 8, at clause 3, states that Congress has the power to regulate foreign and interstate commerce. Like the necessary and proper clause, the commerce clause has been used to expand the realm of the national government.

Article VI contains another important provision, the **"supremacy" clause**. The relevant part of Article VI provides that "This Constitution, and the Laws of the United States which shall be made in Pursuance thereof; and all Treaties made, or which shall be made, under the Authority of the United States, shall be the supreme Law of the Land; and the Judges in every State shall be bound thereby, any Thing in the Constitution or Laws of any State to the Contrary notwithstanding." In other words, any state or local law that conflicts with the Constitution or a treaty of the United States is invalid. Also, any state or local law that conflicts with any national law, when the policy area is exclusively national, is invalid.

Finally, the Civil War Amendments—Amendments Thirteen, Fourteen, and Fifteen—contributed to an increase in federal power. The Fourteenth Amendment, for example, which was adopted in 1868, increased the authority of the national government as against the states in regard to civil liberties. A post-Civil War amendment, it protects due process and equal protection rights of all persons in the United States. The amendment further provides that Congress "shall have power to enforce, by appropriate legislation, the provisions of this article." Legislation enacted to enforce this and the other Civil War Amendments limits the authority of the states.

Dual and Cooperative Federalism

The balancing of national and state powers has not been an easy task. How exactly is the Tenth Amendment to be construed—as a limitation upon the national authority, or as a truism? How far does Congress's power over interstate commerce extend? What is necessary and proper?

TERMS

---

commerce clause[†] The clause in Article I, § 8, of the Constitution that gives Congress the power to regulate commerce between the states and between the United States and foreign countries. Federal statutes that regulate business and labor ... are based upon this power.

supremacy clause[†] The provision in Article VI of the Constitution that "this Constitution and the laws of the United States ... shall be the supreme law of the land, and the judges in every state shall be bound thereby."

The Philosophy of States' Rights

The framers were careful to preserve the sovereignty of the states. Three delegates to the Constitutional Convention (Gerry, Mason, and Randolph) refused to sign the Constitution because it extended too much power to the national government and, accordingly, took too much power from the states and the people. The states' rights controversy continues even today. But why did the framers believe so strongly in state, rather than federal, power? There are three answers.

First, they feared centralized power. These men had experienced the centralized power of the British monarchy and were of the belief that absolute power corrupts absolutely. They saw even lesser powers as having the same relative corruptive consequence.

Second, the framers knew that localized government is more responsive to local needs. Local leaders are members of the community; they live, work, and worship together. Accordingly, they are more sensitive to local concerns.

Third, it was a generally held belief at the time republics had to be small to be successful. One of the antifederalist writers of the time, Brutus (a pseudonym), opposed the Constitution for this reason. In one of his essays, he quoted Montesquieu's *Spirit of Laws:*

> It is natural to a republic to have only a small territory, otherwise it cannot long subsist. In a large republic there are men of large fortunes, and consequently of less moderation; these are trusts too great to be placed in any single subject; he has interest of his own; he soon begins to think that he may be happy, great and glorious, by oppressing his fellow citizens; and that he may raise himself to grandeur on the ruins of his country. In a large republic, the public good is sacrificed to a thousand views; it is subordinate to exceptions, and depends on accidents. In a small one, the interest of the public is easier perceived, better understood, and more within the reach of every citizen; abuses are of less extent, and of course are less protected.

Brutus stated that the

> territory of the United States is of vast extent; it now contains near three million souls, and is capable of containing much more than ten times that number. Is it practicable for a country, so large and so numerous as they will soon become, to elect a representation, that will speak their sentiments, without their becoming so numerous as to be incapable of transacting public business? It certainly is not.[3]

Different theories have been developed concerning the nature of the federal–state relationship. One theory is that the federal government and state governments are coequal sovereigns. This is known as **dual federalism**. Under this approach, the Tenth Amendment is read

TERMS

dual federalism   The theory that the national government and the state governments are coequal sovereigns. The national government is supreme only when its jurisdiction is explicitly granted by the Constitution.

Amicus

Traditions of the Supreme Court of the United States

The Supreme Court met for the first time on February 2, 1790, in New York City, the nation's first capital. John Jay was the Court's first Chief Justice. The Court has many long-standing practices, some dating back to the Court's first sessions.

By statute, the Court's term begins the first Monday of October, every year. The Court operates under a continuous single term designated by the month and year (for example, the October 1998 Term). Public sessions begin at 10:00 A.M. and close at 3 P.M. There are no public sessions on Thursdays or Fridays. Wednesdays are split between oral arguments in the morning and a conference of the Justices in the afternoon. Thursdays are reserved for conducting research, preparing opinions, and the like. The Justices meet on Fridays to discuss and decide pending cases and petitions for certiorari. Approximately twelve cases are argued during the Monday, Tuesday, and Wednesday sessions. Public sessions in May and June are used to announce the Court's decisions. When all the decisions have been announced, the Court recesses for the summer. Although in recess, the Court continues to manage petitions for certiorari during the summer.

At the Justices' conferences, the Chief Justice begins the discussion by explaining his position and what he expects his final vote to be. The most senior Associate Justice then does the same, and the process continues until the least senior Associate Justice has made a statement. After a vote is finalized, the Chief Justice assigns a Justice to write the Court's opinion, if the Chief Justice is in the majority. If not, the most senior Associate Justice in the majority makes the assignment.[4] The opinion is circulated among the Justices in the majority for comment. An opinion may be amended at this stage if the Justices unanimously agree. A Justice who is in the majority but does not want to join in the majority's opinion may write a concurring opinion. This means that the Justice agrees with the outcome, but not necessarily with the Court's rationale. Justices in the minority may draft dissenting opinions for publication.

Chief Justice Fuller initiated a practice during the late nineteenth century that continues today, the "conference handshake." Before each session and prior to their conferences, the Justices shake hands. Through this, they symbolize their cooperation and harmony, in spite of any differences of opinion they have.

A visitor to the Courtroom may notice that the Justices' chairs are different. The practice of each Justice selecting his or her own chair is another tradition of the Court.

Six Justices constitutes a quorum; although rare, there have been cases in which a quorum could not be reached due to recusals and absences. The Chief Justice is seated in the center chair. The senior Associate Justice is seated to the Chief Justice's immediate right, the Justice next in seniority is seated to the Chief Justice's immediate left, and so on, alternating from right to left.

Since at least 1800, the Justices have worn black robes. Chief Justice Jay and other Justices initially wore robes with a red facing, emulating English judges, but this practice was discontinued. Similarly, a wig was worn by at least one Justice initially, but this practice did not continue.

Quill pens are also a tradition of the Court. A white quill pen is placed at each counsel table before each session.

In the Court's early years, attorneys appeared wearing formal attire, including tails. Today, this practice is followed by attorneys appearing on behalf of the government. It is optional for others. Most attorneys today appear in dark suits.[5] ▐▐▐

broadly and the supremacy, necessary and proper, and commerce clauses are read narrowly. Only if the national government clearly has jurisdiction are its laws supreme over the states. Further, the Tenth Amendment is construed as establishing a particular sphere of state power; that is, it is considered an independent source of states' rights. As a result, there is a large group of exclusive state powers, a smaller group of exclusive federal powers, and few, if any, concurrently held powers. This approach predominated until the early twentieth century.

Another theory, **cooperative federalism**, asserts that the national government is supreme in the scheme. Using this approach, the supremacy, necessary and proper, and commerce clauses are read expansively, whereas the Tenth Amendment is interpreted as not creating any specific state powers. Dual federalists, alternatively, view the Tenth Amendment as an independent source of states' rights. It is seen as establishing a state domain upon which the national government may not encroach. Under the cooperative federalism approach, the Tenth Amendment is viewed as a truism, a negative statement of state power. No domain is staked out; rather, the states are left with whatever the national government cannot lawfully regulate. In addition, there is a large area over which the federal and state governments exercise concurrent jurisdiction, albeit with federal law reigning supreme. Intrastate commercial ventures that affect interstate commerce are examples.

Another characteristic of cooperative federalism is increased interaction between the states and national government (and local forms of government) in an effort to effectively regulate and administer law and programs. The "war on drugs" waged during the Reagan and Bush administrations is an example of cooperative federalism, as the law enforcement agencies of the national government worked more closely with their counterpart state agencies, including sharing and coordinating resources, all toward policy objectives that were identical or substantially similar.

This aspect of cooperative federalism is a product of the political branches, the executive and legislative. The judiciary has little to do with the cooperative aspect because it does not engage in creation or development of programs and therefore does not interact with state authorities in the administration of those programs. The judiciary usually becomes involved when there is a dispute over jurisdiction;

TERMS

cooperative federalism   The theory that the national government is supreme to the state governments. The powers of the national government are read broadly and the Tenth Amendment is read as not granting any specific powers to the states.

accordingly, it is normally concerned with defining the relative powers of the national and state governments.

The judiciary has had to deal with federalism issues in three contexts, and through its decisions in these contexts, it has advanced the supremacy of national power. First, under the **preemption doctrine**, state laws are invalidated if they interfere or conflict with national legislation. For example, the federal government has preempted state regulation of aviation. Thus, a state cannot enact airline safety regulations, because the federal government has completely regulated the area.

Second, state laws that interfere with interstate commerce, even if largely unregulated by the federal government, are invalidated. This is known as the **dormant commerce clause doctrine**. Pursuant to this doctrine, laws that discriminate against out-of-state market participants have been invalidated. Hence, a state law that prohibited the sale of milk produced outside New York at a lower price than milk produced within the state was held unconstitutional.[6]

Third, through the **intergovernmental immunity doctrine**, the national government possesses greater immunity from state regulation than the states do from federal regulation. That is, the federal government has greater authority to impose obligations upon the states than vice versa. Accordingly, federal overtime and wage laws apply against the states, but similar state laws do not protect federal employees. These three doctrines are discussed more fully in Chapter 7.

Which theory has been applied in the United States? Both. The two theories have been applied by the Court cyclically. As discussed in Chapter 1, the Marshall Court was strongly nationalist. It operated under a cooperative federalism approach. The same was true of the

---

TERMS

preemption[†]   The doctrine that once Congress has enacted legislation in a given field, a state may not enact a law inconsistent with the federal statute. ... A similar doctrine also governs the relationship between the state government and local government.

preemption doctrine   Doctrine that state laws that interfere with federal laws are invalid pursuant to the supremacy clause.

dormant commerce clause doctrine   The idea that state laws that unduly burden interstate commerce, even if the subject is unregulated by the national government, are invalid under federalism principles, because the regulation of interstate and foreign commerce belongs exclusively to the federal government.

intergovernmental immunity doctrine   The doctrine that both the states and the national government possess some immunity from the regulation of the other under federalism principles. Generally, the federal government enjoys greater immunity than do the states.

post-Civil War and late New Deal Courts. It was also true of the Burger Court in its late years.

The Taney Court, Pre-New Deal Court, and the early Burger Court followed the dual federalism approach. Notice that the Burger Court is split between the two theories. This is because the Court issued two opinions, only seven years apart, reaching opposite conclusions concerning the allocation of power between the national and state governments.[7]

In many respects, it is easy to understand why the federal government would today possess broader authority than during the framers' time. At the time the Constitution was created, most commercial activities occurred locally. Industries were small and affected their local areas only. Travel and mobility were much more limited than today. National communication was minimal. People's social lives did not stretch far beyond their local communities.

Today, industries are large and have the ability to significantly affect not only other states, but also the nation and even the world. Through cyberspace and other forms of high-tech communication, nearly all persons are connected. Travel is no longer a local matter. Long-distance air, land, and sea carriers have become commonplace, as have immigration and emigration. These changes have caused an increase in the federal government's sphere. In some instances, the need for uniformity of law has caused the federal government to become involved. In others, the impetus has been the lack of resources of the states. In still others, social, technological, or political change has converted what was once a traditional state issue into a national one.

State and National Powers Compared

Some powers are held exclusively by the national government, others are held exclusively by the states, and some are held concurrently (see Figure 2-1). Then there are some actions that neither may take, because of rights retained by the people.

The powers of the national government are set out in the Constitution. Many of these are found in Article I, which enumerates the powers of Congress. Examples of exclusive national powers are coining money, declaring war, conducting foreign diplomacy, making treaties, regulating interstate and international commerce, establishing a post office, taxing imports and exports, regulating naturalization of citizenship, and establishing bankruptcy law.

Article II, which establishes the national executive, grants to the President of the United States the responsibility of conducting foreign

FIGURE 2-1
Comparing
State and
Federal Powers

Exclusive National Powers
Coining money
Foreign diplomacy
Making treaties
Regulating interstate and foreign
    commerce
Establishing a post office
Taxing imports and exports
Regulating naturalization of
    citizenship
Regulating immigration and
    emigration
Establishing bankruptcy law

Exclusive State Powers
Providing for the health and
    welfare of state citizens
General police and fire protection
Licensing most professions
Providing education

Concurrently Held Powers
Taxing citizens
Chartering banks
Constructing roads
Borrowing money
Eminent domain
Punishing crime

Powers Denied to Both
Ex post facto laws
Bills of attainder
Other encroachments upon
    civil rights protected by
    the Constitution

diplomacy and negotiating treaties. Treaties must be ratified by the Senate, however. The states are forbidden from engaging in diplomacy and entering into agreements with other nations.

Although the sovereignty of the states has diminished since the Constitution was created, certain areas remain within the exclusive domain of the states. Regulating for the health and welfare of citizens is within the state sphere. Providing police and fire protection is another matter within a state's control. These functions make up what is generally referred to as the **police power**. The licensing of professions, such as physicians, plumbers, electricians, and attorneys, is regulated by the states. Education has also been a traditional state function. Just as the national government has the exclusive right to regulate interstate and foreign commerce, the states possess the exclusive right to regulate intrastate commerce.

Finally, some powers are held concurrently. The power to tax citizens, charter banks and corporations, and build roads are examples.

TERMS

police power † The power of government to make and enforce laws and regulations necessary to maintain and enhance the public welfare and to prevent individuals from violating the rights of others.

If the power over a policy area has been delegated to the federal or state governments, the delegatee is generally permitted to engage in regulation of any type, civil, administrative, or criminal. Frequently, the result is an overlapping of administrative functions, as well as civil and criminal laws. For example, the United States Department of Transportation has overlapping jurisdiction with state agencies charged with highway administration. Also, robbery of a federally insured or chartered bank is a violation of both state and federal law. The state in which the robbery occurred has jurisdiction pursuant to its general police powers, and the federal government has jurisdiction by virtue of its charter or insurance coverage.

Finally, civil rights, or rights of the people, are a limitation upon the power of both the states and the national government. Some of these rights are found in the original Constitution. For example, Article I forbids Congress from enacting ex post facto laws and bills of attainder. The Bill of Rights also protects a number of civil rights, such as freedom from self-incrimination, freedom of the press, freedom of assembly, and freedom from cruel and unusual punishment. The rights specifically mentioned in the Constitution are not intended to be exclusive. The Tenth Amendment, often referred to as the *state rights amendment*, also reserves powers to the people. Further, the Ninth Amendment reserves rights not mentioned in the Constitution exclusively to the people. It states, "The enumeration in the Constitution, of certain rights, shall not be construed to deny or disparage others retained by the people." To date, the courts have not read this amendment as reserving any particular rights.

Be aware, however, that the Supreme Court has determined that the Bill of Rights was intended to be a limitation upon the national government, not the states. However, the Court has also determined that the Fourteenth Amendment's due process clause "incorporates" most of the amendments. Any amendment incorporated applies against the states. Nearly every amendment has been incorporated, and therefore the Bill of Rights limits the powers of the states as well as the national government.[8] See Chapter 5 for a thorough discussion of **incorporation**.

The debate over the balancing of federal and state powers continues today. Proponents of states' rights claim that the national government,

---

TERMS

incorporation   The Bill of Rights was intended to be applied only against the national government. However, the Supreme Court determined that most of the rights contained therein were "incorporated" by the due process clause of the Fourteenth Amendment. A right is *incorporated* if it is fundamental and necessary to an ordered liberty. Once incorporated, the right applies against the states.

through all three of its branches, has emasculated state sovereignty. The national government has extended its power in two primary ways. First, the sphere of the national government's jurisdiction has widened considerably, through a liberal reading of the Constitution's delegation of powers to the national government (i.e., commerce and necessary and proper clauses) and a narrow interpretation of the Tenth Amendment. This has already been mentioned and is the subject of further discussion in Chapter 5.

Second, if the national government wants to effectuate a policy objective that falls within the exclusive (or concurrent) jurisdiction of the states, it may impose its will on the states through economic coercion. It does this by attaching conditions to subsidies, grants, and appropriations made to the states. For example, to further the national government's policy of racial integration at public events, one condition placed on money awarded to states is that it may not be used to fund segregated functions. The 55-mile-per-hour speed limit is another example. The regulation of state and local highways is outside the direct regulation of the national government. When the federal government wanted to impose a nationwide 55-mile-per-hour speed limit, it accomplished that aim by threatening to withhold funding from states that did not adopt the 55-mile-per-hour limit. The federal government similarly coerced the states to come into compliance with federal clean air laws by threatening to withhold federal highway funds.[9]

Various Presidents have attempted to address states' rights concerns, such as Presidents Nixon and Ford, who advocated a "new federalism," whereby the federal government would place fewer conditions on the use of federal subsidies. President Carter implemented rules requiring federal administrative officers to work directly with state officials to accomplish policy objectives. President Carter's approach has been termed *shared and cooperative federalism*. President Reagan advocated states' rights, claiming that power should be returned to the states; however, little power was actually transferred during his administration.

As we have seen, not only the political branches of government have struggled with the complexity of federalism. The Supreme Court has wavered between dual and cooperative federalism, with its approach being dependent upon the ideology of its members.

Undoubtedly, the debate over the allocation of powers between the states and national government will continue as an inherent feature of a federalist system like that of the United States. The vacillation between dual and cooperative federalism will also continue, as a result of political, social, and economic factors. At times when national or international concerns consume the nation's attention and conscience, such as war and economic crisis, cooperative federalism will predominate. During periods when there are no pressing national problems, dual federalism is more likely to predominate.

§ 2.2 Separation of Powers

Under the Articles of Confederation, there was no national judiciary. Also, there was no independent executive, as the President was a member of, and selected by, the Congress. The framers were heavily influenced by the theories of philosophers John Locke and Charles de Montesquieu. These men advanced the theory that, to avoid tyranny, a separation or division of governmental power must exist. To the framers, separation of powers was more than a theory. They had had experience with a centralized authority, the English crown, and had found it arbitrary and unjust. Concerning the centralization of powers, James Madison stated that "[t]he accumulation of all power legislative, executive and judiciary in the same hands, whether hereditary, self-appointed, or elective, may justly be pronounced the very definition of tyranny."[10]

Although the phrase "separation of powers" does not appear in the Constitution, the framers embodied the principles in the document. Hence, there is a horizontal division of governmental power, just as there is a vertical division (federalism) (see Figure 2-2).

Horizontally, the national government's powers are divided among three branches, the legislative, executive, and judicial. This division is found in the first three articles of the Constitution. Article I establishes Congress and sets forth its powers. Congress comprises two chambers, the House of Representatives and the Senate. Article II establishes the Presidency and also sets forth the powers of the executive. Article III establishes the Supreme Court and such inferior courts as Congress may

FIGURE 2-2
Dividing
Governmental
Power

		SEPARATION OF POWERS		
		Executive	*Legislative*	*Judicial*
FEDERALISM	*United States*	*President* ▪ Second-level executive officials	*Congress* ▪ Senate ▪ House	*Federal courts* ▪ Article III ▪ Supreme Court ▪ appeals courts ▪ trial courts
	States	*Governor* ▪ Second-level officials	*State legislatures* ▪ typically bicameral	*State courts* (Non-Article III) ▪ highest court ▪ intermediate appeal ▪ trial

establish and sets forth the powers of the judiciary. Congress has exercised the authority to create lower judicial tribunals. Today, there are three levels of federal courts. The trial level courts are called *district courts*. Appeals are taken to the courts of appeals, which are divided into thirteen circuits. Finally, the Supreme Court sits at the apex of the judiciary. In addition, there are a few specialty courts in the federal system. See Figure 2-3, which diagrams the federal court structure.

The authority and responsibilities of the three branches are not equally well defined by the Constitution. Congress's authority is the best defined, with the President's and the judiciary's falling second and third, respectively.

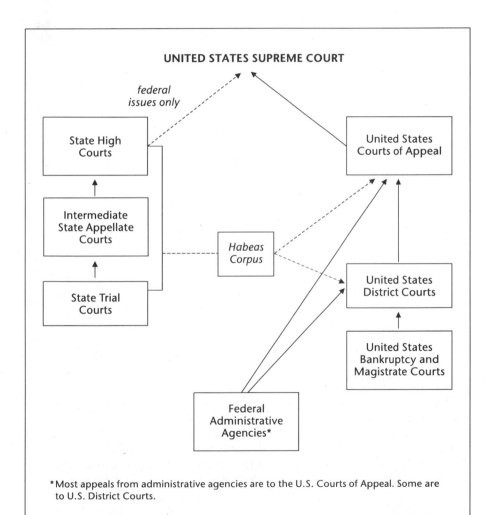

FIGURE 2-3
Courts and Appellate Procedure

Congress is responsible for making the nation's laws; the President is responsible for administering and enforcing the nation's laws, conducting foreign affairs, and negotiating treaties, and is the commander-in-chief of the military; the judiciary is responsible for administering justice, resolving disputes, and interpreting the law. Today, the judiciary also plays a role in preserving the balance of powers and protecting civil liberties.

As a general proposition, one branch may not exercise the functions of any other coordinate branches. However, no one function is vested entirely in one branch. The framers went one step further in preventing abuse—they incorporated a system of checks and balances.

§ 2.3 Checks and Balances

Although the framers did intend to separate the three governmental branches, they did not intend for the branches to be "wholly unconnected with each other."[11] The branches do come into contact with one another on occasion. For example, executive officials and judges may testify at congressional hearings concerning their functions and needs. The President, Justices of the Supreme Court, and the entire Congress assemble for the President's State of the Union address. The branches also come into contact (albeit often indirect) as a result of the many checks and balances found in the Constitution.

Through checks and balances, the framers prevented one branch from possessing absolute authority over any particular function. Rather, the functions delegated to one branch are "checked" by, or shared with, another branch. This provides balance to the system by keeping each branch accountable to its coordinate branches. Several checks can be found in the Constitution (see Figure 2-4).

Congress is responsible for making the law. It is checked in this function by the President, who may veto legislation. The President is then checked by Congress, which can override a veto with a two-thirds majority. Also, Congress enacts laws, but it depends on the President to enforce them. The judiciary also checks Congress. Legislation that conflicts with the Constitution may be declared void by the courts.

The President conducts foreign affairs and negotiates treaties. Congress, the Senate in particular, must ratify treaties. The President is the commander-in-chief of the military, but Congress possesses significant authority over the military as well. It is charged with making rules regulating the military and is responsible for declaring war. The President has been delegated the authority to nominate federal judges and other governmental officers, but the appointments are final only after

Power	Checked By
President negotiates treaties	Senate ratification
President nominates judges and officers	Senate confirmation
Congress enacts laws	Presidential approval and judicial review
Presidential veto	Congressional override
President is commander-in-chief of the military	Congress declares war and creates rules regulating the military
Courts exercise judicial review	Impeachment by Congress and constitutional amendment process
Elected officials are not responsive to public	People, through the vote

FIGURE 2-4
Examples of Checks and Balances

Senate confirmation. As a check on both the President and the judiciary, Congress holds the power of impeachment. Finally, through judicial review, the judiciary checks the President's actions for constitutionality.

The judiciary is also checked. Article III judges are nominated by the President and the Senate must approve the nominations. Congress has the authority to remove cases from the appellate jurisdiction of the Supreme Court and, presumably, could limit the jurisdiction of lower courts. Also, because the courts inferior to the Supreme Court were created by Congress, they could be abolished by Congress. As previously mentioned, judges may be removed through impeachment by Congress. The states and Congress (the people) check the constitutional pronouncements of the Court through the amendment process.

Therefore, it is obvious that no branch is completely independent in the performance of its functions. Because of these checks, interbranch cooperation, especially between Congress and the President, is increased and the potential for unlawful, unethical, and unreasonable governmental behavior is decreased.

Another method of checking government is through the varying methods of selecting governmental officials. This power is diffused, that is, no one entity is responsible for choosing the representatives of the people. Even within Congress, for example, two methods of selection were incorporated by the original framers: members of the House of Representatives were elected directly by the people, and senators were chosen by state legislatures. The method of selecting senators by the states did not change until the Seventeenth Amendment was adopted in 1913. Today, both houses are selected by direct election.

The President is elected by the Electoral College, a small group of people chosen at the state level nationwide. Federal judges are nominated by the President and must be confirmed by the Senate. Other federal officials, such as diplomats and Cabinet officials, must undergo the same process.

Federalism, separation of powers, and checks and balances are all intended to prevent tyranny and the usurpation of state sovereignty. In the following five chapters, these issues are examined more closely. In Chapters 3, 4, 5, and 6, the powers of the national legislative, executive, and judicial branches are discussed. Chapter 7 discusses a particular separation of powers problem, that of delegations to administrative agencies. The powers of the states as opposed to the national government are explored in Chapter 8.

Summary

Even though the framers wanted to increase the national government's power from its weak position under the Articles of Confederation, they did not want to centralize all governmental power into one hand or groups of hands. Instead, they controlled power through structure. First, they created a federation. Second, they further divided federal power into three departments or branches. These power divisions are not absolute, however. The federal and state governments often share jurisdiction and the three branches of the federal government check each other. These additional features of the United States government are intended to protect the people against tyranny.

The precise relationship between the federal and state governments is continually being redefined. The social, economic, and political circumstances of each case determine the legal outcome of any jurisdictional conflicts. The Supreme Court has vacillated between the dual and cooperative federalism perspectives since the Constitution was enacted. There is no question, however, that the federal government has experienced enormous growth and increases in power during the past 200 years. Some of this can be attributed to population growth and the globalization of economic, travel, political, and social aspects of the world. Other factors, such as internal politics, have also contributed to the current federal scheme. Whether a devolution or shift of powers from the federal government to the states will occur remains to be seen. But for now, the Supreme Court has interpreted the Tenth Amendment as a truism, not an independent source of states' rights, while constitutional delegations of power to Congress (e.g., the commerce and necessary and proper clauses) are being interpreted expansively.

Review Questions

1. Define federalism and separation of powers.

2. Why did the framers separate governmental powers?

3. List two powers held exclusively by the federal government, two held exclusively by the state governments, and two concurrently held.

4. Identify two checks and balances provided for in the Constitution.

5. Briefy describe the functions of each of the three branches.

Review Problems

1. Compare and contrast dual and cooperative federalism. Which do you believe the framers intended? Should the framers' intent matter today? Explain your answers.

2. Congress enacts the following statute:

   Section One TRAFFIC LAWS: FTPA; exclusive national jurisdiction

   The Federal Traffic Police Administration is hereby established. It shall have jurisdiction over all traffic offenses defined by federal law. The federal government shall be the source of all traffic laws and law enforcement on all roads, paved and unpaved, in the United States.

   Section Two TRAFFIC LAWS: FTT; Trials

   A system of Federal Traffic Tribunals is hereby established. The FTT shall be located within the Department of Justice. The FTT shall have exclusive jurisdiction over every traffic violation charge in the United States. The judges of the tribunal shall be appointed by the Attorney General and may be removed by the Attorney General without cause.

   Under further provisions, all traffic offenses are characterized as criminal and punishment varies from small fines to several years in prison (e.g., vehicular manslaughter, 10 years). Is this statute constitutional? Explain fully.

Notes

1 *The Federalist* No. 47.

2 *The Federalist* No. 45.

3 Essay published in the *New York Journal* on October 18, 1787, taken from *The Creation of the Constitution* 109–111. Opposing Viewpoints Series (Greenhaven Press 1995).

4 *See* William H. Rehnquist, "Sunshine in the Third Branch," 16 *Washburn L. Rev.* 559, n.1 (1977).

5 Stephen McAllister, "Practice Before the Supreme Court of the United States," 64 *J. Kan. B. Ass'n* 25 (Apr. 1995); Wright, Miller, and Cooper, 13 *Fed. Prac. and Procedure, Juris 2d* § 3507 (1984).

6 *Baldwin v. G.A.F. Seelig, Inc.*, 294 U.S. 511 (1935).

7 The two cases are *National League of Cities v. Usery*, 426 U.S. 833 (1976) and *San Antonio Independent School District v. Rodriguez*, 411 U.S. 1 (1973).

8 The amendments that have not been incorporated are the right to a jury trial in civil cases (Seventh amendment), the right to grand jury indictment (Fifth amendment), and the right to have a twelve-person jury (Sixth amendment and case law).

9 For a discussion of this topic, *see* William Klein, "Pressure or Compulsion? Federal Highway Fund Sanctions of the Clean Air Act Amendments of 1990," 26 *Rutgers L.J.* 855 (1995).

10 *The Federalist* No. 47.

11 *The Federalist* No. 48.

CHAPTER 3

THE JUDICIARY: ITS ROLE AND JUDICIAL REVIEW

§ 3.1 The Federal Court System

Chapters 3 through 6 the three branches of the federal government in detail. Because of the special role the judiciary plays in constitutional law, that branch is examined first, followed by the legislative and executive branches, respectively. The discussion begins with the structure of the federal court system.

Article III, § 1, of the federal Constitution provides that the "judicial power of the United States, shall be vested in one Supreme Court, and such inferior Courts as the Congress may from time to time ordain and establish." There is no mention of the number of judges that shall sit on the Supreme Court nor how or what lower courts may be established. Further, the jurisdictional statement (which is discussed later in this chapter) is vague. It is true, as shown in Chapters 5 and 6, that the framers gave considerably more attention to defining the legislative and executive branches. This probably reflects their fears that the executive and legislative branches posed a greater threat to freedom and state sovereignty than did the judiciary. Alexander Hamilton said that although the executive "holds the sword of the community," and the legislature holds the purse strings and the power to make the laws, the judiciary,

> on the contrary, has no influence over either the sword or the purse; no direction either of the strength or of the wealth of the society, and can take no active resolution whatever. It may truly be said to have neither FORCE nor WILL but merely judgment; and must ultimately depend upon the aid of the executive arm even for the efficacy of its judgments ... . It proves incontestably that the judiciary is beyond comparison the weakest of the three departments of power.[3]

The framers expressly created the Supreme Court. They left the number of justices constituting the Court to Congress (through legislation involving the President) to determine. Initially, the number was set at six—one Chief Justice and five Associate Justices—by the Judiciary Act of 1789. The number changed to five between 1801 and 1807. In

1807 it rose to nine justices. In 1837, the Court had its greatest number of justices, ten. In 1866, the number returned to seven, and in 1869 the number again became nine, where it has remained ever since.

Franklin D. Roosevelt, displeased with decisions of the Court that invalidated some of his New Deal reforms, proposed increasing the size of the Court. He proposed that one additional Justice be appointed for every Justice over the age of 70. Had his proposal become law, he would have been able to appoint six new Justices, increasing the size of the Court to fifteen. The proposal was unsuccessful, but represents the boldest attempt yet by a President to control the ideology of the Court.

The Supreme Court sits at the apex of the judiciary of the United States and for the most part exercises **appellate jurisdiction**. Appeals from the United States Courts of Appeals and from the highest courts of the states (on federal issues) are taken to the Supreme Court. In rare instances, the Supreme Court acts as a court of **original jurisdiction**, which means that a case does not come to the Court by appeal, but rather is initiated in the Supreme Court. See Figure 2-3 for a chart of the federal court system. The original and appellate jurisdiction of the Supreme Court is discussed at greater length in Chapter 4.

Congress immediately created inferior federal courts through the Judiciary Act of 1789. Through that statute, three circuit courts of appeals and thirteen district courts were created. Initially, there were no circuit judges. Circuit court panels were comprised of one district judge and two Supreme Court Justices.

The organization of the system has since changed. Today, there are eleven geographical circuits with a court of appeals in each. There are two additional courts of appeals, one in the District of Columbia and another for the Federal Circuit. Hence, there are thirteen courts of appeals in the federal system.

The courts of appeals are the intermediate-level appellate courts of the federal system. (See Figure 3-1, which diagrams the judicial circuits of the United States.) These courts hear appeals from district courts, specialty courts, and, in some instances, administrative tribunals. Each court of appeals has many associate judges (e.g., eleven) and one chief judge. Cases are usually heard by three judges, although a court may sit **en banc** so that all the members of the court hear a single case.

TERMS

appellate jurisdiction[†] The authority of one court to review the proceedings of another court or of an administrative agency.

original jurisdiction[†] The jurisdiction of a trial court, as distinguished from the jurisdiction of an appellate court.

en banc[†] [French for] "on the bench." A court, particularly an appellate court, with all the judges sitting together (sitting en banc) in a case.

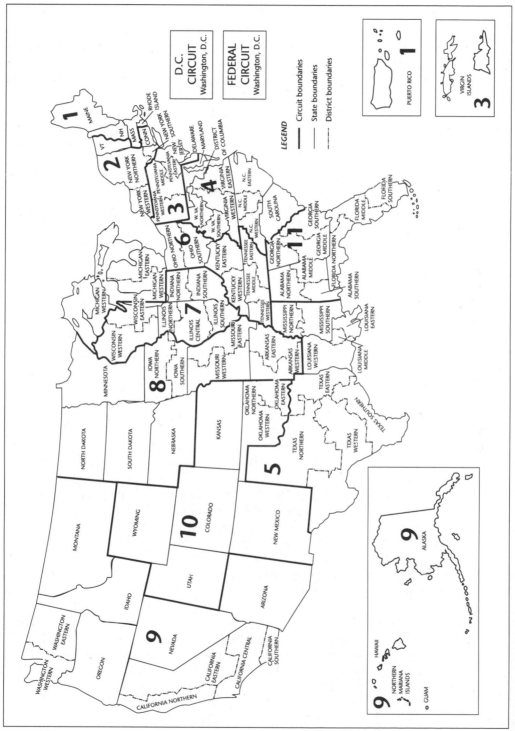

FIGURE 3-1 United States Courts of Appeals and United States District Courts

In addition, there are ninety-four district courts in the United States. These are the federal trial courts. Each state has at least one district court and larger states have as many as four. Districts may be further geographically divided into divisions.

The number of judges in each district varies according to need. District judges usually sit individually. However, Congress has provided for three-judge district courts in particular cases. Even when a three-judge court is statutorily mandated, one judge may be designated as the chief of the panel and be delegated the authority to make some decisions alone, such as whether preliminary injunctions or stays should be ordered. All three judges must sit, however, at trial. In most three-judge district court trials, appeal is taken directly to the Supreme Court. See Chapter 4 for a discussion of when three-judge district courts are required.

Finally, Congress has created a number of specialty courts. The Claims Court, the Court of International Trade, the Tax Court, and the Court of Customs and Patent Appeals are examples. In addition, a system of bankruptcy courts and U.S. magistrate-judges handles a considerable amount of the federal caseload.

§ 3.2 Federal Judges

The framers considered several proposals for the appointment of federal judges: first, selection by the President alone; second, selection by Congress alone; third, selection by Congress with the advice and consent of the President; fourth, selection by the President with the advice and consent of Congress, specifically, the Senate.[4] Their decision is embodied in Article II, § 2, of the Constitution, which provides that the President "shall nominate, and by and with the Advice and Consent of the Senate, shall appoint ... Judges of the supreme Court." First, a nominee is selected by the President. The language of the clause appears to anticipate senatorial participation in the form of "advice." The final nomination decision is, however, exclusively the President's. That nomination is sent to the Senate for "consent," that is, the Senate may either deny or confirm the nomination.

The Constitution does not specify criteria for confirmation; rather, this is left to the political branches to determine. In recent years, the process has been criticized as being too political, focusing too much on the candidates' ideology and not enough on the candidates' objective abilities and qualifications.

Amicus

The First Justices of the Supreme Court

President George Washington signed the Judiciary Act of 1789 on September 24, 1789. The Judiciary Act established the three circuit courts and thirteen district courts that initially made up the inferior courts of the United States. In addition, the Judiciary Act fixed the number of Supreme Court Justices at six. Unlike justices today, these men did not sit in one location. Justices were required to "ride a circuit" hearing appeals. Many justices wrote of the extreme hardship imposed by circuit riding.

On the same day President Washington signed the Judiciary Act into law, he announced his first nominees to the Court. He selected John Jay as Chief Justice and James Wilson, John Rutledge, John Blair, William Cushing, and Robert H. Harrison as Associate Justices. Robert Harrison declined the position, even though he had been confirmed by the Senate. In his place President Washington nominated James Iredell. All the nominees were confirmed by the Senate.

John Jay was born on December 12, 1745. He studied philosophy, Latin, Greek, and law at King's College, which is now Columbia University. During his career, he practiced law, served in the Continental Congress, fought for ratification of the Constitution, authored a number of the *Federalist Papers,* and was a diplomat, New York's first Chief Justice, Governor of New York, and Chief Justice of the United States. He resigned as the nation's first Chief Justice to become the Governor of New York. Later, President John Adams asked Jay to rejoin the Court, but Jay refused, stating that

the efforts repeatedly made to place the Judicial Department on a proper footing have proved fruitless. I left the bench perfectly convinced that under a system so defective, it would not obtain the energy, weight and

dignity which are essential to its affording due support to the national Government, nor acquire the public confidence and respect which, as the last resort of justice in the nation, it should possess. Hence I am induced to doubt both the propriety and expediency of my returning to the bench under the present system.

James Wilson was born in Scotland in 1742 and moved to the United States in 1765. He studied the classics and initially intended to enter the clergy. However, law and politics were to be his life. His career included a successful law practice, service as a delegate to the Constitutional Convention, and service as one of the first Justices of the Supreme Court.

John Rutledge was born in South Carolina in 1739. He was home-schooled until he studied law in England. In addition to being one of the first Justices of the Supreme Court, he was a delegate to the first Continental Congress, Governor of South Carolina, and a delegate to the Constitutional Convention. Rutledge resigned in 1791 to assume the Chief Justiceship of the South Carolina Court of Common Pleas. In 1795, Washington appointed Rutledge to serve as Acting Chief Justice until he could be confirmed as Chief Justice. However, between the time of his appointment and his confirmation hearings, he became embroiled in a political controversy (he opposed the Jay Treaty) that was to prove fatal to his nomination. The Senate did not confirm him; thus, he is the only person to have sat as Chief Justice without confirmation.

John Blair, Jr., was born in Virginia in 1732. He studied law at William and Mary in England. His career included being a member of the Virginia House of Burgesses and Chief Justice of the General Court of Virginia; he was also a delegate to the Constitutional Convention and Associate Justice of the Supreme Court.

William Cushing was born in Massachusetts in 1732. He studied the classics at Harvard and planned to enter theology, but later decided to pursue a career in law. He practiced law in his early years and eventually was appointed judge to the Supreme Court of Massachusetts. Although not a delegate to the Constitutional Convention, Cushing was an advocate of the new Constitution at the Massachusetts ratification convention. He served as the senior Associate Justice under Chief Justice Jay.

James Iredell was born on October 5, 1751, in England. He studied law and came to the United States as an official of the English government. He later became an opponent of English legislative domination of the colonies.

He was a judge in North Carolina and an advocate of the Constitution, as well as one of the first Justices of the Supreme Court.

As you can see, the nation's first Justices all played an important role in the development and ratification of the Constitution. In addition to having legal and judicial experience, they knew politics. This pattern continued for many years. During the first decade of the Court, a total of twelve justices sat. Six had been delegates to the Constitutional Convention, four had served in the Confederation Congress, and two had served in the new Congress. Many were delegates to their state ratification conventions and only one, Samuel Chase, had not served at either the Constitutional Convention or a state ratification convention.[5] ▥

Another criticism of the selection process and the lifetime tenure rule (discussed later in this section) is that they create a **countermajoritarian institution**, an institution whose members are not elected by, or directly accountable to, the people. In fact, they are only marginally accountable even to the people's elected representatives.

Clearly, the Court is countermajoritarian in structure. But is it countermajoritarian in practice? Research indicates that the Court is largely a majoritarian institution, responding to public opinion:

> Empirically, the results of our analysis are easily summarized. For most of the period since 1956, a reciprocal relationship appears to have existed between the ideology of the public mood in the United States and the broad ideological tenor of Supreme Court decisions. ... [T]he evidence suggests that public opinion exercises important influence on the decisions of the Court even in the absence of changes in the composition of the Court or in the partisan and ideological makeup of

---

TERMS

countermajoritarian institution Because its members are not elected by the people, are not accountable to the people, and are not required to consider public opinion in their decision making, the Supreme Court is considered by most to be a countermajoritarian institution. This does not mean, however, that the Court has historically been countermajoritarian in its decision making.

Congress and the presidency. That the effects of public opinion take five years, on average, to register on the Court's decisions probably reflects both the time it takes for a change in public opinion to be reflected in presidential elections and the time required before a newly elected president has a Court vacancy to fill. ... [T]he results appear to reassure those committed to democratic principles and concerned about the countermajoritarian potential of the Court. Our analyses indicate that for most of the period since 1956, the Court has been highly responsive to majority opinion. Its decisions not only have conformed closely to the aggregate policy opinions of the American public but have thereby reinforced and helped legitimate emergent majoritarian concerns.[6]

The findings correlating public opinion and the Court's decisions include only fundamental changes in public opinion, not ordinary fluctuations or mood swings. Interestingly, the strong correlation between public opinion and the Court's decision began to diminish in 1981, when the Court's decisions became increasingly more conservative and the public mood became increasingly more liberal. The result was that the Court was more countermajoritarian under Presidents Reagan and Bush than under the previous administrations.[7]

Why did the framers establish an institution with a countermajoritarian potential? The framers believed strongly in the independence of the judiciary. Although they created a republican form of government, they believed that the will of the majority should be checked in some circumstances. This is because, upon occasion, such as during times of national emergency, the popular will may be at odds with republican, democratic principles. It is the duty of the judiciary to keep a cool, deliberative, rational head. It should not ride the waves of popularism. The judiciary, as an institution, should be the nation's democratic conscience. If the judiciary were dependent upon the people directly, or upon one of the other two political branches, this role could not be fulfilled.

Once confirmed, federal judges receive lifetime tenure. Also, the Constitution prohibits Congress from decreasing the salaries of federal judges during their tenure. These provisions were intended to shield the judiciary from overreaching by the other two branches. By assuring judges lifetime tenure and income, Congress cannot coerce judges; thereby, the independence of the judiciary is protected. Remember that the framers believed that an independent judiciary was necessary to protect civil liberties. Alexander Hamilton stated, in the *Federalist Papers,* the following about the selection process and lifetime appointment:

> If, then, the courts of justice are to be considered as the bulwarks of a limited Constitution against legislative encroachments, this consideration

will afford a strong argument for the permanent tenure of judicial offices, since nothing will contribute so much as this to that independent spirit in the judges which must be essential to the faithful performance of so arduous a duty.

This independence of the judges is equally requisite to guard the Constitution and the rights of individuals from the effects of those ill humors which the arts of designing men, or the influence of particular conjunctures, sometimes disseminate among the people themselves, and which, though they speedily give place to better information, and more deliberate reflection, have a tendency, in the meantime, to occasion dangerous innovations in the government, and serious oppressions of the minor party in the community. ...

That inflexible and uniform adherence to the rights of the Constitution, and of individuals, which we perceive to be indispensable in the courts of justice, can certainly not be expected from judges who hold their offices by a temporary commission. Periodical appointments, however regulated, or by whomsoever made, would in some way or other, be fatal to their necessary independence. If the power of making them was committed either to the executive or legislature there would be danger of an improper complaisance to the branch which possessed it; if to both, there would be an unwillingness to hazard the displeasure of either; if to the people, or to persons chosen by them for the special purpose, there would be too great a disposition to consult popularity to justify a reliance that nothing would be consulted but the Constitution and the laws.

There is yet a further weighty reason for the permanency of the judicial offices ... . [A] temporary duration in office which would naturally discourage such characters from quitting a lucrative line of practice to accept a seat on the bench would have a tendency to throw the administration of justice into the hands less able and less well qualified to conduct it with utility and dignity.[8]

John Marshall declared the same principle during the Virginia constitutional convention. "I have always thought, from my earliest youth until now, that the greatest scourge an angry Heaven ever inflicted upon an ungrateful and sinning people was an ignorant, a corrupt, or a dependent judiciary."[9]

Lifetime appointment is not absolute. Judges may be removed by Congress. Article III provides that judges shall remain in office during "good behavior." Article II, § 4, allows removal of any civil officer of the national government, including a judge, for treason, bribery, or other high crimes and misdemeanors.

Article I vests the power of impeachment in the House of Representatives. However, impeachment is not removal, it is an accusation. The Senate tries impeachment cases and decides whether to remove the accused official. There are two other methods of ending the appointment of a federal judge: death and retirement.

Federal and State Judges: Then and Now

Through the Judiciary Act of 1789, six Supreme Court Justiceships were created (one Chief Justice and five Associate Justices). Additionally, Congress provided for thirteen district judgeships. In total, nineteen federal judicial positions were created. At the same time, there were approximately 100 state judges.

Compare those numbers to contemporary figures. In 1988, there were 575 district judges, 168 appellate judges, 280 bankruptcy judges, 284 magistrate-judges, and 9 Supreme Court Justices in the federal system, totalling 1,316 federal judges. In 1990, there were 28,658 state court judges sitting in 15,642 courts.

Source of contemporary state statistics: Judicial Council of California, National Center for State Courts (1996).
Source of contemporary federal statistics: R. Katzmann, *Judges and Legislators* 60 (Washington, D.C.: Brookings 1988).

Today, there are ninety-four district courts, some with multiple judges, and thirteen appellate courts. In addition, Congress has created a number of courts and judgeships that are considered *legislative courts* rather than *constitutional courts*. Whether a court is legislative or constitutional largely depends on the status of the judges who sit on the court. If the judges are empowered under Article III of the Constitution—and therefore must undergo the nomination and confirmation process, are assured lifetime tenure, and cannot have their pay reduced—the court is constitutional. District, appellate, and Supreme Court judges are all constitutional judges.

In contrast, if the judges do not have these characteristics, they are empowered by Congress and not the Constitution. The United States Claims Court, the United States Court of International Trade, the United States Tax Court, and administrative law tribunals are examples of non-Article III courts. The judges of these courts are federal judicial officers, but they are not empowered by the Constitution; rather, their positions are created by Congress and are not formally part of the judicial branch. For this reason, they are commonly referred to as *Article I judges*.

In addition to the judges who sit on the foregoing non-Article III courts, Congress has created a system of bankruptcy courts, presided over by bankruptcy judges. Also, through the Federal Magistrate Act, a system of magistrate-judges was created to relieve some of the burden on district judges.

Neither bankruptcy judges nor magistrate-judges undergo the nomination and confirmation process. Instead, Congress has delegated the appointment power to Article III judges. Also, such judges do not benefit from lifetime appointment. Bankruptcy judges are appointed for fourteen years and magistrate-judges for seven years. Both may be reappointed. Through appointment by Article III judges and other measures, Congress has created a degree of independence (from Congress and the executive) for these non-Article III judges. Nevertheless, there are some limitations upon what functions they may perform, as they are not constitutionally empowered. For example, magistrate-judges may not preside over the critical stages of a felony criminal trial without the consent of the parties.[10] Also, at present, it appears that bankruptcy judges may not preside over jury trials.[11] Regardless, both these types of judicial officers are valuable members of the federal judiciary.

§ 3.3 Formal and Informal Controls on the Federal Judiciary

As will be discussed later in this chapter, through judicial review, a court may declare executive, congressional, or state action void as unconstitutional. This is an awesome and controversial power. Regardless, it is a well-established power.

Now consider the federal judiciary. As you have learned, federal judges are appointed for life. They are assured no decrease in their salaries. They are, for the most part, independent. Does this mean that the United States is governed by an imperial and unconstrained judiciary? No, there are a number of formal and informal constraints on the judiciary (see Figure 3-2). Our discussion begins with formal constraints.

Formal Constraints

First, the political branches are responsible for the selection of judges. The President nominates a candidate. The Senate must confirm the nomination before it can become final. Through this process, the political branches control the membership of the Court. As one would expect, presidents have always tended to nominate individuals who hold ideologies similar to their own. However, ideology has increased in importance lately, and contemporary presidents and Senates have increasingly probed deeper into the backgrounds, philosophies, and records of candidates.

In spite of efforts to nominate persons with a particular judicial philosophy, presidents occasionally end up dissatisfied with their selections. President Eisenhower appointed Earl Warren as Chief Justice. Later he said of this choice that it was "[t]he greatest damn-fool mistake

---

CONTROLS ON FEDERAL JUDICIAL POWER—SUMMARY

Formal

1. Presidential nomination and senate confirmation of Article III judges

2. Removal through impeachment

3. Congressional control of jurisdiction

4. Congressional control of number of justices and lower federal courts

5. Justiciability requirements

6. Constitution and statutory amendments intended to reverse judicial decisions

7. Congressional control of increases in salaries and provision of other resources

Informal

1. Judicial reliance on executive branch for the enforcement of orders

2. Public opinion

3. Interest in preserving the integrity of the judiciary

FIGURE 3-2 Controls on Federal Judicial Power—Summary

I ever made!" President Truman remarked that "whenever you put a man on the Supreme Court, he ceases to be your friend."[12]

The effect a President can have on the philosophy of the nation's judiciary can be profound. This is especially true of two-term presidents and periods during which successive presidents are of the same ideological fabric. For example, Presidents Reagan and Bush appointed over 600 federal judges, out of a total of only 828 federal judges.[13] Even if a small percentage prove to be philosophically disappointing to the nominator, these two presidents have had a significant and long-lasting effect on the judiciary.

Removal of judges by Congress is the second formal control on the judiciary. The House of Representatives has the power to impeach a justice. An article of impeachment is the equivalent of bringing charges. However, the Constitution limits impeachment to removal from office. Once a judge is impeached, the Senate tries the matter. A two-thirds vote is required to remove a justice. Either house, or both, may assign their respective responsibilities to a committee that will hear the evidence and report its findings and recommendations.

Only one Supreme Court Justice, Samuel Chase, has ever been impeached, and he was not convicted by the Senate. Twelve appellate and district judges have been impeached and seven of those were convicted. Many others have resigned because of controversy or impending impeachment.[14]

Third, as you will see later in this chapter, Congress possesses significant authority to control the types of cases that may be heard by the judiciary. It can do this because the Constitution grants to Congress the authority to control the **jurisdiction** of the Court in some circumstances. *Jurisdiction* refers to the authority of a court to hear a case. If a court has the authority to hear a case, then it has jurisdiction.

Fourth, Congress determines the number of Justices to sit on the Supreme Court. However, if Congress were to try to use this power to influence the Court's decision making, by packing the Court with members of a particular ideological view, it would have to have a President who shared their philosophy, because the nominations must be made by the executive. As previously discussed, Franklin D. Roosevelt proposed a court-packing plan that was defeated in Congress. The size of the Supreme Court has not been changed since 1870 when it was finally set at nine.

Fifth, so-called *justiciability requirements* also are controlling factors. A number of doctrines limit the power of the Court to render decisions. Mootness, ripeness, standing, political question, and case or controversy requirements all limit the authority of the judiciary. See Chapter 4.

Sixth, the Court's decisions can be changed through political processes. An unfavorable interpretation of a statute can be changed by congressional amendment of the law. Although more difficult than amending a statute, unfavorable constitutional decisions can be changed through the Article IV amendment process. See § 1.5 for a description of the process of amending the Constitution. The Constitution has been amended four times to reverse Supreme Court decisions:

1. The Eleventh Amendment, which provides for state immunity in federal court. Enacted in response to *Chisholm v. Georgia,* 2 U.S. (2 Dall.) 419 (1793).

2. The Fourteenth Amendment, which provides for due process and equal protection in the states. Enacted, partly, in response to *Dred Scott v. Sandford,* 60 U.S. (19 How.) 393 (1856).

TERMS

jurisdiction[†]   A term used in several senses: 1. In a general sense, the right of a court to adjudicate lawsuits of a certain kind. 2. In a specific sense, the right of a court to determine a particular case; in other words, the power of the court over the subject matter of, or the property involved in, the case at bar. 3. In a geographical sense, the power of a court to hear cases only within a specific territorial area.

3. The Sixteenth Amendment, which provides for the federal income tax. Enacted in response to *Pollock v. Farmer's Loan & Trust Co.*, 157 U.S. 429 (1895), in which the Court ruled a federal income tax unconstitutional.

4. The Twenty-Sixth Amendment, which provides that all individuals age eighteen and older possess the right to vote in state and national elections. Enacted in response to *Oregon v. Mitchell*, 400 U.S. 112 (1970).

Seventh, although the pay of Article III judges may not be decreased, Congress does control increases and the provision of other resources to the courts.

Informal Constraints

The Court is also constrained by informal forces. The most significant informal force is the Court's inability to enforce its own commands. The Court does not have a battery of officers, an army, or the administrative network necessary to enforce its orders. The framers vested the executive with the responsibility of enforcing the law. This includes enforcement of court orders.

Some legal scholars believe that some Justices fear that the integrity of the Court would be put in jeopardy if the Court were to issue an order knowing that the President would refuse to enforce its mandate. President Andrew Jackson once responded to a decision of the Supreme Court by stating, "John Marshall has made his decision, now let him enforce it."[15] This fear constrains the Justices to making decisions that they believe the President will enforce. To issue a decision that will not be enforced would result in disrespect for the Court and could potentially set a devastating precedent that the executive may be selective in the orders it wishes to enforce.

Similarly, judicial decision making may be limited by public opinion. Directly, the Court has been insulated from such concerns through lifetime tenure and assured salaries. Justices do not, however, live in a special dormitory separated from society. They are exposed to the media, family, friends, and acquaintances. They may not consider public opinion directly, but surely they have some awareness of contemporary issues, norms, and beliefs that then influences their conceptions of what is just, fair, and expected by the people. Justice Rehnquist stated, concerning the influence of public opinion on judicial decision making, that:

> Judges, so long as they are relatively normal human beings, can no more escape being influenced by public opinion in the long run than can people working at other jobs. And, if a judge on coming to the

bench were to decide to hermetically seal himself off from all manifes-
tations of public opinion, he would accomplish very little; he would
not be influenced by the state of public opinion at the time he came to
the bench.[16]

There have been a few cases in the Supreme Court's history about
which it is speculated that public opinion and political pressures
unduly influenced the Court's decision making. For example, in the
early 1930s the Court invalidated several statutes (or portions thereof)
that were critical parts of President Roosevelt's New Deal plan. These
decisions were met with considerable resistance from the President,
Congress, and the public. President Roosevelt attempted his famous
court-packing scheme as a result, and Congress considered limiting the
appellate jurisdiction of the Court. By 1937, the Court had changed its
approach and thereafter upheld statutes that it previously might have
invalidated.[17]

In *Korematsu v. United States*,[18] the internment of Japanese residents—many of them citizens of the United States—during World War
II was challenged. The Court upheld the government's actions and
many jurists believe it did so because of political and public pressures.
Of course, the fact that the nation was embroiled in a war with Japan
was a significant factor. As you will learn in Chapter 6, the authority of
the President is greater during war than peace.

In most cases the effect of public opinion on the judiciary is fairly
subtle. Nevertheless, it is a factor that must be considered when analyzing judicial decision making.

§ 3.4 The Role of the Federal Judiciary

What role does the judiciary play in a republican form of government? This is the first question that must be addressed. Once answered,
a second question must be asked: what roles do the state and federal
courts play in our federal republic?

Historically, courts have served two primary functions: dispute resolution and the administration of criminal justice. The former refers to
the process of adjudicating civil claims made by individuals, business
entities, or governmental entities against others. The latter refers to the
adjudication of criminal cases.

In colonial America, both of these functions were performed by
state and local courts. Prior to the new Constitution, there were no national courts. This was one of the weaknesses of the Articles of Confederation.

The new Constitution did create a national judiciary: it specifically established the Supreme Court. Further, it provided that Congress could create inferior federal courts. What role were these courts to play in the new system? Clearly, the framers did not intend for federal courts to displace state courts. The traditional jurisdiction of state courts was to continue. To the framers, there was no question that most disputes and criminal cases belonged in state courts. At the Constitutional Convention, antifederalists opposed creating a national judiciary, fearing that it would usurp the authority of state courts. Similarly, the federalists strongly favored creating a national judiciary to protect the United States from the states. They compromised by creating only the Supreme Court, leaving the inferior courts to Congress, and by delegating most judicial authority to the states.

The framers had personally observed the economic and political turmoil caused by a lack of national unity, interstate conflicts, and conflicts between the national and state governments under the Articles of Confederation. Therefore, certain disputes were delegated to the federal judiciary so that a national perspective would be part of judicial decision making. Cases in which the United States is a party are the most obvious example.

Diversity jurisdiction is another form of federal jurisdiction. Cases involving disputes between a citizen of one state and another state, between two states, between citizens of different states, or between a foreign nation or one of its citizens and a state or one of the state's citizens are examples of diverse cases. Federal jurisdiction also extends to cases involving ambassadors, public ministers, and consuls.

Finally, there is federal jurisdiction any time national law is at issue, whether constitutional, statutory, treaty, administrative, or other. This is known as **federal jurisdiction** or *federal question jurisdiction*. These forms of jurisdiction are recognized in the Constitution. Generally, they are considered permissive grants of jurisdiction. That is, they do not automatically create federal jurisdiction; rather, they permit federal jurisdiction to be assumed. Congress has enforced the provisions primarily through two statutes, one providing for diversity of citizenship jurisdiction[19] and the other for federal question jurisdiction.[20]

Since the adoption of the new Constitution, the federal judiciary has grown significantly, both in size and in jurisdiction. The increase in

---

TERMS

diversity jurisdiction[†]   The jurisdiction of a federal court arising from diversity of citizenship, when the jurisdictional amount has been met.

federal jurisdiction[†]   The jurisdiction of the federal courts. Such jurisdiction is based upon the judicial powers granted by Article III of the Constitution and by federal statutes.

jurisdiction is mostly attributable to federal question jurisdiction. As the national government has extended its sphere through the necessary and proper and commerce clauses, the jurisdiction of the federal judiciary has grown concomitantly. The Reconstruction amendments (Thirteen through Fifteen) and civil rights legislation enacted to enforce them have also contributed to the expansion of the jurisdiction of federal courts, probably far beyond what the framers imagined.

Although federal courts hear a large variety of cases today, including many the framers did not anticipate, they have not usurped the role of state courts. In fact, over 95 percent of all civil and criminal cases are heard by state courts.

Another role the judiciary plays is that of guardian and protector. This role has two related features. First, the judiciary acts as the guardian of liberty, justice, and civil liberties. Second, the judiciary acts as a governmental referee, overseeing the state and federal governments to be sure that separation of powers and federalism principles are adhered to.

It is the obligation of the courts to stand between the government and the individual, checking the government's behavior and shielding the individual from any wrongs by the government. Alexander Hamilton wrote that "[t]he courts were designed to be an intermediate body between the people and the legislature, in order, among other things, to keep the latter within the limits assigned to their authority."

This role extends beyond protection of the individual to protection of minorities. The United States is a *republic,* an impure form of democracy. Majority rule is the benchmark of governmental decision making in a democracy. However, the framers also recognized the dangers attendant to majoritarianism. A small group, a minority, can be disadvantaged for the benefit of the majority. The judiciary, with its counter-majoritarian attributes, is responsible for protecting minorities from the abuses of the community. Alexander Hamilton commented on this role of the judiciary:

> The independence of judges is equally requisite to guard the Constitution and the rights of individuals from the effects of those ill humors which the arts of designing men, or the influence of particular conjunctures, sometimes disseminate among the people themselves, and which, though they speedily give place to better information, and more deliberate reflection, have a tendency, in the meantime, to occasion dangerous innovations in the government, and serious oppressions of the minor party in the community. ... [I]t is not to be inferred from this principle that the representatives of the people, whenever a momentary inclination happens to lay hold of a majority of their constituents incompatible with the provisions in the existing Constitution, would, on that account, be justifiable in a violation of those provisions; or that the

courts would be under a greater obligation to connive at infractions in this shape than when they had proceeded wholly from the cabals of the representative body. Until the people have, by some solemn and authoritative act, annulled or changed the established form, it is binding upon themselves collectively, as well as individually; and no presumption, or even knowledge, of their sentiment can warrant their representatives in a departure from it prior to such an act. But it is easy to see that it would require an uncommon portion of fortitude in the judges to do their duty as faithful guardians of the Constitution, where legislative invasions of it had been instigated by the major voice of the community.[21]

Today this function is more critical than ever, and it is likely to continue to increase in significance. At the time the Constitution was adopted, the United States was largely homogeneous. Today, the United States is a pluralistic and heterogeneous nation. There simply are more minorities that require attention today than there were 200 years ago.

Do you agree that a countermajoritarian institution (in structure) is required to preserve individual liberties and to protect minorities? How far should the judiciary take this principle? Slavery, and later the segregation of blacks from the white community, are examples of the oppression feared by Hamilton. Slavery was not ended by the judiciary. That occurred through the political branches and a civil war. It was, however, the judiciary that ended the separate-but-equal doctrine. Bear in mind that the term *minorities,* as used by Hamilton, refers to any minority, not just racial or ethnic groups. Political, religious, and social minorities are included. Do you believe that homosexuals should be treated as minorities within the context of this discussion?

Another important function served by the judiciary is the interpretation of law. While adjudicating cases, all courts must read the law and determine what it means. This is called *interpretation.* The most important document interpreted is the Constitution. The most influential interpretation of that document comes from the Supreme Court.

§ 3.5 Constitutional Interpretation

The Constitution does not state how it is to be interpreted. In many ways, the issue of what method of interpreting the Constitution should be used parallels the question of what is the role of the judiciary in the United States. We have delegated the authority to make policy to the legislative and, to a lesser degree, the executive branches, which are accountable to the people through the voting booth. However, federal judges are not elected, and once installed, they leave office only through death, retirement, or impeachment. Therefore, the issue is whether the Constitution should be interpreted in a manner that permits justices to consider policy matters. Should they be guided by their own ideologies? The nation's?

The most common methods of interpreting the Constitution are originalism, modernism, historical literalism, contemporary literalism, and democratic reinforcement (see Figure 3-3).

Originalism

Originalists follow the so-called doctrine of **original intent**. It is not truly a constitutional doctrine; rather, it is an approach to interpreting the Constitution. Originalists hold that the Constitution should be interpreted to mean what the framers originally intended it to mean.

They contend that by examining the records from the Constitutional Convention, letters written by the framers, the *Federalist Papers* and related publications, the records from the state ratification debates, and other documents, it is possible to determine the framers' intent. Originalists assert that by using this approach, the Court's decision will be less normative. Said another way, decisions will not be the result of the personal opinions (beliefs, mores, biases, etc.) of Justices; they will be "objectively" arrived at. This being so, the Court's decisions will be more predictable and stable and will be perceived as objective, not as a product of the Court's ideological bent. Thereby, the institution itself will be more respected. Originalists argue that once the original intent has been declared, change can come only through the amendment process.

Opponents of the original intent approach argue that the very premise of originalism is unfounded. They ask how one intent can be attributed to the entire group of framers. Individual delegates may have had different reasons for supporting a particular provision of the Constitution.

Also, because the document was ratified by the states, should the intent of all the participants at the state conventions be considered? Maybe the intent of the framers is not even relevant—after all, the

---

TERMS

original intent [†]   A term applied to the view of some scholars and jurists that judicial interpretation of the Constitution should be based on the words of the Constitution itself and the framers' "original intent," not on a contemporary understanding of the Constitution in the context of current realities. Adherents of this doctrine are sometimes referred to as *strict constructionists*.

CONSTITUTION INTERPRETATION METHODS

Method	Description	Evidence
Originalism	Constitution is interpreted and applied in a manner consistent with the framers' intentions	<ul><li>Convention records</li><li>Writings of the framers and their contemporaries (e.g. *Federalist Papers*)</li><li>Ratification debate records</li><li>Laws of the era and preexisting constitution</li></ul>
Modernism/ Instrumentalism	Constitution is interpreted and applied in contemporary terms	<ul><li>Objective indicators of public values</li><li>Social scientific evidence</li></ul>
Literalism— historical	Constitution is interpreted and applied by focusing on its terms, syntax, and other linguistic features that were in use at the time of adoption/ ratification	<ul><li>Text of the Constitution</li><li>Evidence of language use at time of adoption/ratification</li></ul>
Literalism— contemporary	Constitution is interpreted and applied by focusing on its terms, syntax, and other linguistic features that are currently in use	<ul><li>Text of the Constitution</li><li>Evidence of contemporary language use</li></ul>
Democratic/ normative reinforcement	Constitution is interpreted and applied in a manner that reinforces the document's underlying democratic themes	<ul><li>Evidence of framers' intentions</li><li>Structure/organization inherent in Constitution</li><li>Objective evidence of reinforcement of norms</li></ul>

FIGURE 3-3 Methods of Interpreting the Constitution

Constitution is a document of the people. Should an attempt to understand the people's general beliefs and attitudes be made? Furthermore, there is evidence that some provisions were intentionally drafted vaguely (such as the due process clause of the Fifth Amendment), so that the precise meaning could be developed at a later date. What of these provisons? There is also some evidence that the framers did not intend for their subjective intentions to live in perpetuity. For example, James Madison believed that a document must speak for itself and that any meaning derived from its reading should not be displaced by a contrary finding of original intent. He also stated, "[a]s a guide in expounding and applying the provisions of the Constitution, the debates and incidental decisions of the Convention can have no authoritative character." He believed that the "public meaning" of the Constitution should prevail over the individual intentions of the framers. Public meaning could be shown, according to Madison, through precedent and consensus. That is, if there is consensus in the government and with the people as to what the Constitution means, and they have acted accordingly for some time, then the meaning is established, regardless of any original intent.[22]

It is also argued that original intention cannot be discerned in most instances, because the framers did not consider every possibility. This is especially true when one considers the significant changes the nation has seen since the Constitution was ratified. The industrial revolution, technological revolution, rapid modernization, population explosion (there were fewer than four million people in the United States at the time the Constitution was ratified), and changes in social, political, and economic attitudes brought with them problems that could not have been foreseen by the framers.

Opponents also disagree with the conclusion that predictability and stability will be assured. Courts can differ in their interpretation of intent and even in the method of determining original intention; therefore, decisions could be changed because of differences in opinion concerning the framers' original intentions.

Modernism

Many of those who criticize originalism are **modernists**, also known as *instrumentalists*. Associate Justice William Brennan, Jr., was of this ideological group. He contended that the Constitution should be interpreted as if it were to be ratified today—a "contemporary ratification" or "living constitution" approach. Originalists discover the meaning of the Constitution by examining the intent of the framers. Modernists find meaning by reading the language of the Constitution in light of contemporary life. Through this approach, the judiciary contributes to the social and moral evolution of the nation. Some oppose this method as countermajoritarian. That is, they contend that it is not the function of nine unelected individuals to make policy decisions for

---

TERMS

modernism An approach to interpreting the Constitution that allows courts to consider changes in social, economic, and political forces.

the nation. Proponents hold that, as an institution, the Court must engage in this form of decision making to perform its function of shielding the individual from governmental excesses and to assure that its decisions will be respected.

In addition to the philosophies previously mentioned, the adherents of this school oppose the doctrine of original intention because it causes the Constitution to become dated and out-of-touch with contemporary problems. They contend that the Constitution's strength comes from its dynamic, flexible nature. Although it affirmatively establishes certain principles, it does so in language that permits it to change as America changes—not drastic changes, but change within certain parameters. Change outside of the perimeters of reason must occur by amendment. Justice Brennan said:

> We current justices read the Constitution in the only way that we can: as Twentieth Century Americans. We look to the history of the time of framing and to the intervening history of interpretation. But the ultimate question must be, what do the words of the text mean in our time. For the genius of the Constitution rests not in any static meaning it might have had in a world that is dead and gone, but in the adaptability of its great principles to cope with current problems and current needs … . As augmented by the Bill of Rights and the Civil War Amendments, this text is a sparkling vision of the supremacy of the human dignity of every individual. This vision is reflected in the very choice of democratic self-governance: the supreme value of a democracy is the presumed worth of each individual. And this vision manifests itself most dramatically in the specific prohibitions of the Bill of Rights … . It is a vision that has guided us as a people throughout our history, although the precise rules by which we have protected fundamental human dignity have been transformed over time in response to both transformations of social condition and evolution of our concepts of human dignity.[23]

Justice Brennan is in good company. Associate Justice Benjamin Cardozo commented that "the great generalities of the Constitution have a content and a significance that vary from age to age."[24] Chief Justice Fred Vinson responded to originalists by stating, "To those who would paralyze our government in the face of impending threat by encasing it in a semantic straitjacket, we must reply that all concepts are relative."[25]

Modernists do not discard original intention or stare decisis; they recognize them as factors in judicial decision making. But the needs of society are also taken into account, as is the nature of the dispute that gave rise to the case before the Court. To the modernist, the framers could not anticipate every issue that would be presented to the Court, nor did they try. It is the duty of the Court to read the Constitution and apply its terms in a manner that gives due deference to the nation's history and customs, as well as contemporary conditions and public expectations.

The results of scientific research may also play a role in judicial decision making. Judges following the modernist tradition are more likely to be receptive to the use of scientific data than if they were following another method. For example, in *Brown v. Board of Education,*[26] the evidence produced by social scientists indicating that segregation has detrimental effects on black people was relied upon in striking down the separate-but-equal doctrine. Critics charge that, by its nature, much scientific data, particularly the results of social science research, are unreliable and are used by the Court only to justify policy objectives (social engineering), a task better left to Congress and the states.

Reference to contemporary values may also be part of modern analysis. For example, the Eighth Amendment prohibits cruel and unusual punishments. The Court applies both original and modern approaches in Eighth Amendment cases. First, all punishment believed by the framers to be cruel and unusual are forever forbidden. Second, the Court has held that the Eighth Amendment is not "bound by the sparing humanitarian concessions of our forebears" and that punishments must be in accord with "evolving standards of decency that mark the progress of a maturing society."[27] The Court has said that when necessary to determine contemporary values, it will look to "objective factors," such as how other states punish the crime in question, how the jurisdiction in question punishes other crimes, and (in death penalty cases) how often sentencing juries choose the punishment.

Historical and Contemporary Literalism

Another approach to interpreting the Constitution is **literalism**, also known as *textualism*. This method focuses on the actual text of the Constitution. Literalists believe that the words of the document must be examined first. Words have objective meaning that may differ from the drafters' intentions. Language is paramount, not the intentions of the framers. The framers were particular in their choice of language, and accordingly, those words should be respected. The first tenet

════════════════════════ TERMS ════════════════════════

literalism   An approach to interpreting the Constitution that focuses on the literal meanings of its words, rather than on other factors, such as the original intent of the framers. There are two forms of literalism, historical and contemporary. *Historical literalism* defines terms in the context of when the particular provision being considered was ratified. *Contemporary literalism* uses contemporary definitions.

of literalism is the **plain meaning rule**, which states that if the meaning of a term is immediately apparent, then that meaning must be accepted and applied, regardless of any other factors.

However, the meanings of words change. The phrase "modern means of production" is historically contextual. It has a different meaning in 1999 than it did in 1799. The same can be said of the language of the Constitution. Does the phrase "cruel and unusual punishment" mean the same today as it did in 1791?

Those in the historical literalism camp believe that the meaning of the words at the time the provision was ratified must be used. This approach is similar to originalism. However, do not confuse the two approaches. An originalist may transcend the language of the document in order to find the original intent; a literalist would not.

There is a second group of literalists that advocate contemporary literalism, that is, the view that contemporary definitions should be applied. They are similar to modernists, but focus on language more than a modernist does.

Historical literalists assert, as do originalists, that their method deemphasizes the effect the ideologies of judges have on decisions, and further, that it makes the law more predictable and stable. Contemporary literalists concede that because the meanings of terms evolve, this method may result in slightly less stability. Nevertheless, they believe that they strike the proper balance between keeping the Constitution current and preventing justices from engaging in policy making.

Democratic Reinforcement

Another approach to interpreting the Constitution has been termed *democratic* or *representation reinforcement.* Proponents of this theory suggest that the framers did not intend to establish a set of specific substantive principles. Rather, they created a document that defines the processes, structures, and relationships that constitute the foundation of the American democracy. The first three articles of the Constitution, for example, establish the structure of the national government, define the powers of the national government and its actors, and establish the procedures that must be followed in deciding who will occupy high government positions. Even rights usually thought of as purely

TERMS

plain meaning rule [†]   The rule that in interpreting a statute whose meaning is unclear, the courts will look to the "plain meaning" of its language to determine legislative intent. The plain meaning rule is in opposition to the majority view of statutory interpretation, which takes legislative history into account.

substantive have procedural or structural aspects. For example, the First Amendment's religion clauses are recognized as protecting the individual's substantive right to choose and exercise religious beliefs, but it also establishes a structure separating governmental and religious institutions. Although structural components of the Constitution are generally easy to define, substantive portions are not. This is because the language of the Constitution is vague or broad when it comes to substance. "Due process," "equal protection," and "cruel and unusual punishments" are examples.

From these facts, some analysts glean that the framers did not intend to establish a precise set of substantive laws. Rather, they intended to define the who, what, where, and when of substantive rulemaking. Following this theory, judicial interpretation should be guided by the general republican principles underlying the Constitution. However, the analysis is contemporary. The basic republican themes established by the framers are used as a base, but those themes are interpreted within the context of contemporary society. By allowing change in this way, constitutional law actually reflects the will of people. Accordingly, the Supreme Court is not viewed as a countermajoritarian institution, but one that reinforces democracy and republicanism.[28]

The Interpretation Process

Few judges can be said to subscribe exclusively to any one approach. The same judge may favor originalism for one issue and modernism for another. This does not necessarily mean that the judge is inconsistent; rather, each judge develops his or her own approach to interpretation. For example, all judges must begin with the language of the Constitution. Nearly all judges believe they have an obligation to enforce language that is plain and clear on its face. In this sense, they are literalists subscribing to the plain meaning doctrine. However, exceptions to this rule can be found. For example, in *Hans v. Louisiana*, 134 U.S. 1 (1890), the Court determined that the Eleventh Amendment shields states from suits by their citizens in federal courts, regardless of the plain language of the amendment, which provides for state immunity in federal courts from suits filed only by citizens of other states or other nations. The Eleventh Amendment reads:

> The Judicial power of the United States shall not be construed to extend to any suit in law or equity, commenced or prosecuted against one of the United States by Citizens of another State, or by Citizens or Subjects of any Foreign State.

Many originalists and modernists subscribe to the plain meaning doctrine. However, when the meaning of a term is not plain, they diverge into their respective approaches. They may again find themselves on similar tracks if the originalist cannot determine what the intent of the framers was or if it is determined that the framers intended to create an evolutionary concept. In such cases, the originalist finds herself on another track, possibly the same track as the modernist.

In some cases, interpretation is guided by customs, practices, and the common law. If a practice is long-standing, it is more likely to be found consistent with the Constitution than if it were new.

Common-law decisions predating the Constitution may also be considered. For example, processes that were approved at common law have traditionally been approved under the Fifth and Fourteenth Amendments' due process clauses. In fact, many constitutional provisions are codifications of common-law doctrines and thus the common law is depended upon to shed light on the meaning of the Constitution. For example, the Court said of the Fourth Amendment's probable cause and warrants requirements that the "provision was not intended to establish a new principle but to affirm and preserve a cherished rule of the common law designed to prevent the issue of groundless warrants."[29] This is only one example of many instances in which reference to the common law is part of interpretation of the Constitution.

The effect that a particular decision will have on the nation, the nation's institutions (including the Court itself), and the parties to the case before the Court are also factors in judicial decision making.[30] For example, in *Bibb v. Navajo Freight Lines*,[31] the issue was whether a state could require trucks engaged in interstate commerce to comply with its safety requirements. In support of its decision holding that states may not regulate interstate trucking in this manner, the Court pointed out the consequence of an opposite decision: disruption of interstate commerce would result from differing safety requirements. The Court reasoned that truck drivers would be forced to stop at the border of every state and reconfigure their trucks to be in compliance with the next state's safety regulations. In short, the effect of a Court ruling permitting such state regulation would be disruption of the interstate trucking industry.

A judge may also consider the interpretations of other actors, such as Congress, the President, or administrative agencies. Even though it is not required of the Supreme Court, in some cases it has exhibited deference to the interpretations of its coordinate branches when there is no dispute between them.

Although there are proponents and opponents of every approach discussed here, there is no one correct method. Justices differ in their approaches and legal scholars differ sharply on the subject as well. Be aware of the different methods and look for their application in the cases in this text. Understanding them will increase your understanding of constitutional law and will also enhance your ability to predict the outcome of future cases.

Stare Decisis, Canons, and Practices Affecting Interpretation

A number of rules and practices also affect constitutional judicial decision making. **Stare decisis** is an important rule. This common-law doctrine (the name of which translates from Latin as "let the decision stand") actually comes from the Latin phrase, *stare decisis et non quieta movere* or "stand by matters that have been decided and do not disturb what is tranquil." Stare decisis is a legal principle that requires courts to respect precedent. It dates back to medieval England and was so well established by the eighteenth century that Blackstone included it in his famous *Commentaries.* The doctrine of stare decisis holds that if a court has established a legal principle that applies to a certain set of facts, it should adhere to that principle in future cases with identical or substantially similar facts. If the new case is different from the prior case in issues of law or fact, the doctrine is not applicable.

As a matter of policy, the courts adopted the practice of respecting precedent in order to make the law predictable, stable, and secure. Three additional benefits are derived from the doctrine: uniformity, efficiency, and constraint. If state courts and lower federal courts were not bound by the decisions of the Supreme Court, the Constitution and other federal laws would not have one meaning and application, but several. The Supreme Court said of the importance of following precedent that "[u]nless we wish anarchy to prevail within the federal judicial system, a precedent of this Court must be followed by the lower federal courts no matter how misguided the judges of those courts may think it to be."[32]

As for efficiency, Justice Cardozo commented that "[t]he labor of judges would be increased almost to the breaking point if every past decision could be reopened in every case, and one could not lay one's own course of bricks on the secure foundation of the courses laid by others who had gone before him."[33] In addition, adherence to precedent is "a basic self-governing principle within the Judicial Branch,

---

TERMS

stare decisis[†] [Latin for] "standing by the decision." Stare decisis is the doctrine that judicial decisions stand as precedents for cases arising in the future. It is a fundamental policy of our law that, except in unusual circumstances, a court's determination on a point of law will be followed by courts of the same or lower rank in later cases presenting the same legal issue, even though different parties are involved and many years have elapsed.

which is entrusted with the sensitive and difficult task of fashioning and preserving a jurisprudential system that is not based upon an arbitrary discretion."[34]

Having a legal question answered has its own value, even if it is answered wrongly. "The Court has noted in the past that stare decisis is a principle of policy, ... and it is usually the wise policy, because in most matters it is more important that the applicable rule of law be settled than it be settled right."[35]

Courts are bound only by their own decisions and the decisions of courts superior to them. For example, the Supreme Court is superior to all other courts, state and federal, in interpreting national law, and therefore its decisions are binding upon them all. In regard to issues of state law, the high court of each state is the final arbiter and even the Supreme Court is bound by that court's declarations.

Unlike the decisions of the Supreme Court, which have national precedential authority, the decisions of the U.S. courts of appeals are binding only upon the courts within their geographical circuits. For example, the Eleventh Circuit includes Alabama, Georgia, and Florida, so the decisions of the court of appeals for that circuit are precedent for the state and federal courts in those states. A decision of a district court is precedent within its district only. These limitations concern the precedential value of interpretive decisions, not the power of these courts to issue process or orders.

Courts must defer to precedent set by a superior court. As a matter of policy, courts should also respect their own prior decisions. However, a court may overturn a prior decision. The Supreme Court did this in *Brown v. Board of Education,*[36] wherein it set aside the separate-but-equal doctrine that it established in *Plessy v. Ferguson.*[37] The Court also did this in *Payne v. Tennessee,*[38] which overruled its decision in *Booth v. Maryland.*[39] In *Booth* the Supreme Court had held that the Eighth Amendment's prohibition of cruel and unusual punishments forbade the use of victim impact evidence at an offender's sentencing. This holding was reversed in *Payne,* only four years after *Booth* was issued.

The extent to which a Supreme Court Justice will respect stare decisis depends on many factors: the nature of the prior decision, including the nature of the decision-making process; how squarely the precedent fits the case before the Court; the age of the decision; whether citizens or legislators have acted in reliance on a previous decision; whether settled rights or obligations will be dislodged by a change; the ideologies of the Justices that issued the prior decision; the number of Justices that joined in the prior majority opinion; whether the decision accomplished its objectives; what the results of reversing or reaffirming the prior decision will be; how the parties before the Court will be affected by the decision; any subsequent social, political, or economic changes the nation has undergone; and the Justices' conclusions concerning the propriety of the prior decision. Of course, a particular Justice's approach to constitutional interpretation will determine which of these factors, if any, will be considered, and the weight to be given to each. For example, an originalist would not be interested in subsequent social, political, or economic changes. The originalist would be interested, however, in the decision-making process. Particularly, she would want to know whether the Court used an originalist approach. Presumably, a Justice is more likely to vote to set aside precedent if it is based on an approach contrary to her own than she would if a decision with which she disagrees was reached using her favored approach.

It is generally accepted that because the high Court's constitutional decisions can be altered only through the amendment process, they should have less precedential effect than interpretations of statutes, which can be freely amended by Congress. The Court has stated that respect for precedent is strongest "in the area of statutory construction, where Congress is free to change this Court's interpretation of its legislation."[40]

There may be a qualification of the general rule that constitutional precedents are more freely reversed than statutory precedents: precedents that have been relied upon that secure fundamental individual liberties should not be changed without significant justification.

> To overturn a constitutional decision is a rare and grave undertaking. To overturn a constitutional decision that secured a fundamental personal liberty to millions of persons would be unprecedented in our 200 years of constitutional history. Although the doctrine of stare decisis applies with somewhat diminished force in constitutional cases generally ... even in ordinary constitutional cases "any departure from ... stare decisis demands special justification" ... . This requirement of justification applies with unique force where, as here, the Court's abrogation of precedent would destroy people's firm belief, based on past decisions of this Court, that they possess an unabridgeable right to undertake certain conduct.[41]

Two principles are reflected here. The first concerns reliance interests. As public reliance on a precedent increases, so does the role stare decisis should play. Otherwise, the public's ability to rely on and predict the law will be hindered. Also, precedents securing fundamental rights should not be set aside as freely as other constitutional precedents.

A judge who does not regularly adhere to stare decisis is commonly referred to as an *activist*. More broadly, **judicial activism** describes two

---

TERMS

judicial activism 1. Use of judicial decisions to engage in social engineering. 2. A judicial philosophy that gives little deference to precedent and, therefore, commonly results in the abrogation of prior decisions.

phenomena: a pattern by a judge of disrupting precedent in favor of his own conceptions and beliefs; and a pattern of using judicial decisions to engage in social engineering or policy making. In recent years, activism has been associated with political and legal liberalism. For example, the Warren Court is noted (and often criticized by conservatives) for its judicial activism in the social engineering and policy-making context. However, activism transcends ideology. The "conservative" Rehnquist Court may prove to be as activist as the "liberal" Warren Court.

A Justice faces a dilemma when confronting precedent with which she disagrees. On the one hand, stare decisis serves laudable objectives. On the other hand, the individual Justice has sworn to uphold and defend the Constitution. The two are at odds when a Justice believes that precedent runs afoul of the Constitution. This difficulty is not new. In 1851, Justice Roger Taney said that if a "former decision was founded in error, and that the error, if not corrected, must produce serious public as well as private inconvenience and loss, it becomes our duty not to perpetuate it."[42] In another opinion, the Supreme Court stated that "[s]tare decisis is not an inexorable command; rather, it is a principle of policy and not a mechanical formula of adherence to the latest decision."[43] It is generally agreed that stare decisis plays a larger role in nonconstitutional cases than in constitutional ones. Associate Justice William O. Douglas commented that

> The place of stare decisis in constitutional law is even more tenuous. A judge looking at a constitutional decision may have compulsions to revere past history and accept what was once written. But he remembers above all else that it is the Constitution which he swore to support and defend, not the gloss which his predecessors may have put upon it. So he comes to formulate his own views, rejecting some earlier ones as false and embracing others.[44]

Associate Justices William Brennan, Jr., and Thurgood Marshall were notorious for their approach to death penalty cases. Even though the Court held that capital punishment is not inherently cruel and unusual in *Gregg v. Georgia*[45] in 1976, both men refused to adhere to this ruling and dissented in every denial of certiorari in death penalty appeals, on the theory that the punishment was in fact violative of the Eighth Amendment's cruel and unusual punishments prohibition. Justice Brennan, while acknowledging that judges have a general obligation to follow precedent, said of his practice in death penalty cases:

> I must add a word about a special kind of dissent: the repeated dissent in which a justice refuses to yield to the views of the majority although persistently rebuffed by them. ... For me ... the fatal constitutional infirmity of capital punishment is that it treats members of the human race as nonhumans, as objects to be toyed with and discarded ... . This is an interpretation to which a majority of my fellow justices—not to

mention, it would seem, a majority of my fellow countrymen—do not subcribe. Perhaps you find my adherence to it, and my recurrent publication of it, simply contrary, tiresome, or quixotic. Or perhaps you see in it a refusal to abide by the judicial principle of stare decisis, obedience to precedent. ... Yet, in my judgment, when a justice perceives an interpretation of the text to have departed so far from its essential meaning, that justice is bound, by a larger constitutional duty to the community, to expose the departure and point toward a different path. ... [T]his type of dissent constitutes a statement by the judge as an individual; "Here I draw the line."[46]

Although it does so only with gravest caution, the Supreme Court has discarded precedent on many occasions. For example, from 1971 to 1991, the Supreme Court overruled thirty-three of its prior constitutional decisions.[47] In total, the Court has reversed itself on over 200 occasions, and three-quarters of those were constitutional decisions.[48] Regardless, stare decisis continues to be the rule, so a party seeking to overturn precedent has the burden of convincing the Court that it should disregard its previous decisions.

A judge can avoid the issue of stare decisis by determining that a prior case is not precedent for the case at bar. This can occur in two ways. First, if it is determined that the case **sub judice** is different in fact from a previous case, then the previous case has no, or limited, precedential influence. This is known as **distinguishing on the facts**. Of course, the facts must differ to such a degree that it is illogical to apply the earlier case to the one sub judice.

Second, a judge can avoid a prior decision by framing the issues differently than the court did in the prior case. For example, suppose a state supreme court determined that the state's constitutional due process requirement does not confer greater rights on a criminal defendant than does the due process clause of the Constitution of the United States in regard to a confession made to the police. In a later case, the state supreme court could avoid this decision by recharacterizing the issue as one of the right to be free from self-incrimination under the state constitution, rather than due process. In so doing, the court could reach a different result from the prior case even though the facts are identical, and it can do so without reversing itself.

TERMS

sub judice [†] Before the court for consideration and determination.
distinguish [†] To explain why a particular case is not precedent or authority with respect to the matter in controversy.
distinguishing on the facts Choosing not to apply a rule from a previous case because its facts differ from the case sub judice.

Judicial decision making is also affected by the **canons of construction and interpretation**. The canons are a set of rules governing the interpretation of written law, such as statutes and constitutions. The canons have been developed by the courts through the common law.

A number of canons have been recognized by the Supreme Court. For example, the strict necessity rule limits the exercise of judicial review to cases in which it is strictly necessary. Under this canon, constitutional issues are not to be adjudicated if a case can be adequately adjudicated on nonconstitutional grounds.

Another rule under which the Court operates is the presumption that statutes are constitutional. Accordingly, the burden of persuasion falls upon the party challenging a statute to prove that it is violative of the constitution.

Similarly, another canon holds that if two or more reasonable constructions of a statute are possible, a court is to select a construction that is consistent with the Constitution, and thereby uphold the statute, if possible. Associate Justice Louis Brandeis stated, "[w]hen the validity of an act of the Congress is drawn in question, and even if a serious doubt of constitutionality is raised, it is a cardinal principle that this Court will first ascertain whether a construction of the statute is fairly possible by which the question may be avoided."[49] Of course, if every reasonable interpretation leads to the conclusion that the law is unconstitutional, it must be so declared.

Another interpretation rule provides that, if possible, an unconstitutional provision of a statute (or other law) is to be severed from the statute to allow the remainder to continue to be enforceable. For the **severability rule** to apply, the court must determine that removal of the unconstitutional portion does not disrupt the nature or thwart the objectives of the law.[50]

Certain practices also affect constitutional adjudication. The Supreme Court has long engaged in the **avoidance** of constitutional issues. That is, the Court will address constitutional issues only if necessary. In most cases, the Court will decide a case upon nonconstitutional grounds rather than delving unnecessarily into constitutional issues.

TERMS

canons of construction and interpretation   A set of judicially created rules that govern the interpretation of written law, such as statutes, regulations, and constitutions.

severability rule   A rule of interpretation that allows a court to remove unconstitutional portions from a law and leave the remainder intact.

avoidance   The Supreme Court's practice of avoiding constitutional issues by deciding cases upon nonconstitutional grounds.

The Court also avoids constitutional issues in another way. If a case has reached the Supreme Court via appeal from a state high court, the Supreme Court may **remand** the case to the state for further consideration if it appears that the case can be disposed of through state law.[51] However, the process of deciding whether to grant certiorari weeds most of these cases out before the appeal is heard by the Court.

To avoid policy making, the Court usually limits its decisions to the facts of the specific cases or cases before it. By tailoring its opinions and orders to fit a specific case, it is less likely to create wide-sweeping constitutional mandates.

There are problems with relying on canons and practices, however. First, the canons may themselves be in conflict. For example, cases can be found to support the principle that if a provision has a plain meaning, that obvious meaning must be enforced regardless of outcome or policy. Other decisions require courts to set aside interpretations that lead to absurd results. Even further, at least one Supreme Court case permits an examination into legislative intent at any time, regardless of a statute's plain meaning. In *United States v. American Trucking Ass'n,* the Court said, "when aid to construction of the meaning of words, as used in the statute, is available, there certainly can be no 'rule of law' which forbids its use, however clear the words may appear on 'superficial examination.' "[52] Although *American Trucking* involved the interpretation of a statute, by analogy the reasoning could be extended to constitutional interpretation.

The second problem with rules of interpretation is that the Supreme Court is not consistent in their application. The rules have been developed by the courts and can be disregarded by them as well. Third, it is not always easy to determine whether a rule is truly a canon or simply a principle intended to apply in an individual case.

In the following chapters you will learn a number of other ways in which constitutional adjudication is avoided by the Supreme Court. For example, the Constitution limits the Court's jurisdiction to "cases or controversies." Therefore, abstract or hypothetical disputes may not be heard. An *abstract case* is one through which an individual challenges a law on constitutional grounds, even though he or she has

---

TERMS

remand[†] n. The return of a case by an appellate court to the trial court for further proceedings, for a new trial, or for entry of judgment in accordance with an order of the appellate court.
v. To return or send back.

not been harmed by it. Also prohibited to federal courts is hypothetical jurisdiction. *Hypothetical jurisdiction* refers to the issuance of advisory opinions, a practice not permitted because no genuine case exists. For example, the President may not request advice from the Supreme Court concerning possible prospective action, such as whether it would be constitutional to commit troops in some nation. A number of other limiting doctrines stem from the Article III case-or-controversy requirement. If an issue is political, the Court may refuse to hear it under the self-imposed political question doctrine. Further, the Court defers to the decision making of its coordinate branches in some circumstances. In such cases, the Court's decision-making role is diminished.

As is apparent, understanding constitutional adjudication is not an easy task. All the factors discussed here, and many to be discussed in the remainder of this text, affect constitutional adjudication. If you read the cases closely, paying attention to context, patterns, and trends, you will find that your understanding of constitutional law is greatly enhanced.

§ 3.6 Judicial Review

What is a court to do when faced with applying a statute (or other law or action) that is contrary to the Constitution? Must it defer to another branch's (or state's) determination that the law is constitutional? What if there is no evidence that the other branch has considered the constitutional propriety of its action? These questions were answered by the adoption of judicial review by the Supreme Court.

The doctrine of judicial review provides that the judiciary may invalidate actions of other governmental actors that are violative of the Constitution. The Constitution does not expressly grant this power to the judiciary. The power extends from the judiciary's authority to interpret and declare the meaning of law. (See Figure 3-4 for a summary.)

Historical Basis

Recall that one of the functions performed by courts in the United States is protection of individual liberties. Through judicial review, the courts act to control the government and thus protect individual rights.

FIGURE 3-4
Summary of
Judicial Review

JUDICIAL REVIEW—A SUMMARY

Defined: The power of the judiciary to review the acts of its coequal branches (and possibly its co-sovereign) for constitutionality. An unconstitutional act is declared void.

Structure: Diffused. With the exception of a few local courts, all courts in the United States, both federal and state, possess the power of judicial review.

Source (federally): Not expressly provided for in the Constitution. Implicit in the general grant of judicial power in Article III. *Marbury v. Madison* is the landmark case on judicial review.

Impact: Less than 1 percent of all federal statutes are invalidated by the Supreme Court.

In the early years of the British monarchy, the Crown was sovereign and virtually unchecked. However, theories of **natural law** and **natural rights** eventually led the Crown to acknowledge that certain laws and rights were fundamental and superior to the monarch's imperative. This occurred in 1215 when the feudal nobles of England coerced King John into signing the Magna Carta, a document that recognized particular natural rights. Though a landmark in law, the Magna Carta did not declare rights for all Englishmen and was hardly what contemporary western cultures would consider a comprehensive declaration of human rights. Further, the Magna Carta fell into disuse and the abuses it was intended to curb resurfaced.

However, natural law theories were later used by philosophers, such as John Locke and Charles Montesquieu, to advance theories of representative government, separation of powers, and use of the judiciary to protect individuals from governmental abuse. These philosophers advanced the theory that sovereignty rests not with the monarch but with the people. Natural law theories were the foundation of both the French Declaration of Rights and the French Revolution and their United States counterparts.

TERMS

natural law [†] A term referring to the concept that there exists, independent of manmade law, a law laid down (depending upon one's beliefs) by God or by nature, which human society must observe in order to be happy and at peace.

natural right [†] A right existing under natural law, independent of manmade law.

England, from which the United States as a nation derived its common law, does not have a written constitution, at least not in the sense that the United States has one. Nor is there an independent judiciary in that nation. Parliament is the highest body (except for the symbolic role the Crown continues to play) in the nation. It is not only responsible for the making of law, but also, through the House of Lords, sits at the apex of the English judiciary.

Generally, parliamentary law is supreme. The British insist, however, that they have a constitution, that is, a body of fundamental law. What could be supreme to parliamentary law in a system in which Parliament is supreme?

The English Constitution is not found in one written document. Instead, there are a number of laws that, taken together, make up the British fundamental law. First, certain common-law principles and customs are so sacred that they are considered part of England's fundamental law. Second, several acts of Parliament are considered fundamental. For example, the Bill of Rights of 1689 established that the monarch must be Protestant, that the Crown could not raise an army without parliamentary approval, that the Parliament was the supreme lawmaker, and that Protestant subjects possessed a right to petition the Crown and bear arms. It also prohibited excessive fines and cruel and unusual punishment. The Act of Settlement of 1701 is also considered part of England's fundamental law. Through this act, the proposition that the Crown ruled through Parliament was furthered. For example, it provides, in part, that the Crown must have the consent of Parliament to remove judges.

In spite of apparent parliamentary supremacy, the thought that Parliament is limited by a higher form of law (natural law) can be found as early as 1610. In *Dr. Bonham's Case,* Lord Coke wrote that "[w]hen an Act of Parliament is against common right and reason, or repugnant, or impossible to be performed, the common law will controul [sic] it, and adjudge such Act to be void."[53] Regardless of this famous statement by Lord Coke, which was made during a period when natural law theory was popular, judicial review is not recognized in England. This is largely due to Parliament's self-restraint. It has not attempted, in recent times, to abrogate any fundamental freedoms, such as the freedom of the press. If it did, the issue of parliamentary supremacy might be reconsidered.

The framers of the United States Constitution were heavily influenced by natural law and natural rights theories. Natural law was the foundation of the Declaration of Independence and the American Revolution. The framers believed that certain matters were beyond the control of government and that certain rights were inalienable. Further, they believed in the role of the courts as guardians of freedom. It is not surprising, considering this history, that eight of the thirteen states had expressly adopted judicial review even before the new Constitution was written. A number of statements by delegates during the Constitutional Convention indicate that they intended for the judiciary to possess the power. For example, the delegates considered establishing a council comprised of the President and a number of Justices of the Supreme Court to review legislation for constitutionality. The proposal was opposed and rejected as unnecessary because it was thought that the judiciary possessed the power to nullify unconstitutional laws. Again, natural law was the foundation of this belief. James Madison stated at the convention that "a law violating a constitution established by the people ... would be considered by judges as null and void." The proposal was thus rejected.

The same argument was made by delegates who opposed giving Congress the authority to veto laws that are contrary to the national constitution. It was argued that the interests of the national government would be adequately guarded by the national judiciary, which possesses the power to negate state laws that contravene the national constitution.

Alexander Hamilton later wrote in the *Federalist Papers,* "where the will of the legislature declared in its statutes, stands in opposition to that of the people, declared in the constitution, the judges ought to be governed by the latter, rather than the former. They ought to regulate their decisions by the fundamental laws." Further, he stated that the power to declare unconstitutional legislative acts void belonged to the judiciary.[54]

John Marshall stated that "[i]f they [Congress] were to make a law not warranted by any of the powers enumerated, it would be considered by the judges as an infringement of the Constitution which they are to guard. They would not consider such a law as coming under their jurisdiction. They would declare it void." Luther Martin, James Wilson, and others made similar statements.[55]

There is also evidence that judicial review was practiced in state courts before 1789. In *The American Doctrine of Judicial Supremacy,*[56] Haines traces the history of the doctrine back to state and colony courts. The idea that legislative enactments were to be limited by natural law, natural rights, or a written constitution is found in the state efforts to create constitutional tribunals. These groups were known as *councils of censors* and *councils of revision* and existed in Pennsylvania, New York, and Vermont. The Pennsylvania Constitution of 1776 provided that the Constitution was not to be violated and established a council, composed of persons chosen from each city and county, charged with overseeing the constitutionality of executive and legislative branch actions. In addition, this body was delegated the authority to pass public censures, to order impeachments, to recommend that unconstitutional laws be repealed, and to call constitutional conventions.

Vermont's council of censors was nearly identical in structure to Pennsylvania's. New York, in contrast, did not elect laymen to sit on its council. Rather, the governor, chancellor, and justices of the state supreme court sat together on a council of revision, which reviewed bills for constitutionality before they became law. The group possessed veto power, but its vetoes could be overridden by a two-thirds majority vote in the state legislature.

All three councils were eventually abolished. They are important to constitutional history, however, because they illustrate that the framers did not embrace the English concept of legislative supremacy.

There is additional, more direct, evidence of support for judicial review. In several cases that predate the Constitution, judicial review was either exercised or recognized. For example, *Holmes v. Walton*,[57] a 1780 decision from New Jersey, involved a statute that provided for a six-man jury. The defendant objected, claiming that a twelve-man jury was required by the state constitution. The court agreed and invalidated the statute. There are other examples.[58]

In summary, the concept of judicial review was not new when the Supreme Court first invoked it to nullify a law in 1803. However, there is also evidence that the framers did not intend for the judiciary to possess the power. After all, if the framers had intended it, why was it not explicitly provided for in the Constitution? Possibly, they did not specifically mention judicial review because they believed it to be inherent in the judicial power, which they granted wholly to the judiciary in Article III. In the end, the evidence is inconclusive about whether the framers intended for the courts to possess the power of judicial review.

Court Decisions and Opinions   **SIDEBAR**

Many of the decisions made by judges are written. Many of these are published. The higher the court, the more likely it is that its decisions will be published.

The decisions of the Supreme Court are published in the *United States Reports* (abbreviated as U.S.), a federal government publication. In addition, West Publishing Company reports the Supreme Court's decisions in the *Supreme Court Reporter* (S. Ct.). Lawyers Cooperative Publishing Company also publishes these decisions in the *Lawyers Edition,* which is now in its second series (L. Ed. or L. Ed. 2d). These last two sources are *parallel* to the official U.S reporter. Generally, cite only the official reporter when available. All cites indicate the court, volume, page, and year the decision was rendered. The volume precedes the court and the page on which the case begins follows the court designation:

Roe v. Wade, 410 U.S. 113, 93 S. Ct. 705, 35 L. Ed. 2d 147 (1973)

This citation shows that the case *Roe v. Wade* can be located in volume 410 of the United States Reports at page 113. The decision was issued in 1973. This citation style is used for all reported court decisions.

United States Courts of Appeals decisions are reported in the *Federal Reporter,* now in the third series (F., F.2d, F.3d). Not only are the reporter volume and page part of the cite, but so is the specific court that issued the decision:

> *FSK Drug Corp. v. Perales,* 960 F.2d 6 (2d Cir. 1992)

The parenthetical information indicates that the decision was rendered by the U.S. Court of Appeals for the Second Circuit.

District court decisions are published in the *Federal Supplement* (F. Supp.) and are cited as such:

> *Wimberg v. University of Evansville,* 761 F. Supp. 587 (S.D. Ind. 1989)

This decision was issued by the U.S. District Court for the Southern District of Indiana.

State court decisions are reported in a system of regional reporters. Some states have their own official reporters as well.

Congressional Action

The power of judicial review can be traced to decisions of the Supreme Court as far back as 1796.[59] However, the landmark case of *Marbury v. Madison* was where the Court first used judicial review to invalidate federal action.

SIDEBAR

Briefing Cases

Appendix A provides a discussion of reading and briefing cases.

Chief Justice Marshall carefully constructed this opinion. He did not want a confrontation with the President, for fear that the judiciary as an institution would be harmed. At the same time, Marshall wanted both to establish the Court's authority and to announce that the President's actions were unlawful. He accomplished this by ruling against Marbury, due to a lack of jurisdiction, and thereby avoiding a direct confrontation with the executive, but simultaneously declaring that the judiciary can check the actions of the other branches for constitutionality and that the President had acted improperly. How exactly did he reach these conclusions?

First, he found that Marbury had been properly appointed and that President Jefferson (through his Secretary of State James Madison) had wrongly withheld his commission. To avoid a potentially harmful confrontation with the executive, however, the Court did not order the President to deliver the commission. Rather, the Court concluded that

MARBURY v. MADISON
5 U.S. (1 Cranch) 137 (1803)

[The following historical background will make understanding this case easier. Federalist President John Adams lost his reelection bid to Republican Thomas Jefferson in 1800. Additionally, the Federalists also lost their majority in Congress. To extend the influence of the Federalist Party beyond Adams's administration, Congress and President Adams attempted to fill the judiciary with federalists. Sixteen new circuit judge positions were created by Congress (previously, Justices of the Supreme Court and district judges sat as circuit judges). The size of the Supreme Court was decreased by one, to prevent the new administration and Congress from replacing retiring Associate Justice William Cushing. Chief Justice Oliver Ellsworth retired early so that Adams could nominate his replacement. President Adams nominated his Secretary of State, John Marshall, to become the new (third) Chief Justice. The Senate quickly confirmed Marshall's nomination. Congress also created forty-two new justices of the peace for the District of Columbia. The final days of the Adams administration were hurried and hectic. Adams's nominations for the justice of the peace positions were confirmed only one day before the new President was to be inaugurated. President Adams signed the commissions and gave them to John Marshall, who was then still Secretary of State, for delivery. Marshall, however, was unable to deliver four of the justice of the peace commissions before the Jefferson administration assumed power. President Jefferson ordered his Secretary of State, James Madison, not to deliver the commissions. William Marbury was one of the four men who did not receive their commissions. Marbury filed suit against Madison in the Supreme Court seeking an order (a writ of mandamus) compelling delivery of the commissions.

The suit was filed in 1801, but no decision was rendered until 1803 because the new administration effectively canceled the 1802 term. It did this by first changing the two terms of the Court, beginning in 1802, from February and August to June and December. Then in April 1802, before the Court held its first session, Congress again changed the Court's term to every February. Therefore, the Court did not meet from December 1801 to February 1803. In addition, the new Republican Congress repealed the circuit judgeships created by the lame duck Federalist Congress.

Although highly controversial, both politically and constitutionally, these actions were never ejudicially reviewed. By the time the case was heard by the Supreme Court, Marshall had assumed the position of Chief Justice. In fact, he authored the Court's opinion.]

Chief Justice Marshall delivered the Court's decision. [Vote: 4–0–2. Cushing and Moore did not participate.]

* * *

In the order in which the court has viewed the subject, the following questions have been considered and decided.

1st. Has the applicant a right to the commission he demands?

2ndly. If he has a right, and that right has been violated, do the laws of his country afford him a remedy?

3rdly. If they do afford him a remedy, is it a mandamus issuing from this court?

The first object of inquiry is, 1st. Has the applicant a right to the commission he demands?

His right originates in an act of congress passed in February 1801, concerning the district of Columbia ... [which provides] "that there shall be appointed ... such number of discreet persons to be justices of the peace as the president of the United States shall, from time to time think expedient, to continue in office for five years. ...

It is therefore, decidedly the opinion of the court, that when a commission has been signed by the president [after confirmation by the Senate], the appointment is made; and that the commission is complete, when the seal of the United States has been affixed to it by the secretary of state. ...

Mr. Marbury, then, since his commission was signed by the President and sealed by the secretary of state, was appointed; and as the law creating the office, gave the officer a right to hold for five years, independent of the executive, the appointment was not revocable, but vested in the officer legal rights, which are protected by the laws of this country.

To withhold his commission, therefore, is an act deemed by the court not warranted by law, but violative of a vested legal right.

This brings us to the second inquiry; which 2ndly. If he has a right, and that right has been violated, do the laws of his country afford him a remedy?

The very essence of civil liberty certainly consists in the right of every individual to claim the protection of the laws whenever he receives an injury. One of the first duties of government is to afford that protection. ...

[The Court found that the President and his immediate subordinates are entitled to immunity from the judicial process when performing certain discretionary functions, but not necessarily when performing ministerial functions.] ... But where a specific duty is assigned by law, and individual rights depend upon the performance of that duty, it seems equally clear that the individual who considers himself injured, has a right to resort to the laws of his country for a remedy ... .

It is then the opinion of the court ... [t]hat, having this legal title to the office, he has a consequent right to the commission; a refusal to deliver which, is a plain violation of that right, for which the laws of his country afford him a remedy.

It remains to be inquired whether,

3rdly. He is entitled to the remedy for which he applies. This depends on, 1st. The nature of the writ applied for, and, 2dly. The power of this court.

1st. The nature of the writ. [The Court explained that at common law writs of mandamus could be used to compel government officers to take actions required by law.]

This, then, is a plain case for a mandamus, either to deliver the commission, or a copy of it from the record; and it only remains to be inquired,

Whether it [the writ of mandamus] can issue from this court.

The act to establish the judicial courts of the United States authorizes the supreme court "to issue writs of mandamus, in cases warranted by the principles and usages of law, to any courts appointed, or persons holding office, under the authority of the United States."

The secretary of state, being a person holding an office under the authority of the United States, is precisely within the letter of the description; and if this court is not authorized to issue a writ of mandamus to such an officer, it must be because the law is unconstitutional, and therefore absolutely incapable of conferring the authority, and assigning the duties which its words purport to confer and assign.

The constitution vests the whole judicial power of the United States in one supreme court, and such inferior courts as congress shall, from time to time, ordain and establish. This power is expressly extended to all cases arising under the laws of the United States; and consequently, in some form, may be exercised over the present case; because the right claimed is given by a law of the United States.

In the distribution of this power it is declared that "the supreme court shall have original jurisdiction in all cases affecting ambassadors, other public ministers and consuls, and those in which a state shall be a party. In all other cases, the supreme court shall have appellate jurisdiction."

It has been insisted, at the bar, that as the original grant of jurisdiction, to the supreme and inferior courts, is general, and the clause, assigning original jurisdiction to the supreme court, contains no negative or restrictive words; the power remains to the legislature, to assign original jurisdiction to that court in other cases than those specified in the article which has been recited; provided those cases belong to the judicial power of the United States.

If it had been intended to leave it in the discretion of the legislature to apportion the judicial power between the supreme and inferior courts according to the will of that body, it would certainly have been useless to have proceeded further than to have defined the judicial power, and the tribunals in which it should be vested. The subsequent part of the section is mere surplusage, is entirely without meaning, if such is to be the construction. If congress remains at liberty to give this court appellate jurisdiction, where the constitution has declared their jurisdiction shall be original; and original jurisdiction where the constitution has declared it shall be appellate; the distribution of jurisdiction, made in the constitution, is form without substance.

Affirmative words are often, in their operation, negative of other objects than those affirmed; and in this case, a negative or exclusive sense must be given to them or they have no operation at all.

It cannot be presumed that any clause in the constitution is intended to be without effect; and therefore such a construction is inadmissible, unless words require it. ...

When an instrument organizing fundamentally a judicial system, divides it into one supreme, and so many inferior courts as the legislature may ordain and establish; then enumerates its powers, and proceeds so far to distribute them, as to define the jurisdiction of the supreme court by declaring the cases in which it shall take the original jurisdiction, and that in others it shall take appellate jurisdiction; the plain import of the words seems to be, that in one class of cases its jurisdiction is original, and not appellate; in the other it is appellate, and not original. If any other construction would render the clause inoperative, that is an additional reason for rejecting such other construction, and for adhering to their obvious meaning.

To enable this court then to issue a mandamus, it must be shown to be an exercise of appellate jurisdiction, or to be necessary to enable them to exercise appellate jurisdiction. ...

It is an essential criterion of appellate jurisdiction, that it revises and corrects the proceedings in a cause already instituted, and does not create that cause. Although, therefore, a mandamus may be directed to courts, yet to issue such a writ to an officer for the delivery of a paper, is in effect the same as to sustain an original action for that paper, and therefore seems not to belong to appellate, but to original jurisdiction. Neither is it necessary in such a case as this, to enable the court to exercise its appellate jurisdiction.

The authority, therefore, given to the supreme court, by the act establishing the judicial courts of the United States, to issue writs of mandamus to public officers, appears not to be warranted by the constitution; and it becomes necessary to inquire whether a jurisdiction, so conferred, can be exercised.

The question, whether an act, repugnant to the constitution, can become the law of the land, is a question deeply interesting to the United States; but, happily, not of an intricacy proportioned to its interest. It seems only necessary to recognize certain principles, supposed to have been long and well established, to decide it.

That the people have an original right to establish, for their future government, such principles as, in their operation, shall most conduce to their own happiness, is the basis, on which the whole American fabric has been erected. The exercise of this original right is a very great exertion; nor can it, nor ought it to be frequently repeated. The principles, therefore, so established, are deemed fundamental. And as the authority, from which they proceed, is supreme, and can seldom act, they are designed to be permanent.

This original and supreme will organizes the government, and assigns, to different departments, their respective powers. It may either stop here; or establish certain limits not to be transcended by those departments.

The government of the United States is of the latter description. The powers of the legislature are defined, and limited; and that those limits may not be mistaken, or forgotten, the constitution is written. To what purpose are powers limited, and to what purpose is that limitation committed to writing, if these limits may, at any time, be passed by those intended to be restrained? The distinction, between a government with limited and unlimited powers, is abolished, if those limits do not confine the persons on whom they are imposed, and if acts prohibited and acts allowed, are of equal obligation. It is a proposition too plain to be contested, that the constitution controls any legislative act repugnant to it; or, that the legislature may alter the constitution by an ordinary act.

Between these alternatives there is no middle ground. The constitution is either a superior, paramount law, unchangeable by ordinary means, or it is on a level with ordinary legislative acts, and like other acts, is alterable when the legislature shall please to alter it.

If the former part of the alternative be true, then a legislative act contrary to the constitution is not law; if the latter part be true, then written constitutions are absurd attempts, on the part of the people, to limit a power, in its own nature illimitable.

Certainly all those who have framed written constitutions contemplate them as forming the fundamental and paramount law of the nation, and consequently the theory of every such government must be, that an act of the legislature, repugnant to the constitution, is void.

This theory is essentially attached to a written constitution, and is consequently to be considered, by this court, as one of the fundamental principles of our society. It is not therefore to be lost sight of in the further consideration of this subject.

If an act of the legislature, repugnant to the constitution, is void, does it, notwithstanding its invalidity, bind the courts, and oblige them to give it effect? Or, in other words, though it be not law, does it constitute a rule as operative as if it was a law? This would be to overthrow in fact what was established in theory; and would seem, at first view, an absurdity too gross to be insisted on. It shall, however, receive more attentive consideration.

It is emphatically the province and duty of the judicial department to say what the law is. Those who apply the rule to particular cases, must of necessity expound and interpret that rule. If two laws conflict with each other, the courts must decide on the operation of each.

So if a law be in opposition to the constitution; if both the law and the constitution apply to a particular case, so that the court must either decide that case conformably to the law, disregarding the constitution; or conformably to the constitution, disregarding the law; the court must determine which of these conflicting rules governs the case. This is of the very essence of judicial duty.

If then the courts are to regard the constitution; and the constitution is superior to any ordinary act of the legislature, the constitution, and not such ordinary act, must govern the case to which they both apply.

Those then who controvert the principle that the constitution is to be considered, in court, as a paramount law, are reduced to the necessity of maintaining that courts must lose their eyes on the constitution, and see only the law.

This doctrine would subvert the very foundation of all written constitutions. It would declare that an act, which, according to the principles and theory of our government, is entirely void; is yet, in practice, completely obligatory. It would declare, that if the legislature shall do what is expressly forbidden, such act, notwithstanding the express prohibition, is in reality effectual. It would be giving to the legislature a practical and real omnipotence, with the same breath which professes to restrict their powers within narrow limits. It is prescribing limits, and declaring that those limits may be passed at pleasure.

That it thus reduces to nothing what we have deemed the greatest improvement on political institutions—a written constitution—would itself be sufficient, in America, where written constitutions have been viewed with so much reverence, for rejecting the construction. But the peculiar expressions of the constitution of the United States furnish additional arguments in favour of its rejection.

The judicial power of the United States is extended to all cases arising under the constitution.

Could it be the intention of those who gave this power, to say that, in using it, the constitution should not be looked into? That a case arising under the constitution should be decided without examining the instrument under which it arises?

This is too extravagant to be maintained.

In some cases then, the constitution must be looked into by the judges. And when they open it at all, what part of it are they forbidden to read, or to obey?

There are many other parts of the constitution which serve to illustrate this subject.

It is declared [in the Constitution] that "no tax or duty shall be laid on articles exported from any state." Suppose a duty on the export of cotton, of tobacco, or of flour; and suit instituted to recover it. Ought judgment to be rendered in such a case? Ought the judges to close their eyes on the constitution, and only see the law?

The constitution declares that "no bill of attainder or ex post facto law shall be passed."

If, however, such a bill should be passed and a person should be prosecuted under it; must the court condemn to death those victims whom the constitution endeavors to preserve?

"No person," says the constitution, "shall be convicted of treason unless on the testimony of two witnesses to the same overt act, or on confession in open court."

Here the language of the constitution is addressed especially to the courts. It prescribes, directly for them, a rule of evidence not to be departed from. If the legislature should change that rule, and declare one witness, or a confession out of court, sufficient for conviction, must the constitutional principle yield to the legislative act?

From these, and many other selections which might be made, it is apparent, that the framers of the constitution contemplated that instrument, as a rule for the government of the *courts,* as well as of the legislature.

Why otherwise does it direct judges to take an oath to support it? This oath certainly applies, in an especial manner, to their conduct in their official character. How immoral to impose it on them, if they were to be used as the instruments, and the knowing instruments, for violating what they swear to support!

The oath of office, too, imposed by the legislature, is completely demonstrative of the legislative opinion on this subject. It is in these words, "I do solemnly swear that I will administer justice without respect to persons, and do equally right to the poor and to the rich; and that I will faithfully and impartially discharge all the duties incumbent on me as _____, according to the best of my abilities and understanding, agreeably to *the constitution,* and laws of the United States."

Why does a judge swear to discharge his duties agreeable to the constitution of the United States, if that constitution forms no rule for his government? If it is closed upon him, and cannot be inspected by him?

If such be the real state of things, this is worse than solemn mockery. To prescribe, or to take this oath, becomes equally a crime.

It is also not entirely unworthy of observation, that in declaring what shall be the *supreme* law of the United States generally, the *constitution* itself is first mentioned; and not the laws of the United States generally, but those only which shall be made in *pursuance* of the constitution, have that rank.

Thus, the particular phraseology of the constitution of the United States confirms and strengthens the principle, supposed to be essential to all written constitutions, that a law repugnant to the constitution is void; and that *courts,* as well as other departments, are bound by that instrument.

The rule must be discharged.

---

it could not issue the writ of mandamus because it lacked jurisdiction over the case.

Congress had included a provision in the Judiciary Act of 1789 that provided the Supreme Court with original jurisdiction to issue writs of mandamus against public officials. Marshall found that the Constitution's statement of original jurisdiction was exclusive, could not be extended by Congress, and did not provide for original jurisdiction in mandamus cases. Therefore, that provision of the Judiciary Act was unconstitutional.

Marshall then had to address the issue of whether the Court had the authority to invalidate (by not enforcing) a coequal branch's actions. For a number of reasons, he concluded that the judiciary did possess such authority. Marshall posed the problem: what is the judiciary to do when faced with applying a statute that is repugnant to the Constitution? Because the Constitution is the higher form of law, it must be followed and not the statute. This does not address the central issue, however; that is, why is the Supreme Court the final word on the meaning of the Constitution? Why should it not defer to the legislature's interpretation? Marshall concluded that it is the responsibility of the judiciary to declare the meaning of the law. In his words, "[i]t is emphatically the province and duty of the judicial department to say what the law is." If two laws conflict, it is a court that must decide which governs a case. "This is of the very essence of judicial duty," said Marshall. Because the Constitution is the highest form of law in the land, a court must choose to apply it over any other law.

In support of his conclusions, Marshall pointed to several provisions of the Constitution. Recall that there is no express delegation of judicial review in the Constitution. First, Article III, § 2, provides that the "judicial Power shall extend to all Cases ... arising under this Constitution." Implicit in this assertion is the belief that the judicial power includes being the final arbiter of the meaning of the Constitution. After all, could not the judicial power extend to all cases arising under the Constitution even though the judiciary defers to the legislature's interpretations of the Constitution?

Second, Marshall pointed to particular provisions in the Constitution to establish that the framers intended for the courts to independently determine the meaning of the Constitution, regardless of legislation. For example, the treason provision requires the testimony of two witnesses to the same overt act, or a confession, before a person may be convicted of treason. Marshall reasoned that the framers would not want a court to enforce a law that allowed conviction for treason upon the testimony of one person. Therefore, Marshall concluded that the framers intended the Constitution to bind the judiciary, as well as the other branches. This being so, courts must independently interpret, comply with, and enforce the Constitution.

One other constitutional provision was relied upon by Marshall. The supremacy clause of the Constitution declares that the laws of the national government are the supreme laws of the United States. Marshall noted that, in declaring what laws are supreme, the framers mentioned the Constitution first. He deduced from this that the Constitution is paramount to statutes and other law.

Finally, Marshall noted that judges are required to take an oath of office. Through that oath judges swear to uphold the laws of the nation, including the Constitution. In order to uphold the Constitution, he asserted, it must be interpreted and treated as paramount law.

For these reasons, Marshall concluded that Congress had improperly conferred original jurisdiction upon the Court, and that the Court therefore lacked the authority to issue the mandamus. For the first time, judicial review was used to nullify federal action—particularly, an act of Congress. In addition to concluding that the judiciary can review congressional actions, Marshall also stated that executive actions can be reviewed. This statement was **dictum**, however, because the Court had determined that it lacked jurisdiction to issue the mandamus. Regardless, the power has since extended over the executive branch as well.

Executive Action

The Burger Court reiterated in the *Nixon* tapes case what the Marshall Court stated in *Marbury v. Madison* 171 years earlier: it is the duty of the judiciary to say what the law is. This does not mean that the executive and legislative branches should not make their own interpretations; it simply means that the judiciary is final word on the subject. Consider the sensitivity of issuing an order to a coequal branch. Consider further the enforcement aspect of such an order. The Court has no method of enforcing its orders—it is the duty of the executive to enforce court orders. As such, it is uncomfortable to courts to order the executive branch to do something the executive opposes.

President Nixon complied with the order, thereby averting a constitutional crisis. Even though he supplied all the tapes, the eighteen-minute erasure remains a mystery. Impeachment looming, President Nixon resigned on August 9, 1974, thus becoming the only President ever to resign. Additional litigation later resulted from the Watergate affair. Some of the other prominent cases are discussed further in Chapter 6, which discusses the role, authority, and responsibilities of the President.

―――――――――――――――― TERMS ――――――――――――――――

dictum (obiter dictum) [†]   [E]xpressions or comments in a court opinion that are not necessary to support the decision made by the court; they are not binding authority and have no value as precedent. If nothing else can be found on point, an advocate may wish to attempt to persuade by citing cases that contain dicta.

UNITED STATES v. NIXON
418 U.S. 683 (1974)

[On June 17, 1972, members of President Richard Nixon's committee for reelection were caught burglarizing the Democratic National Headquarters in the Watergate Hotel in Washington, D.C.

Archibald Cox, the special prosecutor appointed to investigate the Watergate affair, asked the President to produce documents and audiotapes recorded by the President of conversations in the Oval Office. President Nixon refused to provide the documents and recordings to the special prosecutor. Cox then sought and obtained court orders compelling the President to produce the requested documents and tapes.

Enraged, President Nixon ordered the Attorney General to fire the special prosecutor. The Attorney General resigned rather than comply. President Nixon then ordered the second highest official in the Department of Justice to discharge the special prosecutor. That official also resigned. Finally, Solicitor General Robert Bork acquiesced and fired the special prosecutor, in what became known as the "Saturday Night Massacre." A new Special Prosecutor, Leon Jaworski, was appointed. He continued the Watergate investigation, eventually obtaining indictments against several White House officials. President Nixon was not indicted, but was named as a co-conspirator in the indictments. At this point, impeachment was being considered by Congress.

Both Congress and Jaworksi insisted that the President produce the previously requested tapes and documents. Special Prosecutor Jaworski sought and obtained a subpoena compelling complete production by President Nixon. President Nixon responded by producing the documents and edited versions of the audiotapes, one of which included an eighteen-minute period that appeared to have been erased. Additionally, on May 1, 1974, President Nixon moved to quash the subpoena, claiming executive privilege. The district court denied the motion. Because of the significance and sensitivity of the case, the Supreme Court granted certiorari before the court of appeals heard the appeal.]

Chief Justice Burger delivered the opinion of the Court. [Vote: 8–0–1. Justice Rehnquist did not participate.]

* * *

[W]e turn to the claim that the subpoena should be quashed because it demands "confidential conversations between a President and his close advisors that it would be inconsistent with the public interest to produce." The first contention is a broad claim that the separation of powers doctrine precludes judicial review of a President's claim of privilege. The second contention is that if he does not prevail on the claim of absolute privilege, the court should hold as a matter of constitutional law that the privilege prevails over the subpoena *duces tecum*.

In the performance of assigned constitutional duties each branch of the Government must initially interpret the Constitution, and the interpretation of its powers by any branch is due great respect from the others. The President's counsel, as we have noted, reads the Constitution as providing an absolute privilege of confidentiality for all Presidential communications. Many decisions of this Court, however, have unequivocally reaffirmed the holding of *Marbury v. Madison* (1803) that "it is emphatically the province and duty of the judicial department to say what the law is."

No holding of the Court had defined the scope of judicial power specifically relating to the enforcement of a subpoena for confidential Presidential communications for use in a criminal prosecution, but other exercises of power by the Executive Branch and the Legislative Branch have been found invalid as in conflict with the Constitution. ...

Notwithstanding the deference each branch must accord the others, the "judicial power of the United States" vested in the federal courts by Art. III, Sec. 1, of the Constitution can no more be shared with the Executive Branch than the Chief Executive, for example, can share with the Judiciary the power to override a Presidential veto. Any other conclusion would be contrary to the basic concept of separation of powers and the checks and balances that flow from the scheme of a tripartite government. We therefore reaffirm that it is the province and duty of this Court "to say what the law is" with respect to the claim of privilege presented in this case.

In support of his claim of absolute privilege, the President's counsel urges two grounds, one of which is common to all governments and one of which is peculiar to our system of separation of powers. The first ground is the valid need for protection of communications between high Government officials and those who advise and assist them in the performance of their manifold duties; the importance of this confidentiality is too plain to require further discussion. Human experience teaches that those who expect public dissemination of their remarks may well temper candor with a concern for appearances and for their own interests to the detriment of the decisionmaking process. Whatever the nature of the privilege of confidentiality of Presidential communications in the exercise of Art. II powers, the privilege can be said to derive from the supremacy of each branch within its own assigned area of constitutional duties. Certain powers and privileges flow from the nature of enumerated powers; the protection of the confidentiality of Presidential communications has similar constitutional underpinnings.

The second ground asserted by the President's counsel in support of the claim of absolute privilege rests on the doctrine of separation of powers. Here it is argued that the independence of the Executive Branch within its own sphere insulates the President from a judicial subpoena in an ongoing criminal prosecution, and thereby protects confidential Presidential communications.

However, neither the doctrine of separation of powers, nor the need for confidentiality of high-level communications, without more, can sustain an absolute, unqualified Presidential privilege of immunity from judicial process under all circumstances. The President's need for complete candor and objectivity from advisers calls for great deference from the courts. However, when the privilege depends solely on the broad, undifferentiated claim of public interest in the confidentiality of such conversations, a confrontation with other values arises. Absent a claim of need to protect military, diplomatic, or sensitive national security secrets, we find it difficult to accept the argument that even the very important interest in confidentiality of Presidential communications is significantly diminished by production of such material for *in camera* inspection with all the protection that a district court will be obliged to provide.

The impediment that an absolute, unqualified privilege would place in the way of the primary constitutional duty of the Judicial Branch to do justice in criminal prosecutions would plainly conflict with the function of the courts under Art. III. In designing the structure of our Government and dividing and allocating the sovereign power among three co-equal branches, the Framers of the Constitution sought to provide a comprehensive system, but the separate powers were not intended to operate with absolute independence. ... To read the Art. II powers of the President as providing an absolute privilege as against a subpoena essential to enforcement of criminal statutes on no more than a generalized claim of the public interest in confidentiality of nonmilitary and nondiplomatic discussions would upset the constitutional balance of "a workable government" and gravely impair the role of the courts under Art. III.

Since we conclude that the legitimate needs of the judicial process may outweigh Presidential privilege, it is necessary to resolve those competing interests in a manner that preserves the essential functions of each branch. The right and indeed the duty to resolve that question does not free the Judiciary from according high respect to the representations made on behalf of the President.

The expectation of a President to the confidentiality of his conversations and correspondence, like the claim of confidentiality of judicial deliberations, for example, has all the values to which we accord deference for the privacy of all citizens and, added to those values, is the necessity for protection of the public interest in candid, objective, and even blunt or harsh opinions in Presidential decisionmaking. A President and those who assist him must be free to explore alternatives in the process of shaping policies and making decisions and to do so in a way many would be unwilling to express except privately. These are the considerations justifying a presumptive privilege for Presidential communications. The privilege is fundamental to the operation of Government and inextricably rooted in the separation of powers ... .

But this presumptive privilege must be considered in light of our historic commitment to the rule of law. This is nowhere more profoundly manifest than in our view that "the twofold aim [of criminal justice] is that guilt shall not escape or innocence suffer." We have elected to employ an adversary system of criminal justice in which the parties contest all issues before a court of law. The need to develop all relevant facts in the adversary system is both fundamental and comprehensive. The ends of criminal justice would be defeated if judgments were to be founded on a partial or speculative presentation of the facts. The very integrity of the judicial system and public confidence in the system depend on full disclosure of the facts, within the framework of the rules of evidence. To ensure that justice is done, it is imperative to the function of courts that compulsory process be available for the production of evidence needed either by the prosecution or by the defense.

In this case the President challenges a subpoena served on him as a third party requiring the production of materials for use in a criminal prosecution; he does so on the claim that he has a privilege against disclosure of confidential communications. He does not place his claim of privilege on the ground they are military or diplomatic secrets. As to these areas of Art. II duties the courts have traditionally shown the utmost deference to Presidential responsibilities ... .

No case of the Court, however, has extended this high degree of deference to a President's generalized interest in confidentiality. Nowhere in the Constitution, as we have noted earlier, is there any explicit reference to a privilege of confidentiality, yet to the extent this interest relates to the effective discharge of a President's powers, it is constitutionally based.

The right to the production of all evidence at a criminal trial similarly has constitutional dimensions. The Sixth Amendment explicitly confers upon every defendant in a criminal trial the right "to be confronted with the witnesses against him" and "to have compulsory process for obtaining witnesses in his favor." Moreover, the Fifth Amendment also guarantees that no person shall be deprived of liberty without due process of law. It is the manifest duty of the courts to vindicate those guarantees, and to accomplish that it is essential that all relevant and admissible evidence be produced.

In this case we must weigh the importance of the general privilege of confidentiality of Presidential communications in performance of the President's responsibilities against the inroads of such a privilege on the fair administration of criminal justice. The interest in preserving confidentiality is weighty indeed and entitled to great respect. However, we cannot conclude that advisers will be moved to temper the candor of their remarks by the infrequent occasions of disclosure because of the possibility that such conversations will be called for in the context of a criminal prosecution.

On the other hand, the allowance of the privilege to withhold evidence that is demonstrably relevant in a criminal trial would cut deeply into the guarantee of due process of law and gravely impair the basic function of the courts. ...

We conclude that when the ground for asserting privilege as to subpoenaed materials sought for use in a criminal trial is based only on the generalized interest in confidentiality, it cannot prevail over the fundamental demands of due process of law in the fair administration of criminal justice. The generalized assertion of privilege must yield to the demonstrated, specific need for evidence in a pending criminal trial.

State Action

As previously discussed, the federal judiciary exercises constitutional review over the actions of its two coequal branches. Does it possess the same power over the states?

The Supreme Court answered this question for the first time in 1810 when it declared a Georgia statute unconstitutional.[60] Six years later, the Supreme Court issued *Martin v. Hunter's Lessee,* wherein it asserted the power of judicial review over the decisions of the states' high courts.

Today, the power of the federal courts to review state actions is well established. All federal courts, whether district, appellate, or Supreme, possess the constitutional power of judicial review. Federal courts may review the actions of any governmental entity (local, state, or national) for compliance with the Constitution, provided the Court has jurisdiction and there is not some other limiting doctrine.

State courts also exercise judicial review as to both state and federal law. Under the supremacy clause of Article VI, state courts must apply federal law, even if contrary to their own state's laws. This also means that state judges have an obligation to nullify state laws that are violative of the Constitution. Further, state judges may declare federal laws that are violative of the Constitution void. Of course, the decision will have precedential effect only within each particular court's geographical jurisdiction. Through its appellate jurisdiction, the Supreme Court eventually will have an opportunity to review state court decisions interpreting the Constitution. In some instances, review by a lower federal court is possible.

Shield or Sword?

Although the power of judicial review is well established today, the debate over whether the framers intended for the judiciary to have the exclusive power, or whether it ought to have that power, continues. Is judicial review a shield with which the judiciary protects the individual and the integrity of our system, or is it a sword used by judges to maintain a judicial supremacy over the coordinate branches and the states?

The frequency of invocation of the judicial review power by the Supreme Court is informative. Since 1790, the Supreme Court has declared approximately 1,500 acts of local, state, and federal government unconstitutional.[61] This may appear significant, but it represents only a small fraction of a percent of the total laws enacted. Congress enacted over 60,000 laws from 1790 to 1990, and the Supreme Court declared less than 1 percent unconstitutional.[62]

MARTIN v. HUNTER'S LESSEE
14 U.S. (1 Wheat.) 304 (1816)

Justice Story delivered the opinion of the Court. [Vote 6–0–1. Chief Justice Marshall did not participate.]

[Denny Martin, a citizen and resident of England, inherited a 300,000-acre tract of Virginia land in 1781 from his uncle, Lord Fairfax, who had been living in the United States. However, a Virginia statute forbade "enemies" of the United States from inheriting property. Therefore, Virginia took possession of the property and began selling it. The state sold some of the land to Hunter. Simultaneously, Martin began selling the property. One tract of the land was sold to Chief Justice John Marshall and his brother. For this reason, Marshall did not participate in this case.

Martin contested the state's assertion that he had no interest in the land. Martin prevailed at the trial level; however, that decision was reversed by the Court of Appeals of Virginia, the court of last resort in Virginia. The decision of the Virginia appellate court was appealed to, and reversed by, the Supreme Court of the United States. The Supreme Court held that the Virginia statute was unconstitutional because it conflicted with the Treaty of Paris. The Virginia Court of Appeals was ordered to enforce the decision by recognizing Martin's interests.

The Virginia Court of Appeals refused to comply with the order. Further, it concluded that the provision of the Judiciary Act of 1789 that endowed the Supreme Court with appellate jurisdiction in the case was unconstitutional and, hence, void. The Virginia Court of Appeals was asserting, in essence, that it was not subordinate to the Supreme Court and that it had the authority to independently interpret the Constitution of the United States. Martin again appealed to the Supreme Court for relief.]

* * *

The questions involved in this judgment are of great importance and delicacy. Perhaps it is not too much to affirm, that, upon their right decision, rest some of the most solid principles which have hitherto been supposed to sustain and protect the constitution itself. The great respectability, too, of the court whose decisions we are called upon to review, and the entire deference which we entertain for the learning and ability of that court, add much to the difficulty of the task which has so unwelcomely fallen upon us. It is, however, a source of consolation, that we have had the assistance of the most able and learned arguments to aid our inquiries; and that the opinion which is now to be pronounced has been weighed with every solicitude to come to a correct result, and matured after solemn deliberation.

Before proceeding to the principal questions, it may not be unfit to dispose of some preliminary considerations which have grown out of the arguments at the bar.

The constitution of the United States was ordained and established, not by the states in their sovereign capacities, but emphatically, as the preamble of the constitution declares, by "the people of the United States." There can be no doubt that it was competent to the people to invest the general government with all the powers which they might deem proper and necessary; to extend or restrain these powers according to their own good pleasure, and to give them a paramount and supreme authority. As little doubt can there be, that the people had a right to prohibit to the states the exercise of any powers which were, in their judgment, incompatible with the objects of the general compact; to make the powers of state governments, in given cases, subordinate to those of the nation, or to reserve to themselves those sovereign authorities which they might not choose to delegate to either. The constitution was not, therefore, necessarily carved out of existing state institutions, for the powers of the states depend upon their own constitutions; and the people of every state had the right to modify and restrain them, according to their own views of policy or principle. On the other hand, it is perfectly clear that the sovereign powers vested in the state governments, by their respective constitutions, remained unaltered and unimpaired, except so far as they were granted to the government of the United States.

These deductions do not rest upon general reasoning, plain and obvious as they seem to be. They have been positively recognized by one of the articles in amendment of the constitution, which declares, that "the powers not delegated to the United States by the constitution, nor prohibited by it to the states, are reserved to the *states* respectively, or *to the people.*"

The government, then, of the United States, can claim no powers which are not granted to it by the constitution, and the powers actually granted, must be such as are expressly given, or given by necessary implication. On the other hand, this instrument, like every other grant, is to have reasonable construction, according to the import of its terms; and where a power is expressly given in general terms, it is not to be restrained to particular cases, unless that construction grow out of the context expressly, or by necessary implication. The words are to be taken in their natural and obvious sense, and not in a sense unreasonably restricted or enlarged.

The constitution unavoidably deals in general language. It did not suit the purposes of the people, in framing this great charter of our liberties, to provide for minute specifications of its powers, or to declare the means by which those powers should be carried into execution. It was foreseen that this would be a perilous and difficult, if not an impracticable, task. The instrument was not intended to provide merely for the exigencies of a few years, but was to endure through a long lapse of ages, the events of which were locked up in the inscrutable purposes of Providence. It could not be foreseen what new changes and modifications of power might be indispensable to effectuate the general objects of the .charter; and restrictions and specifications, which at the present, might seem salutary, might, in the end, prove the overthrow of the system itself. Hence its powers are expressed in general terms, leaving to the legislature, from time to time, to adopt its own means to effectuate legitimate objects, and to mould and model the exercise of its powers, as its own wisdom, and the public interests, should require.

With these principles in view, principles in respect to which no difference of opinion ought to be indulged, let us now proceed to ... consideration of the great question as to the nature and extent of the appellate jurisdiction of the United States ... .

If the constitution meant to limit the appellate jurisdiction to cases pending in the courts of the United States, it would necessarily follow that the jurisdiction of these courts would, in all the cases enumerated in the constitution, be exclusive of state tribunals. How otherwise could the jurisdiction extend to *all* cases arising under the constitution, laws, and treaties of the United States, or *to all cases* of admiralty and maritime jurisdiction? If some of these cases might be entertained by state tribunals, and no appellate jurisdiction as to them should exist, then the appellate power would not extend to *all,* but to *some,* cases. If state tribunals might exercise concurrent jurisdiction over all or some of the other classes of cases in the constitution without control, then the appellate jurisdiction of the United States might, as to such cases, have no real existence, contrary to the manifest intent of the constitution. Under such circumstances, to give effect to the judicial power, it must be construed to be exclusive; and this not only when the *casus faederis* [federal cause of action] should arise directly, but when it should arise, incidentally, in cases pending in state courts. This construction would abridge the jurisdiction of such court far more than has been ever contemplated in any act of Congress.

On the other hand, if, as has been contended, a discretion be vested in congress to establish, or not to establish, inferior courts at their own pleasure, and congress should not establish such courts, the appellate jurisdiction of the supreme court would have nothing to act upon, unless it could act upon cases pending in state courts. ...

It must, therefore, be conceded that the constitution not only contemplated, but meant to provide for cases within the scope of the judicial power of the United States, which might yet depend before state tribunals. It was foreseen that in the exercise of their ordinary jurisdiction, state courts would incidentally take cognizance of cases arising under the constitution, the laws, and treaties of the United States. Yet to all these cases the judicial power, by the very terms of the constitution, is to extend. ...

It has been argued that such an appellate jurisdiction over state courts is inconsistent with the genius of our governments, and the spirit of the constitution. That the latter was never designed to act upon state sovereignties, but only upon the people, and that if the power exists, it will materially impair the sovereignty of the states, and the independence of their courts. We cannot yield to the force of this reasoning; it assumes principles which we cannot admit, and draws conclusions to which we do not yield our assent.

It is a mistake [to assert] that the constitution was not designed to operate upon states, in their corporate capacities. It is crowded with provisions which restrain or annul the sovereignty of the states in some of the highest branches of their prerogatives. The tenth section of the first article contains a long list of disabilities and prohibitions imposed upon the states. Surely, when such essential portions of state sovereignty are taken away, or prohibited to be exercised, it cannot be correctly asserted that the constitution does not act upon the states. The language of the constitution is also imperative upon the states as to the performance of many duties. It is imperative upon the state legislatures to make laws prescribing the time, places, and manner of holding elections for senators and representatives, and for electors of president and vice-president. And in these, as well as some other cases, congress have a right to revise, amend, or supersede the laws which may be passed by state legislatures. ... The courts of the United States can, without question, revise the proceedings of the executive and legislative authorities of the states, and if they are found to be contrary to the constitution, may declare them to be of no legal validity. Surely the exercise of the same right over judicial tribunals is not a higher or more dangerous act of sovereign power.

Nor can such a right be deemed to impair the independence of state judges. ... In respect to the powers granted to the United States, they are not independent; they are expressly bound to obedience by the letter of the constitution; and if they should unintentionally transcend their authority, or misconstrue the constitution, there is no more reason for giving their judgments an absolute and irresistible force, than for giving it to the acts of the other co-ordinate departments of state sovereignty. ...

It is further argued, that no great public mischief can result from a construction which shall limit the appellate power of the United States to cases in their own courts; first, because state judges are bound by an oath to support the constitution of the United States, and must be presumed to be men of learning and integrity; and, secondly, because congress must have an unquestionable right to remove all cases within the scope of the judicial power from the state courts to the courts of the United States, at any time before final judgment, though not after final judgment. As to the first reason—admitting that the judges of the state courts are, and always will be, of as much learning, integrity, and wisdom, as those of the courts of the United States, (which we very cheerfully admit,) it does not aid the argument. It is manifest that the constitution has proceeded upon a theory of its own ... . The constitution has presumed (whether rightly or wrongly we do not inquire) that state attachments, state prejudices, state jealousies, and state interests, might sometimes obstruct, or control, or be supposed to obstruct or control, the regular administration of justice. Hence, in controversies between states; between citizens of different states ... it enables the parties, under the authority of congress, to have the controversies heard, tried, and determined before the national tribunals. ... In respect to other enumerated cases—the cases arising under the constitution, laws, and treaties of the United States ... reasons of higher and more extensive nature, touching the safety, peace, and sovereignty of the nation, might well justify a grant of exclusive jurisdiction.

This is not all. A motive of another kind, perfectly compatible with the most sincere respect for state tribunals, might induce the grant of appellate power over their decisions. That motive is the importance and even necessity of *uniformity* of decisions throughout the whole United States, upon all subjects within the purview of the constitution.

Judges of equal learning and integrity, in different states, might differently interpret a statute, or a treaty of the United States, or even the constitution itself: If there were no revising authority to control these jarring and discordant judgments, and harmonize them into uniformity, the laws, the treaties, and the constitution of the United States would be different in different states, and might, perhaps, never have precisely the same construction, obligation, or efficacy, in any two states. ...

On the whole, the court are of the opinion, that the appellate power of the United States does extend to cases pending in state courts ... .

It is the opinion of the whole court, that the judgment of the court of appeals of Virginia, rendered on the mandate in this cause, be reversed, and the judgment of the district court, held at Winchester, be, and the same is hereby affirmed.

Former Judge Robert Bork asserted the proposition that the Court is continually deferring less to the decisions of the states and its coordinate branches. For example, he points out that during the 93-year period from 1803 to 1896, the Court declared 19 acts of Congress and 167 state laws unconstitutional. In the 27 years from 1897 to 1924, the Court declared 28 acts of Congress and 212 state laws unconstitutional. Between 1940 and 1970, the Court held about the same number of acts of Congress unconstitutional, but the number of state laws invalidated increased to 278. According to Judge Bork,

> With each successive case, the Court shrinks the sphere of legislative decision making and expands the role of the judiciary: We observe ... the increasing importance of the one counter-majoritarian institution in the American democracy ... . What is worrisome is that so many of the Court's increased number of declarations of unconstitutionality are not even plausibly related to the actual Constitution. This means that we are increasingly governed not by law or elected representatives but by an unelected, unrepresentative, unaccountable committee of lawyers applying no will but their own."[63]

It is generally agreed by constitutional scholars that the Court is playing a larger role than it had in the past. But Judge Bork's other assertions—that the Court is doing this at the expense of legislative power and that many of the Court's decisions are not well grounded in the Constitution—are the subject of considerable debate.

The theory that there is a negative correlation between the power of the Court and its coordinate branches and the states assumes that the power of government as a whole has not changed since 1789; that governmental power is a zero-sum game. However, it is possible that the power of the Court has increased concomitantly with the increase in power of government. Today, government regulates the personal and commercial life of its citizens to a much greater degree than it did just 100 years ago. Therefore, possibly, the enlargement of the role of the

Court has not meant a decrease in the power of legislatures. Judge Bork's assertion that the Court's decisions are not "plausibly related" to the Constitution is also easier understood when one knows his constitutional ideology: he is an originalist.

In any event, the total number of laws invalidated by the Court remains small. In instances in which the Court has nullified a law, it has generally been successful in protecting the individual from arbitrary and unreasonable governmental actions and in helping its coordinate branches, the states, and the federal government maintain the delicate balance of power conceived by the framers.

In addition, the Court has created a number of rules and doctrines governing its decision making that are intended to respect the integrity and independence of the other branches, as well as of the states. Some of these have been discussed, such as the presumption that legislation is constitutional and the rule requiring the Court to construe a statute as constitutional, if reasonable. Also, through the political question doctrine, the Court refuses to adjudicate cases that are inherently political in nature or involve disputes that are best resolved by the executive or legislative branches. Therefore, it appears that the Court can serve the "guardian and protector" function while not excessively interfering with the functions of its coordinate branches or of the states.

The judiciary plays its role in the system through its administration of justice. That is, federal courts do not make rules on their own initiative; rather, they make decisions of law within the context of adjudication of cases. Importantly, the authority of the federal courts to hear cases, which is referred to as *jurisdiction,* is limited. The jurisdiction of the federal courts is examined in Chapter 4.

A Diffused Model

Recall that all courts, state and federal, may be called upon to interpret the Constitution. Through Article VI of the Constitution, state courts have an obligation to apply federal law even if contrary to their own state's laws. Section 2 of Article VI reads:

> This Constitution, and the Laws of the United States, which shall be made in Pursuance thereof; and all Treaties made, or which shall be made, under the Authority of the United States, shall be the supreme Law of the Land; and the Judges in every State shall be bound thereby, any Thing in the Constitution or Laws of any State to the Contrary notwithstanding.

Hence, the power of judicial review is diffused to all state and federal courts (except that certain limited-jurisdiction courts, such as traffic courts, may not possess this authority). Every day, every judge stands as a barrier between potentially oppressive government conduct and the citizen.

Not all systems operate in this manner. For example, there is no judicial review whatsoever in some nations; nations with a socialist legal system usually fall into this category. In others, judicial review is concentrated in one tribunal or court. For example, the Constitutional Council in France is the only body in that nation that may declare a law unconstitutional, and that body falls outside the judiciary. Germany also employs a concentrated model of judicial review. Unlike France, however, the power is held by a judicial entity, the *Bundesverfassungsgericht*.[64] These examples illustrate the significance of judicial review in the United States (see Figure 3-5). Simply stated, judicial review is an important part of American legal culture.

Of course, a court's power of judicial review is limited by stare decisis. If a higher court has already interpreted the Constitution in a particular manner, a lower court may not render a conflicting reinterpretation. Recall, however, that a court may distinguish a case under review from a prior binding case. To do so, the court must determine that the facts of the prior case are so dissimilar as to make it useless as precedent. Also, in certain rare instances a lower court will interpret a case in a manner that is inconsistent with a precedential case. Finding that a precedential case is so old that its law is no longer viable is an example. Such decisions may, of course, be reviewed by higher courts.

As a practical matter, judges in lower courts are less likely to declare laws unconstitutional than are judges of higher courts. Similarly, state

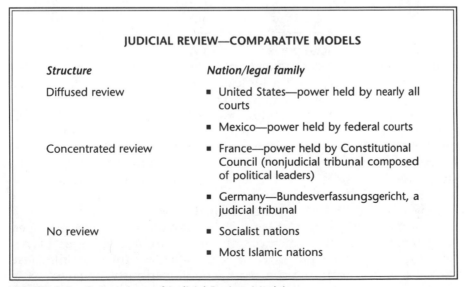

JUDICIAL REVIEW—COMPARATIVE MODELS

Structure	Nation/legal family
Diffused review	■ United States—power held by nearly all courts
	■ Mexico—power held by federal courts
Concentrated review	■ France—power held by Constitutional Council (nonjudicial tribunal composed of political leaders)
	■ Germany—Bundesverfassungsgericht, a judicial tribunal
No review	■ Socialist nations
	■ Most Islamic nations

FIGURE 3-5 Comparison of Judicial Review Models

judges are less likely to declare acts of Congress or the President uncon- stitutional than are federal courts. Although federal trial courts and state courts both hear cases involving federal issues, various procedural and substantive laws increase the likelihood that a case of national sig- nificance will first be resolved by a federal court or, in rare circum- stances, by the Supreme Court.

Summary

Although the framers intended for most cases to remain in the state courts, they also determined that a national judiciary was necessary to protect the newly formed national government from the states and, to a lesser degree, to protect individuals from the excesses of govern- ments. The latter function has increased in importance as a result of the expansion of federal jurisdiction, particularly in the area of civil rights. Today, federal courts play an important role in checking states and state officials and generally in the preservation of individual liberties.

The power of the federal courts is not, however, unbounded. Several formal institutional and informal limits exist to control the power of federal courts. In addition, even though federal jurisdiction has grown significantly in the past 100 years, most judicial power continues to re- side in the states.

The power of the judiciary to review the acts of its coordinate branches and the states for constitutionality is significant. Although not specifically provided for in the Constitution, Chief Justice John Marshall stated in *Marbury v. Madison* that the power is inherent in the general grant of judicial power found in Article III. Accordingly, all Ar- ticle III judges possess the power of judicial review. This diffusion of power establishes significant judicial power in the American political and legal systems. Judicial review is used every day in courts across the land when judges review statutes, other written law, and the actions of government officials such as law enforcement officers) for constitution- ality. Although the power is frequently invoked, data indicate that courts do not use it often to invalidate legislation. Of course, this is a subjective determination, and many jurists argue that it is used too fre- quently and that it is used in important policy cases that would be more properly decided by elected representatives.

Interpretation of the Constitution is a function all judges must per- form. There are as many methods of interpretation as there are judges. Regardless, most constructions can be classified as primarily originalist, modernist, literalist, or normative. The Constitution is silent as to whether the framers' intentions are to be followed and there is no other concrete evidence in the matter. In reality, most judges treat the Constitution as a living document, while adhering to the plain meaning rule or original intent when the outcome is clear and obvious.

The judiciary has become an important institution in American legal culture. the public expects courts to be available to redress their injuries and protect them from governmental abuse. The federal courts have come to play a unique role and their jurisdiction will likely continue to increase in the future.

Review Questions

1. What is meant by the assertion that the Supreme Court is a countermajoritarian institution?

2. Briefly describe the roles the Supreme Court plays in the United States governmental system.

3. Chart the structure of the current federal court system, noting the names of the courts at each level. Which courts were established under the Constitution? Which by Congress?

4. Briefly distinguish between originalism, modernism, and historical and contemporary literalism as methods of interpreting the Constitution.

5. Define *stare decisis*. When does it apply and what does *distinguishing on the facts* mean?

6. What is the rule of severability?

7. Define *certiorari*.

8. What is judicial review and in what Supreme Court case did Chief Justice Marshall announce the power on behalf of the federal judiciary?

9. The United States employs a diffused model of judicial review. What does this mean?

10. State two informal and two formal constraints on federal judicial power.

Review Problems

1. State statute provides that individuals convicted of vandalism of private or public property may be whipped with ten to twenty lashes. A defendant

subject to this statute asserts that it is prohibited by the Eighth Amendment as a cruel and unusual punishment. You are the trial judge. What information do you need to decide the issue?

2. The equal protection clause of the Fourteenth Amendment extends the equal protection of laws to all people. Historically, the clause has applied to immutable conditions such as race and gender. State statute prohibits homosexuals from adopting children. Sam, a homosexual, was denied an adoption. He is preparing to reapply. He has filed a complaint in federal court seeking an order enjoining the enforcement of the law in the future. Using a modern interpretive approach, what information would be relevant?

Notes

[1] *Addresses and Papers of Charles Evans Hughes (N.Y. 1908)*.

[2] Jerome Frank, "Words and Music," 47 *Colum. L. Rev.* 1259, 1269 (1947).

[3] Robert Katzmann, ed., *Judges and Legislators* 32 (Brookings 1988).

[4] *The Federalist* No. 78.

[5] Strauss and Sunstein, "The Senate, The Constitution and the Confirmation Process," 101 *Yale L.J.* 1491 (1992).

[6] *See* William Mishler and Reginald S. Sheehan, "The Supreme Court as a Countermajoritarian Institution? The Impact of Public Opinion on Supreme Court Decisions," 87 *Am. Pol. Sci. Rev.* 87, 96–97, (Mar. 1993).

[7] *Id.* at 97–98.

[8] *The Federalist* No. 78.

[9] Robert Katzman, ed., *Judges and Legislators* 32 (Brookings 1988).

[10] *Gomez v. United States,* 490 U.S. 858 (1989).

[11] *Granfinanciera S.A. v. Nordberg,* 492 U.S. 33 (1989).

[12] *New York Times,* Apr. 7, 1994, at A13.

[13] *See* Peter Schuck, "Public Law Litigation and Social Reform [book review]," 102 *Yale L.J.* 1763, 1786 (1993).

[14] Emily Field van Tassel, "Resignations and Removals: A History of Federal Judicial Service—and Disservice—1789–1992," 142 *U. Pa. L. Rev.* 333, 335 (1993).

[15] Richard M. Frank, "The Scorpions' Dance: Judicially Mandated Attorney's Fees—The Legislative Response and Separation-of-Powers Implications," 1 *Emerging Issues St. Const. Law* 73 (1988), citing H. Hockett, *Political and Social Growth of the United States* 502 (1937).

[16] Mishler and Sheehan, supra n. 5, at 89.

[17] *See* Daniel Hall, *Administrative Law* ch. 2 (Delmar/Lawyers Cooperative Publishing Co. 1994).

[18] 323 U.S. 214 (1944).

[19] 28 U.S.C. § 1332.

[20] 28 U.S.C. § 1331.

[21] *The Federalist* No. 78.

[22] *See* H. Jefferson Powell, "The Original Understanding of Original Intent," 98 *Harv. L. Rev.* 885 (1985).

[23] William J. Brennan, Jr., "The Constitution of the United States: Contemporary Ratification," 27 *S. Tex. L. Rev.* 433 (1986).

[24] Benjamin Cardozo, *The Nature of the Judicial Process* 17 (1921).

[25] *Dennis v. United States,* 341 U.S. 494 (1951). For further discussion of the Eighth Amendment's cruel and unusual punishments clause, see Daniel Hall, "When Caning Meets the Eighth Amendment: Whipping Offenders in the United States," 4 *Widener J. Pub. L.* 903 (1995).

[26] 347 U.S. 483 (1954).

[27] *Ford v. Wainwright,* 477 U.S. 399, 406 (1986) (further citations omitted); *Trop v. Dulles,* 356 U.S. 86, 101 (1958).

[28] *See* John H. Ely, *Democracy and Distrust: A Theory of Judicial Review* (Harvard University Press 1980).

[29] *McGrain v. Daugherty,* 273 U.S. 135, 156 (1927).

[30] *See* Johnson and Canon, *Judicial Policies: Implementation and Impact* (Congressional Quarterly Press 1984) for further discussion of this topic.

[31] 359 U.S. 520 (1959).

[32] *Rummel v. Estelle,* 445 U.S. 263, 375 (1980).

[33] Benjamin Cardozo, *The Nature of the Judicial Process* 149 (1921).

[34] *Patterson v. McLean Credit Union,* 491 U.S. 164, 172 (1989); Alexander Hamilton, *The Federalist* No. 78.

[35] *Holder v. Hall,* 114 S. Ct. 2581, 2618 (1994) (concurring opinion).

[36] 347 U.S. 483 (1954).

[37] 163 U.S. 537 (1896).

[38] 501 U.S. 808 (1991).

[39] 482 U.S. 496 (1987).

[40] *Illinois Brick Co. v. Illinois,* 431 U.S. 720, 736 (1977).

[41] *Webster v. Reproductive Health Services, Inc.,* 492 U.S. 490, 558 (1989) (concurring/dissenting opinion), citing *Arizona v. Rumsey,* 467 U.S. 203, 212 (1984).

[42] *Genesee Chief v. Fitzhugh,* 12 How. 443 (1852).

[43] *Helvering v. Hallock,* 309 U.S. 106, 119 (1940), cited in *Payne v. Tennessee,* 111 S. Ct. 2597, 2609 (1991).

[44] William O. Douglas, "*Stare Decisis,*" 49 Colum. L. Rev. 735, 736 (1949).

[45] 428 U.S. 153 (1976).

[46] William J. Brennan, Jr., "In Defense of Dissents," 37 *Hastings L.J.* 427, 437–38 (1986).

[47] *Payne v. Tennessee,* 111 S. Ct. 2597, 2610 (1991).

[48] *See* Paul Linton, *"Planned Parenthood v. Casey:* The Flight From Reason in the Supreme Court," 13 *St. Louis U. Pub. L. Rev.* 15 n. 273 (1993), citing an unpublished work by A. Blaustein and C. Willner entitled *Stare Decisis.*

[49] *Ashwander v. TVA,* 297 U.S. 288, 346 (1936).

[50] *See Alaska Airlines v. Brock,* 480 U.S. 678 (1987); *Immigration & Naturalization Service v. Chadha,* 462 U.S. 919 (1983).

[51] *Government & Civic Employees Organizing Committee v. Windsor,* 353 U.S. 364 (1957).

[52] *United States v. American Trucking Ass'n,* 310 U.S. 534 (1940). *See also Cass v. United States,* 417 U.S. 72 (1974).

[53] 8 Co. Rep. 107(a) (1610).

[54] *The Federalist* No. 78.

[55] Haines, *The American Doctrine of Judicial Supremacy* 136 (2d ed. 1959).

[56] *Id.*

[57] Austin Scott, *Holmes v. Walton; The New Jersey Precedent,* Rutgers College Publication No. 5, 4 *Am. Hist. Rev.* 456 (Apr. 1899).

[58] Id., chs. V and VI.

[59] *See Hylton v. United States,* 3 Dall. 171 (1796), wherein the Court implicitly exercised the power by reviewing and upholding a federal taxing statute.

[60] *Fletcher v. Peck,* 10 U.S. (6 Cranch) 87 (1810).

[61] L. Baum, *The Supreme Court,* 4th ed. (Congressional Quarterly Press 1992).

[62] *Id.;* C. Herman Pritchett, *Constitutional Law of the Federal System* (Prentice-Hall 1984), citing in part Sen. Doc. No. 134, 93d Cong., S127–S135 (1974), provides the following numbers: between 1865 and 1979 the Court held 120 acts of Congress unconstitutional; between 1953 and 1969 (Warren Court), 25 acts of Congress were held unconstitutional; between 1969 and 1979 (Burger Court), 21 acts of Congress were held unconstitutional; and between 1789 and 1974 848 acts of state and local government were held unconstitutional. *See also* Henry J. Abraham, *The Judicial Process,* 4th ed. 271 (Oxford University Press 1980); *Constitution of the United States: Analysis and Interpretation,* S. Doc. No. 16, 99th Cong. (1982).

[63] Robert H. Bork, *The Dangers of Political Law: The Tempting of America: The Political Seduction of Law* 130 n. 1 (Free Press 1989).

[64] Philip B. Reichel, *Comparative Criminal Justice Systems* 163 (Prentice-Hall 1994).

CHAPTER 4

THE JUDICIARY: JURISDICTION

§ 4.1 Federal Judicial Jurisdiction

Article III, § 1, of the Constitution provides that the "judicial power of the United States shall be vested in one Supreme Court, and such inferior Courts as the Congress may from time to time ordain and establish." Only the existence of the Supreme Court is assured by the Constitution. However, the framers empowered Congress to create additional federal courts. This was done by the first Congress through the Judiciary Act of 1789, and even more federal courts (and restructuring of existing federal courts) were added by later congressional action.

Because the Supreme Court was established by the Constitution, it is commonly known as a *constitutional court* or an *Article III* court. Some lower federal courts are Article III courts also. Others derive their jurisdiction entirely from Congress and, as a result, are known as *legislative courts* or *Article I* courts. There has even been an executive court (Article II court) in U.S. history. These courts are discussed more fully later in this chapter. The distinction between Article III courts and other courts is important. Jurisdiction, appointment procedures, length of appointment, and authority differ among Article III and other courts (see Figure 4-1).

Case-and-Controversy Requirement

Article III provides that the judicial power of federal courts extends to cases and controversies. An actual case or dispute must exist before an Article III court has jurisdiction. Because of this and other limitations, federal courts are considered **courts of limited jurisdiction**, as opposed to **courts of general jurisdiction**.

TERMS

court of limited jurisdiction [†]   A court whose jurisdiction is limited to civil cases of a certain type or which involve a limited amount of money, or whose

FIGURE 4-1

FEDERAL COURTS—CONSTITUTIONAL SOURCES

	Nature	*Examples*
ARTICLE I	Creation by President pursuant to treaty or military powers. Ad hoc in nature.	Tiede Court
ARTICLE II	Creation by Congress. May be ad hoc or permanently established.	U.S. Magistrate-Judges, Bankruptcy judges, Administrative law judges
	Judges are not "constitutionally established," so no lifetime tenure or salary guarantee.	
ARTICLE III	Supreme Court created by Constitution; district and circuit judges provided for by Constitution but established by Congress. Lifetime tenure and salary guarantees.	Chief Justice, Associate Justices, District judges, Court of Appeals judges

Therefore, federal courts do not have jurisdiction over hypothetical cases, nor can they issue **advisory opinions**. For example, Congress may not petition the Supreme Court to decide whether a proposed law, if enacted, would be constitutional. In such a case there is no dispute, no injury. However, if the law is enacted and enforced against a person who believes it unconstitutional, then there is jurisdiction, because there is a genuine dispute between the government and the individual resisting enforcement of the law. The Supreme Court was forced

TERMS

jurisdiction in criminal cases is confined to petty offenses and preliminary hearings. A court of limited jurisdiction is sometimes called a *court of special jurisdiction*.

court of general jurisdiction [†]   Generally, another term for trial court; that is, a court having jurisdiction to try all classes of civil and criminal cases except those which can be heard only by a court of limited jurisdiction.

advisory opinion [†]   A judicial interpretation of a legal question requested by the legislative or executive branch of government. Typically, courts prefer not to give advisory opinions.

advisory opinion   A judicial opinion concerning a legal issue over which no dispute or controversy exists. Federal courts are generally prohibited from rendering advisory opinions.

to resolve this issue early in the nation's history.[3] Thomas Jefferson, while Secretary of State to President George Washington, requested an advisory ruling on treaty matters. Chief Justice John Jay refused to issue an opinion because there was no case or controversy.

Similarly, private parties cannot consent to, or create, jurisdiction in Article III courts when there is no genuine dispute. Nor can Congress declare a party to have interest when it does not. That was the issue in the 1991 case of *Muskrat v. United States*.[4] *Muskrat* involved a set of statutes that changed the ownership of Cherokee tribal property to individual ownership and also concerned rights of alienation of that property. One statute provided that certain individuals could sue to test the constitutionality of the laws in the Court of Claims, with appeal to the Supreme Court. A group of plaintiffs brought an action, as provided for in the statute, before they were engaged in a real dispute over ownership. As provided for by the law, the United States was made a party to the case. The Supreme Court held that Congress had improperly granted jurisdiction to the federal courts because the law did not require an actual controversy in its jurisdictional provision. The Court concluded that Congress had created a mechanism for individuals to circumvent the case-or-controversy requirement. Adding the United States as a party was specious, because the United States was not claiming ownership of any of the properties in dispute, nor did it have any other genuine interest in the outcome of the case. If there had been an ownership dispute between two citizens over a piece of land, or if the government had voided a sale or lease because the contract violated the alienation provisions of the law, then the case-or-controversy requirement would have been satisfied.

The case-or-controversy requirement was intended by the framers to limit the authority of the judiciary. If the rule were otherwise, the judiciary could act as a superlegislature and superexecutive, issuing opinions and orders and voiding the laws and actions of the other branches as it pleased. Hence, the case-or-controversy provision preserves the integrity of the doctrine of separation of powers.

The case-or-controversy requirement affects only Article III courts. Article I and Article II courts, therefore, may issue advisory opinions. Hence, Congress may establish a court whose responsibility it is to render advisory opinions to both Congress and the executive. Of course, the decisions rendered by such a body could be only advisory and would not directly influence Article III judicial decision making.

The case-or-controversy requirement is also at issue when considering **declaratory relief**. Generally, parties seek money damages (legal

---
TERMS

declaratory judgment (declaratory relief) [†]   A judgment that specifies the rights of the parties but orders no relief. Nonetheless, it is a binding judgment

relief) or an order from a court requiring or prohibiting some action (equitable relief). For example, in a breach-of-contract case, the plaintiff may seek compensation for losses resulting from the breach. He may also request an order requiring the defendant to complete the contract (specific performance). These are the standard legal and equitable remedies sought by plaintiffs. They create no case-or-controversy problem.

In some instances, however, a plaintiff may request that a court review a case and declare the respective rights and obligations of the parties before there has been an injury. That is, in fact, the purpose of declaratory relief. Even though no injury has occurred, the Supreme Court has held that Article III courts have jurisdiction, so long as there is a genuine controversy between two or more parties.[5]

In the *Wallace* case, an appeal from the Supreme Court of Tennessee, the Supreme Court addressed the issue of whether declaratory relief is permitted under the case or controversy requirement. According to this case, the issue is not what form of remedy is **prayed** for; rather, it is the nature of the case itself. Actual injuries and damages do not have to be present to establish Article III jurisdiction, but there must be real parties—adversaries—who have a genuine dispute.

Federal Question and Diversity Jurisdiction

Federal judicial jurisdiction is further limited by Article III, § 2, to cases that involve federal legal issues or where diversity of citizenship exists. Congress has enacted statutes controlling the precise contours of judicial jurisdiction. This is because the Constitution delegated to Congress the authority to define jurisdiction. In doing so, Congress may not increase the jurisdiction of the judicial branch beyond the limits set by the Constitution. Do not be surprised when you learn that Congress has declared diversity jurisdiction to be narrower than allowed by the Constitution. A more thorough discussion of congressional control of federal judicial jurisdiction follows in this chapter.

Federal Question Jurisdiction

As to the first form of jurisdiction, Article III, § 2 states that the judicial power "shall extend to all Cases, in Law and Equity, arising under

─────────────────────── **TERMS** ───────────────────────

and the appropriate remedy for the determination of an actionable dispute when the plaintiff is in doubt as to his or her legal rights.

prayer[†] Portion of a bill in equity or a petition that asks for equitable relief and specifies the relief sought.

NASHVILLE, CINCINNATI, & ST. LOUIS RAILWAY v. WALLACE
288 U.S. 249 (1933)

Mr. Justice Stone delivered the opinion of the Court.

Appellant brought suit in the Chancery Court of Davidson County, Tenn., under the Uniform Declaratory Judgments Act of that state, chapter 29, Tennessee Public Acts 1923, to secure a judicial declaration that a state excise tax levied on the storage of gasoline ... as applied to appellant, [was] invalid under the commerce clause and the Fourteenth Amendment of the Federal Constitution. A decree for appellees was affirmed by the Supreme Court of the State, and the case comes here from appeal under section 237(a) of the Judicial Code (28 USCA § 344(a)).

After the jurisdictional statement required by Rule 12 (28 USCA § 354) was submitted, this Court, in ordering the cause set down for argument, invited the attention of counsel to the question "whether a case or controversy is presented, in view of the nature of the proceedings in the state courts." This preliminary question, which has been elaborately briefed and argued, must first be considered, for the judicial power with which this Court is invested by article 3, § 1, of the Constitution, extends by article 3, § 2, only to "cases" and "controversies"; if no "case" or "controversy" is presented for decision, we are without power to review the decree of the court below.

In determining whether this litigation presents a case within the appellate jurisdiction of this Court, we are concerned, not with form, but with substance. Hence, we look not to the label which the Legislature has attached to the procedure followed in the state courts, or to the description of the judgment which is brought here for review, in popular parlance, as "declaratory," but to the nature of the proceeding which the statute authorizes, and the effect of the judgment rendered upon the rights which the appellant asserts.

Section 1 of the Tennessee Declaratory Judgments Act confers jurisdiction on courts of record "to declare rights ... whether or not further relief is or could be claimed" and provides that "no action or proceeding shall be open to objection on the ground that a declaratory judgment or decree is prayed for. The declaration may be either affirmative or negative in form and effect; and such declaration shall have the force and effect of a final judgment or decree." By section 2 it is provided that "any person ... whose rights, status or other legal relations are affected by a statute ... may have determined any question or construction or validity arising under the ... statute ... and obtain a declaration of rights ... thereunder."

Under section 6, the court may refuse to render a declaratory judgment where, if rendered, it "would not terminate the uncertainty or controversy giving rise to the proceeding." ...

The statute has been often considered by the highest court of Tennessee, which has consistently held that its provisions may only be invoked when the complainant asserts rights which are challenged by the defendant, and presents for decision an actual controversy to which he is a party, capable of final adjudication by the judgment or decree to be rendered. ...

Proceeding in accordance with this statute, appellant filed its bill of complaint in the state chancery court, joining as defendants the appellees, the Attorney General and the state officials charged with the duty of collecting the gasoline privilege tax imposed by the Tennessee statute. The complaint alleged that appellant is engaged in purchasing gasoline outside the state, which it stores within the state pending its use within and without the state in the conduct of appellant's business as an interstate rail carrier; that appellees assert that the statute taxes the privilege of storing gasoline within the state and is applicable to appellant; that they have demanded payment of the tax in a specified amount and have determined to enforce their demand; and that, under the circumstances alleged, the statute as applied to appellant is invalid under the commerce clause and the Fourteenth Amendment. [The chancery court found the tax to be lawful and dismissed the complaint.]

... Obviously the appellant, whose duty to pay the tax will be determined by the decision of this case, is not attempting to secure an abstract determination by the Court of the validity of a statute ... or a decision advising what the law would be on an uncertain or hypothetical state of facts ... . Thus the narrow question presented for determination is whether the controversy before us, which would be justiciable in this Court if presented in a suit for injunction, is any the less so because through a modified procedure appellant has been permitted to present it in the state courts, without praying for an injunction ... .

While the ordinary course of judicial procedure results in a judgment requiring an award of process or execution to carry it into effect, such relief is not an indispensable adjunct to the exercise of the judicial function. ...

The issues raised here are the same as those which under old forms of procedure could be raised only in a suit for an injunction or one to recover the tax after its payment. But the Constitution does not require that the case or controversy requirement should be presented by traditional forms of procedure, invoking only traditional remedies. The judiciary clause of the Constitution defined and limited judicial power, not the particular method by which that power might be invoked. ... The states are left free to regulate their own judicial procedure. Hence changes merely in the form or method of procedure by which federal rights are brought to final adjudication in the state courts are not enough to preclude review of the adjudication of this Court, so long as the case retains the essentials of an adversary proceeding, involving a real, not hypothetical, controversy, which is finally determined by judgment below. ... Accordingly, we must consider the constitutional questions raised by the appeal. [The Supreme Court then concluded that the tax was constitutional.]

the Constitution, the Laws of the United States, and Treaties made, or which shall be made, under their Authority." The section continues by specifying jurisdiction in particular cases, including those that involve federal public officials such as ambassadors and cabinet officers. This provision is enforced by a federal statute, 28 U.S.C. § 1331. Accordingly, cases founded upon federal law may be heard by federal courts. *This is known as federal question jurisdiction.* Recall, however, that federal claims may also be heard by state courts, unless Congress declares otherwise. The opposite is not true. Federal courts do not freely hear state claims.

Federal question jurisdiction extends beyond constitutional claims. The previously mentioned provision refers to all laws and treaties of the United States. This includes statutes, administrative regulations, executive orders, and similar proclamations. Accordingly, all of the following are examples of cases in which federal question jurisdiction is found:

1. A plaintiff sues a police officer and a police department for violating a federally secured constitutional right, such as the right to be free from unreasonable searches and seizures (Fourth Amendment).

2. A plaintiff sues a private employer to recover unpaid overtime income under the Fair Labor Standards Act.

Amicus

The Many Seats of the Supreme Court

The Supreme Court has met in more than a dozen locations. The Court met for the first time on February 2, 1790, in the Royal Exchange Building in New York City. The Royal Exchange Building served as the nation's temporary capitol. The first floor of the building was a farmers' market. The Court held its sessions on the second floor, within earshot of the market. The capitol was moved from New York City to Philadelphia in February 1791 and housed in Independence Hall. However, the Court's stay in Independence Hall was short-lived. It was moved to Philadelphia City Hall in August of the same year.

The Supreme Court conducted its sessions in Philadelphia City Hall until 1801, at which time the entire national government was again relocated, this time to Washington, D.C. Although the White House and Capitol had been provided for, and were sufficiently finished, no provision for a judiciary building had been made. Therefore, the Court was given space in the Capitol basement. This is only one of six different locations within the Capitol that the Court would occupy. After the Capitol was damaged by British soldiers in 1814 (during the War of 1812), the Court was forced to meet outside the Capitol in several different locations.

The Court returned to the Capitol in 1817 to dungeon-like quarters. In 1819, the Court was again relocated to new quarters that had been restored after the fire set by the British soldiers in 1814. The Court was again relocated in 1860 to the old Senate Chamber. The Court remained in this location until 1935, when it moved into the Supreme Court Building (which was actually completed in 1939). The construction of a separate building for the Court was supported and urged by President William Howard Taft (who would eventually serve as Chief Justice), who believed that a separate facility symbolized the independence of the judiciary. The Court continues to reside in this building today. The total cost of construction, which began in 1929, was less than $10 million. The old Senate Chamber than was converted into a courtroom has been preserved and may be visited today. The Supreme Court's sessions are public and may be attended by any person. ▐▐

---

3. The administrators of a nuclear power plant sue to enjoin the enforcement of an administrative regulation, promulgated by the Nuclear Regulatory Commission, that they contend was created in an improper manner.

4. A plaintiff sues the United States for breach of contract after the President orders that the employment of the plaintiff and other striking employees of the federal government be terminated.

There are thousands of "laws" of the United States. As you can see from these examples, such laws govern more than the relationship between the government and its citizens. Relationships between individuals are also subject to federal regulation.

Diversity of Citizenship Jurisdiction

There is a second form of federal judicial jurisdiction: **diversity of citizenship** jurisdiction. Again the jurisdictional statement is found in Article III, § 2, which provides that federal judicial jurisdiction includes controversies between two or more states, between citizens of different states, and between a citizen or state of the United States and a foreign nation or one of its citizens. This form of jurisdiction is commonly known as **diversity jurisdiction.** Diversity jurisdiction arises most frequently in cases in which a citizen of one state sues a citizen of another state. For example, diversity jurisdiction might exist if a citizen of New York were to injure a citizen of Florida in an automobile accident while vacationing in Florida. The injured Floridian is not required to file his personal injury action in New York; rather, using diversity jurisdiction, he may be able to establish jurisdiction in a federal district court located in Florida.

Congress enacted a statute, 28 U.S.C. § 1332, that brings diversity jurisdiction to life. The Supreme Court has interpreted that statute as conferring narrower jurisdiction than the Constitution allows. In particular, the Supreme Court held that *complete diversity* of citizenship is required before a federal court may exercise jurisdiction in cases of multiple defendants and plaintiffs.[6] That is, every plaintiff must be diverse from, or from a different location than, every defendant. If any plaintiff is from the same forum as any of the defendants in the case, then jurisdiction is destroyed.

Consider this example. John and Samantha, husband and wife, live in New York. They are sitting in their automobile, which was manufactured in Michigan by a company incorporated in Michigan and purchased in New York at a dealership incorporated in New York, in the driveway to their home. Unexpectedly, as a result of negligent design, the car slips out of park into drive and runs into their garage door. They suffer both property damage and personal injury. If the couple decides to sue both the manufacturer and the distributor in Michigan, they must file their negligence action in a Michigan court, because complete diversity does not exist to establish federal court jurisdiction.

TERMS

diversity of citizenship [†]   A ground for invoking the original jurisdiction of a federal district court, the basis of jurisdiction being the existence of a controversy between citizens of different states.

diversity jurisdiction [†]   The jurisdiction of a federal court arising from diversity of citizenship, when the jurisdictional amount has been met.

Recall that the preceding Florida motorist example stated that diversity jurisdiction *may* exist. This is because more than diversity of citizenship must be shown. Pursuant to 28 U.S.C. § 1332, not the Constitution, an additional requirement must be met to establish diversity jurisdiction: a minimum amount in controversy. A plaintiff must have a minimum amount of damages before he or she can invoke federal jurisdiction. Otherwise, the case belongs in state court. The amount is set by Congress and is currently $50,000, though it is likely that this amount will increase in the next few years.[7]

Accordingly, there are two requirements to establish diversity jurisdiction. First, there must be complete diversity of the parties; second, there must be a minimum amount in controversy. (By the way, no specific amount in controversy is required to establish federal question jurisdiction.)

It is easy to understand why the framers would want federal question cases to be heard by federal courts. But why diversity cases? The purpose of diversity jurisdiction is to avoid local bias. The nation was different in 1789. People were less mobile and were more closely affiliated with their communities. The framers believed that the possibility of local prejudice in state courts was too great. Accordingly, they created diversity jurisdiction to bring traditional state cases out of state court into a federal forum, where it was assumed that the foreign person would receive fair treatment. Why would a noncitizen receive fairer treatment in a federal court in Virginia than in a state court in Virginia? It was thought that because federal judges are appointed by, paid by, and owe their allegiance to the federal government, they will not bring local bias to the courtroom. In addition, unlike most state judges, they have lifetime appointments, which allow them to make unpopular decisions without fearing for their jobs. Whether diversity jurisdiction makes sense today is heavily debated. There have been proposals to abolish diversity jurisdiction, but to date Congress has opted merely to reduce the number of cases subject to diversity jurisdiction (by increasing the amount-in-controversy requirement) rather than to eliminate it altogether.

Pendent Jurisdiction, Removal, and Other Practice Issues

The relationship and coordination between the federal and state court systems can be complex. Plaintiffs must sometimes choose between filing in federal or state court (due to concurrent jurisdiction), and the defendant may disagree with the plaintiff's choice of forum. As the preceding discussion shows, a forum decision involves more than strategic considerations—there are constitutional concerns as well.

Pendent Jurisdiction

The framers of the Constitution intended for state trial courts to have general jurisdiction over both state and federal claims. It remains true today that federal claims may be filed in state courts, unless otherwise provided by statute. Federal courts, in contrast, possess limited jurisdiction. As a result, federal courts are generally prohibited from hearing state claims. There are exceptions. For example, through **pendent jurisdiction**, a federal court may hear a state claim if the state claim is related to a legitimate federal claim. Claims are *related* if they stem from a "common nucleus of operative facts." The federal claim provides the basis of the federal court's jurisdiction and the state claim is heard in the interests of efficiency. As an example, assume that Defendant Don, a local police officer, is sued by Perry Plaintiff under a federal civil rights statute. Perry claims that Don used excessive force while arresting Perry. Perry files his action in federal court, using the federal civil rights statute to establish jurisdiction. Through pendency, Perry may also attach his state claims for deprivation of civil rights, assault and battery, and intentional infliction of emotional distress. If the rule were otherwise, a plaintiff who desires to have a federal claim heard in federal court would have to file any state claims separately in state court. This is judicially inefficient and more costly in time and expenses for the litigants.

Removal

If a plaintiff files an action in federal court when no federal jurisdiction exists, the case should be dismissed under Federal Rule of Civil Procedure 12. In cases of concurrent jurisdiction, is the plaintiff's choice of forum final? No. The Supreme Court has held that defendants have a right to have their cases heard in federal court when such jurisdiction exists, even if the plaintiff originally filed in state court. Defendants enforce this constitutional principle through **removal** procedures. *Removal* is the term used to describe the process of transferring a case from state court to federal court. For removal to be proper, there must be concurrent jurisdiction at the time the action is originally filed. Removal in the United States occurs automatically after a defendant has

---

TERMS

pendent jurisdiction[†]   The rule that, even though there is no diversity of citizenship, a federal court has the right to exercise jurisdiction over a state matter if it arises out of the same transaction as a matter already before the federal court.

removal of case[†]   [T]he transfer of a case from a state court to a federal court.

complied with all the procedural requirements (e.g., filing a petition for removal with the federal court, serving the petition on the parties, and serving a notice on the state court). Congress has provided that, in certain circumstances, a criminal case may be removed from state court to federal court. In the criminal context, the purpose of removal is to preserve the sovereignty of the federal government and to assure a fair trial to particular criminal defendants. Otherwise, the states could interfere with the functioning of the federal government by harassing federal officials through criminal proceedings.

Whether the action is civil or criminal, a federal official sued in state court may remove the case to the federal district court in which the action is pending, if the suit concerns the performance of her official duties.[8] Similarly, 28 U.S.C. § 1442(a) provides for removal of cases, whether civil or criminal, filed against members of the United States armed forces for actions taken in the course of their duties. 28 U.S.C. § 1443 provides for removal of certain civil rights cases.

Removal of criminal cases is the same as for civil: the defendant must file a notice of, and petition for, removal.[9] Improperly removed actions are remanded to the state court from which they came.[10] Cases that are improperly removed (no federal jurisdiction) are returned to the state court through **remand** procedures. At both removal and remand stages, constitutional and statutory jurisdiction issues must be resolved.

The case-and-controversy requirement of Article III, as well as the dual kinds of jurisdiction (federal question and diversity), form the foundation of federal jurisdiction (see Figure 4-2). With an understanding of those subjects, you are now prepared to examine the jurisdictions of the Supreme Court and lower federal courts more specifically.

§ 4.2 Supreme Court Jurisdiction

Article III, § 2, clause 2, states:

In all Cases affecting Ambassadors, other public Ministers and Consuls, and those in which a State shall be a Party, the supreme Court shall have original Jurisdiction. In all the other Cases before mentioned, the

---

TERMS

---

remand[†]   The return of a case by an appellate court to the trial court for further proceedings, for a new trial, or for entry of judgment in accordance with an order of the appellate court.

FIGURE 4-2

FEDERAL JUDICIARY—JURISDICTION

Two forms of federal judicial jurisdiction are authorized by Article III of the Constitution. Both have been implemented by Congress via statute.

Federal Question	*Diversity of Citizenship*
Law: 28 U.S.C. § 1331	Law: 28 U.S.C. § 1332
Jurisdiction: Cases arising under the federal Constitution or other federal law	Jurisdiction: Cases in which all plaintiffs are from different states from all defendants (complete diversity) and there is a minimum amount in controversy ($50,000)

Removal: Cases originally filed in state court, but for which federal jurisdiction exists, may be removed to federal court by the defendant. 28 U.S.C. § 1441.

Remand: Improperly removed cases (no federal jurisdiction) may be returned to the state courts from which they were removed. 28 U.S.C. § 1447.

supreme Court shall have appellate Jurisdiction, both as to Law and Fact, with such Exceptions, and under such Regulations as the Congress shall make.

Original Jurisdiction

Article III, § 2, delegates to the Supreme Court original jurisdiction in all "[c]ases affecting Ambassadors, other public Ministers and Consuls, and those in which a State shall be a Party." Congress has implemented this provision through statutes. *Marbury* taught us that Congress may not extend the Supreme Court's original jurisdiction beyond this constitutional limit. Nevertheless, Congress may decide whether the Supreme Court's original jurisdiction is exclusive or is held concurrently with other courts.[11]

By statute, 28 U.S.C. § 1251, the Supreme Court is required to hear cases between two or more states. (This statute and the other jurisdictional statutes discussed in this section can be found in Appendix D. You may want to refer to those statutes during this discussion.) Section 1251 jurisdiction is exclusive; therefore, no other court may originally hear these cases. The Supreme Court has ruled, however, that the statute does not confer exclusive jurisdiction over cases involving political subdivisions of states, such as counties and municipalities.[12] Few of these cases come to the Supreme Court, but when one does, the Court usually refers it to a **special master** to conduct the trial and make findings of fact. Otherwise, the Court actually sits as a trial court, receiving evidence in addition to hearing the arguments of counsel.

As to cases involving ambassadors, public ministers, and other public officials of foreign nations, or disputes between the United States and a state, or disputes between a state and citizens of another state or aliens, the Supreme Court has concurrent original jurisdiction with the federal district courts. In such cases, the Supreme Court is unlikely to accept jurisdiction; accordingly, the true court of original jurisdiction is the district court. The Supreme Court stated in one case that "[i]t has long been this Court's philosophy that our original jurisdiction should be invoked sparingly."[13] The seriousness of the claims and the availability of an alternate forum are important factors in the decision of whether to deny original jurisdiction. The Court has stated that its policy is justified because it needs to reserve time for its appellate duties.

Although 28 U.S.C. § 1251 was enacted to implement the Court's original jurisdiction, the Court has stated that such legislation is unnecessary, because the constitutional delegation of original jurisdiction is self-executing.[14] Said another way, the Constitution itself is the basis of the Supreme Court's original jurisdiction and Congress is not needed to make this so. Further, Congress may not eliminate this jurisdiction. Although self-execution of constitutional provisions is the norm, in some circumstances, they are not. If a constitutional provision is not self-executing, some additional action, commonly a statute, is necessary to make it enforceable.

Appellate Jurisdiction

Article III, § 2, clause 2 provides that in all cases in which the Supreme Court does not have original jurisdiction, but there is federal judicial power, the Supreme Court has appellate jurisdiction. The clause continues by stating that this appellate jurisdiction is subject to "regulations" and "exceptions" by Congress. Before delving into congressional control of the Court's appellate jurisdiction, let us examine the forms of appellate jurisdiction, certiorari, and appeal by right.

The Supreme Court receives far more appeals than it can hear. In recent years the Court has entertained only a small percentage of the cases

─────────── **TERMS** ───────────

special master[†]   A person appointed by the court to assist with certain judicial functions in a specific case.

brought to it. In fact, less than 2 percent of cases are granted certiorari. See Figure 4-3 for a breakdown of cases filed with the court over a three-year period.

Most of the cases heard by the Court arrive through certiorari procedure. *Certiorari* is a common-law writ ordering a lower court to transmit

---

SUPREME COURT FILINGS AND CASES

The Supreme Court receives thousands of petitions for certiorari each year. Most come to the Court in the form of a petition to proceed *in forma pauperis* (IFP). This is a request to proceed without paying the required fees. Statistically, IFPs are less likely to be granted than are paid petitions. The Court also receives a small number of original case petitions yearly. The data in this figure reflect the total cases on the Court's docket each term, whether newly filed or carried over from the prior term.

	October Term, 94–95	October Term, 93–94	October Term, 92–93
Cases on Docket			
Paid cases	2138	2100	2062
IFP cases	5574	5332	4792
Original cases	11	12	12
Total cases	7723	7444	6866
Cases Granted Review			
Paid cases	117	75	137
IFP cases	15	25	27
Original cases	11	12	12
Total cases	143	112	176
Percentage of Cases on the Docket Granted Review			
	1.8%	1.5%	2.5%[15]

FIGURE 4-3 United States Supreme Court: Filings and Cases Heard

a file to a higher court for review. The Supreme Court (as well as state appellate courts) uses certiorari to control its caseload. Individuals desiring Supreme Court review petition the Court to grant the writ. Under the **rule of four**, if any four justices vote in favor of granting certiorari, the case is placed on the docket. Granting the writ does not indicate which party will prevail, but only that the Court feels the case is of sufficient importance to be heard. Certiorari is purely discretionary. The Court decides, upon its best judgment, what cases it will hear. It is prone to entertain cases that pose novel issues of federal law (also known as *cases of first impression*), especially constitutional law; cases in which there is a conflict in interpretation of federal law between state high courts or U.S. courts of appeals; and case wherein a state high court or U.S. court of appeals has failed to follow the Supreme Court's precedents.[16] 28 U.S.C. § 1254 provides that any party to a civil or criminal action in a U.S. court of appeals may petition for certiorari. Also, a court of appeal may certify a question to the Supreme Court when it needs guidance or instructions. Under 28 U.S.C. § 1257, any party to a case before a state high court may petition for certiorari when one of the following occurs:

1. The validity of a treaty is questioned
2. The validity of a federal statute is questioned
3. A state statute is challenged as violative of federal law, whether constitutional, statutory, or other
4. A party asserts a title, right, privilege, or commission secured by federal law.

If, after granting a writ of certiorari, a majority of the Court determines that the case should not be heard, it is removed from the Court's docket and the decision of the lower court stands. A denial of a petition for a writ of certiorari also leaves the lower court's decision intact. A denial of certiorari has no precedential value, because no decision concerning the merits of the case is rendered.

A second avenue to the Supreme Court is through appeal by right. Unlike certiorari, the Supreme Court must hear cases of this nature. Appeals have always been outnumbered by certiorari, but since amendments to 28 U.S.C. §§ 1254 and 1257 in 1988, the number of appeals has fallen, because cases that previously came to the Court through appeal

---

TERMS

rule of four[†]   An internal rule of the Supreme Court, which provides that a case will be reviewed by the Court if four justices wish it to be reviewed.

were shifted to certiorari procedure. Today, the only cases that come to the Court by appeal are those in which three-judge district courts were empaneled. Few cases today require a three-judge district court, so these cases constitute only a small percentage of the high Court's business. Pursuant to 28 U.S.C. § 1253, appeals from orders granting or denying injunctive relief from three-judge district courts may be appealed directly to the Supreme Court. 28 U.S.C. § 2284 establishes that three-judge district courts are required whenever specified by Congress through special legislation and in political apportionment cases. That is, if a congressional district or state legislative district is challenged as being improperly apportioned, a three-judge district court, as opposed to the usual one-judge court, must hear the case.

There are several instances, which occur infrequently, in which a three-judge district court is required with direct appeal to the Supreme Court; for example, enforcement of the Twenty-sixth Amendment (voting rights) by the United States against the states,[17] civil rights actions filed by the Attorney General of the United States in employment cases[18] and cases concerning access to public accommodations,[19] actions by the United States against a state to enjoin a poll tax,[20] and actions filed by members of Congress concerning the constitutionality and enforcement of certain spending statutes.[21] In recent years, Congress has decreased the number of cases in which mandatory appeals were possible. Less than 1 percent of the Court's total caseload has come through mandatory appeals in recent years.

In some cases, appeal to the Supreme Court from a district court follows neither appeal nor certiorari procedure. Rather, a hybrid procedure is followed by which direct appeal to the Court is permitted but the appeal is discretionary. For example, a party in antitrust litigation may bring an appeal directly to the Supreme Court from the district court. However, the Supreme Court may dispose of the appeal "in the same manner as any other direct appeal ... or in its discretion, deny the direct appeal and remand the case to the court of appeals."[22]

Also, as a matter of procedure, there must be a quorum of Justices (five) before the Court may hear an appeal (certiorari or mandatory). A quorum may not be present because of vacancies on the Court or recusal of Justices (e.g., when a Justice has an interest in the case). By statute, the Chief Justice may remand a case to a United States Court of Appeals for hearing if a quorum cannot be reached. The decision of the court of appeals is final in such a case. In cases brought through certiorari, the judgment of the court from which the appeal is brought (i.e. court of appeals or state high court) is treated as affirmed if the qualified Justices determine that a quorum does not exist and will not exist during the Court's next term.[23]

SIDEBAR

Law Clerks

Nearly all federal judges employ at least one attorney, usually a recent law graduate, as a judicial law clerk. Although federal clerkships at all levels are prestigious, the most highly coveted are those for Supreme Court Justices. Each Justice of the Supreme Court has at least three clerks. Justice Horace Gray was the first to employ (at his own expense) a recent law school graduate to serve as secretary or law clerk.

Most clerks serve for only one or two years, although some clerks have served for longer periods. Clerks are appointed by, and exclusively serve, individual Justices. Excepting the attorneys of the parties during oral arguments and the other members of the Court, law clerks are the only attorneys with whom a Justice may confer. As a result, the law clerk becomes an important sounding board and source of ideas for many Justices.

Selection criteria for law clerks vary, but it is common for Justices to hire clerks from particular law schools (perhaps where the Justice studied), from particular geographic areas of the country, who have prior clerking experience, and are personally compatible. For example, Oliver Wendell Holmes, Jr., Louis Brandeis, and William Brennan favored Harvard Law School graduates. Justices William O. Douglas and Earl Warren favored individuals from the western United States. A former clerk stated that the best clerk for Justice Hugo Black was an Alabama boy who went to an Alabama law school.

The duties of a clerk are defined by his or her Justice and vary significantly. Dean Acheson, who clerked for Justice Brandeis, commented that he wrote the footnotes of opinions. Clerks to Justices Butler and Murphy, in contrast, wrote nearly all the opinions of those Justices. Justice Warren would have his clerks prepare a draft opinion from which he would cast his final opinion. Most Justices have their law clerks conduct legal research, prepare memoranda examining legal issues and parties' briefs, and screen petitions for certiorari. Justice Frankfurter used his law clerks to lobby the clerks of other Justices, and sometimes the Justices themselves, in an effort to "line up" votes.

The degree to which law clerks influence the development of the law is unknown, but it is unquestionable that as the caseload of all federal courts has increased, so has the role clerks play.

Source: David O'Brien, *Storm Center: The Supreme Court in American Politics,* 3d ed. (W.W. Norton 1993).

Recall that Article III, § 2, clause 2 provides that Congress may establish "exceptions" to the appellate jurisdiction of the Supreme Court. The structure of the clause makes it clear that the exceptions provision applies only to the Court's appellate jurisdiction and not its original jurisdiction. To what extent may Congress regulate the Court's appellate jurisdiction? Like many other clauses, the exceptions provision is vague. May Congress eliminate the Court's appellate jurisdiction entirely? This appears to be more than an "exception." What types of exceptions may Congress announce? May the jurisdiction of the Court be revoked as to a single case or during the pendency of a case? What role does the doctrine of separation of powers play in the exceptions analysis? These are difficult questions. The leading case in this area is *Ex parte McCardle*.

McCardle stands for the proposition that Congress possesses broad authority over the Supreme Court's appellate jurisdiction. Some jurists interpret the exceptions clause (and the *McCardle* decision) as granting Congress nearly absolute control over the Supreme Court's appellate jurisdiction. Justice Frankfurter interpreted the exceptions clause in this literal manner. He said that "Congress cannot give this Court any appellate power; it may withdraw appellate jurisdiction once conferred and it may do so even while a case is *sub judice*."[24]

Whether the Supreme Court would interpret the exceptions clause this broadly today is questionable. Justice Douglas stated in a 1962 opinion that "[t]here is a serious question whether the *McCardle* case could command a majority view today."[25] There are several reasons to believe that congressional authority over the Court's appellate jurisdiction might be interpreted more narrowly than advanced by Justice Frankfurter. First, *McCardle* was issued at a time when the federal courts played less of a role in government than today. Increasingly, the public has looked to the Court to maintain the balance of government and to secure civil liberties. Accordingly, separation of powers principles could be used to block the wholesale elimination of the Court's appellate jurisdiction. Indeed, distinguished jurist Henry Hart stated that the exceptions clause cannot be used to "destroy the essential role of the Supreme Court in the constitutional plan."[26] Today, the Court's essential role may be its status as referee of the relationships between the federal government's branches, between the states and the federal government, between states, and between governments and citizens. If this is accepted, Congress would be prohibited from using the exceptions clause to prevent review of its actions that are alleged to violate civil liberties or separation of powers. To date, the Supreme Court has not announced such a limitation upon Congress's authority under the exceptions clause.

The second limitation upon the exceptions clause has a separation of powers foundation. Congress may not use the exceptions clause to exercise a judicial power. That is, Congress may not use the exceptions clause to decide an individual case. Any withdrawal of jurisdiction must be neutral. To be neutral, such a law would have to apply generally, as opposed to applying to an individual or specific group of individuals. Congress may not use the exceptions clause to direct the outcome of a specific case. The issue of selective withdrawal of jurisdiction came before the Court in *United States v. Klein*.

EX PARTE MCCARDLE
74 U.S. (7 Wall.) 506 (1869)

[McCardle, a civilian, was arrested and detained by military authorities. He was charged with printing "incendiary and libelous" articles in a newspaper in violation of the Reconstruction Acts. Alleging unlawful detention, McCardle sought habeas corpus (judicial review of the constitutionality of detention) in the United States Court of Appeals. When this was denied, he appealed to the U.S. Supreme Court under a statute allowing such an appeal. The Supreme Court received the case and heard arguments but, before it issued a decision, Congress repealed the statute under which McCardle had appealed. President Andrew Johnson (who was involved in his own impeachment at the time) vetoed the bill, but it was overriden by two-thirds votes in both houses of Congress.]

Chief Justice Chase delivered the opinion of the Court.

The first question necessarily is that of jurisdiction; for, if the act of March, 1868, takes away the jurisdiction defined by the act of February, 1867, it is useless, if not improper, to enter into any discussion of other questions.

It is quite true, as was argued by the counsel for the petitioner, that the appellate jurisdiction of this court is not derived from acts of Congress. It is, strictly speaking, conferred by the Constitution. But it is conferred "with such exceptions and under such regulations as Congress shall make."

It is unnecessary to consider whether, if Congress had made no exceptions and no regulations, this court might not have exercised general appellate jurisdiction under rules prescribed by itself. For among the earliest acts of the first Congress, at its first session, was the act of September 24th, 1789, to establish the judicial courts of the United States. That act provided for the organization of this court, and prescribed regulations for the exercise of its jurisdiction.

The source of that jurisdiction, and the limitations of it by the Constitution and by statute, have been on several occasions subjects of consideration here. In the case of *Durousseau v. United States* [6 Cranch 312, 3 L. Ed. 232 (1810)] particularly, the whole matter was carefully examined, and the court held, that while "the appellate powers of this court are not given by the judicial act, but are given by the Constitution," they are, nevertheless, "limited and regulated by that act, and by such other acts as have been passed on the subject." The court said, further, that the judicial act was an exercise of the power given by the Constitution to Congress "of making exceptions to the appellate jurisdiction of the Supreme Court." "They have described affirmatively," said the court, "its jurisdiction, and this affirmative description has been understood to imply a negation of the exercise of such appellate power as is not comprehended within it."

The principle that the affirmation of appellate jurisdiction implies the negative of all such jurisdiction not affirmed having been established, it was an almost necessary consequence that acts of Congress, providing for the exercise of jurisdiction, should come to be spoken of as acts granting jurisdiction, and not as acts making exceptions to the constitutional grant of it.

The exception to appellate jurisdiction in the case before us, however, is not an inference from the affirmation of other appellate jurisdiction. It is made in terms. The provision of the act of 1867, affirming the appellate jurisdiction of this court in cases of *habeas corpus* is expressly repealed. It is hardly possible to imagine a plainer instance of positive exception.

We are not at liberty to inquire into the motives of the legislature. We can only examine into its power under the Constitution; and the power to make exceptions to the appellate jurisdiction of this court is given by express words.

What, then, is the effect of the repealing act upon the case before us? We cannot doubt as to this. Without jurisdiction the court cannot proceed at all in any cause. Jurisdiction is the power to declare the law, and when it ceases to exist, the only function remaining to the court is that of announcing that fact and dismissing the cause.

And this is not less clear upon authority than upon principle. ...

[T]he general rule, supported by the best elementary writers, is, that "when an act of the legislature is repealed, it must be considered, except as to transactions past and closed, as if it never existed." ...

It is quite clear, therefore, that this court cannot proceed to pronounce judgment in this case, for it has no longer jurisdiction of the appeal; and judicial duty is not less fitly performed by declining ungranted jurisdiction than in exercising firmly that which the Constitution and laws confer. ...

The appeal of the petitioner in this case must be dismissed for want of jurisdiction.

The Court concluded in *Klein* that Congress was not eliminating appeals in a class of cases. Rather, it was using jurisdiction to decide specific cases—a judicial function. In addition to attempting to usurp judicial power, the Court also held that Congress was usurping executive power. This is in direct conflict with the doctrine of separation of powers, so the statute was held void. Even in *McCardle,* the Court referred to state cases in which state courts had invalidated state laws dealing with judicial jurisdiction as interfering with the judicial power. This principle appears to be a well-entrenched limitation upon the exceptions clause.

Third, the exceptions clause may be limited by other constitutional provisions. In cases wherein a congressional decision to limit jurisdiction conflicts with another constitutional provision, the Court would be forced to decide which provision prevails. For example, there is considerable First Amendment jurisprudence concerning whether governments may allow displays or exhibits of a religious nature (a Christian manger scene, for example) on public property. The plaintiffs in these cases are often individuals of other religious faiths. It would be unconstitutional (violative of equal protection, as guaranteed by the Fifth and Fourteenth Amendments) for Congress to withdraw the Supreme Court's appellate jurisdiction in cases in which Muslims, Jews, Hindus, or people of other faiths were plaintiffs.

The issue appears to be one, at least in part, of legislative motive. In such a case, Congress's motive would be to direct the outcome of a specific class of cases. The line between a neutral law and an improperly motivated law is thin. Even more, motive-based tests are tricky. They create evidence problems: how does a plaintiff prove that Congress had a particular motive? Legislative history may be used, but often it does not reflect the true intentions of legislators. In any event, it is likely that a jurisdictional statute that encroaches upon equal protection or due process will be invalidated. Through dicta, the Court has stated as much.[27]

The final issue is that of complete withdrawal. The Supreme Court handed down *Ex parte Yerger*[28] during the same year it decided *McCardle.* The Court held that it had jurisdiction to hear an appeal in *Yerger,* even

UNITED STATES v. KLEIN
80 U.S. 128 (1871)

[Klein sued to recover property that had been seized by the United States during the Civil War. Pursuant to the authorizing statute, to be eligible to recover his property, a claimant had to prove that he did not aid the Confederacy. Klein received a presidential pardon (pursuant to a general pardon offered by the President to all citizens who aided the Confederacy) for his war activities. In his petitition to recover his property, Klein relied on a Supreme Court decision that declared pardons to be conclusive proof that an individual did not aid in the rebellion. Klein won his case at the trial level, in the U.S. Court of Claims, but while his appeal to the Supreme Court was pending, Congress enacted a statute reversing the Supreme Court's earlier decision. That statute declared that this specific pardon was irrebuttable proof that the pardoned citizen had aided the Confederacy. The statute further required cases in the Court of Claims to be dismissed, thereby denying the return of property, if the claimant had accepted the pardon without a disclaimer ("I accept the pardon even though I did not support the enemy"). Finally, the Supreme Court's jurisdiction over appeals from the Court of Claims in these cases was withdrawn.]

Mr. Chief Justice Chase delivered the opinion of the court.

The Court of Claims is thus constituted one of those inferior courts which Congress authorizes, and has jurisdiction of contracts between the Government and the citizen, from which appeal regularly lies to this Court.

Undoubtably, the Legislature has complete control over the organization and existence of that court and may confer or withhold the right of appeal from its decisions. And if this Act did nothing more, it would be our duty to give it effect. If it simply denied the right of appeal in a particular class of cases, there could be no doubt that it must be regarded as an exercise of the power of Congress to make "such exceptions from the appellate jurisdiction" as should seem to it expedient.

But the language of the proviso shows plainly that it does not intend to withhold appellate jurisdiction except as a means to an end. Its great and controlling purpose is to deny to pardons granted by the President the effect which this court had adjudged them to have. ...

It seems to us that this is not an exercise of the acknowledged power of Congress to make exceptions and prescribe regulations of the appellate power.

The court is required to ascertain the existence of certain facts and thereupon to declare that its jurisdiction on appeal has ceased, by dismissing the bill. What is this but to prescribe a rule for the decision of a cause in a particular way? ...

We must think that Congress has inadvertently passed the limit which separates the legislative from the judicial power.

It is of vital importance that these powers be kept distinct. The Constitution provides that the judicial power of the United States shall be vested in one Supreme Court and such inferior courts as Congress shall from time to time ordain and establish. The same instrument, in the last clause of the same article, provides that in all cases other than those of original jurisdiction "the Supreme Court shall have appellate jurisdiction both as to law and fact, with such exceptions and under such regulations as the Congress shall make."

The Congress has already provided that the Supreme Court shall have jurisdiction of the judgments of the Court of Claims on appeal. Can it prescribe a rule in conformity with which the court must deny to itself the jurisdiction thus conferred, because and only because its decision, in accordance with settled law, must be adverse to the Government and favorable to the suitor? This question seems to us to answer itself.

The rule prescribed is also liable to just exception as impairing the effect of a pardon, and thus infringing the constitutional power of the Executive.

It is the intention of the Constitution that each of the great coordinate departments of the Government—the Legislative, the Executive and the Judicial—shall be, in its sphere, independent of the others. To the Executive alone is intrusted the power of pardon; and it is granted without limit. It blots out the offense pardoned and removes all its penal consequences. ...

Now, it is clear that the Legislature cannot change the effect of such a pardon any more than the Executive can change a law. Yet this is attempted by the provision under consideration. [The motion to dismiss was denied and the judgment of the Court of Claims was affirmed.]

though the case was similar to *McCardle*. Jurisdiction was present in *Yerger,* however, because the appeal was brought through certiorari procedure and not through the repealed statute that was at issue in *McCardle*. The Court held that Congress had only withdrawn one method of reaching the Court and that the Court's discretion to grant certiorari had not been withdrawn. Some commentators have suggested that the outcome in *McCardle* would have been different if the holding in *Yerger* had not been possible. That is, repeal of a remedy is valid so long as other remedies are available to an aggrieved party. The *McCardle* Court recognized that the repeal of appellate jurisdiction at issue was limited. "Counsel seems to have supposed, if effect be given to the repealing act in question, that the whole appellate power of the court, in cases of habeas corpus, is denied. But this is an error. The act of 1868 does not except from the jurisdiction any cases but appeals from Circuit Court under the act of 1867."[29] It may be that if Congress had eliminated all classes of appeals in habeas corpus cases, or if it had eliminated habeas corpus in all federal courts, the decision might have been different. The issue is, what is an exception? The use of the term *exception* itself indicates that the Supreme Court will retain the bulk of its appellate jurisdiction outlined in the Constitution. Many interpretations are possible. Can an exception be horizontal (that is, withdrawing jurisdiction that affects many classes of cases, such as excepting all cases that arise out of the Fourteenth Amendment), vertical (withdrawing jurisdiction in one type of case only, such as school prayer), or both? Can Congress except all cases arising during a specified period of time (e.g., the Supreme Court shall not hear any appeals from cases arising between January 1, 1997 and January 1, 1998)? Can Congress except cases arising in certain regions of the nation (e.g., the Supreme Court shall not hear any appeals from cases arising out of the Seventh Circuit Court of Appeals)? Although no such cases have been litigated, the former is likely violative of separation of powers and the latter violative of equal protection. Exception to jurisdiction in particular cases, as discussed earlier, is the clearest case for overreaching by Congress.

Finally, Congress could use the exceptions clause to control the Court's review of cases by subject matter (e.g., the Supreme Court shall not hear any appeals from cases involving abortion rights). That issue has not reached the Court and it is unknown whether such a law would be constitutional. The following factors would be considered for this determination:

1. What is being excepted from review? Does the withdrawal conflict with another constitutional provision, such as due process or equal protection?
2. Is the withdrawal of jurisdiction neutral?
3. Does the withdrawal of jurisdiction comport with separation of powers principles?
4. Does the withdrawal interfere with the Court's performance of its essential role?
5. Does the withdrawal of jurisdiction leave the states to decide federal constitutional law?

This is not a precise formulation, and this area of law is uncertain.[30] It does, however, provide a good guide as to whether a congressional withdrawal of jurisdiction would be valid.

There are arguments favoring a broad interpretation of the exceptions clause. Proponents of the countermajoritarian theory contend that congressional control over the Court's jurisdiction is not only proper, but also necessary, to check the Court. Otherwise, the Court is likely to become a body of philosopher-kings. Of course, individuals who subscribe to the literal school of interpretation contend that the clause is unambiguous—Congress has been delegated the authority to decide the what and when of the Supreme Court's appellate jurisdiction. Remember, withdrawal of Supreme Court jurisdiction does not mean that no court will hear the case. Rather, a state or federal appellate court will become the court of final resort.

On the other side, a more narrow interpretation of the clause insulates the Supreme Court from riding the wave of public opinion. Recall that the nation was founded upon the ideal of limited government and individual freedom. Although other courts, state and federal, may enforce the law in a fair and neutral manner, the Supreme Court's place at the top of the judicial hierarchy gives the law uniformity. If the Court's appellate jurisdiction is eliminated in an area, lower court decisions (those of state high courts, United States courts of appeals, etc.) would become final. As a result of conflicting interpretations, citizens in different geographic areas of the country could be treated differently under the Constitution. For example, affirmative action could be lawful in some areas but violative of equal protection in others.

Also, a narrow reading of the clause preserves the integrity of the Court in the tripartite system. To give Congress plenary authority over the Court's jurisdiction is like allowing the fox to guard the henhouse, as one of the roles of the Court (at least since *Marbury*) is to review the actions of its coordinate branches (see Figure 4-4).

§ 4.3 Lower Courts' Jurisdictions

Article III Courts

Although Article III expressly creates only the Supreme Court, it provides that Congress may create "inferior Courts." Courts created under this provision, like the Supreme Court, are commonly known as *constitutional courts* or *Article III courts*. Although these courts are established by Congress, the Constitution is the source of their existence. As Article III entities, these courts are limited in jurisdiction to "cases and controversies." Congress may not extend their jurisdiction beyond the Constitution's limits. Judges of Article III courts are assured lifetime tenure and no reduction in pay. Certain classes of cases, as well as certain parts of cases, must be heard by Article III judges.

The first Congress established Article III lower courts in the Judiciary Act of 1789. Through that statute, three circuit courts of appeals and thirteen district courts were created. Initially, there were no circuit judges. Circuit court panels were comprised of one district judge and two Supreme Court Justices.

SUPREME COURT JURISDICTION

Original: Cases involving ambassadors, other public ministers, and consuls, and those in which a state is a party.

Congressional control: Congress may not extend the Court's original jurisdiction. It may, however, provide that the Court's original jurisdiction is held concurrently with other federal courts or that it is exclusive.

Appellate: All cases where federal judicial power exists and the Court does not have original jurisdiction.

Congressional control: Congress may establish "regulations" and "exceptions." The extent of congressional control is undefined.

FIGURE 4-4 The United States Supreme Court—Jurisdiction

The organization of the system has since changed. Today, there are eleven geographical circuits with a court of appeals in each. There are two additional courts of appeals, one in the District of Columbia and another for the Federal Circuit. Hence, there are thirteen courts of appeals in the federal system.

These courts represent the intermediate-level appellate courts of the federal system. (See Figure 2-3 for a diagram of the federal appellate circuits.) They hear appeals from district courts, specialty courts, and, in some instances, administrative tribunals.

In addition, there are ninety-four district courts in the United States. These are the federal trial courts. Each state has at least one district court and larger states have as many as four. Districts may be further geographically divided into divisions. The number of judges in each district varies according to need.

It is generally agreed that, because since Congress possesses the power to create these courts, it has control over their jurisdiction. Recall, however, that as Article III courts their jurisdiction cannot be extended by Congress beyond the Constitution's case-and-controversy, diversity, and federal question limitations. But it appears that, within those limitations, Congress has nearly total control over the cases that may be entertained by these courts.

> It would seem to follow, also, that, having a right to prescribe, Congress may withhold from any court of its creation jurisdiction of any of the enumerated controversies. Courts created by statute can have no jurisdiction but such as the statute confers.[31]

Similarly, the Court stated that:

> As regards the inferior courts to be established, Congress may give them such jurisdiction, both original and appellate, within the limits of the Constitution, as it may see fit to confer … . The whole subject is remitted to the unfettered discretion of Congress.[32]

Of course, some jurists argue that Congress may have control over the jurisdiction of lower courts, but its authority is not **plenary**. Rather, jurisdictional declarations must be consonant with other constitutional mandates, as was previously discussed in regard to Supreme Court appellate jurisdiction. In the extreme, it has been argued that, because of the importance of federal courts in assuring due process and equal protection of citizens, Congress could not totally eliminate the lower federal courts today. It appears that Congress may not totally eliminate relief for a constitutional deprivation. For example, it is generally accepted

<hr>

TERMS

plenary[†]   Full; complete.

that Congress may withdraw cases from being heard in state courts. Also, Congress may withhold the original jurisdiction of lower federal courts and the appellate jurisdiction of the Supreme Court. In such cases, no court would possess jurisdiction to resolve the federal constitutional claim. Although the jurisdictional mandates may be valid individually, as a whole they are constitutionally unsound. Whether the line is drawn at this extreme point, or earlier, is unknown.

This analysis applies only to constitutionally secured rights. If a right is established by Congress, it may eliminate that right or withhold the jurisdiction of all courts to enforce the right while leaving it intact. Recall, however, that state judges have an obligation to follow federal law, even if contrary to their own state's law. Thus, a citizen may assert the federal Constitution as a defense to state action. Congress cannot withdraw this remedy from the state courts. However, this example refers to cases involving the federal government. For example, suppose Congress enacts a new environmental statute that prohibits the owners of wetlands from building on or otherwise developing their property. These types of laws are often challenged as constituting a taking of property under the Fifth Amendment. In a taking, the federal government is required to compensate the property owner. It is hard to imagine that it would be constitutionally sound to withdraw jurisdiction from every state and federal court in such a case. In fact, it appears that the framers intended for all federal claims to be heard by a federal court. At the inception of the new Constitution, this role could be handled by the Supreme Court. Today, however, the Court cannot hear all these cases. Therefore, lower courts are now not a luxury—they are a constitutional necessity.

Through diversity and federal question jurisdiction, federal courts hear nearly all the cases allowed by the Constitution. Congress could expand the jurisdiction of the federal courts if it wished. For example, the statute providing for diversity jurisdiction has been interpreted as limiting that jurisdiction to cases of complete diversity (all defendants diverse from all plaintiffs), although the Court has held that the Constitution permits incomplete diversity.[33] Also, several statutes limit original and appellate jurisdiction directly, such as a statute that generally forbids federal courts from enjoining state court proceedings.[34]

Article I and Article II Courts

Congress may establish nonconstitutional courts. The judges of these courts are not entitled to lifetime tenure, their pay may be reduced while they are in office, and they need not be selected through the constitutional nomination and confirmation process. These courts are commonly referred to as *Article I courts*. The Constitution's jurisdictional limitations do not apply to these courts. Accordingly, Congress may delegate to these tribunals hypothetical questions and other nondisputes.

There are many Article I judges and courts in the federal system. The United States Bankruptcy Courts, U.S. Magistrate-Judges, military courts, territorial courts, the Claims Court, the Tax Court, and some District of Columbia courts are examples.

Although their nonconstitutional nature enables Article I judges to perform some functions prohibited to Article III judges, it also limits their authority in particular instances. Article I judges may not be delegated the authority to perform an essential judicial function. For example, in some instances a litigant may possess a right to appear before a constitutionally empowered judge. In such a case, an Article I judge may not render the final decision in the case, nor may he or she preside over some critical stage of the proceeding.

This is true of U.S. Magistrate-Judges. These official positions are the creation of Congress, although they reside within the judicial branch. The system of magistrates was created in an effort to reduce the burden on district judges without establishing new Article III judgeships. Congress was careful to keep magistrates accountable to Article III judges and therefore less susceptible to constitutional challenge. Magistrates are appointed by, and may be removed by, Article III judges. The decisions of magistrates are reviewed, **de novo**, by Article III judges. Party consent is required before a magistrate may conduct a trial.

Under the Federal Magistrates Act,[35] certain responsibilities are delegated to magistrates (though their actions are reviewable by district judges) and district judges are empowered to delegate further responsibilities. However, in *Gomez v. United States*[36] and *Peretz v. United States*,[37] the Court ruled that a magistrate may not preside over the critical stages of a criminal trial over the objection of one of the parties. Because Congress carefully drafted the Magistrates Act, however, magistrates may preside over nearly all other pretrial and trial proceedings, subject to review by a district judge. If Congress were to amend the Magistrates Act to make the decision of a magistrate final, it would likely be invalid.

An interesting question, which remains open today, is whether federal bankruptcy judges may conduct jury trials. The Seventh Amendment preserves the right to a jury in federal common-law cases when the amount in controversy exceeds $20. There is no right to a jury trial in equity cases. Although most of the legal issues presented to bankruptcy judges are equitable in nature, some are not.

TERMS

de novo[†]   Anew; over again; a second time.

In 1989, the Supreme Court issued *Granfinanciera, S.A. v. Nordberg,*[38] in which it ruled that litigants in bankruptcy actions involving a common-law issue possess a right to have those disputes heard by a jury. The Supreme Court did not answer the next logical question: whether Article I bankruptcy judges may preside over bankruptcy-related jury trials. This question has not been answered by the Court and there is a split of authority among the lower federal courts.[39] The powers and limitations of non-Article III tribunals are discussed in greater depth in Chapter 7.

In total, the federal courts dispose of a significant amount of litigation annually. In 1993, the district courts handled 275,850 cases; courts of appeals, 50,000 cases; and bankruptcy courts, 896,000 cases. The Supreme Court had 5,832 cases on its docket during that year. What is amazing is that this accounts for less than 5 percent of all litigation in the United States (the remainder falls into the state courts).

Congress has created a number of specialty courts. The Court of Claims, the Court of International Trade, the Tax Court, and the Court of Customs and Patents Appeals are examples. The Court of Claims was created by statute in 1855. It has jurisdiction over most claims against the United States.[40]

Finally, there are the anomalous courts established by the executive under Article II of the Constitution. These are rare, but known to the law. For example, the State Department established a court in Berlin, West Germany, in 1978 to try airline hijackers. The hijackers were not terrorists, but East Germans who had commandeered a plane and forced it to land in West Germany, in an attempt to escape the repression of the Eastern Bloc. The United States, West Germany, and East Germany were signatories to an international agreement criminalizing hijacking, and the United States continued to have authority over its section of West Germany as a residual power from World War II. East Germany insisted on prosecution and West Germany convinced the United States to try the individuals under United States authority. Hence, a court was created under the authority of the President.

The defendants were tried by a jury and convicted. An Article III judge, Herbert Stern, was selected to try the matter, and he caused the State Department some consternation by applying United States constitutional law. The State Department insisted that the Constitution has no force outside the United States and that the defendants were not entitled to the rights and protections found therein, such as the right to a jury trial. Judge Stern disagreed and ruled that the defendants were protected by the Constitution; accordingly, they were entitled to due process and a jury trial. As to the claim that the court was an Article II tribunal subject to orders from the Secretary of State, Judge Stern stated that "[d]ue process requires that if the United States convenes this Court, it must come before the Court as a litigant and not as a commander." The judge was careful to distinguish the case from military courts martial, espionage cases, and military trials during times of war, in which the outcomes would be different.[41]

Interesting issues are raised by such a case. Can courts be established under Article II to try criminal cases? Unquestionably, such a court could not be used within the United States. But what about international circumstances such as those presented in the Berlin case? What about international war crimes trials, such as the Nuremburg trials? If permitted, to what extent must the judge be independent? Also, to what extent does the Constitution apply in such a case? These questions have not been answered and are as much political as they are legal.[42]

Administrative Tribunals

As discussed in greater detail in Chapter 7, administrative agencies perform "quasi-judicial" functions. Also, as discussed earlier, these agencies are not Article III tribunals. Accordingly, they are limited by the Constitution to a greater extent than are Article III judges in some ways; in others, they may possess broader jurisdiction than Article III judges. For example, an agency can be delegated the authority to render advisory opinions. However, because such an agency is not constitutionally empowered, its interpretations of law would not be binding on Article III courts. Similarly, the case-or-controversy requirement that limits the jurisdiction of federal courts has no constitutional effect on administrative agencies.

The jurisdictional authority of administrative agencies is established by Congress. Administrative tribunals are characterized as informal, when compared to courts, and operate under a different set of procedural and evidentiary rules than do court proceedings. There are over 1,000 administrative law judges (ALJs) in the federal administrative system. ALJs hear more cases each year than do all the federal courts combined. One agency alone, the Social Security Administration, hears more cases than the entire civil docket of the federal courts.[43] Greater detail about the powers, limits, and role of administrative tribunals is provided in Chapter 7.

§ 4.4 Limitations on Federal Judicial Power

As previously discussed, Article III limits the jurisdiction of federal courts to actual cases and controversies. Article III courts may not hear hypothetical cases, no matter how important to the nation. Article III is also the source of other limitations.

Additionally, other constitutional provisions, such as the Eleventh Amendment, restrict the power of federal courts. A case that may be heard by a federal court is said to be *justiciable,* and the following rules are known, in combination, as the **justiciability doctrine**. What follows is a discussion of the most significant limitations on federal judicial power.

Ripeness and Mootness

As previously pointed out, Article III limits the jurisdiction of federal courts to genuine disputes. This rule affects the timing of lawsuits.

Ripeness

If a suit is filed before a harm has occurred or before the threat of harm is imminent, there is no genuine dispute and hence no jurisdiction. The case is said to be *unripe.*

The most significant decision in this area is the 1947 Supreme Court decision in *United Mine Workers v. Mitchell.*[44] This case centered around the Hatch Act, a federal statute that prohibited executive branch employees from participating in political campaigns. One employee had violated the statute, but several employees challenged it. The Court heard the case and concluded that only the employee who was subject to punishment for actually violating the statute had presented a justiciable claim. The other employees had presented their claim prematurely. The Court stated that "[a] hypothetical threat is not enough. We can only speculate as to the kinds of political activity the appellants desire to engage in or as to the contents of their proposed public statements ... . Should the courts [hear such cases,] they would become the organ of political theories."[45]

Similarly, if a law is not enforced and there is no reason to believe that it will be enforced, an action seeking to have the law declared unconstitutional is not ripe. This occurred in *Poe v. Ullman,*[46] in which a law criminalizing the use of contraceptives was challenged. The Court found that because the law was not enforced, there was no justiciable issue.

TERMS

justiciability doctrine   Rules that limit the authority of federal courts to hear cases, such as ripeness, mootness, political question, and standing.

Mootness

Just as a case may be filed prematurely, it may also be heard by a court too late to be justiciable. A case for which the disputed issues have been resolved or dissipated during litigation is moot. Consider a hypothetical example. Latoya is the president of SITUS (State Income Tax is Unlawful Society). At each monthly SITUS meeting, Latoya burns the state flag in protest of the state income tax. In January, the state legislature enacts a statute criminalizing desecration of the state flag. Latoya receives a letter the following week from the local prosecutor indicating that if she continues her practice she will be prosecuted under the new law. Latoya responds by filing a petition asking the federal district court to declare the law unconstitutional under the First Amendment. During the pendency of the suit, the prosecutor comes to believe that the law is unconstitutional and issues a public statement that no person will be prosecuted under the new law. This action renders the case moot.

An example of mootness that reached the Supreme Court is *DeFunis v. Odegaard*.[47] DeFunis was denied admission to the University of Washington Law School in 1971. He filed an action in state court seeking an order declaring the admissions process violative of equal protection. DeFunis claimed that minority applicants were unlawfully favored for admission. He prevailed at the trial level and an order was issued to the university to admit him. During his legal studies, the Supreme Court of Washington reversed the trial court's decision. The Supreme Court issued a stay of that court's decision and set the matter for hearing. By the time the case reached the Supreme Court, DeFunis was in his third year of law school, and the university indicated that he would be allowed to complete his graduate degree regardless of the outcome of the appeal. Due to these facts, the Supreme Court held that the case was moot.

Important to the mootness inquiry is whether an action is filed by an individual or on the behalf of a class. Individual actions become moot more easily than do **class actions**. For example, had DeFunis filed his action on behalf of all caucasian applicants, past and future, who were or might be discriminated against as a result of the university's

---

TERMS

class action[†] An action brought by one or several plaintiffs on behalf of a class of persons. A class action may be appropriate when there has been injury to so many people that their voluntarily and unanimously joining in a lawsuit is improbable and impracticable. In such a situation, injured parties who wish to do so may, with the court's permission, sue on behalf of all. A class action is sometimes referred to as a representative action.

affirmative action policy, the entire action might not have been dismissed as moot.[48]

Exceptions to Mootness

There are exceptions to the mootness doctrine. The first concerns behavior that is **capable of repetition yet evading review.** Three elements must be proved to satisfy this test. First, there must have been a legal or factual issue when the case was filed which became moot during the pendency of the proceedings. Second, the harm at issue must be capable of recurring. Third, the nature of the issue must be such that it evades review. Typically, a case evades review because its facts change before review can be had. That was true in the well-known case of *Roe v. Wade,*[49] wherein the Supreme Court held that women possess the right to elect to abort pregnancies, in some circumstances.

Roe, a plaintiff using a **pseudonym,** challenged a Texas statute that prohibited her from obtaining an abortion. By the time the case reached the Court, there was no chance that Roe was still pregnant (at least not the pregnancy that was the basis of her complaint), as two years had passed. Regardless, the Supreme Court heard the case. The Court stated that

> the normal 266-day human gestation period is so short that the pregnancy will come to term before the usual appellate process is complete. If that termination makes a case moot, pregnancy litigation seldom will survive much beyond the trial stage, and appellate review would be effectively denied. Pregnancy provides a classic justification for a conclusion of non-mootness. It truly could be capable of repetition yet evading review.[50]

A second exception to mootness applies in cases when the defendant appears to have stopped the alleged violation in order to avoid judicial review. This is commonly referred to as the **voluntary cessation of illegal acts** doctrine. This is similar to the capable of repetition yet

---

TERMS

capable of repetition yet evading review An exception to the mootness doctrine, which provides that if an alleged harm may be repeated, but by its nature cannot be judicially determined in the normal legal process, that harm may become the basis of jurisdiction.

pseudonym A fictitious name. A plaintiff may sometimes be permitted to file a case using a fictitious name, if the plaintiff has a legitimate interest in protecting his or her privacy, such as when the facts of the case are embarrassing or the plaintiff's life may be threatened.

voluntary cessation of illegal acts An exception to the mootness doctrine, which provides that if an alleged harm has been ceased in order to

evading review rule, except that the defendant is responsible for the case becoming moot. If it appears that such an action is intended only to avoid review and that the behavior may resume, jurisdiction to hear the case exists.

A third exception applies when the actual subject of litigation becomes moot but **collateral consequences** continue to linger. For example, assume that a state punishes thefts of items valued at less than $100 with a fine and no more than three months' imprisonment. It is not possible for a case to be reviewed by an appellate court before the sentence is served. Even though the sentence may have been completed, there are collateral consequences: an offender may be placed on probation, sentences in future convictions may be enhanced due to the conviction, and the offender may be stigmatized in the community. For these reasons, the issue is justiciable even though the actual sentence has been fully served. So long as a party has some interest, tangible or intangible, in the litigation, the case is not moot.

Parties may not create fictional disputes in order to get a legal question answered. For example, in *United States v. Johnson*,[51] the plaintiff sued his landlord, alleging that the rent he paid was in excess of what federal regulations permitted. The United States intervened (which explains why it is in the case title) in defense of the law. The trial court ruled that the law was unconstitutional. The United States then sought reconsideration because it claimed that the original parties had acted in collusion to create jurisdiction. In support of this, the United States pointed out that the plaintiff had brought the suit (using a fictitious name) at the defendant's request, the plaintiff's counsel had never met the plaintiff, and, most importantly, the defendant had paid the plaintiff's attorney fees. Based upon these facts, the Supreme Court found that the parties were attempting to have a legal question answered, not to have a dispute resolved.

Standing

Standing is concerned with *who* may file a claim or assert a defense—in other words, who may be a plaintiff or defendant. An individual must

---

TERMS

avoid review, and there is a reasonable likelihood that the harm will reoccur or be recommenced, then the case may be heard.

collateral consequences An exception to the mootness doctrine, which provides for jurisdiction in cases in which the primary issue is moot, but secondary—*collateral*—issues remain.

standing The legal capacity to bring and to maintain a lawsuit. A person is without standing to sue unless some interest of his or hers has been adversely

have standing to be a party to litigation. To have standing, a party must have a genuine interest in the outcome of the litigation. A party must possess "such a personal stake in the outcome of a controversy as to assure that concrete adverseness which sharpens the presentation of issues upon which the Court so largely depends for illumination of difficult constitutional questions."[52]

In some cases, standing may be evident from a statute. Congress may have created a right and expressly provided that certain classes of individuals have standing to enforce the created right. In other cases, such as when Congress creates a right but does not express who should have standing, and in cases in which a constitutional right is asserted, standing is more problematic.

Generally, standing exists if three requirements are met. This test was announced by the Supreme Court in *Baker v. Carr*.[53]

1. The plaintiff must have suffered an injury in fact; and
2. The injury must have been caused by the challenged action; and
3. A favorable decision will redress the injuries suffered.

Injury in Fact

What is an *injury in fact*? Clearly, tangible injuries, such as personal and financial, satisfy this requirement. As examples, a physician who performs abortions has standing to challenge a statute proscribing that procedure[54]; owners of bookstores have standing to challenge a law that restricts the display of sexually explicit materials, because the law may reduce sales.[55]

Although a mere metaphysical or intellectual interest is not adequate to establish standing, in recent years the Court has expanded the injury-in-fact category to include aesthetic, conservational, and recreational injuries. In the *Morton* case, the Court held that a personal interest in the environment is adequate to establish standing.[56]

Although the Court held that an aesthetic, conservational, or recreational interest is adequate to establish standing, it also held that such an interest must be held by the party asserting the harm. Hence, had Sierra Club held its meetings at Mineral King, for example, standing could have been found.

Another way a special interest group can establish standing is by representing individuals who have suffered an injury in fact. The lesson of *Sierra Club* was not learned by the plaintiffs in *Lujan v. Defenders of*

─────────── TERMS ───────────

affected or unless he or she has been injured by the defendant. The term "standing to sue" is often shortened simply to "standing."

SIERRA CLUB v. MORTON
405 U.S. 727 (1972)

The Mineral King Valley is an area of great natural beauty nestled in the Sierra Nevada Mountains in Tulare County, California, adjacent to Sequoia National Park. It has been part of the Sequoia National Forest since 1926, and is designated as a national game refuge by special Act of Congress. Though once the site of extensive mining activity, Mineral King is now used almost exclusively for recreational purposes. Its relative inaccessibility and lack of development have limited the number of visitors each year, and at the same time have preserved the valley's quality as a quasi-wilderness area largely uncluttered by the products of civilization.

The United States Forest Service, which is entrusted with the maintenance and administration of national forests, began in the late 1940s to give consideration to Mineral King as a potential site for recreational development. Prodded by a rapidly increasing demand for skiing facilities, the Forest Service published a prospectus in 1965, inviting bids from private developers for the construction and operation of a ski resort that would serve as a recreation area. The proposal of Walt Disney Enterprises, Inc., was chosen from those of six bidders, and Disney received a three-year permit to conduct surveys and explorations in the valley in connection with its preparation of a complete master plan for the resort.

The final Disney plan, approved by the Forest Service in January 1969, outlines a $35 million complex of motels, restaurants, swimming pools, parking lots, and other structures designed to accommodate 14,000 visitors daily. ...

Representatives of the Sierra Club, who favor maintaining Mineral King largely in its present state, followed the progress of recreational planning for the valley with close attention and increasing dismay. They unsuccessfully sought a public hearing on the proposed development in 1965, and in subsequent correspondence with officials of the Forest Service and the Department of the Interior, they expressed the Club's objections to Disney's plan as a whole and to particular features included in it. In June 1969 the Club filed the present suit in the United States District Court for the Northern District of California, seeking a declaratory judgment that various aspects of the proposed development contravene federal laws and regulations governing the preservation of national parks, forests, and game refuges, and also seeking preliminary and permanent injunction restraining federal officials involved from granting their approval or issuing permits ... .

The first question presented is whether the Sierra Club has alleged facts that entitle it to obtain judicial review of the challenged action. Whether a party has sufficient stake in an otherwise justiciable controversy to obtain judicial resolution of that controversy is what has traditionally been referred to as the question of standing to sue. Where the party does not rely on any specific statute authorizing invocation of the judicial process, the question of standing depends upon whether the party has alleged such a "personal stake in the outcome of the controversy," ... as to ensure that "the dispute sought to be adjudicated will be presented in an adversary context and in a form historically viewed as capable of judicial resolution." ...

The injury alleged by the Sierra Club will be incurred entirely by reason of the change in the uses to which Mineral King will be put, and the attendant change in the aesthetics and ecology of the area. Thus, in referring to the road to be built through Sequoia National Park, the complaint alleged that the development "would destroy or otherwise adversely affect the scenery, natural and historic objects and wildlife of the park and would impair the enjoyment of the park for future generations." ...

The trend of cases arising [under federal law] authorizing judicial review of federal agency action has been toward recognizing that injuries other than economic harm are sufficient to bring a person within the meaning of the statutory language, and toward discarding the notion that an injury that is widely shared is *ipso facto* not an injury sufficient to provide the basis for judicial review. We noted this development in [a prior case], in saying that the interest alleged to have been injured "may reflect 'aesthetic, conservational, and recreational' as well as economic values." But broadening the categories of injury that may be alleged in support of standing is a different matter from abandoning the requirement that the party seeking review must himself have suffered an injury.

Some courts have indicated a willingness to take this latter step by conferring standing upon organizations that have demonstrated "an organizational interest in the problem" of environmental or consumer protection. ... But a mere "interest in a problem," no matter how qualified the organization is in evaluating the problem, is not sufficient in itself [to establish standing].

[The Court found that there was no standing because the Sierra Club had failed to allege that it or its members used the Mineral King site.]

Wildlife.[57] *Lujan* centered around the Endangered Species Act (ESA), a statute intended to protect animal species from extinction. The ESA provided that agencies were not to commit acts that were likely to jeopardize the continued existence of an endangered species.

Pursuant to the ESA, the Fish and Wildlife Service and National Marine Fisheries Service jointly promulgated regulations stating that the ESA applied to agency actions in foreign nations. The agencies later changed their position and promulgated a regulation stating that the ESA had force only in the United States and on the high seas. This action was challenged by the plaintiffs, who sought an order compelling the Secretary of the Interior to issue a regulation restoring the ESA's international scope.

The Supreme Court held that the plaintiffs did not have standing. The plaintiff wildlife preservation organizations relied upon the affidavits of two members to establish standing. In those affidavits, the members asserted that they had been abroad and intended at some unknown date to return, and that they had an interest in observing endangered species while abroad. The Court found this interest inadequate to confer standing. The Court reiterated the principles set out in *Sierra Club v. Morton*; that is, an organization can maintain an action so long as at least one member of that organization can individually establish standing, the organization can adequately represent the member's interest, and the subject of the lawsuit is one in which the organization has a special interest and expertise. An intent to return to a foreign land at some unplanned and unknown date is too conjectural and hypothetical to confer standing.

It would have been easy to satisfy the standing requirements in *Lujan*. Had a member been a scientist who studied endangered species abroad, there would have been standing. Also, Justice Kennedy, in a concurring opinion, asserted that if the members had obtained airline tickets and made plans to visit one of the areas in dispute, there would have been standing.

Causation

In addition to proving an injury in fact, a plaintiff must also show a nexus between the injury and the alleged act. In terms of governmental conduct, a plaintiff must prove that the injury was caused by the government's conduct.

Allen v. Wright teaches that there must be a connection between the injury in fact and the conduct alleged to be unlawful. The injury must be "fairly traceable" to the conduct to satisfy this prong of the standing test. It is not always easy to determine when an injury is fairly traceable. In *Duke Power Co. v. Carolina Environmental Study Group*,[58] a federal statute that limited the liability of the owners of nuclear power plants for nuclear accidents was at issue. The plaintiff lived near the site where a plant was to be constructed and would suffer environmental injury in the event of an accident. The plaintiff challenged the law, claiming that it increased the likelihood that the plant would be built; accordingly, his potential injuries would be fairly traceable to the statute. The Court agreed. The line between *Allen v. Wright* and *Duke Power* is thin.

Administrative Law Standing

In most administrative law cases, standing issues revolve around an enabling statute. Even though Congress may not expand federal court jurisdiction beyond what is permitted in Article III, Congress may create a right and grant standing to enforce that right to a class of individuals. The enabling statute may thus provide standing even when traditional standing law does not. However, in most instances, standing in administrative cases parallels traditional standing law.

If a plaintiff is suing under a statute, he must prove that his injury is within the zone of interests intended to be protected by that law to have standing. If he does so, then he has standing to challenge an agency's conduct. *Association of Data Processing Service Organizations v. Camp*[59] is such a case. The plaintiffs in *Camp* challenged a ruling by the Comptroller of the Currency which declared that banks could make data processing services available to each other and bank customers. The plaintiffs were in the business of selling these services and did not want the additional competition. The Court found that, as competitors, the plaintiffs would suffer some financial injury; accordingly, they met the injury-in-fact prong of the standing test. Then the Court determined that, to meet the second prong of the test, they would have to prove that they were in the zone intended to be protected by law. The plaintiffs claimed that

ALLEN v. WRIGHT
468 U.S. 737 (1984)

[This case was filed by several parents of black schoolchildren. They sued the Internal Revenue Service (IRS) for declaratory and injunctive relief, claiming that the IRS had an obligation to deny tax-exempt status to schools that discriminated against children on the basis of race. The parents claimed that this behavior of the IRS undermined desegregation. The parents prevailed at the lower levels.]

Justice O'Connor delivered the opinion of the Court.

Article III of the Constitution confines the federal courts to adjudicating actual "cases" and "controversies." As the Court explained in *Valley Forge Christian College v. Americans United for Separation of Church and State, Inc.,* 454 U.S. 464, 471–476 (1982), the "case or controversy" requirement defines with respect to the Judicial Branch the idea of separation of powers on which the Federal Government is founded. The several doctrines that have grown up to elaborate that requirement are "founded in concern about the proper—and properly limited—role of the courts in a democratic society." ... The case-or-controversy doctrines state fundamental limits on federal judicial power in our system of government.

The Art. III doctrine that requires a litigant to have "standing" to invoke the power of a federal court is perhaps the most important of these doctrines. "In essence the question of standing is whether the litigant is entitled to have the court decide the merits of the dispute or of particular issues." Standing doctrine embraces several judicially self-imposed limits on the exercise of federal jurisdiction, such as the general prohibition on a litigant's raising another person's legal rights, the rule barring adjudication of generalized grievances more appropriately addressed in the representative branches, and the requirement that a plaintiff's complaint fall within the zone of interests protected by the law invoked. [The] requirement of standing, however, has a core component derived directly from the Constitution. A plaintiff must allege personal injury fairly traceable to the defendant's allegedly unlawful conduct and likely to be redressed by the requested relief. ...

Like the prudential component, the constitutional component of standing doctrine incorporates concepts concededly not susceptible of precise definition. The injury alleged must be, for example, "distinct and palpable," ... not "abstract" or "conjectural" or "hypothetical." [The] injury must be "fairly" traceable to the challenged action, and relief from the injury must be "likely" to follow from a favorable decision. [These principles] cannot be defined so as to make application of the constitutional standing requirement a mechanical exercise. ...

Respondents [parents] allege two injuries in their complaint to support their standing to bring this lawsuit. First, they say that they are harmed directly by the mere fact of Government financial aid to discriminatory private schools. Second, they say that the federal tax exemptions to racially discriminatory private schools in their communities impair their ability to have their public schools desegregated.

[Respondents'] first claim of injury [might be] a claim simply to have the Government avoid the violation of law alleged in respondents' complaint. Alternatively, it might be a claim of stigmatic injury, or denigration, suffered by all members of a racial group when the Government discriminates on the basis of race. Under neither interpretation is this claim of injury judicially cognizable.

This Court has repeatedly held that an asserted right to have the Government act in accordance with law is not sufficient, standing alone, to confer jurisdiction on a federal court. ...

Neither do they have standing to litigate their claims based on the stigmatizing injury often caused by racial discrimination. There can be no doubt that this sort of noneconomic injury is one of the most serious consequences of discriminatory government action and is sufficient in some circumstances to support standing.

[This Court's] case makes clear, however, that such injury accords a basis for standing only to "those persons who are personally denied equal treatment" by the challenged conduct. ... [If] the abstract stigmatic injury were cognizable, standing would extend nationwide to all members of the particular racial groups against which the Government was alleged to be discriminating by its grant of tax exemption to a racially discriminatory school, regardless of the location of that school. ... Recognition of standing in such circumstances would transform the federal courts into "no more than a vehicle for the vindication of the value interests of concerned bystanders." It is in their complaint's second claim of injury that respondents allege harm to a concrete, personal interest that can support standing in some circumstances. The injury they identify—their children's diminished ability to receive an education in a racially integrated school—is, beyond any doubt, not only judicially cognizable but, as shown in *Brown v. Board of Education* ... one of the the the most serious injuries recognized in our legal system. Despite the constitutional importance of curing the injury alleged by respondents, however, the federal judiciary may not redress it unless standing requirements are met. In this case, respondents' second claim of injury cannot support standing because the injury alleged is not fairly traceable to the Government conduct respondents challenge as unlawful.

The illegal conduct challenged by respondents is the IRS's grant of tax exemptions to some racially discriminatory schools. The line of causation between that conduct and desegregation of respondents' schools is attenuated at best. From the perspective of the IRS, the injury to respondents is highly indirect and "results from the independent action of some third party not before the court."

The diminished ability of respondents' children to receive a desegregated education would be fairly traceable to unlawful IRS grants of tax exemptions only if there were enough racially discriminatory private schools receiving tax exemptions in respondents' communities for withdrawal of those exemptions to make an appreciable difference in public-school integration. Respondents have made no such allegation. It is, first, uncertain how many racially discriminatory private schools are in fact receiving tax exemptions. Moreover, it is entirely speculative [that] withdrawal of a tax exemption from any particular school would lead the school to change its policies. [It is also] speculative whether any given parent of a child attending such a private school would decide to transfer the child to public school as a result of any changes in educational or financial policy made by the private school once it was threatened with loss of tax-exempt status. It is also pure speculation whether, in a particular community, a large enough number of the numerous relevant school officials and parents would reach decisions that collectively would have a significant impact on the racial composition of the public schools.

The links in the chain of causation between the challenged Government conduct and the asserted injury are far too weak for the chain as a whole to sustain respondents' standing. ...

The idea of separation of powers that underlies standing doctrine explains why our cases preclude the conclusion that respondents' alleged injury "fairly can be traced to the challenged action" of the IRS. That conclusion would pave the way generally for suits challenging, not specifically identifiable Government violations of law, but the particular programs agencies establish to carry out their legal obligations. ...

The Constitution, after all, assigns to the Executive Branch, and not to the Judicial Branch, the duty to "take Care that the Laws be faithfully executed." ...

"The necessity that the plaintiff who seeks to invoke the judicial power stand to profit in some personal interest remains an Art. III requirement." Respondents have not met this fundamental requirement. The judgment of the Court of Appeals [which had ruled in the respondents' favor] is accordingly reversed, and the injunction issued by that court is vacated.

the Comptroller's ruling was contrary to statutes regulating banks. The Court ruled that as a competitor who might suffer economic loss, the association had standing. See Chapter 7 for further discussion of standing and administrative law.

Citizen and Taxpayer Standing

As *Allen v. Wright* taught, having a generalized interest in the affairs of government does not give one standing to challenge governmental actions. Status as a citizen does not provide a sufficient interest to give one standing to challenge governmental conduct. Similarly, being a taxpayer does not give a person standing to challenge the expenditure of public funds in most circumstances. *Flast v. Cohen*[60] represents an exception to this general rule. *Flast* involved a challenge to a statute that provided financing for reading, arithmetic, and other nonreligious courses in religious schools. The plaintiff, a taxpayer, filed an action alleging that the expenditure violated the establishment clause of the First Amendment.

The Court held that taxpayers may have standing if a nexus between the taxpayers' status and the expenditure can be shown and it can be further shown that the statute exceeds a constitutional limitation. The plaintiff in *Flast* satisfied these requirements because the Court found that the expenditure was significant, that the plaintiff was in the group of taxpayers whose funds were being spent, and that the First Amendment was clearly implicated. Note that the First Amendment was "implicated." No actual violation need be found to confer standing. On the contrary, standing is a preliminary matter. At this stage, a court must only decide that the Constitution is implicated (somehow involved). If so, then the party has standing and the case proceeds further. When standing is found to exist, a person is allowed to participate in the proceedings, but no final decision has been rendered on the merits.

Although *Flast* continues to be the law, the Court seriously limited its scope in a 1982 decision, *Valley Forge Christian College v. Americans for Separation of Church & State, Inc.*[61] In that case, a delegation of authority from Congress to the Secretary of Health, Education, and Welfare (now Secretary of Education) that allowed the Secretary to transfer surplus property at discounted rates to schools for educational use was at issue. The plaintiffs complained that the Secretary's transfer of property to a Christian school at a 100 percent discount violated the Constitution. The Court disagreed and upheld the transfer because the delegation from Congress to the Secretary was not made under Congress's taxing and spending power, but under the property clause of Article IV of the Constitution. Furthermore, the Court stated that because the decision to award the grant was made by an administrative agency, not Congress, the taxpayer lacked standing. Said another way, a taxpayer only has standing to challenge the actual body responsible for levying a tax or authorizing an expenditure of tax revenues.

As a general rule, one person does not have standing to assert the rights of another. There are exceptions to this rule. First, a close personal relationship may pave the way to third-party standing. Parents may stand in for their children and guardians for their wards, for example. A professional relationship may also suffice to establish third-party standing. In *Singleton v. Wulff*,[62] it was held that a doctor has standing to assert a patient's privacy interest in securing an abortion against a statute prohibiting that medical procedure. In support of this decision, the Court pointed out that the physician-patient relationship is intimate and that the patient could be deterred from asserting her claim by potential public embarrassment.

Association Standing

Sierra Club v. Morton establishes that a special interest organization may represent its members in federal courts. Organizational representation is permitted so long as at least one of the organization's members has standing; the organization will adequately represent the members' interest, and participation by the individual member is unnecessary; and the issues of the case fall within the purview of the organization's expertise and mission.[63] Organizational representation is most common in environmental, labor (unions representing workers), and consumer protection cases.

Government Standing and Parens Patriae

The government does not have to meet the association test to represent its citizens. A state, or the federal government, may file actions or intervene in actions when a public interest exists. The government's interest in the health and welfare of its citizens is adequate to confer standing. The state stands in **parens patriae** to its citizens. It may obtain injunctive relief on behalf of the public. For example, a state agency may obtain an injunction prohibiting unlawful business practices. In addition, the government may seek to have individuals compensated when a governmental interest is involved. Thus, the state may seek compensation for those individuals harmed by a company's unlawful business practices. In actions against other states or the federal

---

TERMS

parens patriae [Latin for] "the parent of the country."

government, a state may seek declaratory and injunctive relief, but it has no standing to present the claims of individuals who are seeking damages.[64]

Congressperson Standing

Members of Congress have filed civil cases challenging both presidential and congressional action on many occasions. The issue is whether a person's status as a member of Congress establishes standing to challenge governmental actions. The courts have held that in some cases it may.

For the case-or-controversy requirement to be satisfied, a congressperson must establish:

1. That she suffered a distinct and palpable injury
2. That the injury was fairly traceable to the act that is the subject of the complaint
3. That a remedy is available that will redress the injury.[65]

An act that diminishes the member's influence or nullifies his legislative vote is "distinct and palpable." For example, in *Goldwater v. Carter,*[66] it was decided that a congressman had standing to challenge President Carter's decision to terminate a treaty with the Republic of China without first obtaining Senate approval. Because the integrity of a Senator's vote was in question, standing existed. Note, however, that the Court found in favor of the President on the larger issue: it held that the President could unilaterally terminate the treaty.

Another case illustrates the point. In *Kennedy v. Sampson,*[67] it was decided that a member of Congress has standing to seek an order requiring executive branch officials to recognize the existence of a law. A bill had been passed and presented to the President. The presentment indicated that the bill could be returned to the Secretary of the Senate if the Senate was in recess. The Senate went into its Christmas recess, but the President never returned the bill. In spite of the rule that bills not returned in ten days become law, the executive branch refused to recognize the law. Because this action had the effect of nullifying Senator Kennedy's vote, he had standing to challenge it. Furthermore, he prevailed in the larger issue: the court found that the bill had become law. The Supreme Court did not review this decision.

Members of Congress generally lack standing to challenge acts of Congress, because they have available to them the best remedy: using their position to advocate and vote to amend or repeal the law. Similarly, a member does not have standing to protect the executive or judicial branches from legislative encroachments.[68] (Members of those branches do, of course, have standing in such circumstances.)

BAKER v. CARR
369 U.S. 186 (1962)

[Tennessee citizens brought suit challenging a state statute enacted in 1901 that established the apportionment for the General Assembly (state legislature). The voters claimed that, because of changes in population demographics, the statute caused some citizens to have less vote than others.]

Mr. Justice Brennan delivered the opinion of the Court.

[The Court holds] that this challenge to an apportionment presents no nonjusticiable "political question." ...

Of course the mere fact that the suit seeks protection of a political right does not mean it presents a political question. Such an objection "is little more than a play upon words." Rather, it is argued that apportionment cases, whatever the actual wording of the complaint, can involve no federal constitutional right except one resting on the guaranty of a republican form of government, and that complaints based on that clause have been held to present political questions which are nonjusticiable.

We hold that the claim pleaded here neither rests upon nor implicates the Guaranty Clause. ...

We have said that "In determining whether a question falls within [the political question] category, the appropriateness under our system of government of attributing finality to the action of the political departments and also the lack of satisfactory criteria for a judicial determination are dominant considerations." The nonjusticiability of a political question is primarily a function of the separation of powers. Much confusion results from the capacity of the "political question" label to obscure the need for case-by-case inquiry. Deciding whether a matter has in any measure been committed by the Constitution to another branch of government, or whether the action of that branch exceeds whatever authority has been committed, is itself a delicate exercise in constitutional interpretation, and is a responsibility of this Court as ultimate interpreter of the Constitution.

Foreign relations: There are sweeping statements to the effect that all questions touching foreign relations are political questions. Not only does resolution of such issues frequently turn on standards that defy judicial application, or involve the exercise of a discretion demonstrably committed to the executive or legislature; but many such questions uniquely demand single-voiced statement of the Government's views. Yet it is error to suppose that every case or controversy which touches foreign relations lies beyond judicial cognizance. Our cases in this field seem invariably to show a discriminating analysis of the particular question posed, in terms of history of its management by the political branches, of its susceptibility to judicial handling in the light of its nature and posture in the specific case, and of the possible consequences of judicial action. ...

Validity of enactments: In *Coleman v. Miller,* this Court held that the questions of how long a proposed amendment to the Federal Constitution remained open to ratification, and what effect a prior rejection had on a subsequent ratification, were committed to congressional resolution and involved criteria of decision that necessarily escaped the judicial grasp. Similar considerations apply to the enacting process: "The respect due to coequal and independent departments," and the need for finality and certainty about the status of a statute contribute to judicial reluctance to inquire whether, as passed, it complied with all requisite formalities. ...

Prominent on the surface of any case held to involve a political question is found a textually demonstrable constitutional commitment of the issue to a coordinate political department; or a lack of judicially discoverable and manageable standards for resolving it; or the impossibility of deciding without an initial policy determination of a kind clearly for nonjudiciable discretion; or the impossibility of a court's undertaking independent resolution without expressing lack of respect due coordinate branches of government; or an unusual need for unquestioning adherence to a political decision already made; or the potentiality of embarrassment from multifarious pronouncements by various departments on one question.

Unless one of these formulations is inextricable from the case at bar, there should be no dismissal for nonjusticiability ... .

But it is argued that this case shares the characteristics of decisions that constitute a category not yet considered, cases concerning the Constitution's guaranty [of] a republican form of government. ...

Luther v. Borden, though in form simply an action for damages for trespass was, as Daniel Webster said in opening argument for the defense, "an unusual case." The defendants, admitting an otherwise tortious breaking and entering, sought to justify their action on the ground that they were agents of the established lawful government of Rhode Island, which State was then under martial law to defend itself from active insurrection; that the plaintiff was engaged in that insurrection; and that they entered under orders to arrest the plaintiff. The case arose "out of the unfortunate political differences which agitated the people of Rhode Island in 1841 and 1842," which had resulted in a situation wherein two groups laid competing claims to recognition as the lawful government. The plaintiff's right to recover depended upon which of the two groups was entitled to such recognition. ...

Clearly, several factors were thought by the Court in *Luther* to make the question there "political": the commitment to the other branches of the decision as to which is the lawful state government; the unambiguous action by the President, in recognizing the charter government as the lawful authority; the need for finality in the executive's decision; and the lack of criteria by which a court could determine which form of government was republican.

But the only significance that *Luther* could have for our immediate purposes is in its holding that the Guaranty Clause is not a repository of judicially manageable standards which a court could utilize independently in order to identify a State's lawful government. ...

We come, finally, to the ultimate inquiry whether our precedents as to what constitutes a

nonjusticiable "political question" bring the case before us under the umbrella of that doctrine. A natural beginning is to note whether any of the common characteristics which [we] have been able to identify and label descriptively are present. We find none: the question here is the consistency of state action with the Federal Constitution. We have no question decided by a political branch of government coequal with this Court. Nor do we risk embarrassment of our government abroad, or grave disturbance at home if we take issue with Tennessee as to the constitutionality of her action here challenged. Nor need the appellants, in order to succeed in this action, ask the Court to enter upon policy determinations for which judicially manageable standards are lacking. Judicial standards under the Equal Protection Clause are well developed and familiar, and it has been open to courts since the enactment of the Fourteenth Amendment to determine, if on the particular facts they must, that a discrimination reflects *no* policy, but simply arbitrary and capricious action.

This case does, in one sense, involve the allocation of political power within a State, and the appellants might conceivably have added a claim under the Guaranty Clause. Of course, as we have seen, any reliance on that clause would be futile. But because any reliance on the Guaranty Clause could not have succeeded it does not follow that appellants may not be heard on the equal protection claim which in fact they tender. True, it must be clear that the Fourteenth Amendment claim is not so enmeshed with those political question elements which render Guaranty Clause claims nonjusticiable as actually to present a political question itself. But we have found that not to be the case here.

[Reversed and remanded.]

Mr. Justice Frankfurter, whom Mr. Justice Harlan joins, dissenting.

The Court today reverses a uniform course of decision established by a dozen cases, including one by which the very claim now sustained was unanimously rejected only five years ago. ...

[In] its earliest opinions this Court has consistently recognized a class of controversies which do not lend themselves to judicial standards and judicial remedies. ...

1. The cases concerning war or foreign affairs, for example, are usually explained by the necessity of the country's speaking with one voice in such matters. ...
2. The Court has been particularly unwilling to intervene in matters concerning the structure and organization of the political institutions of the States. ...
4. The Court has refused to exercise its jurisdiction to pass on "abstract questions of political power, of sovereignty, of government." ...
5. The influence of these converging considerations [the court restated the issues that were considered political in prior cases] has been decisive of the settled line of cases, reaching back more than a century, which holds that Art. IV, § 4, of the Constitution, guaranteeing to the States "a Republican Form of Government," is not enforceable through the courts. ...

The present case involves all the elements that have made the Guarantee Clause cases non-justiciable. ...

[Appellants] invoke the right to vote ... [but] they are permitted to vote and their votes are counted. [Appellants'] complaint is simply that the representatives are not sufficiently numerous or powerful. [To allow jurisdiction] will add a virulent source of friction and tension in Federal-state relations. ...

Also, like all citizens, a member's generalized objection to the manner in which the executive branch enforces a law, or does not enforce a law, is not adequate to confer standing.[69]

Third-Party Standing

As a general proposition, one party may not assert another's constitutional rights. The theory is that constitutional rights are personal. This rule is important in the criminal law context.

A criminal defendant may not assert another person's constitutional rights in an effort to have evidence excluded at trial. For example, Sam is at Norma's home. He forgets to take his briefcase with him when he leaves her home. He has cocaine in the briefcase. Later that day the police conduct a search of Norma's home, looking for evidence of an unrelated crime. They discover the briefcase and its contents, but the search is later determined to be unlawful by a court. Accordingly, any evidence seized may not be used to prosecute Norma. However, the contents of the briefcase may be used to prosecute Sam (Norma implicated him) because he does not have standing to assert Norma's Fourth Amendment right to be free from unlawful searches and seizures.

This doctrine applies to the assertion of all constitutional rights and in all contexts, whether civil, criminal, or administrative. Recall from the preceding discussion of standing that organizations may establish standing to represent their members if they can prove that at least one member satisfies the traditional standing test and that the subject of the litigation is related to the purposes of the organization.

Political Questions

Another limitation upon judicial power is the so-called **political question** doctrine. The Supreme Court has long held that certain cases are nonjudiciable due to their political nature. The theory holds that the political branches—the executive and legislative—are better equipped to deal with these political issues than is a court of law.

The political question doctrine is based somewhat upon Article III, but primarily upon separation principles. It is a self-imposed restraint of judicial power. The doctrine applies in cases where it otherwise appears that judicial jurisdiction exists. Because of this, courts are careful not to extend their jurisdiction too far. Chief Justice John Marshall said in *Cohens v. Virginia*[70] that

> It is most true that this court will not take jurisdiction if it should not; but it is equally true, that it must take jurisdiction when it should. The judiciary cannot, as the legislature may, avoid a measure because it approaches the constitution. ... [W]e have no more right to decline the exercise of jurisdiction which is given, than to usurp that which is not given. The one or the other would be treason to the constitution.

However, this same Chief Justice stated in *Marbury v. Madison* that political questions "can never be made in this court."[71]

The Court has not been entirely consistent in its application of the doctrine, and the phrase "political question" is really a misnomer. Nearly all cases before courts, especially the Supreme Court, have political aspects. That does not mean they are not heard. The political question doctrine is more concerned with keeping the judiciary out of the business of the executive and legislative branches than with avoiding questions of politics.

One of the first Supreme Court cases that dealt with the political question doctrine was *Luther v. Borden,* which is discussed in *Baker v. Carr.* In *Baker,* the Court announced the factors or issues that implicate the political question doctrine. Justice William Brennan, writing for the Court, stated that the presence of any of the following suggest a political question:

1. The case involves a power that is delegated by the Constitution to the legislative or executive branch of government and not to the courts

2. There are no judicially discoverable and manageable standards for resolving the issue of the case

---

TERMS

political question [†]   A nonjudicial issue. The political question doctrine states that, under the Constitution, certain questions belong to the nonjudicial branches of the federal government to resolve.

3. It is impossible to decide the case without an initial policy determination of a kind clearly for nonjudiciable discretion

4. It is impossible for the court to undertake independent resolution without expressing lack of respect due the coordinate branches of government

5. There is an unusual need for unquestioning adherence to a political decision already made

6. There is the potential of embarrassment from multifarious pronouncements by various departments on one question.

These standards reflect separational, functional, and political concerns. The Court decided, in *Baker v. Carr,* that the issue of whether legislative apportionment satisfies equal protection is not a political question, because the issue does not pose a separation of power issue and there are judicial standards to be applied in such Fourteenth Amendment cases.

An examination of other political question cases illustrates these points. Similar to *Baker v. Carr,* the courts have held that political **gerrymandering** cases are justiciable.[72] *Luther* teaches that controversies arising under the guaranty clause of the Constitution are not likely to be justiciable, but the facts in *Luther* are important. After a small rebellion, each of two groups claimed to be the lawful government, even though the President had already announced which government was legitimate. Further, there were no meaningful standards to guide a court in determining what government is legitimate.

Coleman v. Miller,[73] a 1939 Supreme Court decision, illustrates a case that was nonjudiciable because its core question was delegated by the Constitution to one of the Court's coordinate branches. Several issues were raised in *Coleman* concerning the constitutional amendment process, including whether a state that rejected an amendment can later ratify it and whether an amendment has been ratified within an appropriate period of time. The Supreme Court found these two issues to be within the purview of Congress and not fit for judicial review.

The plaintiff in *Powell v. McCormack,*[74] Adam Clayton Powell, Jr., had been elected to the House of Representatives, but, because of allegations of misuse of public funds and unbecoming conduct, the House refused to seat him. The issues centered around two provisions of the Constitution. Article I, § 5, clause 1, states that "[e]ach House shall be

────────────── TERMS ──────────────

gerrymandering † Manipulating the boundary lines of a political district to give an unfair advantage to one political party or to dilute the political strength of voters of a particular race, color, or national origin.

the Judge of the Elections, Returns, and Qualifications of its own members." Clause 2 of the same section provides that "[e]ach House may determine the Rules of its Proceedings, punish its Members for disorderly Behavior, and, with the Concurrence of two thirds, expel a Member."

The Court stated, in dicta, that a congressional decision to expel a member would be nonjusticiable as a political question because the Constitution clearly delegates such decisions to Congress. However, the Court concluded that Powell had not been expelled because he was never permitted to take his place in the House. Accordingly, the Court treated the case as arising under the former clause.

The Court held that congressional authority to exclude members under this clause is narrower than its authority to expel sitting members. The Court reasoned that the Constitution provides that a house may exclude a member because of lack of qualification, such as not satisfying the age or citizenship requirements, but that it does not permit a house to exclude elected representatives for other reasons. Accordingly, a court could not review a decision to exclude a member that is based upon the qualifications clause. For example, if Congress were to exclude an elected representative because it determined that the representative did not satisfy the age requirement, there could be no judicial review under the political question doctrine. It would not violate separation principles, however, for a court to review exclusions for other reasons, as such power has not been delegated to Congress. Because there was no question that Powell satisfied the Constitution's qualification requirements, the Court ordered that he be seated in the House.

In 1984, Frank McCloskey and Richard McIntyre were opposing candidates in the closest congressional election in history. The initial vote count showed McCloskey a winner by 72 votes. However, after a recount, the Indiana Secretary of State declared McIntyre the victor by 34 votes. The House of Representatives intervened and conducted its own investigation and recount. The House's recount showed McCloskey to be the winner, by only four votes. The final count was 116,645 to 116,641.

McIntyre challenged the decision in state court. McCloskey removed the case to the United States District Court for the Southern District of Indiana. That court held the issue to be nonjusticiable. This decision of the trial court was affirmed on appeal. The appellate court stated that issues concerning what votes count is one left to the appropriate house of Congress, not to the judiciary.[75]

Impeachment cases are also nonjusticiable. The House of Representatives impeaches officials and the Senate tries impeachment cases. Other than providing that the Chief Justice shall preside at the Senate trial, the Constitution does not establish a role for the judiciary in such actions. Accordingly, the decisions to impeach and convict are political and they are finally decided in the appropriate house of Congress.

Foreign Affairs, National Security, and Military

It is also generally accepted that foreign affairs, national security, and military questions are not judiciable. The Court stated of this policy:

> The President, both as Commander-in-Chief and as the Nation's organ for foreign affairs, has available intelligence services whose reports are not and ought not to be published to the world. It would be intolerable that courts, without the relevant information, should review and perhaps nullify actions of the Executive taken on information properly held secret. Nor can courts sit in camera in order to be taken into executive confidences.
>
> But even if courts could require full disclosure, the very nature of executive decisions are wholly confided by our constitution to the political departments of government.[76]

The decision to declare war is left to Congress. The decision to negotiate a treaty and in most cases, whether a treaty is in effect, and whether a treaty has been violated by a foreign power, is left to the President. Whether to recognize a foreign government is also a political question. The Supreme Court has refused to decide whether the United States was dealing with the proper representative of a foreign nation while negotiating a treaty. This is an executive decision.[77] The decision of whether a state of war exists between nations was also held to be a political question best left to the executive.[78] In *United States v. Alvarez-Machain,*[79] the Court was faced with an unlawful abduction of a criminal defendant by U.S. authorities. The defendant was kidnapped in Mexico and returned to the United States for trial. The Court concluded that it had jurisdiction to determine whether the United States/Mexico extradition treaty had been violated but, since it had not, the decision on whether to return the man to Mexico belonged to the President. This is logical, as a treaty provides a court with standards from which it can render a decision. Beyond that, the decision rests upon political considerations that are beyond the competence of the judiciary.

Exceptions

Although these issues represent the clearest cases of political questions, there may be exceptions. Recall that the Court stated in *Baker v. Carr* that "it is error to suppose that every case or controversy which touches foreign relations lies beyond judicial cognizance."

NIXON v. UNITED STATES
113 S. Ct. 732 (1993)

Chief Justice Rehnquist delivered the opinion of the Court.

Petitioner Walter L. Nixon, Jr., asks this court to decide whether Senate Rule XI, which allows a committee of Senators to hear evidence against an individual who has been impeached and to report that evidence to the full Senate, violates the Impeachment Trial Clause, Art. I, Section 3, cl. 6. That Clause provides that the "Senate shall have the sole Power to try all impeachments." But before we reach the merits of such a claim, we must decide whether it is "justiciable," that is, whether it is a claim that may be resolved by the courts. We conclude that it is not.

Nixon, a former Chief Judge of the United States District Court for the Southern District of Mississippi, was convicted by a jury of two counts of making false statements before a federal grand jury and sentenced to prison. ... The grand jury investigation stemmed from reports that Nixon had accepted a gratuity from a Mississippi businessman in exchange for asking a local district attorney to halt the prosecution of the businessman's son. Because Nixon refused to resign from his office as a United States District Judge, he continued to collect his judicial salary while serving out his prison sentence. ...

On May 10, 1989, the House of Representatives adopted three articles of impeachment for high crimes and misdemeanors. ... After the House presented the articles to the Senate, the Senate voted to invoke its own Impeachment Rule XI, under which the presiding officer appoints a committee of Senators to "receive evidence and take testimony." ... The Senate committee held four days of hearings. ... [The Senate then convicted Nixon.]

Nixon thereafter commenced the present suit, arguing that Senate Rule XI violates the constitutional grant of authority to the Senate to "try" all impeachments because it prohibits the whole Senate from taking part in the evidentiary hearing. ... [Nixon lost at both the trial and appellate levels].

A controversy is nonjusticiable—i.e. involves a political question—where there is "a textually demonstrable constitutional commitment of the issue to a coordinate political department; or a lack of judicially discoverable and manageable standards for resolving it ... ."

In this case we must examine Art. I, Section 3, cl. 6, to determine the scope of the authority conferred upon the Senate by the Framers regarding impeachment. It provides:

> "The Senate shall have the sole Power to try all Impeachments. When sitting for that Purpose, they shall be on Oath or Affirmation. When the President of the United States is tried, the Chief Justice shall preside: And no person shall be convicted without the Concurrence of two thirds of the Members present."

The language and structure of the Clause are revealing. The first sentence is a grant of authority to the Senate, and the word "sole" indicates that this authority is reposed in the Senate and nowhere else. The next two sentences specify requirements to which the Senate proceedings shall conform: the Senate shall be on oath or affirmation, a two-thirds vote is required to convict, and when the President is tried the Chief Justice shall preside.

Petitioner argues that the word "try" in the first sentences imposes by implication an additional requirement on the Senate in that the proceeding must be in the nature of a judicial trial. From there the petitioner goes on to argue that this limitation precludes the Senate from delegating to a select committee the task of hearing the testimony of witnesses, as was done pursuant to Senate Rule XI. " 'Try' means more than simply 'vote on' or 'review' or 'judge.' In 1787 and today, trying a case means hearing the evidence, not scanning a cold record." Brief for Petitioner 25. Petitioner concludes from this that courts may review whether or not the Senate "tried" him before convicting him.

There are several difficulties with the position which lead us ultimately to reject it. The word "try," both in 1787 and later, has considerably broader meanings than those to which petitioner would limit it. Older dictionaries define *try* as "to examine" or "to examine as a judge." See 2 S. Johnson, *A Dictionary of the English Language* (1785). In more modern usage the term has various meanings. For example, *try* can mean "to examine or investigate judicially," "to conduct the trial of," or "to put to the test by experiment, investigation, or trial." *Webster's Third New International Dictionary* ... .

Petitioner submits that "try," as contained in T. Sheridan, *Dictionary of the English Language* (1796), means "to examine as a judge; to bring before a judicial tribunal." Based on the variety of definitions, however, we cannot say that the Framers used the word "try" as an implied limitation on the method by which the Senate might proceed in trying impeachments. ...

The conclusion that the use of the word "try" in the first sentence of the Impeachment Trial Clause lacks sufficient precision to afford any judicially manageable standard of review of the Senate's actions is fortified by the existence of the three very specific requirements that the Constitution does impose on the Senate when trying impeachments: the members must be under oath, a two-thirds vote is required to convict, and the Chief Justice presides when the President is tried. These limitations are quite precise, and their nature suggests that the Framers did not intend to impose additional limitations on the form of the Senate proceedings by the use of the word "try" in the first sentence.

... We think that the word "sole" is of considerable significance. Indeed, the word "sole" appears only one other time in the Constitution—with respect to the House of Representatives' sole Power of Impeachment. ... The common sense meaning of the word "sole" is that the Senate alone shall have authority to determine [whether] an individual should be acquitted or convicted. The dictionary definition bears this out. "Sole" is defined as "having no companion," "solitary," "being the only one," and "functioning ... independently and without assistance or interference." ... If the courts may review the actions of the Senate in order to determine whether that body "tried" an impeached official, it is difficult to see how the Senate would be "functioning ... independently and without assistance or interference."

Nixon asserts that the word "sole" has no substantive meaning. To support his contention, he argues that the word is nothing more than a mere "cosmetic edit" added by the Committee of Style after the delegates had approved the substance of the Impeachment Trial Clause. ... [W]e must presume that the Committee's reorganization or rephrasing accurately captured what the Framers meant in their unadorned language. ... Second, carrying Nixon's argument to its logical conclusion would constrain us to say that the second to last draft would govern in every instance where the Committee of Style added an arguably substantive word. Such a result is at odds with the fact that the Convention passed the Committee's version, and with the well established rule that the plain language of the enacted text is the best indicator of intent. ...

The history and contemporary understanding of the impeachment provisions support our reading of the constitutional language. The parties do not offer evidence of a single word in the history of the Constitutional Convention or in contemporary commentary that even alludes to the possibility of judicial review in the context of impeachment powers. ...

There are two additional reasons why the Judiciary, and the Supreme Court in particular, were not chosen to have any role in impeachments. First, the Framers recognized that most likely there would be two sets of proceedings for individuals who commit impeachable offenses— the impeachment trial and a separate criminal trial. In fact, the Constitution explicitly provides for two separate proceedings. See Art. I, Sec. 3, cl. 7. The Framers deliberately separated the two forums to avoid raising the specter of bias ... .

Second, judicial review would be inconsistent with the Framers' insistence that our system be one of checks and balances. In our constitutional system impeachment was designed to be the only check on the Judicial Branch by the Legislature. ... For the foregoing reasons, the judgment of the Court of Appeals is Affirmed.

Where is the limit? Consider the following hypothetical case. The Constitution expressly delegates to Congress the authority to declare war. In spite of this, Presidents often initiate wars. The power of the executive in this area is now recognized, primarily due to historical precedent. What if the President were to commit troops or order other military action after Congress had considered and rejected the idea of declaring war? What if the President refused to engage in war after Congress declared it? Whether this would be nonjusticiable is unknown, but may represent an extreme political case in which the Court might intervene.

Finally, in the political question arena, there is *United States v. Nixon*.[80] The Watergate prosecutor subpoenaed certain documents and tapes from President Nixon. The President claimed executive privilege as to the information and also claimed that his actions were nonjusticiable as political questions. The Court rejected the nonjusticiability claim and ordered that the prosecutor be permitted an in camera inspection of the documents. The Court reasoned that the issues of the case were traditionally vested in the judiciary: specifically, whether evidence that is relevant to an ongoing criminal investigation should be produced. Accordingly, the courts were to determine the extent of the President's immunity under the executive privilege doctrine. See Chapter 6 for a discussion of executive privilege.

Abstention

In spite of Chief Justice John Marshall's statement in *Cohens v. Virginia*[81] that the Court has no right to relinquish jurisdiction, it does in abstention cases.[82] There are three forms of abstention. The first occurs when there is an unsettled state law issue; the second arises when a federal court is faced with an issue that has traditionally been left to state courts to decide; and the third when comity principles demand it. The first two forms of abstention occur most often in diversity of citizenship cases.

Unsettled State Law

As to the first situation, a federal court will abstain from hearing a case, but will retain jurisdiction, whenever a case rests upon an unsettled issue of state law. Even though jurisdiction exists, the federal court will stay the case until a state court has had an opportunity to resolve the state legal issue. This occurs most often when diversity of citizenship is used to establish federal judicial jurisdiction, but the underlying state legal issue is controversial and unresolved. The more sensitive the state legal issue, the more likely it is that abstention will be invoked. Also, if it is possible that a state court's interpretation of its laws or orders will avoid a federal constitutional issue, the likelihood of abstention is increased. For example, suppose that there are two possible interpretations of a state statute, one that raises federal constitutional issues and one that does not. A federal court may abstain from resolving the issue in hopes that a state court will interpret the statute in the manner that avoids the federal constitutional issue.

To facilitate the process and policy underlying abstention, many states have enacted certification procedures through which a federal court can certify questions of state law to be presented to the state high courts for resolution. This can occur during the pendency of the federal proceeding. If no certification procedure is available, the plaintiff must initiate a new state court action to have the state issues answered. This does not preclude federal judicial review; rather, it postpones such review until the state court has rendered its decision. Whatever procedure is used, abstention usually delays resolution of a case.

Traditional State Law Issues

Abstention may be declared in a second class of cases. Questions that have traditionally been resolved by state courts, or otherwise strike at the heart of traditional state powers, are left to state courts to answer. For example, domestic issues, such as divorce and child custody, have belonged to the states. The Supreme Court announced this as early as 1859.[83] Accordingly, federal courts abstain from hearing domestic cases even if diversity jurisdiction can be established. Consider the marriage of Herman and Mariza, for example. Recall that to establish diversity jurisdiction, there must be a diversity of citizenship between the plaintiff and the defendant and the amount in controversy must exceed $50,000. Herman and Mariza were married in Oregon and remained there until they separated in 1998. Herman moved to Florida and Mariza moved to Maryland at that time. The total value of their marital property is $200,000. Using these facts, federal court diversity jurisdiction exists. However, because this area of law is left to the states, no federal court will entertain the case. Similarly, federal courts abstain from estate and probate cases.

Younger Doctrine

Federal courts also generally abstain from interfering with pending state court cases, even if a federal constitutional issue is raised. If a criminal defendant in state court, for example, alleges that his federal constitutional rights are being violated, he may not obtain federal court intervention in most instances. Rather, the federal issues must be resolved through the appellate and habeas corpus processes. This is generally known as the **Younger doctrine**, after the 1971 Supreme Court case that announced the principle.[84] Pursuant to the *Younger* doctrine, federal courts are to abstain from interfering with state court criminal cases unless a federal constitutional right is asserted, the defendant will suffer irreparable harm without intervention, the harm will be both great and immediate, and the state authorities are acting in bad faith. This is a rigorous standard for a state criminal defendant to meet; as a result, *Younger* demands abstention in nearly all cases.

Younger has been extended to civil cases as well. For *Younger* to apply in a civil proceeding, the "[s]tate's interests in the proceeding [must be] so important that exercise of the federal jurisdiction power would disregard the comity between the states and National Government."[85] Enforcement of judgments and contempt proceedings are examples of important state interests. *Younger* may also apply to administrative proceedings.[86]

An individual has standing to seek federal intervention if a prosecution has been initiated or there is a legitimate and serious threat of impending prosecution. If a federal court decides that intervention is appropriate, it will issue an injunction staying the state court proceeding so that it may hear the federal issue. In some instances, the case may be brought to final judgment in the federal court; in others the federal issue will be resolved and the case remanded to the state court for final adjudication.

The Supreme Court has stated that there are three policy reasons for the *Younger* abstention doctrine. First, as a general rule, equity does not operate except when a party has no adequate remedy at law. Because a party seeking federal review is in a state court of law, equity is generally unavailable. This hurdle can be overcome by showing that the state courts will not hear the constitutional claim. However, failure to raise the issue in the state court is not adequate. Second, *comity*—that is, respect for federalism principles—also justifies the doctrine. Third, federal courts avoid constitutional issues whenever possible. It is possible that the state court, if allowed to proceed, will deal with the case in a manner that does not implicate the federal constitution.

TERMS

Younger **doctrine**   The doctrine, drawn from *Younger v. Harris*, that federal courts will abstain in most cases from interfering with state court proceedings, even if federal constitutional issues are present. Except in extreme cases, federal review of federal constitutional issues must wait until appeal or habeas corpus review.

Sovereign Immunity and the Eleventh Amendment

In old England, the Crown could not be held accountable for its actions. This is the historical source of **sovereign immunity**. This doctrine was accepted and adopted by the states and national government early in United States history, albeit not without criticism. However, in the United States, the people are regarded as sovereign, not the state. One court said that "[i]n preserving the sovereign immunity theory, courts have overlooked the fact that the Revolutionary War was fought to abolish that 'divine right of the kings' on which the theory was based."[87]

Regardless of any controversy, sovereign immunity continues to be the law for both states and the federal government. Local forms of government are not protected by this immunity, however.

In 1793, the Supreme Court handed down *Chisholm v. Georgia,*[88] wherein it decided that the citizen of one state could sue another state in federal court. Believing that it was shielded from suits by the doctrine of sovereign immunity, Georgia refused to defend itself and a default judgment was entered against it. The public response was sure and swift. The Eleventh Amendment was initiated and ratified in five years. That Amendment reads:

> The Judicial power of the United States shall not be construed to extend to any suit in law or equity, commenced or prosecuted against one of the United States by Citizens of another State, or by Citizens or Subjects of any Foreign State.

The intention of the Eleventh Amendment is clear. States shall be immune from suit in federal court from cases filed by citizens of other states or nations. It was, in the opinion of its drafters, a ratification of the doctrine of sovereign immunity. Because a case may not be prosecuted in federal court does not necessarily mean that a party is without a remedy, though. If a state has waived immunity in its own courts, the plaintiff may pursue her action there.

In spite of its plain language to the contrary, the Supreme Court interpreted the Eleventh Amendment as barring suits by citizens against their own states in *Hans v. Louisiana.*[89] This decision was based upon original intention analysis.

There are several exceptions to the Eleventh Amendment. First, states are not immune from actions brought by other states or the United States. This includes actions filed by the United States on behalf of citizens,

---

TERMS

sovereign immunity[†] The principle that the government—specifically, the United States or any state of the United States—is immune from suit except when it consents to be sued.

even if the citizens could not have filed the actions themselves. For example, the United States Department of Labor was permitted to prosecute a case against a state alleging that the state was violating the federal labor rights of certain employees. The employees themselves would have been barred from bringing such an action.[90]

Second, a state may waive its immunity. This is normally accomplished through state statute. A waiver must be clearly expressed in a statute or must be implied strongly.[91] A court may not read a waiver into a law.

A third exception to the Eleventh Amendment applies to political subdivisions of states. Counties, municipalities, districts, and other governmental subdivisions are not shielded by the Eleventh Amendment. State agencies do, however, fall under the immunity of the amendment.

To address special interstate issues, two or more states will sometimes join with the federal government in the creation of an agency. In such cases, the Eleventh Amendment may shield the agency with immunity. This was the issue in *Hess v. Port Authority,*[92] a 1994 Supreme Court case. Two states (New York and New Jersey) and the federal government created a port authority. Employees of the port who were injured while on the job sued the authority for their damages under the Federal Employers Liability Act. The authority claimed that it was immune from being sued in federal court.

The Supreme Court held that in determining whether such bilateral agencies are immune, a court should consider whether the states and federal government intended for the agency to be immune and the degree to which the agency is independent and self-sustaining. If an agency's losses directly affect the state treasury, then the agency is most likely immune. In *Hess,* the Court stated that because the agency paid its own debts and generated its own revenues, it was sufficiently independent of the states to fall outside the protection of the Eleventh Amendment.

 SIDEBAR

Personal and Official Capacities

Lawsuits against government officials may be filed in "official capacity" or "personal capacity." Generally, a claim filed in official capacity makes the government itself a party. Claims against individuals are personal and usually do not make the employer-government a real party in interest. The title of the claim is not dispositive; the issue is who will bear the burden of any resulting judgment.

Fourth, state officials may be sued in federal court for unconstitutional actions. The theory underlying this exception is that unconstitutional acts are by their nature not state action. Such a suit must be directed against the official and not the state. Thus, suits seeking declaratory and injunctive relief against public officials are permitted. So are suits alleging that a state official violated a person's constitutional rights. However, if the suit seeks money from the state treasury, then it is barred, regardless of whether it is filed against an individual in her personal or official capacity. In such a case, the real party is the state, not the public official.

Injunctive relief against state officers requiring compliance with federal law is permitted. Damages are not permitted. Although these injunctions appear to be against the state, the Supreme Court has held that they are not and that such lawsuits must name the public official rather than the state as the defending party. The trial court may use its contempt powers to prod state officials into compliance. Oddly, the Supreme Court has held that both the official and state may be fined for refusals to comply.[93] The fact that a state will expend state funds while complying with an injunction does not mean that it is a real party in Eleventh Amendment terms. For example, an order to desegregate will involve costs to a state, but these expenditures are ancillary.

Fifth, Congress may authorize suits against states in federal courts in some instances. This congressional power stems from Amendments Thirteen through Fifteen (Civil War amendments prohibiting slavery, assuring due process, etc.), Nineteen (women's right to vote), Twenty-three (no poll taxes), and Twenty-six (franchise of eighteen-year-olds). These amendments specifically provide that Congress may enact legislation to enforce their mandates. Because these amendments postdate the Eleventh Amendment, they are interpreted as limitations upon both state sovereignty (Tenth Amendment) and state immunity (Eleventh Amendment). For example, a state can be sued in federal court for refusing to permit eighteen-year-old citizens the vote, and individuals can sue their states to collect the costs of cleaning up environmental toxins that are the responsibility of the state.[94]

Congress has enacted many civil rights statutes prohibiting discrimination in many sectors of life, including employment and access to public facilities. These laws are generally designed to apply to private parties. Congress may, but usually does not, extend the remedies under these laws to state action. Congressional intent to abrogate state immunity will not be inferred lightly; rather, there must be an "unequivocal expression of congressional intent." This issue was addressed by the Supreme Court in *Atascadero State Hospital v. Scanlon*, a 1985 case.

Federal sovereign immunity continues to be recognized by the courts. This is not as serious a barrier as it was 100 years ago, as Congress has waived immunity in most cases. For example, through the Federal Tort Claims Act,[95] the United States permits individuals to prosecute cases against it for certain torts. There are other similar laws.[96] In cases in which the United States has not waived immunity, the court is to dismiss the case.

ATASCADERO STATE HOSPITAL v. SCANLON
473 U.S. 678 (1985)

Justice Powell delivered the opinion of the Court.

This case presents the question whether States and state agencies are subject to suit in federal court by litigants seeking retroactive monetary relief under § 504 of the Rehabilitation Act of 1973 ... or whether such suits are proscribed by the Eleventh Amendment.

Respondent, Douglas James Scanlon, suffers from diabetes mellitus and has no sight in one eye. In November 1979, he filed this action against petitioners, Atascadero State Hospital and the California Department of Mental Health, in the United States District Court for the Central District of California, alleging that in 1978 the hospital denied him employment ... solely because of his physical handicaps. Respondent charged that the hospital's discriminatory refusal to hire him violated § 504 of the Rehabilitation Act of 1973. ...

Petitioners moved for dismissal of the complaint on the ground that the Eleventh Amendment barred the federal court from entertaining respondent's claims. ... In January 1980, the District Court granted petitioner's motion to dismiss the complaint on the ground that respondent's claims were barred by the Eleventh Amendment. On appeal, the United States Court of Appeals for the Ninth Circuit affirmed [on different grounds]. ... We granted certiorari ... vacated the judgment ... and remanded the case for further consideration. ... On remand, the Court of Appeals reversed the judgment of the District Court. It held that "the Eleventh Amendment does not bar [respondent's] action because the State, if it has participated in and received funds from programs under the Rehabilitation Act, has implicitly consented to be sued ... ."

The [court of appeals] decision in this case is in conflict with those of the Courts of Appeals for the First and Eighth Circuits. ... We granted certiorari to resolve this conflict. ...

The Eleventh Amendment provides: "The Judicial power of the United States shall not be construed to extend to any suit in law or equity, commenced or prosecuted against one of the United States by Citizens of another State, or by Citizens or Subjects of any Foreign State." As we have recognized, the significance of this Amendment "lies in its affirmation that the fundamental principle of sovereign immunity limits the grant of judicial authority in Art. III" of the Constitution. ...

There are, however, certain well-established exceptions to the reach of the Eleventh Amendment. For example, if a State waives its immunity and consents to suit in federal court, the Eleventh Amendment does not bar the action. ... Moreover, the Eleventh Amendment is "necessarily limited by the enforcement provisions of § 5 of the Fourteenth Amendment," that is, by Congress' power to enforce, by appropriate legislation, the substantive provisions of the Fourteenth Amendment. ...

But because the Eleventh Amendment implicates the fundamental constitutional balance between the Federal Government and the States, this Court consistently has held that these exceptions apply only when certain specific conditions are met. Thus, we have held that a State will be deemed to have waived its immunity "only where stated by the most express language or by such overwhelming implication from the text as [will] leave no room for any other reasonable construction. ... Likewise, in determining whether Congress in exercising its Fourteenth Amendment powers has abrogated the State's Eleventh Amendment immunity, we have required "an unequivocal expression of congressional intent to overturn the constitutionally guaranteed immunity of the several states." ...

In this case, we are asked to decide whether the State of California is subject to suit in federal court for alleged violations of [the Rehabilitation Act]. ...

Respondent argues that the State of California has waived its immunity to suit in federal court ... . The test for determining whether a State has waived its immunity from federal court jurisdiction is a stringent one. Although a State's general waiver of sovereign immunity may subject it to suit in state court, it is not enough to waive the immunity guaranteed by the Eleventh Amendment. ... As we explained just last Term, "a State's constitutional interest in immunity encompasses not merely whether it may be sued, but where it may be sued." ... In view of these principles, we do not believe that Art. III, § 5, of the California Constitution constitutes a waiver of the State's constitutional immunity. This provision does not specifically indicate the State's willingness to be sued in federal court. Indeed, this provision appears simply to authorize the legislature to waive the State's sovereign immunity. In the absence of an unequivocal waiver ... we decline to find that California has waived its constitutional immunity.

Respondent also contends that in enacting the Rehabilitation Act, Congress abrogated the State's constitutional immunity. ...

Only recently the Court reiterated that "the States occupy a special and specific position in our constitutional system. ..." By guaranteeing the sovereign immunity of the States against suit in federal court, the Eleventh Amendment serves to maintain this balance. "Our reluctance to infer that a State's immunity from suit in the federal courts has been negated stems from recognition of the vital role of the doctrine of sovereign immunity in our federal system." ...

For these reasons, we hold ... that Congress must express its intention to abrogate the Eleventh Amendment in unmistakable language in the statute itself.

In light of these principles, we must decide whether Congress, in adopting the Rehabilitation Act, has chosen to override the Eleventh Amendment. Section 504 of the Rehabilitation Act provides in pertinent part:

"No otherwise qualified handicapped individual in the United States ... shall, solely by reason of his handicap, be excluded from the participation in, be denied the benefits of, or be subjected to discrimination under any program or activity receiving Federal financial assistance or under any program or activity conducted by an Executive agency or by the United States Postal Service."

Section 505, which was added to the Act in 1978, describes ... the available remedies under the Act, including provisions pertinent to this case:

"(a) (2) The remedies, procedures, and rights set forth in title VI of the Civil Rights Act of 1964 ... shall be available to any person aggrieved by any act or failure to act by any recipient of Federal assistance or Federal provider of such assistance ... ."
"(b) In any action or proceeding to enforce or charge a violation of a provision of this subchapter, the court, in its discretion, may allow the prevailing party, other than the United States, a reasonable attorney's fee as part of the costs."

The statute thus provides remedies for violations of § 504 by "any recipient of Federal assistance." There is no claim here that the State of California is not a recipient of federal aid under the statute. But given their constitutional role, the States are not like any other class of recipients of federal aid. A general authorization for suit in federal court is not the kind of unequivocal statutory language sufficient to abrogate the Eleventh Amendment. ... Accordingly, we hold that the Rehabilitation Act does not abrogate the Eleventh Amendment bar to suits against the States.

[The Court concluded by holding that, in itself, state receipt of federal funds also does not abrogate a state's immunity.]

Other Limitations

The federal courts have developed several rules intended to restrain their own power (see Figure 4-5 for a complete list). As a matter of policy, federal courts avoid constitutional issues whenever possible. One

FIGURE 4-5

FEDERAL JUDICIAL JURISDICTION LIMITING DOCTRINES

Doctrine	*Source*
1. Ripeness	1. Art. III
2. Mootness	2. Art. III
3. Standing	3. Art. III
4. Political question	4. Art. III and separation of powers principles
5. Abstention	5. Tenth Amendment
6. Cases against states	6. Eleventh Amendment
7. Canons of construction	7. Judicial restraint

---

canon of statutory construction holds that if multiple interpretations of a statute are possible, some holding the law constitutional and others not, a construction that supports the law's constitutionality is to be selected. Similarly, a court will decide a case without addressing a constitutional issue, if possible (alternative grounds). "It is [the Court's] settled policy to avoid an interpretation of a federal statute that engenders a constitutional issue if a reasonable alternative interpretation poses no constitutional question."[97]

Another canon of construction provides that a statute is presumed constitutional and the burden of proving otherwise lies with the challenger. If part of a statute is held unconstitutional, the remaining parts are to remain viable as long as it is logical to do so. The unconstitutional clauses are to be severed, and the courts should enforce the remaining parts of the law.

Finally, federal judicial review of state court decisions is prevented when the lower court decision is based upon **adequate and independent state grounds**, even if federal claims were presented to that court. Of course, the state-law basis for the decision must be consistent with the United States Constitution for this rule to apply.

This rule is the product of federalism, comity, and economy principles. State courts are the final arbiters of state law. A state high court, usually

---

TERMS

adequate and independent state grounds doctrine   Federal judicial review of a state decision in a case that included both state and federal claims will not occur if the lower court's decision rested upon adequate and independent state law.

entitled State Supreme Court, is the court of last resort for state-law principles. The Supreme Court is a lower court in these terms and is bound by state court interpretations of state laws. Accordingly, if a state court can resolve a case by applying state law without violating federal law, then no federal judicial review of any federal constitutional issues is necessary.

State law is adequate in these cases if it logically resolves the issue without the support of federal constitutional law. The more troubling issue concerns the second prong: independence. Often, the issue is whether a state court decided a case upon state or federal constitutional principles. It is common for a state court to cite both state and federal constitutional provisions in support of a decision. In such cases, the question of whether the state court relied upon federal or state case law, state or federal constitutional history, and the like must be considered. Generally, it must be plain that a decision is made upon state grounds to avoid review of federal legal issues.

§ 4.5 State Court Jurisdiction

State courts possess general jurisdiction. They may hear all state-law cases, whether arising under ordinance, statute, regulation, state constitution, or common law. Also, since the merger of equity and common-law courts in most jurisdictions, state courts entertain claims for equitable relief as well. State courts are, as previously noted, the final interpreters of state law.

In addition, state courts are presumed to have jurisdiction over federal claims and Congress may compel state courts to entertain federal claims.[98] Congress may withdraw state court jurisdiction over federal claims in certain cases,[99] such as when a right and its remedy were created by Congress. However, Congress may not withdraw the authority and obligation of state judges to enforce the United States Constitution. Recall that the supremacy clause, Article VI, commands state judges to treat federal law as supreme, even over their own state's laws. State courts must follow federal precedents when applying federal law.

In a case in which federal jurisdiction exists concurrently with state jurisdiction, and the case was filed in state court, removal to federal court is possible. Removal is optional, so if no party files a petition to remove, the case remains in the state court. As a result of the anti-injunction act and comity doctrines (such as the *Younger* doctrine), federal courts rarely interfere with exclusive state-law cases. However, in extreme cases, if a party will be immediately, greatly, and irreparably harmed and bad faith can be shown to exist at the state level, a federal court may stay its proceedings and review any federal constitutional issues.

State courts are not bound by Article III's case-or-controversy requirement, even when interpreting federal law. Accordingly, a litigant who cannot establish standing in a federal court may be able to have her federal claim heard in state court. This creates a situation where state court interpretations of federal law cannot be reviewed by federal courts.

This paradoxical situation was tempered by the 1989 decision in *Asarco Inc. v. Kadish.*[100] *Asarco* involved a challenge to an Arizona statute that permitted leasing of state-owned mineral rights. A group of taxpayers and public school teachers challenged the statute as violative of federal law. The Arizona Supreme Court ruled in favor of the plaintiffs and invalidated the law. The lessees of the mineral rights appealed to the Supreme Court, which held that the plaintiffs in the state court action (taxpayers and teachers with a generalized interest) were without standing. Regardless, the Supreme Court agreed to review the case because the defendant lessees had suffered a "distinct and palpable" injury from the Arizona Supreme Court decision. (The decision would have been different had the defendant prevailed in the state court and the plaintiffs appealed.)

Thus, it is now possible for the Supreme Court to entertain a case in which standing was lacking at the trial level. In essence, the Court concluded that an adverse decision, even when no standing exists, may itself create an injury that gives rise to standing.[101]

America's state courts continue to be the largest dispensers of justice. Over 95 percent of all cases, civil and criminal, are filed in, and resolved by, state courts.

Summary

Article III only mandates the existence of one federal court: the Supreme Court. But Article III grants Congress the power to establish other courts. The first Congress did this and the federal judiciary has grown continuously since that time. Today, the Supreme Court of eight Associate Justices and one Chief Justice sits at the judicial apex, with the courts of appeals directly below it. Below the appellate courts are the nation's district courts. They are the federal trial courts. All district, appellate, and Supreme Court judges and justices are empowered under Article III. This means that they must undergo the presidential confirmation and senatorial confirmation process. Once sworn, an Article III judge receives the benefit of lifetime tenure and no reduction in salary.

District courts have original jurisdiction over two classes of cases: diversity and federal question. Having only limited jurisdiction, these courts may not freely entertain state-law claims. A few exceptions exist, such as pendent claims. In some circumstances, district courts act in an appellate capacity, such as when they hear appeals from non-Article III courts. The courts of appeals hear appeals from district courts and some administrative agencies and possess general appellate powers. The Supreme Court, pursuant to Article III, possesses both original and appellate jurisdiction. The high Court's original jurisdiction is limited to a narrow class of cases, such as those involving states. The Supreme Court most often acts as appellate court, hearing cases through appeal or certiorari. Appeals must be heard, whereas certiorari is discretionary. Only a few cases (i.e., where three-judge district courts are empanelled) come to the Court by appeal. Otherwise, the Supreme Court receives a majority of its cases through certiorari procedure, and it grants certiorari in only 2 to 5 percent of the cases filed.

Although the power of the federal judiciary is significant, especially in regard to constitutional interpretation, it is limited in many respects. Most cases continue to be litigated in state courts, and the federal courts themselves have created a number of limitations (e.g., abstention) on their power. Congress exercises considerable power over federal courts through its powers to create lower federal courts and to define judicial jurisdiction. Congress may not enlarge the judicial power beyond that provided for in Article III; thus, only genuine controversies may be heard. This prohibits federal courts from entertaining hypothetical disputes and issuing advisory opinions. So long as a genuine dispute exists, however, federal courts may render declaratory judgments, as well as issue injunctions and award damages. Today, federal practice is a specialty within law because federal jurisdiction and procedure are so complex.

Review Questions

1. What article of the Constitution establishes the Supreme Court and defines its jurisdiction?

2. What is the significance of *Marbury v. Madison* to United States constitutional law?

3. Name the two forms of federal judicial jurisdiction.

4. Define the political question doctrine.

5. Define the *Younger* doctrine and state its elements in criminal cases.

6. Define standing and its three primary elements.

7. Define sovereign immunity and explain the importance of the Eleventh Amendment to this concept.

8. Identify the three categories of cases in which a federal court may abstain from exercising jurisdiction.

9. State courts are courts of general jurisdiction and federal courts possess limited jurisdiction. Explain these principles.

Review Problems

Problems 1–3. You are a Justice of the Supreme Court. Consider the following facts for Problems 1 through 3. Congress enacts the following statute:

SUPREME COURT JURISDICTION ACT

Section One   President and Congress: Original Jurisdiction

The President of the United States and Congress, by concurrence of two-thirds of the membership of either House, may petition the Supreme Court to answer any question concerning the constitutionality of executive or legislative acts committed, considered, or proposed.

The Supreme Court shall answer any question posed under this article within sixty days.

Section Two   Acts of War: Original Jurisdiction

Any member of Congress, or any member of the Supreme Court, may petition the Supreme Court to determine whether an executive act of hostility toward another nation furthers the best interests of the United States. The Supreme Court shall have the jurisdiction to hear the case and issue necessary injunctions.

Section Three   Statutory Rights: Appellate Jurisdiction

The Supreme Court shall exercise no appellate jurisdiction over cases in which the primary issue is one of interpretation of a statutory right, unless the Supreme Court provides the only appeal available.

1. Is this section of the statute constitutional? Discuss.

2. Is this section of the statute constitutional? Discuss.

3. Is this section of the statute constitutional? Discuss.

4. Serena Anjuvek applies for a permit, on the behalf of the local Ba'hai club, to hold a public rally to exhibit support for the Ba'hai religion. She applied on June 1 and the application is denied on June 15. The rally is scheduled for July 1. Serena's group has held this rally for five years in a row and this is the first time their application has been denied. They have held every rally in the same public park and have had no violent incidents or complaints. They intend to continue the practice of holding their rally in this park, if permitted. The group brings suit and prevails at the trial level, so

it is permitted to hold its rally. The city appeals the decision, however, and prevails in the state supreme court. Serena appeals to the Supreme Court. The city claims that the issue is moot and that the Supreme Court should refuse jurisdiction. Discuss.

5. The United States model of judicial review is not universal. Other nations employ very different structures. Consider France's system. First, the power of judicial review is concentrated in one body, the Constitutional Council, unlike the United States, where the power is spread among all courts. Second, the Constitutional Council reviews the validity of legislation before it becomes effective. Third, standing is limited to political entities, such as the President. Consider and discuss whether reforming the United States system in such a manner is sensible. Are such methods consistent with American values? With our legal culture?

Notes

1 Virginia Constitutional Convention, 1829–1830 *Debates* 619.

2 *Brown v. Allen,* 344 U.S. 443, 540 (1953).

3 This case and many before it came before the Court through private correspondence. Prior to this instance, individual members of the Court had informally, through letters, rendered advice to the President and other government officials.

4 219 U.S. 346 (1911).

5 *Aetna Life Insurance Co. v. Haworth* 300 U.S. 227 (1937).

6 *Strawbridge v. Curtiss,* 3 Cranch 267 (1806).

7 The amount-in-controversy requirement has increased through the years. A federal courts study committee has recommended that the amount be increased to $100,000.

8 28 U.S.C. § 1442.

9 28 U.S.C. § 1446.

10 28 U.S.C. § 1447.

11 *Ames v. Kansas,* 111 U.S. 449 (1884).

12 *Illinois v. Milwaukee,* 406 U.S. 91 (1972).

13 *Id.* at 93.

14 *California v. Arizona,* 440 U.S. 59, 64 (1979).

15 64 U.S.L.W. 5 (Aug. 8, 1995).

16 See Supreme Court Rule 10.

17 42 U.S.C. § 1973bb. Other voting rights cases for which direct appeal to the Supreme Court is provided can be found at 42 U.S.C. §§ 1971, 1973b, 1973aa-2, and 1973c.

18 42 U.S.C. § 2000e-6.

19 42 U.S.C. § 2000a-5.

[20] 42 U.S.C. § 1973h.

[21] 2 U.S.C. § 922.

[22] 15 U.S.C. § 29.

[23] 28 U.S.C. § 2109.

[24] *National Mutual Insurance Co. v. Tidewater Transfer Co.*, 337 U.S. 582, 655 (1949).

[25] *Glidden Co. v. Zdanok*, 370 U.S. 530 (1962).

[26] Henry Hart, "The Power of Congress to Limit the Jurisdiction of Federal Courts: An Exercise in Dialectic," 66 *Harv. L. Rev.* 1362, 1365 (1953).

[27] *United States v. Bitty*, 208 U.S. 393, 399–400 (1908).

[28] 75 U.S. (8 Wall.) 85 (1869).

[29] 74 U.S. (7 Wall.) 506, 515 (1871).

[30] For a more thorough discussion of congressional authority over the Supreme Court's jurisdiction, *see* Henry Hart, "The Power of Congress to Limit the Jurisdiction of Federal Courts: An Exercise in Dialectic," 66 *Harv. L. Rev.* 1362 (1953); William Dodge, "Congressional Control of Supreme Court Appellate Jurisdiction: Why the Original Jurisdiction Clause Suggests an Essential Role," 100 *Yale L.J.* 1013 (1991); Ratner, "Majoritarian Constraints on Judicial Review: Congressional Control of Supreme Court Jurisdiction," 27 *Vill. L. Rev.* 929 (1982).

[31] *Sheldon v. Sill*, 8 U.S. (How.) 441, 448 (1850).

[32] *Home Life Insurance Co. v. Dunn*, 86 U.S. 214, 226 (1873). *See also The Francis Wright*, 105 U.S. 381 (1881).

[33] *State Farm Fire & Casualty Co. v. Tashire*, 386 U.S. 523 (1967).

[34] 28 U.S.C. § 2283.

[35] 28 U.S.C. § 636.

[36] 490 U.S. 858 (1989).

[37] 501 U.S. 923 (1991).

[38] 492 U.S. 33 (1989).

[39] *See* William Kelleher, III, "The Continuing Saga of Jury Trials in Bankruptcy Court—Is There an Answer? An Argument for Jury Trials in Bankruptcy Court," 2 *Am. Bankr. Inst. L. Rev.* 477 (1994); Conrad Cyr, "The Right to Trial by Jury in Bankruptcy: Which Judge Is to Preside?," 63 *Am. Bankr. L.J.* 53 (1989).

[40] *See* 28 U.S.C. § 1491 *et seq.*

[41] *United States v. Tiede*, 86 F.R.D. 227 (Berlin Ct. 1979).

[42] *See* Farber, Eskridge, and Frickey, *Constitutional Law* 1005–06 (West Publishing 1993), which cites Herbert Stern, *Judgment in Berlin* (1984) for a full discussion of this case. Herbert Stern was the judge in the case.

[43] Resnik, "Regarding 'The Federal Court': Revising the Domain of Federal Court Jurisprudence at the End of the Twentieth Century," 47 Vand. L.R. 1021, 1026 (1994).

[44] 330 U.S. 75 (1947).

[45] *Id.* at 90–91.

46 367 U.S. 497 (1961).

47 416 U.S. 312 (1974).

48 *See Sosna v. Iowa*, 419 U.S. 393 (1975) for a discussion of how class action procedure can be used to save an otherwise moot case.

49 410 U.S. 113 (1973).

50 *Id.* at 124.

51 319 U.S. 302 (1943).

52 *Baker v. Carr*, 369 U.S. 186 (1962).

53 369 U.S. 186 (1962).

54 *Singleton v. Wulff*, 428 U.S. 106 (1976).

55 *Virginia v. American Booksellers Ass'n.*, 484 U.S. 383 (1988).

56 For a more thorough discussion of environmental law, *see* Harold Hickok, *Introduction to Environmental Law* (Delmar/Lawyers Cooperative 1996).

57 524 U.S. 555 (1992).

58 438 U.S. 59 (1978).

59 397 U.S. 150 (1970).

60 392 U.S. 83 (1968).

61 454 U.S. 464 (1982).

62 428 U.S. 106 (1976).

63 *Hunt v. Washington State Apple Advertising Commission*, 432 U.S. 333 (1977).

64 *North Dakota v. Minnesota*, 263 U.S. 365 (1923).

65 *Boehner v. Anderson*, 30 F.3d 156 (D.C. Cir. 1994).

66 617 F.2d 697 (D.C. Cir. 1979).

67 511 F.2d 430 (D.C. Cir. 1974).

68 *Dornan v. Secretary of Defense*, 851 F.2d 450 (D.C. Cir. 1988).

69 *Daughtery v. Carter*, 584 F.2d 1050 (D.C. Cir. 1974).

70 19 U.S. 264 (1821).

71 5 U.S. at 170.

72 *Davis v. Bandemer*, 478 U.S. 109 (1986).

73 307 U.S. 433 (1939).

74 395 U.S. 486 (1969).

75 *McIntyre v. Fallahay*, 766 F.2d 1078 (7th Cir. 1985), citing *Roudenbush v. Hartke*, 405 U.S. 15 (1972).

76 *Chicago & Southern Air Lines v. Waterman Steamship Corp.*, 333 U.S. 103 (1948).

77 *Doe v. Braden*, 57 U.S. (16 How.) 635 (1853).

78 *The Divina Pastora: The Spanish Consul*, 17 U.S. 52 (1819).

79 504 U.S. 655 (1992).

80 418 U.S. 683 (1974).

81 19 U.S. (6 Wheat.) 264, 404 (1821).

82 *See Railroad Commission v. Pullman Co.,* 312 U.S. 496 (1941) and *Colorado River Water Conservation District v. United States,* 424 U.S. 800 (1976) for discussions of abstention.

83 *See Barber v. Barber,* 62 U.S. (21 How.) 582 (1859); *Popovici v. Agler,* 280 U.S. 379 (1930).

84 *Younger v. Harris,* 401 U.S. 37 (1971).

85 *Pennzoil v. Texaco,* 481 U.S. 1, 10 (1987).

86 *Aiona v. Hawaii,* 17 F.3d 1244 (9th Cir. 1993).

87 *Molitor v. Kaneland Community Unit District No. 302,* 18 Ill. 2d 11, 163 N.E.2d 89, 94 (1959).

88 2 U.S. (2 Dall.) 419 (1793).

89 134 U.S. 1 (1890).

90 *Employees of Department of Public Health & Welfare v. Missouri Department of Public Welfare,* 411 U.S. 279 (1973).

91 *Port Authority Trans-Hudson Corp. v. Feeny,* 495 U.S. 299 (1990).

92 115 S. Ct. 394 (1994).

93 *Hutto v. Finney,* 437 U.S. 678 (1978).

94 *Pennsylvania v. Union Gas,* 491 U.S. 1 (1989).

95 28 U.S.C. §§ 1291, 1346, 1402, 1504, 2110, 2401–2402, 2411–2412, 2671–2678, 2680.

96 *See* Daniel Hall, *Administrative Law* ch. 10 (Delmar/Lawyers Cooperative Publishers 1994) for a more thorough discussion of the Federal Tort Claims Act and other statutes through which the United States has waived immunity from liability.

97 *Gomez v. United States,* 490 U.S. 858, 863 (1991).

98 *Testa v. Katt,* 330 U.S. 389 (1947).

99 *The Moses Taylor,* 4 Wall 411 (1867).

100 490 U.S. 605 (1989).

101 For a discussion of this topic and a proposal to apply Article III to state courts hearing federal claims, *see* William Fletcher, "The 'Case or Controversy' Requirement in State Court Adjudication of Federal Questions," 78 *Cal. L. Rev.* 263 (1990).

CHAPTER 5

CONGRESS

Laws are like sausages. It's better not to see them being made.

— *Otto von Bismarck*[1]

§ 5.1 Legislatures Generally

Courts are responsible for resolving disputes. As part of that function, they interpret and apply law. Where does the law come from? Of course, the Constitution is a source of law. In a common-law system, some law is created by the courts. But today, the primary source of lawmaking is legislative bodies. In the United States, these bodies are groups of elected representatives.

Whereas courts are largely reactive (only become involved after a dispute has arisen), legislatures are largely proactive. When a court hears a case, it is concerned with individual facts; legislatures consider large systemic issues. Individual cases are used only as anecdotal evidence. Legislation is concerned with policy issues and large groups of people, whereas courts are usually concerned with dispensing justice among a small number of people. Courts look to the past in resolving disputes; legislatures are concerned with the future.

Legislatures are responsible for making law. In making the law, legislators must consider competing policies and interests. Legislatures are free to enact any law, so long as that law is consonant with the Constitution. Legislatures are free to alter, amend, and abolish the common law of their jurisdictions if they wish, except for the common law that is now embodied in the Constitution.

In a democracy such as the United States, any person may petition his representative to propose a law, but only members of legislatures are authorized to propose new laws to the legislature. A proposed law is referred to as a **bill**. Procedures vary among legislatures, but generally

---

TERMS

bill [†] A proposed law, presented to the legislature for enactment; i.e., a legislative bill.

new bills are sent to committees. These committees review the bill, hold hearings and **mark-up** sessions, and eventually vote on whether the bill should proceed further. If so, the bill may be sent to another committee, to a subcommittee, or to the entire body for vote. In **bicameral** legislatures, additional (conference) committee work may be necessary to resolve any problems that the bill has between the two houses.

If the bill receives congressional approval and is signed by the President (or a presidential veto is overridden by Congress), it becomes a public law or **statute**, which is the written law of the body. Statutes are then compiled and arranged according to subject matter in the process of **codification**. These combined statutes are known as **codes**, such as the Code of Civil Procedure or the Administrative Code.

Congress also adopts resolutions. These are formal statements by Congress but are not intended to be statutes. For example, Congress may by resolution express its opinion to the President concerning a matter that is exclusively executive. Resolutions may be issued by a single house or both, in which case they are referred to as *concurrent*. A **joint resolution** is one passed by both houses and approved by the President. Such a resolution has the force of a statute. Very generally, it provides you with a basis to begin your study of the United States Congress.

SIDEBAR

Positive Law and When a Code Is Not a Law

When a bill is enacted, it becomes a *public law* or *session law*—a statute. The statutes are published by year of enactment, but these compilations can be confusing to the researcher. That is because the text of public laws does not necessarily refer to existing related law. For convenience, public laws are arranged into codes.

TERMS

marking up[†]   The detailed revision of a bill by a legislative committee.

bicameral[†]   Two-chambered, referring to the customary division of a legislature into two houses (a Senate and a House of Representatives).

statute[†]   A law enacted by a legislature; an act.

codification[†]   1. The process of arranging laws in a systematic form covering the entire law of a jurisdiction or a particular area of the law; the process of creating a code. 2. The process of turning a common law rule into a statute.

code[†]   1. The published statutes of a jurisdiction, arranged in systematic form. 2. A portion of the statutes of a jurisdiction, especially the statutes relating to a particular subject.

joint resolution[†]   A resolution adopted by both houses of a state legislature or of Congress. In most jurisdictions, a joint resolution is not a law, although a congressional resolution has the effect of law if it is signed by the president.

A *code* is a group of laws organized by subject matter, such as a code of criminal procedure. As laws are enacted, they are made a part of the existing code. Hence, the organization of codes reflects the current state of the law, not a chronological ordering of enactments.

The first codification of federal statutes occurred in 1874. This was revised in 1878. Between 1878 and 1924, the federal codes fell into disarray. Congress, as well as the public, suffered from legislative confusion. For example, Congress amended laws that had previously been repealed. To remedy the problem, Congress arranged for a new codification of federal statutes in 1924. The new code was completed one year later.

Decisions concerning the states of the law had to be made during the codification process. For example, editorial decisions concerning whether statutes had been "amended" or "repealed" by subsequent statutes were made. The result is that unless a code section is formally enacted into *positive law* by Congress, it is not the final authority of law. Congress has enacted many of the code sections found in the United States Code (U.S.C.), but not all. Generally, the unenacted sections of the United States Code are unquestioned. But, when they are challenged as inaccurate, then a court must resort to the Statutes at Large (Stat.) to determine the state of the law.

§ 5.2 The Structure and Organization of Congress

Article I, § 1, of the Constitution reads:

All legislative Powers herein granted shall be vested in a Congress of the United States, which shall consist of a Senate and House of Representatives.

Accordingly, the United States Congress is bicameral, having both a Senate and a House of Representatives. The second and third sections of Article I describe the requirements for being a senator or representative, as well as the processes of selection.

According to § 4, clause 2, Congress is to assemble at least once yearly beginning on the first Monday in December, unless it selects another day. A public journal of the proceedings is to be maintained, except when the body votes for secrecy. The *Congressional Record* is the official record of Congress and can be found in most public libraries. Records of how members vote are to be kept, so long as one-fifth of the members present at a session desire it.[2] Each house is permitted to make its own rules to govern its proceedings.[3] A house may order that its members be present and can punish absences.[4] The House elects its leaders, including the highest officer of the body, the Speaker of the

House. Similarly, the Senate is empowered to elect its leaders, including the President Pro Tempore (commonly known as the Pro Tem).[5]

Bills may be introduced by any member. If a bill is approved by both houses, it is presented to the President. The President may sign the bill, making it law, or may veto the bill. Vetoes may be overcome by two-thirds votes in both houses. If the President does not return a bill within ten days, it becomes law, unless Congress is adjourned. If adjourned, the bill dies. This is known as a **pocket veto**.

With one exception, a bill may originate in either house. Article I, § 7, clause 1, establishes the exception, as it reads, "[a]ll Bills for raising Revenues shall originate in the House of Representatives." A law that does not have revenue raising as its primary purpose, but raises revenues incidentally, may originate in either house. As an example, a statute that requires federal criminal offenders to pay a special assessment into a crime victims fund is not revenue raising for the purposes of the **origination clause**. The Court has also held that origination claims are justiciable.[6]

Note that neither house of Congress may adjourn longer than three days without the consent of the other house. Also, both houses are required to conduct their work in the same location.[7]

§ 5.3 Membership in Congress

The Constitution has provisions concerning the qualifications a person must possess to be a member of Congress, removal of congresspersons, and related matters.

Qualifications

To be a member of the House of Representatives, a person must be at least twenty-five years old, a citizen of the United States for at least

---

TERMS

pocket veto[†]   The veto of a congressional bill by the president by retaining it until Congress is no longer in session, neither signing nor vetoing it. The effect of such inaction is to nullify the legislation without affirmatively vetoing it. The pocket veto is also available to governors under some state constitutions.

origination clause   Article I, § 7, clause 1, of the United States Constitution, which requires all revenue-raising bills to originate in the House of Representatives.

Amicus

Chief Justice John Marshall

One of the most significant individuals in the history of the Supreme Court and United States constitutional law was John Marshall. He was born in Virginia in 1755 and became the nation's fourth Chief Justice in 1801, in which capacity he served until 1835. He was nominated to that position by President John Adams. Before joining the Court, Marshall had practiced law, served in the Virginia Assembly, served as a representative in Congress, and was Secretary of State to President John Adams.

While on the court, Marshall championed the new Constitution and advanced the Federalist agenda of creating a strong national government. Marshall was a consensus builder on the Court and many important decisions were issued during his tenure, including *Marbury v. Madison* (Court's power of judicial review), *McCulloch v. Maryland* (Congress's power to establish a national bank), and *Gibbons v. Ogden* (supremacy of federal laws and broad national power under the commerce clause). ▮▮▮▮

seven years, and an inhabitant of the state where he will run for election. Members of the House, commonly referred to as congressmen and congresswomen, congresspersons, or members, serve two-year terms. The number of representatives that serve from each state varies according to population. Representatives serve districts and, accordingly, are elected by the voters of each district, not by the voters of the state generally. Each congressperson possesses one vote in the House. There are also a few nonvoting members of the House. For example, the representatives from the District of Columbia, Puerto Rico, and American Samoa may not vote.

To be a senator, a person must be at least thirty years old, a citizen of the United States for at least nine years, and an inhabitant of the state where she will be a candidate for election. Senators serve six-year terms. The terms of the senators are staggered so that the terms of one-third of all senators expire every other year. Every state, regardless of population, has two senators, each with one vote.

Initially, according to Article I, § 3, senators were selected by the state legislatures. This reflected the attitude of the framers concerning the role of the Senate. Unlike the House, which was intended to be a true body of the people, the Senate was a body representing the interests of the states. Many of the framers were troubled by the proportional representation in the House. They feared that the smaller states would be taken advantage of by the larger states. Therefore, the Senate, with its equal representation, was devised. However, populism led to the direct election of senators by the people, now enshrined in the Seventeenth Amendment.

No person may simultaneously serve in Congress and in a "civil Office under the Authority of the United States."[8] This requirement avoids obvious conflicts of interest. It is common practice to allow government officials to keep their positions until the time of election, or in some cases, until they are sworn in as a senator or representative.

The Constitution does not limit the number of terms a person may serve in either house. Concerns that the Congress is filled with professional politicians who have lost touch with the people and have incurred detrimental obligations to special interests prompted some states to enact term limits legislation in the early 1990s. The Republican-controlled Congress of 1994 also promised term limits as part of its "Contract with America." In 1995, however, the Supreme Court invalidated an Arkansas constitutional amendment limiting House members to three terms and senators to two terms. The Court held, that the Constitution establishes qualifications and that it would take a constitutional amendment to change them in *United States Term Limits, Inc. v. Thornton.*[9] The Court found:

1. State-imposed qualification restrictions are contrary to the fundamental principle of our representative democracy and that the people should be empowered to choose whom they please to govern.

2. State-imposed qualifications are inconsistent with the Framers' vision of a uniform national legislature.

3. Historical evidence leads to the conclusion that the qualifications appearing in the Constitution are exclusive and neither Congress nor the states may add to them.

The decision on whether a person possesses the qualifications to be a member of Congress is left to the applicable house. Article I, § 5, clause 1, provides that "[e]ach House shall be the Judge of the Elections, Returns, and Qualifications of its own Members." This has been interpreted to mean that each house has the authority to decide whether a member meets the age, citizenship, and domicile requirements. Also, the decision as to who prevailed in an election belongs to the house in which the candidate would be seated. In other words, if there is a dispute as to what votes should be counted, the final decision rests with Congress, not the state where the election was held or to any court.[10]

If the Senate or House were to exclude a member for one of these reasons, its decision would be unreviewable by a court pursuant to the political question doctrine. However, a decision to exclude persons for other reasons is reviewable, as the clause limits the exclusion power to qualifications. This was the issue in *Powell v. McCormack*[11]: Adam Clayton Powell, Jr., had been elected to the House of Representatives but, due to allegations of misuse of public funds and unbecoming conduct, the House refused to seat him. The Supreme Court held that the issue was justiciable and ordered that he be seated.

Discipline and Punishment

Another provision of the Constitution was also at issue in the *Powell* case. The second clause of Article I, § 5, provides that "[e]ach House may determine the Rules of its Proceedings, punish its Members for disorderly Behavior, and, with the Concurrence of two thirds, expel a member."

Expulsion

The Court concluded that Powell had not been expelled because he had never been seated. The Court also stated, in dictum, that a House's power to expel is much broader than its power to exclude. Still, the language of the clause leads to the conclusion that the power is not plenary. Could Powell have been expelled for behavior that occurred before his election? One reasonable construction of the expulsion clause is that it applies to post-election and not pre-election conduct.

Censorship and Other Discipline

In addition to expulsion, the Constitution allows each house to punish its members in other ways. Censorship is an example. In 1881 the Supreme Court went so far as to state that

> punishment may in a proper case be imprisonment, and that it may be for refusal to obey some rule on that subject made by the House for the preservation of order. So, also, the penalty which each House is authorized to inflict in order to compel the attendance of absent members may be imprisonment, and this may be for a violation of some order or standing rule on that subject.[12]

Again, the decision concerning what conduct warrants punishment, including expulsion, is political. An act need not be criminal to be subject to punishment.

Immunity

Both senators and representatives are entitled to a limited immunity from civil arrest while serving. Article I, § 6, clause 1, expresses that all members of Congress

> shall in all Cases, except Treason, Felony and Breach of the Peace, be privileged from Arrest during their Attendance at the Session of their respective Houses, and in going to and returning from the same; and for any Speech and Debate in either House, they shall not be questioned in any other Place.

The first half of this provision, the freedom from arrest clause, has been interpreted very narrowly. First, it has been held that the clause shields congresspersons from civil, but not criminal, arrest. Accordingly, a congressperson may be arrested, detained, or imprisoned, if convicted during a session of Congress, for any crime, felony, or misdemeanor. The immunity applies only to civil arrests, which were more common at the time the Constitution was ratified than today.

Second, members of Congress are immune from civil arrest, but not civil process. Members may be served with complaints and other process during a session. A congressperson may not, however, be arrested in order to secure his or her testimony at a civil trial. These immunities apply when a congressperson is in transit to and returning from a session of Congress.

The second half of this provision contains the speech and debate clause. No congressperson may be sued or otherwise made to answer for any statements made during congressional proceedings. Unlike the freedom from arrest clause, the speech and debate clause is interpreted broadly. It was the intent of the framers to encourage open and candid debates and discussions in Congress. Fear of civil liability, such as an action for defamation of character, tends to hinder this objective. This provision applies to both civil and criminal cases. Therefore, the government could not use the statements of a congressperson made on the floor of the house in his prosecution for defrauding the government and violating a conflicts of interest law.[13]

The clause has force in any congressional proceeding, whether it be a meeting of the entire house or a committee. Statements made to reporters or during news conferences are not privileged. Although committee reports are privileged, individual dissemination of the same information by members of Congress to the public is not.[14] Such dissemination of information is not considered an essential part of the legislative process.

In addition to statements made in congressional meetings, the clause has been interpreted to grant immunity to members for "things generally done in a session of the House by one of its members in relation to the business before it."[15] This extends the immunity beyond speech to include actions. Actions are protected so long as they are an integral part of the deliberative and communicative processes of committee and house proceedings.

GRAVEL v. UNITED STATES
408 U.S. 606 (1972)

Opinion of the Court by Mr. Justice White.

These cases arise out of the investigation by a federal grand jury into possible criminal conduct with respect to the release and publication of a classified Defense Department study entitled History of the United States Decision-Making Process on Viet Nam Policy. This document, popularly known as the Pentagon Papers, bore a Defense security classification of Top Secret-Sensitive. The crimes being investigated included the retention of public property or records with intent to convert (18 U.S.C. § 641), the gathering and transmitting of national defense information (18 U.S.C. § 793), the concealment or removal of public records or documents (18 U.S.C. § 2071), and conspiracy to commit such offenses and to defraud the United States (18 U.S.C. § 371).

Among the witnesses subpoenaed were Leonard S. Rodberg, an assistant to Senator Mike Gravel of Alaska and a resident fellow at the Institute of Policy Studies, and Howard Webber, Director of M.I.T. Press. Senator Gravel, as intervenor, filed motions to quash the subpoenas and to require the Government to specify the particular questions to be addressed to Rodberg. He asserted that requiring these witnesses to appear and testify would violate his privilege under the Speech or Debate Clause of the United States Constitution, Art. I, § 6, cl. 1.

It appeared that on the night of June 29, 1971, Senator Gravel, as Chairman of the Subcommittee on Buildings and Grounds of the Senate Public Works Committee, convened a meeting of the subcommittee and there read extensively from a copy of the Pentagon Papers. He then placed the entire 47 volumes of the study in the public record. Rodberg had been added to the Senator's staff earlier in the day and assisted Gravel in preparing for and conducting the hearing. Some weeks later there were press reports that Gravel had arranged for the papers to be published by Beacon Press and that members of Gravel's staff had talked with Webber as editor of M.I.T. Press.

The District Court overruled the motions to quash and to specify questions but entered an order proscribing certain categories of questions. ...

The Court of Appeals affirmed the denial of the motions to quash but modified the protective order to reflect its own views of the scope of the congressional privilege. ...

Because the claim is that a Member's aide shares the Member's constitutional privilege, we consider first whether and to what extent Senator Gravel himself is exempt from process or inquiry by a grand jury investigating the commission of a crime. Our frame of reference is Art. I, § 6, cl. 1, of the Constitution:

> "The Senators and Representatives shall receive a Compensation for their Services, to be ascertained by Law, and paid out of the Treasury of the United States. They shall in all Cases, except Treason, Felony and Breach of the Peace, be privileged from Arrest during their Attendance at the Session of their respective Houses, and in going to and returning from the same; and for any Speech or Debate in either House, they shall not be questioned in any other Place."

... [Gravel] points out that the last portion of § 6 affords Members of Congress another vital privilege—they may not be questioned in any other place for any speech or debate in either House. ... [Gravel insists] that the Speech and Debate Clause protects him from criminal or civil liability and from questioning elsewhere than in the Senate, with respect to the events occurring at the subcommittee hearings at which the Pentagon Papers were introduced into the public record. To us this claim is incontrovertible. The Speech or Debate Clause was designed to assure a co-equal branch of the government wide freedom of speech, debate, and deliberation without intimidation or threats from the Executive Branch. ...

Even so, the United States strongly urges that because the Speech or Debate Clause confers a privilege only upon "Senators and Representatives," Rodberg himself has no valid claim to constitutional immunity from grand jury inquiry. ... We agree with the Court of Appeals that for the purpose of construing the privilege a Member and his aide are to be "treated as one." ... It is literally impossible, in view of the complexities of the modern legislative process, with Congress almost constantly in session and matters of legislative concern constantly proliferating, for Members of Congress to perform their legislative tasks without the help of aides and assistants; that the day-to-day work of such aides is so critical to the Members' performance that they must be treated as the latter's alter ego. ...

The United States fears the abuses that history reveals have occurred when legislators are invested with the power to relieve others from the operation of otherwise valid civil and criminal laws. But these abuses, it seems to us, are for the most part obviated if the privilege applicable to the aide is viewed, as it must be, as the privilege of the Senator, and invocable only by the Senator or by the aide on the Senator's behalf, and if in all events the privilege available to the aide is confined to those services that would be immune legislative conduct if performed by the Senator himself. This view places beyond the Speech or Debate Clause a variety of services characteristically performed by aides for Members of Congress, even though within the scope of employment. It likewise provides no protection for criminal conduct threatening the security of the person or property of others, whether performed at the direction of the Senator [or not]. Neither does it immunize Senator or aide from testifying at trials or grand jury proceedings involving third-party crimes where the questions do not require testimony about or impugn a legislative act. Thus our refusal to distinguish between Senator and aide ... does not mean that Rodberg is for all purposes exempt from grand jury questioning.

We are convinced also that the Court of Appeals correctly determined that Senator Gravel's alleged arrangement with Beacon Press to publish the Pentagon Papers was not protected speech or debate within the meaning of Art. I, § 6, cl. 1, of the Constitution.

Historically, the English legislative privilege was not viewed as protecting republication of an otherwise immune libel on the floor of the House. ... [An English case] recognized that "[f]or speeches made in Parliament by a member to the prejudice of any other person or hazardous to the public peace, that member enjoys complete impunity." But it was clearly stated that "if the calumnious or inflammatory speeches should be reported and published, the law will attach responsibility on the publisher." ...

Thus, voting by Members and committee reports are protected; and we recognize today—as the Court has recognized before ... that a Member's conduct at legislative committee hearings, although subject to judicial review in various circumstances, as is legislation itself, may not be made the basis for a civil or criminal judgment against a Member because that conduct is within the "sphere of legitimate legislative activity." ...

But the Clause has not extended beyond the legislative sphere. That Senators generally perform certain acts in their official capacity as Senators does not necessarily make all such acts legislative in nature. ...

Legislative acts are not all-encompassing. The heart of the Clause is speech or debate in either House. Insofar as the Clause is construed to reach other matters, they must be an integral part of the deliberative and communicative processes by which Members participate in committee and House proceedings with respect to the consideration and passage or rejection of proposed legislation or with respect to other matters which the Constitution places within the jurisdiction of either House. ...

Here, private publication by Senator Gravel through the cooperation of Beacon Press was in no way essential to the deliberations of the Senate; nor does questioning as to private publication threaten the integrity or independence of the Senate by impermissibly exposing its deliberations to executive influence. The Senator has conducted his hearings; the record and any report that was forthcoming were available both to his committee and the Senate. Insofar as we are advised, neither Congress nor the full committee ordered or authorized the publication. We cannot but conclude that the Senator's arrangements with Beacon Press were not part and parcel of the legislative process.

There are additional considerations. Article I, § 6, cl. 1, as we have emphasized, does not purport to confer a general exemption upon Members of Congress from liability or process in criminal cases. Quite the contrary is true. While the Speech or Debate Clause recognizes speech, voting, and other legislative acts as exempt from liability that might otherwise attach, it does not privilege either Senator or aide to violate an otherwise valid criminal law in preparing for or implementing legislative acts. If republication of these classified papers would be a crime under an Act of Congress, it would not be entitled to immunity under the Speech or Debate Clause. It also appears that the grand jury was pursuing this very subject in the normal course of a valid investigation. The Speech or Debate Clause does not in our view extend immunity to Rodberg, as a Senator's aide, from testifying before the grand jury about the arrangement between Senator Gravel and Beacon Press or about his own participation, if any, in the alleged transaction, so long as legislative acts of the Senator are not impugned.

We must finally consider, in the light of the foregoing, whether the protective order entered by the Court of Appeals is an appropriate regulation of the pending grand jury proceedings.

Focusing first on paragraph two of the order, we think the injunction against interrogating Rodberg with respect to any act, "in the broadest sense," performed by him within the scope of his employment, overly restricts the scope of grand jury inquiry. Rodberg's immunity, testimonial or otherwise, extends only to legislative acts as to which the Senator himself would be immune. The grand jury, therefore, if relevant to its investigation into the possible violations of the criminal law, and absent Fifth Amendment objections, may require from Rodberg answers to questions relating to his or the Senator's arrangements, if any, with respect to republication or with respect to third-party conduct under valid investigation by the grand jury, as long as the questions do not implicate legislative action of the Senator. Neither do we perceive any constitutional or other privilege that shields Rodberg, any more than any other witness, from grand jury questions relevant to tracing the source of obviously highly classified documents that came into the Senator's possession and are the basic subject matter of inquiry in this case, so long as no legislative act is implicated by the questions.

Because the Speech or Debate Clause privilege applies both to Senator and aide, it appears to us that paragraph one of the order, alone, would afford ample protection for the privilege if it forbade questioning any witness, including Rodberg: (1) concerning the Senator's conduct, or the conduct of his aides, at the June 29, 1971, meeting of the subcommittee; (2) concerning the motives and purposes behind the Senator's conduct, or that of his aides, at that meeting; (3) concerning communications between the Senator and his aides during the term of their employment and related to said meeting or any other legislative act of the Senator; (4) except as it proves relevant to investigating possible third-party crime, concerning any act, in itself not criminal, performed by the Senator, or by his aides in the course of their employment. ...

The judgment of the Court of Appeals is vacated and the cases are remanded to that court for further proceedings consistent with this opinion.

The boundaries of the speech and debate clause immunity were examined in *Gravel v. United States*. The Court held in *Gravel* that a congressman's aide is shielded with immunity to the same extent that the congressman is himself. Further, the Court held that the aide could not be compelled to testify at a grand jury hearing concerning the actions committed by himself and his employer-senator in preparation for the committee hearing. Nor could the aide be compelled to answer questions concerning the senator's motives. These matters go to the heart of the legislative process.

The aide could, however, be required to testify concerning matters that did not directly implicate the deliberative and communicative aspects of the legislative process, such as any knowledge he possessed concerning the private publication of the papers. The private publication of information, even if contained in a public record, is not part of the legislative process and is not shielded by the speech and debate clause.

In 1995, it was held that the speech and debate clause did not foreclose the prosecution of Congressman Daniel Rostenkowski of Illinois for fraud, embezzlement, and misappropriation of congressional funds.[16] Rostenkowski was accused in that case, among other things, of having congressional staff perform personal services, purchasing items from the House store at a reduced rate for personal use, and purchasing automobiles with congressional funds for personal use. The Court found that these acts were not part of the legislative process and, as such, were not protected.

The speech and debate clause provides, when applicable, *absolute immunity*. This means that a member of Congress is not only immune from liability, but is also immune from suit or from having to defend herself. Therefore, members are entitled to an immediate appeal from trial court decisions finding no immunity, under the collateral order doctrine.[17] This is contrary to the general appellate rule that requires appeals to be filed after final judgment is rendered in a case.

As previously discussed, Congress may punish its members. So, even if a member is immune from other processes, her house may sanction her conduct, including inappropriate statements made on the floor of the house. The protections of the speech and debate clause are not extended to state legislators who are sued or prosecuted in federal court.[18]

Vacancies

If a representative or senatorial position becomes vacant in between elections (e.g., by a member's death), the Constitution provides that the governor of the state may call an election to fill the seat

(Art. I, § 2 (representative); Amendment 17 (senator)). Amendment 17 goes further and provides that the legislature of the state may empower the governor to make a temporary senatorial appointment pending replacement by election.

§ 5.4 Congressional Power Generally

Over what matters and peoples may Congress legislate? Recall from earlier discussions that the framers intended to create a limited national government. Through the Tenth Amendment, they affirmatively provided that all powers not "delegated to the United States by the Constitution, nor prohibited by it to the States, are reserved to the States respectively, or to the people." It is clear that the framers intended to carve out a well-defined sphere of authority for the national government that could not be enlarged without amendment. In theory, there are no inherent federal powers. There *is* inherent state power. In fact, all powers not belonging to the people or the national government fall into the jurisdiction of the states. Hence, there is a triad of authority: the federal government, the states, and the people. The power of the people is further buttressed by the Ninth Amendment, which provides that "[t]he enumeration in the Constitution, of certain rights, shall not be construed to deny or disparage others retained by the people."

To understand this triad of power, consider the following analysis. First, determine whether the act in question may be regulated by any government. That is, is this a right of the people? If so, then no further analysis is required. If not, then determine if the federal government may regulate the area. If so, then ask if the states may concurrently regulate the area. (Later in this text, it will be shown that other issues, such as preemption, must be considered at this point.) Finally, if the subject is not delegated to the national government and is not prohibited to any government, then it belongs to the states (see Figure 5-1).

To analyze a problem in these terms, constitutional governmental powers and constitutional civil rights must both be understood. We begin with the powers of Congress. Congress's power is limited to the delegations found in the Constitution. Most of those are found in Article I. What follows is a discussion of the express and implied delegations of power to Congress. As is discussed in the following sections, the concept of a limited national government has fallen away; through several provisions of the Constitution, the national government has increased in both size and jurisdiction. The discussion begins with the commerce clause.

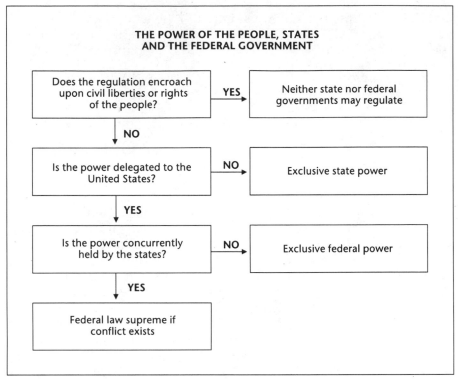

**THE POWER OF THE PEOPLE, STATES
AND THE FEDERAL GOVERNMENT**

FIGURE 5-1   Respective Powers of the People, the States, and the Federal
Government

§ 5.5 Commerce Power

Article I, § 8, clause 3, states that Congress shall have the power to
"regulate Commerce with foreign Nations, and among the several
states, and with the Indian Tribes." This is the **commerce clause**.

State rivalries and conflicts over foreign and interstate commerce
were problems under the Articles of Confederation. The national government was virtually powerless to regulate the area and there was little
uniformity of law. The commerce clause was among several constitutional provisions intended to remedy these problems.

TERMS

commerce clause †   The clause in Article I, § 8, of the Constitution that
gives Congress the power to regulate commerce between the states and between the United States and foreign countries. Federal statutes that regulate business and labor ... are based upon this power.

Early Commerce Clause Cases

The clause delegates the authority to regulate interstate, international, and Indian commerce to the United States. Because the federal government is, in theory, a limited one, it does not have the authority to regulate intrastate commerce. This power is left to the states.

Several troubling issues have surfaced in the commerce area. One concerns a fundamental question. When is commerce interstate in character? The examination of the clause begins with that inquiry.

Chief Justice Marshall defined *interstate commerce* as "commerce that concerns more states than one." According to Chief Justice Marshall, only commerce that is entirely internal is not subject to federal regulation. Further, Congress may regulate activities within states if those activities affect interstate commerce. For example, in 1922 the Court ruled that the Chicago stockyards could be federally regulated because they were a point through which interstate commerce flowed. The Court held that intrastate activities could be regulated if they were part of the "stream or current of commerce."[19] Chief Justice Marshall's broad interpretation of the authority of the federal government to regulate commerce remained the prevailing view until the 1930s.

The New Deal and the Commerce Clause

For a brief period, during the New Deal administration of President Franklin D. Roosevelt, the Court changed its approach to the commerce clause. The Court adopted a more territorial approach to commerce, carving out an area that belonged to the states. In several cases, the Court invalidated New Deal legislation that was intended to remedy the economic depression. In *Railroad Retirement Board v. Alton Rail Co.*,[20] a 1935 decision of the Supreme Court, the Railroad Retirement Act was held to exceed Congress's authority over commerce. The Act governed pensions for railroad employees. In short, the Court found no connection between interstate commerce and the financial security of railroad employees.

Schechter Poultry Corp. v. United States,[21] another 1935 case, represented another defeat for the New Deal's recovery efforts. This case challenged the authority of the President to approve "codes of fair competition" for the poultry industry. The defendant corporation was convicted of violating the code, which had been established by an agency at the direction of the President, over its objections that the delegation to the President was unlawful and that Congress had exceeded its authority under the commerce clause. The Court ruled for the defendant on both counts. The first issue, unlawful delegation of authority to the President, is discussed in Chapter 7. As to the second issue, the

GIBBONS v. OGDEN
22 U.S. (9 Wheat.) 1 (1824)

[New York granted Robert Livingston and Robert Fulton an exclusive license to operate steamships on all New York waterways. Ogden obtained a right to operate a ferry on a New York waterway from Livingston and Fulton. Gibbons, under license from the federal government authorized by federal statute, operated a ship in Ogden's zone. Ogden obtained an injunction in state court prohibiting Gibbons from operating his ship in New York waters.]

Chief Justice Marshall delivered the opinion of the Court. ...

The words are, "Congress shall have the power to regulate commerce with foreign nations, and among the several States, and with the Indian tribes."

The subject to be regulated is commerce; and our constitution being, as was aptly said at the bar, one of enumeration, and not of definition, to ascertain the extent of the power, it becomes necessary to settle the meaning of the word. The counsel for the appellee would limit it to traffic, to buying and selling, or the interchange of commodities, and do not admit that it comprehends navigation. This would restrict a general term, applicable to many objects, to one of its significations. Commerce, undoubtably, is traffic, but it is something more; it is intercourse. It describes the commercial intercourse between nations, and parts of nations, in all its branches, and is regulated by prescribing rules for carrying on that intercourse. The mind can scarcely conceive a system for regulating commerce between nations, which shall exclude all laws concerning navigation, which shall be silent on the admission of vessels of the one nation into the ports of the other, and be confined to prescribing rules for the conduct of individuals, in the actual employment of buying and selling, or of barter.

If commerce does not include navigation, the government of the Union has no direct power over the subject, and can make no law prescribing what shall constitute American vessels, or requiring that they shall be navigated by American seamen. Yet this power has been exercised from the commencement of the government, has been exercised with the consent of all, and has been understood by all to be commercial regulation. All America understands, and has uniformly understood, the word "commerce" to comprehend navigation. ...

If the opinion that "commerce" as the word is used in the constitution, comprehends navigation also, requires any additional confirmation, that additional confirmation is, we think, furnished by the words of the instrument itself ... . The 9th section of the 1st article declares, that "no preference shall be given, by any regulation of commerce or revenue, to the ports of one state over those of another." This clause cannot be understood as applicable to those laws only which are passed for the purposes of revenue, because it expressly applied to commercial regulations; and the most obvious preference which can be given to one port over another, in regulating commerce, relates to navigation. But the subsequent part of the sentence is still more explicit. It is, "nor shall vessels bound to or from one state, be obliged to enter, clear, or pay duties, in another." These words have a direct reference to navigation.

The universally acknowledged power of the government to impose embargoes must also be considered as showing that all America is united in that construction which comprehends navigation in the word commerce. ...

Commerce among the states cannot stop at the external line of each state, but may be introduced into the interior. It is not intended to say that these words comprehend that commerce, which is completely internal, which is carried on between man and man in a State, or between different parts of the same State, and which does not extend to or affect other states [is to be regulated]. ...

Comprehensive as the word "among" is, it may very properly be restricted to that commerce which concerns more States than one. The phrase is not one which would probably have been selected to indicate the completely interior traffic of a State ... . The completely internal commerce of a state, then, may be considered as reserved for the state itself.

But, in regarding commerce with foreign nations, the power of Congress does not stop at the jurisdictional lines of the several states. It would be a very useless power, if it could not pass those lines. ... The deep streams which penetrate our country in every direction, pass through the interior of almost every state ... . If it exists within the States, if a foreign voyage may commence or terminate at a port within a State, then the power of Congress may be exercised within a State.

We are now arrived at the inquiry—What is this power?

It is the power to regulate; that is, to prescribe the rule by which commerce is governed. This power, like all others vested in Congress, is complete in itself, may be exercised to its utmost extent, and acknowledges no limitations, other than those prescribed in the constitution. ...

The power of Congress, then, comprehends navigation, within the limits of every state in the Union; so far as that navigation may be, in any manner, connected with "commerce with foreign nations, or among the several States, or with the Indian tribes." It may, of consequence, pass the jurisdictional line of New York, and act upon the very waters to which the prohibition now under consideration applies. ...

majority held that the intrastate activities of a poultry business did not have sufficient connection to interstate commerce to allow federal regulation.

There were other cases in which the Court read the commerce clause as conferring less federal authority than had previously been allowed.[22] Also, several New Deal statutes were invalidated under excessive delegation and substantive due process theories. These cases are discussed in Chapter 6. (Recall also that these decisions led to President Franklin D. Roosevelt's court-packing plan, previously discussed in Chapter 3).

The Commerce Clause Today

The Court's change in direction occurred in 1937, when the Court upheld the National Labor Relations Act (NLRA), a federal labor statute that governs collective bargaining and unfair labor practices. The Court held that the law's jurisdictional provision, which confined the NLRA's reach to transactions affecting or obstructing commerce, was valid.[23] Under this new approach, the fact that a business may have an economic impact on the nation—regardless of whether it otherwise appears to be intrastate in nature—creates federal jurisdiction. Furthermore, the Tenth Amendment, which had previously been used by the Court to create a state commerce domain, was rejected as a limitation upon federal authority.

Since this time, congressional authority has grown significantly, virtually unchecked by the judiciary. Federal jurisdiction has been found in some cases where common sense leads to the opposite conclusion. In many respects, the power of Congress to regulate has extended into what were once thought to be exclusively state issues. Most notably, Congress now regulates for the general welfare of the people. The power to regulate health, welfare, and security is known as the **police power**. The framers rejected a national police power at the Philadephia Convention in favor of leaving such subjects to the states.

Chief Justice Marshall acknowledged that the police powers rested with the states in *McCulloch v. Maryland,*[24] wherein he announced the **pretext principle**. Marshall, writing for the Court, stated that Congress could enact no law under one of its enumerated powers when its true intent was to regulate a subject that belonged to the states.

Today, the pretext principle has been rendered a dead letter because the Court generally refuses to examine the motives of Congress. That body is now free, so long as a connection to interstate commerce can be established, to regulate for welfare purposes[25]; Congress is no longer limited to strictly commercial concerns. Accordingly, a host of labor laws have been approved, including child labor and occupational safety regulations. The test is whether the statute bears a rational relationship to its objective. If so, it is constitutional. This is not a hard test to satisfy.

Affectation and Cumulative Affects

To what extent must an intrastate regulation relate to commerce to be subject to federal control? In a few early cases, the Court restricted Congress to regulating activities that directly affected interstate commerce. However, since the late 1930s, the power of Congress to regulate activities that indirectly affect interstate commerce has increased. It is through this **affectation doctrine** that Congress often regulates for the general welfare.

TERMS

police power [†] 1. The power of government to make and enforce laws and regulations necessary to maintain and enhance the public welfare and to prevent individuals from violating the rights of others. 2. The sovereignty of each of the states of the United States that is not surrendered to the federal government under the Constitution.

pretext principle A law that is enacted by Congress supposedly under one of its enumerated powers, when the law's true purpose is to regulate a subject belonging to the states, is invalid. Today, the affectation doctrine has made the pretext principle of little significance.

affectation doctrine Rule that provides Congress with authority to regulate intrastate activities that affect interstate commerce. Even though individual

When considering whether an activity indirectly affects interstate commerce, Congress may consider the cumulative effects of seemingly local activity. That is, even though an individual's act may not affect interstate commerce, the cumulative effect of all people who engage in the activity may affect interstate commerce. If so, Congress may regulate the activity. This is the legal issue discussed in *Wickard v. Filburn.*

The following are other examples of congressional regulations approved by the Supreme Court:

1. Congress may regulate surface mining because coal travels in interstate commerce and the environmental effects of the activity may stretch beyond one state.[26]

2. Congress may prohibit discriminatory practices by hotels because such practices affect the interstate travel of black people. The claim that the law was neither moral legislation nor commercial legislation was rejected. The motive of Congress in enacting a regulation under the commerce clause is not material. The issue is whether the activity regulated is interstate in character. If so, the regulation is valid.[27]

3. A locally owned and operated restaurant that served only intrastate customers was subject to federal civil rights laws requiring that it serve black persons because some of the food it served had traveled in interstate commerce.[28]

The Outer Limit

For over sixty years the Supreme Court did not invalidate one act of Congress as exceeding federal authority under the commerce clause. It appeared as though there was no limit to what Congress could regulate, especially in a nation where virtually every enterprise, no matter how small, has contact with people or goods that travel in interstate commerce. And Congress has used its commerce power extensively. Through the commerce clause, Congress regulates the environment, poverty, cyberspace, and criminal matters.

In the criminal law arena, Congress now regulates crimes that once were thought to be local. The Mann Act criminalizes the interstate movement of women for immoral purposes.[29] Movement between states in order to commit domestic violence, including violating protective orders, is a federal crime.[30] The Uniform Flight to Avoid Prosecution Act

TERMS

activity may not affect interstate commerce, the total effect of all individuals who engage in the activity may affect interstate commerce and provide Congress with the jurisdiction to regulate the activity.

WICKARD v. FILBURN
317 U.S. 111 (1942)

[The defendant farmer was penalized $117 for violating the Agricultural Adjustment Act, which set a quota on wheat production. Farmers were prohibited from producing more wheat than allotted. The defendant (Filburn) was a dairy farmer and raised wheat primarily to feed his family and livestock. The defendant sought an injunction prohibiting the Secretary of Agriculture (Wickard) from enforcing the penalty.]

Mr. Justice Jackson delivered the opinion of the Court ... .

It is urged that under the Commerce Clause, [Congress] does not possess the power it has in this instance sought to exercise. The question would merit little consideration but for that this Act extends federal regulation to production not intended in any part to form commerce but wholly for consumption on the farm. [The quotas at issue] not only embrace all that may be sold without penalty but also what may be consumed on the premises. ...

Appellee says that this is a regulation of production and consumption of wheat. Such activities are, he urges, beyond the reach of Congressional power under the Commerce Clause, since they are local in nature, and their effects upon interstate commerce are at most "indirect." In answer the Government argues that the statute regulates neither production nor consumption, but only marketing; and, in the alternative, that if the Act does go beyond the regulation of marketing it is sustainable as a "necessary and proper" implementation of the power of Congress over interstate commerce. ... [The Court reviewed the precedents in the area, including cases requiring activities to directly affect interstate commerce if they are to come under federal authority.]

The Court's recognition of the relevance of the economic effects in the application of the Commerce Clause exemplified by the statement has made the mechanical application of legal formulas no longer feasible. Once an economic measure of the reach of the power granted to Congress in the Commerce Clause is accepted, questions of federal power cannot be decided simply by finding the activity in question to be "production," nor can consideration of its economic effects be foreclosed by calling them "indirect." ... Whether the subject of the regulation in question was "production," "consumption," or "marketing" is, therefore, not material for purposes of deciding the question of federal power before us. That an activity is of local character may help in a doubtful case to determine whether Congress intended to reach it. ... But even if appellee's activity be local and though it may not be regarded as commerce, it may still, whatever its nature, be reached by Congress if it exerts a substantial economic effect on interstate commerce and this irrespective of whether such effect is what might at some earlier time have been defined as "direct" or "indirect."

The parties have stipulated a summary of the economics of the wheat industry. Commerce among the states in wheat is large and important. Although wheat is raised in every state but one, production in most states is not equal to consumption. ...

The wheat industry has been a problem industry for some years. Largely as a result of increased foreign production and import restrictions, annual exports of wheat and flour from the United States during the ten-year period ending in 1940 averaged less than 10 per cent of total production, while during the 1920's they averaged more than 25 per cent. The decline in the export trade has left a large surplus in production which in connection with an abnormally large supply of other grains in recent years caused congestion in a number of markets; tied up railroad cars; and caused elevators in some instances to turn away grains, and railroads to institute embargoes to prevent further congestion. ...

The effect of consumption of homegrown wheat on interstate commerce is due to the fact that it constitutes the most variable factor in the disappearance of the wheat crop. Consumption on the farm where grown appears to vary in the amount greater than 20 per cent of average production.

The total amount of wheat consumed as food varies but relatively little, and use as seed is relatively constant.

The maintenance by government regulation of a price for wheat undoubtedly can be accomplished as effectively by sustaining or increasing the demand as by limiting the supply. The effect of the statute before us is to restrict the amount which may be produced for market and the extent as well to which one may forestall resort to the market by producing to meet his own needs. That appellee's own contribution to the demand for wheat may be trivial by itself is not enough to remove him from the scope of federal regulation where, as here, his contribution, taken together with that of many others similarly situated, is far from trivia. ...

Home grown wheat in this sense competes with wheat in commerce. The stimulation of commerce is a use of the regulatory function quite as definitely as prohibitions or restrictions thereon. This record leaves us in no doubt that Congress may properly have considered that wheat consumed on the farm where grown is wholly outside the scheme of regulation would have a substantial effect in defeating and obstructing [Congress's] purpose to stimulate trade therein at increased prices.

makes flight from one state to another to avoid prosecution of a state crime a federal offense.[31] It is unlawful for certain persons to transport firearms in interstate commerce.[32] The transportation of children in interstate commerce for immoral purposes and the interstate transportation of child pornography are both federal crimes.[33] The Consumer Credit Protection Act, which applies to local extortionate credit transactions (loan-sharking), was upheld on the theory that the cumulative effect of all loan-sharking affects interstate commerce.[34] Congress criminalized carjacking in 1992 in a law codified as 18 U.S.C. § 2119. That statute provides that "whoever, with the intent to cause death or serious bodily harm takes a motor vehicle that has been transported, shipped, or received in interstate or foreign commerce from ... another by force or violence or by intimidation" has committed a federal crime. The law has been upheld as a valid exercise of the commerce power by at least one appellate court.[35]

Unquestionably, these laws are motivated by health and welfare, not commercial, concerns. Again, the Court made it clear in *Heart of Atlanta Motel* and other cases that Congress may exercise police powers. In addition, it also appeared that there was no genuine requirement of affectation; that is, no true connection between interstate commerce and the regulation appeared to be required. This changed with the 1995 decision in *United States v. Lopez*.

Lopez was the first case since the 1940s in which a statute was invalidated as extending federal power under the commerce clause too far. It teaches that there must be a genuine connection between commerce and a regulation before Congress may act. The Court's decision was that the possession of a gun near a school is simply not a commercial activity. Thus, Congress had no authority to regulate it. Remember,

UNITED STATES v. LOPEZ
115 S. Ct. 1624 (1995)

Chief Justice Rehnquist delivered the opinion of the Court.

In the Gun-Free School Zone Act of 1990, Congress made it a federal offense "for any individual knowingly to possess a firearm at [a] place that the individual knows, or has reasonable cause to believe, is a school zone." ... The Act neither regulates a commercial activity nor contains a requirement that the possession be connected in any way to interstate commerce. We hold that the Act exceeds the authority of Congress "[t]o regulate Commerce ... among the several states ... ." U.S. Const., Art. I, § 8, cl. 3.

On March 10, 1992, respondent, who was then a 12th-grade student, arrived at Edison High School in San Antonio, Texas, carrying a concealed .38 caliber handgun and live bullets. Acting upon an anonymous tip, school authorities confronted respondent, who admitted that he was carrying the weapon. He was arrested and charged under Texas law with firearm possession on school premises. ... The next day, the state charges were dismissed after federal agents charged respondent by complaint with violating the Gun-Free School Zone Act of 1990. ... [The defendant was indicted and moved to dismiss the indictment on the ground that the statute was beyond congressional powers. The district court denied the motion and the appellate court reversed the trial court conviction.]

We start with first principles. The Constitution creates a Federal Government of enumerated powers. ... As James Madison wrote, "[t]he powers delegated by the proposed Constitution to the federal government are few and defined. Those which are to remain in the State governments are numerous and indefinite. *The Federalist* No. 45. ... This constitutionally mandated division of authority "was adopted by the Framers to ensure protection of our fundamental liberties." ... [The Court then summarized the history of its commerce clause decisions].

Consistent with this structure, we have identified three broad categories of activity that Congress may regulate under its commerce power. ... First, Congress may regulate the use of the channels of interstate commerce. ... Second, Congress is empowered to regulate and protect the instrumentalities of interstate commerce, or persons or things in interstate commerce, even though the threat may come only from intrastate activities. ... Finally, commerce authority includes the power to regulate those activities having a substantial relation to interstate commerce, ... i.e., those activities that substantially affect interstate commerce. ...

Within the final category, admittedly, our case law has not been clear whether an activity must "affect" or "substantially affect" interstate commerce in order to be within Congress' power to regulate it under the Commerce Clause. ... We conclude, consistent with the great weight of our case law, that the proper test requires an analysis of whether the regulated activity "substantially affects" interstate commerce.

We now turn to consider the power of Congress, in the light of this framework, to [en]act [the Gun-Free School Zone Law]. The first two categories of authority may be quickly disposed of: [the statute] is not a regulation of the use of the channels of interstate commerce, nor is it an attempt to prohibit the interstate transportation of [a] commodity through the channels of commerce; nor can [the statute] be justified as a regulation by which Congress has sought to protect an instrumentality of interstate commerce or a thing in interstate commerce. Thus, if [the statute] is to be sustained, it must be under the third category as a regulation of an activity that substantially affects interstate commerce.

First, we have upheld a wide variety of congressional Acts regulating intrastate economic activity where we have concluded that the activity substantially affected interstate commerce. Examples include the regulation of intrastate coal mining ... instrastate extortionate credit transactions ... restaurants utilizing substantial interstate supplies ... and production and consumption of home-grown wheat. These examples are by no means exhaustive, but the pattern is clear. Where economic activity substantially affects interstate commerce, legislation regulating that activity will be sustained.

Even *Wickard,* which is perhaps the most far reaching example of Commerce Clause authority over intrastate activity, involved economic activity in a way that the possession of a gun in a school zone does not. ...

[The gun-free zone law] is a criminal statute that by its terms has nothing to do with "commerce" or any sort of economic enterprise, however broadly one might define those terms. [The statute] is not an essential part of a larger regulation of economic activity, in which the regulatory scheme could be undercut unless the intrastate activity were regulated. It cannot, therefore, be sustained under our cases upholding regulations of activities that arise out of or are connected with a commercial transaction, which viewed in the aggregate, substantially affects interstate commerce. ...

Second, [the statute] contains no jurisdictional elements which would ensure, through case-by-case inquiry, that the firearm possession in question affects interstate commerce. For example, ... 18 U.S.C. § 1202(a), which made it a crime for a felon to "receiv[e], posses[s], or transpor[t] in commerce or affecting commerce ... any firearm." ... The Court interpreted the possession component of § 1202(a) to require an additional nexus to interstate commerce both because the statute was ambiguous and because "unless Congress conveys its purpose clearly, it will not be deemed to have significantly changed the federal-state balance." ... The [Court in a case arising under § 1202(a)] set aside the conviction because although the Government had demonstrated that [the defendant] had possessed a firearm, it had failed "to show the interpreted statute to reserve the constitutional question whether Congress could regulate, without more, the 'mere possession' of firearms." ... Unlike the statute in [this prior case], [the gun-free school zone statute] has no express jurisdictional element which might limit its reach to a discrete set of firearm possessions that additionally have an explicit connection with or effect on interstate commerce. ...

The Government argues that possession of a firearm in a school zone may result in violent crime and that violent crime can be expected to affect the functioning of the national economy in two ways. First, the costs of violent crime are substantial, and, through the mechanism of insurance, those costs are spread throughout the population. ... Second, violent crime reduces the willingness of individuals to travel to areas within the country that are perceived to be unsafe. ... The Government also argues that the presence of guns in schools poses a substantial threat to the educational process by threatening the learning environment. A handicapped educational process, in turn, will result in a less productive citizenry. That, in turn, would have an adverse effect on the Nation's economic well-being. ...

We pause to consider the implications of the Government's arguments. The Government admits, under its "costs of crime" reasoning, that Congress could regulate not only all violent crime, but all activities that might lead to violent crime, regardless of how tenuously they relate to interstate commerce. ... Similarly, under the Government's "national productivity" reasoning, Congress could regulate any activity that it found was related to the economic productivity of individual citizens: family law ... for example. Under the theories that the Government presents in support of [the statute], it is difficult to perceive any limitation on federal power, even in areas such as criminal law enforcement or education where States historically have been sovereign. Thus, if we were to accept the Government's arguments, we are hard-pressed to posit any activity by an individual that Congress is without power to regulate. ...

For instance, if Congress can, pursuant to its Commerce Clause power, regulate activities that adversely affect the learning environment, then, a fortiori, it also can regulate the educational process directly. Congress could determine that a school's curriculum has a "significant" effect on the extent of classroom learning. As a result, Congress could mandate a federal curriculum for local elementary and secondary schools because what is taught in local schools has a significant "effect on classroom learning" ... and that, in turn, has a substantial effect on interstate commerce. ...

We do not doubt that Congress has authority under the Commerce Clause to regulate numerous commercial activities that substantially affect interstate commerce and also affect the educational process. That authority, though broad, does not include the authority to regulate each and every aspect of local schools.

Admittedly, a determination whether an intrastate activity is commercial or noncommercial may in some cases result in legal uncertainty. But, so long as Congress' authority is limited to those powers enumerated in the Constitution, and so long as those enumerated powers are interpreted as having judicially enforceable outer limits, congressional legislation under the Commerce Clause will always engender "legal uncertainty." ...

These are not precise formulations, and in the nature of things they cannot be. But we think they point the way to a correct decision of this case. The possession of a gun in a local school zone is in no sense an economic activity that might, through repetition elsewhere, substantially affect any sort of interstate commerce. Respondent was a local student at a local school; there is no indication that he had recently moved in interstate commerce, and there is no requirement that his possession of the firearm have any concrete tie to interstate commerce.

To uphold the Government's contentions here, we would have to pile inference upon inference in a manner that would bid fair to convert congressional authority under the Commerce Clause to a general police power of the sort retained to the States. Admittedly, some of our prior cases have taken long steps down that road, giving great deference to congressional action. ... The broad language in these opinions has suggested the possibility of additional expansion, but we decline here to proceed any further. ...

For the foregoing reasons the judgment of the Court of Appeals is Affirmed.

this decision does not forbid the *states* from creating gun-free school zones. States have the authority to enact such laws under their general police powers. The *Lopez* Court identified the things over which Congress may exercise jurisdiction under the commerce clause:

1. The channels of interstate commerce.
2. The instrumentalities of interstate commerce, or persons or things in interstate commerce, even though the threat may come only from intrastate activities.
3. Those activities having a substantial relation to interstate commerce, i.e, those activities that substantially affect interstate commerce.

Lopez was concerned with the third category, and the Court made it clear that an activity cannot be regulated unless it *substantially* affects interstate commerce. The cumulative effect an intrastate activity has on interstate activity can continue to be the basis of federal power, however.

Generally, Congress uses two models to assert its interstate commerce power. First, Congress can make a finding of interstate character for an entire class of cases. For example, in committee reports and a piece of legislation itself, Congress can indicate that it has determined that an activity "substantially affects" interstate commerce. Second, Congress can require that the commerce requirement be satisfied on a case-by-case basis. That is, the elements of a crime or civil action may include an interstate connection, such as requiring proof that drugs have traveled in interstate commerce before allowing federal prosecution for their transportation or sale.

Congressional power under the commerce clause is broad. As the nation and world grow more closely connected, more activities will become subject to federal regulation. *Lopez* teaches, however, that a true nexus between commerce and a regulated activity must exist. If an activity is not commercial and is entirely intrastate in character, its regulation belongs entirely to the states.

The impact of *Lopez* on federal jurisdiction remains to be seen. As of the close of 1995, most lower courts that examined existing federal statutes upheld them. For example, the federal carjacking statute, which criminalizes the forcible taking of an automobile that has been transported, shipped, or received in interstate commerce, was upheld.[36] See Figure 5-2 for a summary of the elements of the congressional commerce power.

FEDERAL COMMERCE POWER—SUMMARY

Article I, § 8, clause 3 provides that Congress shall have the power to "regulate Commerce with foreign Nations, and among the several States, and with the Indian Tribes."

This power may be exercised over:

1. The channels of interstate commerce

2. The instrumentalities of interstate commerce

3. Persons or things in interstate commerce, even though from intrastate commerce

4. Activities having substantial relation to interstate commerce, including activities that substantially affect interstate commerce.

FIGURE 5-2 Federal Commerce Power—Summary

§ 5.6 Taxing, Spending, and Borrowing Powers

For most of the nation's early history, revenues were generated through customs laws (tariffs). Congress imposed the first income tax to finance the Civil War. Various taxes were imposed until the Supreme Court held the federal income tax unconstitutional in *Pollock v. Farmers Loan & Trust Co.*[37] Several proposals to amend the Constitution to allow a federal tax were proposed. One finally passed Congress and was ratified in 1913, as the Sixteenth Amendment. Today, the federal income tax is firmly established.

Other important constitutional provisions provide that Congress has the power to collect taxes and import duties and that all import duties must be uniform throughout the United States.[38] The Constitution also provides that there shall be no federal tax on articles exported from any state.[39]

One issue that the Court has had to deal with in the taxing area is whether Congress may use the federal taxing power to regulate for the general welfare of the people. The Court has generally approved of the use of the taxing power to achieve police power objectives. Again, the Tenth Amendment does not delegate this type of regulation to the states exclusively.

Other constitutional provisions act to limit the taxing power. For example, if a taxing requirement creates a "real and appreciable" possibility of incrimination by the taxpayer, then it is violative of the Fifth Amendment's protection against self-incrimination. Thus, a taxing statute that requires a taxpayer to disclose and pay taxes on money earned from illegal activity (e.g., sale of drugs), but does not protect the information from disclosure to law enforcement officials, is unconstitutional.

The power of Congress to spend is also found in the Constitution. Article I, § 8, clause 1, states that Congress shall have the power to "pay the Debts and provide for the common Defense and general Welfare of the United States." What is the limit of federal spending power? Unquestionably, Congress may spend in furtherance of any of its enumerated powers, such as its power over commerce. May it spend for the general welfare? Again, Congress has broad authority and appropriations will not be invalidated because they concern the general welfare.

Even more, the federal government has used its spending power to coerce the states into complying with federal policies, including those with police power objectives. It does this by attaching conditions to grants to states. If a state does not comply with the conditions, it loses the money. The national fifty-five-mile-per-hour speed limit was achieved in this manner.

This use of the spending power has been approved by the Supreme Court. In *South Dakota v. Dole*,[40] a federal law that withheld highway funds from states that did not prohibit the purchase and consumption of alcohol by individuals under twenty-one years of age was validated. The state objected, claiming that the repeal of Prohibition (Twenty-first amendment) provided the states with control over the issue and that Congress could not interfere. The Court rejected the claim, holding that even though Congress could not regulate the subject directly, it could do so indirectly through its taxing and spending powers. State claims that these conditional grants are violative of the Tenth Amendment have been consistently rejected.

The Constitution delegates other fiscal powers to Congress. The power to coin money belongs to the national government, as does the power to punish counterfeiters.[41] The power to coin money includes the power to establish national banks.[42] Congress may borrow money on behalf of the nation,[43] and is authorized to establish national bankruptcy laws.[44]

§ 5.7 International, War, and Military Powers

Congress and the President share powers over foreign, international, and military affairs. The Constitution does not specifically define what is presidential and what is congressional power. The relationship has been characterized as an "arena of conflict."

The Constitution does state that the President is the commander-in-chief of the military and is responsible for all forms of diplomacy, including the negotiation of treaties. These powers are balanced by the following powers that are expressly delegated to Congress in Article I, § 8:

1. Establishing duties and imports (clause 1).
2. Regulating commerce with foreign nations (clause 3).
3. Establishing uniform rules of naturalization (clause 4).
4. Punishing crimes on the high seas and offenses against the law of nations (clause 10).
5. Declaring war, granting letters of marque and reprisal, and making rules concerning captures on land and water (clause 11).

6. Establishing rules and regulations to govern the United States armed forces (clause 14).

7. Creating and regulating the national militia (clauses 15 and 16).

Article I, § 9, clause 1, provides that Congress shall regulate immigration.

These provisions are clear in delegating to Congress the authority to regulate commerce with foreign nations. Also, Congress alone possesses the power to declare war, although, in reality, presidents have initiated most military encounters without a congressional declaration of war. Congress regulates the military by creating the rules under which it operates, including disciplinary laws, but the President is the commander-in-chief. The relationship between the President and the Congress concerning war making is discussed in Chapter 6.

The power to declare war is much broader than simply making declarations. Congress is empowered to prepare the nation for war and to promote war efforts generally. Accordingly, Congress may demand conscription, seize industries and private property necessary to war efforts, close nonessential businesses, establish price controls and rent controls,[45] and ration foods and supplies. The internment of "enemy aliens" residing in the United States has also been approved by the Court.[46]

The war power extends to postwar recovery efforts as well. For example, laws encouraging the reemployment of returning service personnel would be permissible.

§ 5.8 Emergency Powers

In addition to the national military, the Constitution grants Congress the power to provide for the use of state militias (National Guard units) to suppress insurrections and defend the nation. In addition, Congress may regulate the organization, arming, and disciplining of state militias.[47] This includes delegating to the President the power to call militias into active duty outside the United States without the consent of state executive officials. Federal power is supreme in terms of military affairs.[48]

In times of unrest, Congress may declare martial law in the affected areas of the nation. Congress alone possesses the authority to suspend habeas corpus. Article I, § 9, clause 2 states that "[t]he privilege of the Writ of Habeas Corpus shall not be suspended, unless when in Cases of Rebellion or Invasion the Public Safety may require it."

The greater the emergency, the more governmental action may encroach upon civil liberties. For example, in *Korematsu v. United States,* the Supreme Court upheld the actions taken against Japanese-Americans during World War II.[49] Military officials, under the authority of statute and executive order, excluded Japanese-Americans from certain West Coast areas, established curfews, and interned many in camps. The action was justified, the Court said, by the fear of espionage, sabotage, West Coast invasion by the Japanese Empire, and the disloyalty by some persons of Japanese ancestry on the West Coast.

§ 5.9 Investigatory Powers

To acquire information about the subjects it regulates, Congress conducts investigations. Hearings are a part of the investigatory function. At congressional hearings, witnesses testify and other evidence is received. Hearings educate both members of Congress and the public. The data received are often incorporated into the official record (committee reports, etc.) and are sometimes considered by courts when deciding legislative intent.

Although not expressly stated in the Constitution, a power to conduct hearings is implied in the legislative power. Further, the power to subpoena witnesses, documents, and other evidence is held by both houses of Congress. This power may be delegated to committees and subcommittees.

The power to subpoena carries enforcement powers with it. Recalcitrant witnesses can be held in contempt and jailed by Congress. Congress may conduct the contempt trial and punish witnesses without referring the matter to a court. Regardless, Congress has enacted a statute providing that its contempt cases are to be referred to a federal court for disposition. Once referred, a defendant is entitled to all the rights and privileges afforded any criminal defendant in federal court, even if the right would not have been extended to the defendant if tried by Congress. Today, Congress may punish a contemnor under either its inherent power or this statute.

In addition to punishing witnesses who refuse to testify, Congress may punish other misbehaviors as well. Disruption of congressional proceedings and perjury are examples.

There are limitations upon the congressional investigatory power and, accordingly, its contempt power. First, Congress may not extend an investigation into a matter over which it has no authority to regulate.

Therefore, attempts to expose the private affairs of individuals when there is no possibility of producing legislation is unlawful. However, Congress does have the authority to investigate corruption and incompetence in the other branches.[50]

Second, a committee can punish a witness for refusing to testify only if the appropriate house of Congress has authorized the committee to investigate the subject at issue. Subcommittees must be empowered by the full committee which is empowered by the house.

Third, certain constitutional rights limit the congressional investigatory power. The privilege against self-incrimination, found in the Fifth Amendment, limits the authority of Congress to extract information from witnesses. The committee may inquire into why a defendant believes that his testimony is potentially incriminating in order to determine whether a claim is legitimate. A committee may not, however, demand that a question be answered in order to determine its legitimacy. Also, a Fifth Amendment claim may be overcome by providing **use immunity** to a witness.

The First Amendment also restricts the power of Congress to investigate. Generally, Congress may not punish a witness for refusing to answer questions concerning speech, religion, political beliefs, or association. However, if the public interest in obtaining the information outweighs the individual's interest in nondisclosure, a witness can be compelled to testify. In one case, for example, a witness was legitimately required to answer inquiries about his Communist Party affiliations.[51]

The Fourth Amendment's protection against unreasonable searches and seizures applies to congressional investigations. Therefore, a subpoena that is not supported by probable cause, is overly broad, or is otherwise unreasonable is invalid.

Of course, the due process clause of the Fifth Amendment requires that all actions by investigatory committees be fair. Questions must be clear, what is required of a potential contemnor-witness must be articulated, and the witness should be advised that a refusal to answer may lead to a contempt citation.

Finally, the power of Congress to investigate is limited by structural and institutional forces. Separation of powers principles prevent congressional investigations that delve into matters belonging exclusively to the executive or judicial branches. For example, Congress may not investigate individual court cases. Congress may investigate such cases when considering larger issues, such as whether tort reform is necessary.

TERMS

---

use immunity[†] A guaranty given a person that if he or she testifies against others, his or her testimony will not be used against him or her if he or she is prosecuted for ... involvement in the crime.

§ 5.10 Confirmation and Impeachment Powers

Appointment and Confirmation

The President, Vice-President, and members of Congress are elected officials. Lower executive officials, such as Cabinet members and ambassadors, are appointed. Federal judges are also appointed. The appointment process includes Presidential nomination and Senate confirmation. Or, in the words of the Constitution, the President shall "nominate ... by and with the Advice and Consent of the Senate."[52]

What role the Senate should play in the appointment process is hotly debated. Some commentators would restrain the Senate's role to objective evaluation of the nominee's qualifications and character. According to this view, if a nominee is of good character and is qualified, she should be confirmed regardless of her political beliefs. Other people believe that the Senate should play a more active role and that it may appropriately consider a nominee's political beliefs. In the context of judicial nominations, the issue is whether a judge possesses the favored legal philosophy. The history of the appointments clause sheds little light on the subject and the issue is not likely to be resolved soon.

In recent years, the process has been politicized. The confirmation hearings of Robert Bork (not confirmed to the Supreme Court because he was perceived as too legally conservative), Douglas Ginsburg (nomination to Supreme Court withdrawn after he admitted to marijuana use), Clarence Thomas (confirmed as Associate Justice after controversial hearings wherein he was accused of sexual harassment), and Dr. Henry Foster (confirmed as Surgeon General after a controversy centering around abortion) are examples.

Impeachment

Once confirmed, most executive employees may be removed by the President. In addition, they may be removed by **impeachment**. Other than death and retirement, impeachment is the only method of removing a federal judge. (Figure 5-3 illustrates the impeachment process.)

TERMS

impeachment[†]   The constitutional process by which high elected officers of the United States, including the president, may be removed from office. The accusation (articles of impeachment) is made by the House of

FIGURE 5-3
The
Impeachment
Process

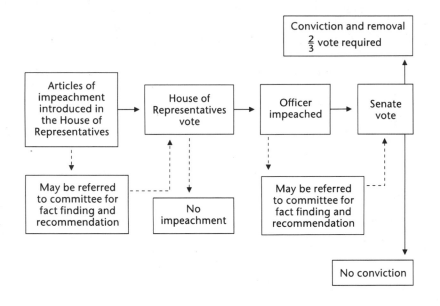

IMPEACHMENT PROCESS

Article II, § 4, provides that the President, Vice President, and all civil officers of the United States shall be removed from office on impeachment for, and conviction of, treason, bribery, or other high crimes and misdemeanors.

Article III, § 1, states that federal judges shall hold their offices during times of good behavior.

Article I, § 2, vests the power of impeachment in the House of Representatives.

Article I, § 3, vests the power to try impeachment cases in the Senate. Article III, § 2, makes it clear that there is *no* right to a jury in impeachment cases.

Conviction and removal
$\frac{2}{3}$ vote required

Articles of impeachment introduced in the House of Representatives → House of Representatives vote → Officer impeached → Senate vote

May be referred to committee for fact finding and recommendation

No impeachment

May be referred to committee for fact finding and recommendation

No conviction

This procedure may occur prior to, after, or simultaneous with any related criminal trial of the officer.

TERMS

Representatives and tried by the Senate, which sits as an impeachment court. Under the Constitution, the grounds for impeachment are "treason, bribery, or other high crimes and misdemeanors."

Article I, § 2, clause 5, vests the power of impeachment in the House of Representatives, and Article I, § 3, clause 6, gives the Senate the responsibility of trying impeachment cases. *Impeachment* is a charge against a public official. Conviction in impeachment cases results in removal from public office. Technically, an official is impeached once charged by the House of Representatives. In common usage, though, the term is used to describe the removal of public officials who have been convicted in the Senate.

The House and Senate may delegate the responsibility of conducting impeachment investigations and hearing evidence to committees. The Constitution requires that a vote of the full house be taken, and a two-thirds majority is required for conviction in the Senate. Impeachment decisions are political questions and are not reviewable by courts. *See Nixon v. United States*, a case involving an impeached and convicted federal judge, in Chapter 4 for a discussion of the political question doctrine in this context. Also, see Figure 5-4 for the actual articles of impeachment against President Nixon, as recommended by the House Judiciary Committee in July 1974.

Famous Impeachments   SIDEBAR

Two of the most famous impeachments in the United States were those of Justice Samuel Chase and President Andrew Johnson. Samuel Chase was impeached by the House of Representatives in 1805. Samuel Chase, a Federalist, had a history of service to the nation. In addition to serving as a Supreme Court Justice, he was a signer of the Declaration of Independence. Justice Chase, while acting as a district judge, made statements from the bench attacking Antifederalist (republican) policies. Eight charges were brought against Justice Chase arising from these statements. His Senate trial lasted one month. He was acquitted by one vote. Interestingly, Aaron Burr, the Vice President of the United States, presided over Chase's trial. At the time of the trial, Aaron Burr was under indictment in two states (New York and New Jersey) for the death of Alexander Hamilton, whom he killed in a duel. Aaron Burr was later tried and acquitted. Both he and Chase were represented by the same lawyer, Luther Martin.

President Andrew Johnson was impeached by the House of Representatives in 1868. Johnson had been President Lincoln's Vice President and assumed the presidency upon Lincoln's assassination. Johnson's reconstruction program was bitterly opposed by Republican members of Congress. Two bills that had the effect of limiting presidential power were vetoed by Johnson. Both vetoes were overridden by two-thirds majorities in both houses. One was the Tenure of Office Act, which restricted the President's power to remove federal officials. When Johnson attempted to remove the Secretary of War, Edwin Stanton, who was a Republican sympathizer, the House of Representatives impeached Johnson. Eleven articles of impeachment were filed, most involving the removal of Stanton. On the first charge, Johnson prevailed by one vote. The Senate adjourned for ten days and

ARTICLES OF IMPEACHMENT AGAINST PRESIDENT RICHARD M. NIXON RECOMMENDED BY THE HOUSE JUDICIARY COMMITTEE

Resolved, That Richard M. Nixon, President of the United States, is impeached for high crimes and misdemeanors, and that the following articles of impeachment be exhibited to the Senate:

Articles of impeachment exhibited by the House of Representatives of the United States of America in the name of itself and of all of the people of the United States of America, against Richard M. Nixon, President of the United States of America, in maintenance and support of its impeachment against him for high crimes and misdemeanors.

Article I

In his conduct of the office of President of the United States, Richard M. Nixon, in violation of his constitutional oath faithfully to execute the office of President of the United States and, to the best of his ability, preserve, protect, and defend the Constitution of the United States, and in violation of his constitutional duty to take care that the laws be faithfully executed, has prevented, obstructed, and impeded the administration of justice, in that:

On June 17, 1972, and prior thereto, agents of the Committee for the Re-election of the President committed unlawful entry of the headquarters of the Democratic National Committee in Washington, District of Columbia, for the purpose of securing political intelligence. Subsequent thereto, Richard M. Nixon, using the powers of his high office, engaged, personally and through his subordinates and agents, in a course of conduct or plan designed to delay, impede, and obstruct the investigation of such unlawful entry; to cover up, conceal and protect those responsible; and to conceal the existence and scope of other unlawful covert activities.

The means used to implement this course of conduct or plan included one or more of the following:

1. Making or causing to be made false or misleading statements to lawfully authorized investigative officers and employees of the United States.

2. Withholding relevant and material evidence of information from lawfully authorized investigative officers and employees of the United States.

3. Approving, condoning, acquiescing in, and counseling witnesses with respect to the giving of false or misleading statements to lawfully authorized investigative officers and employees of the United States and false or misleading testimony in duly instituted judicial and congressional proceedings;

4. Interfering or endeavoring to interfere with the conduct of investigations by the Department of Justice of the United States, the Federal Bureau of Investigation, the Office of Watergate Special Prosecution Force, and Congressional committees;

5. Approving, condoning, and acquiescing in, the surreptitious payment of substantial sums of money for the purpose of obtaining the silence or

FIGURE 5-4 Articles of Impeachment Against President Richard M. Nixon

influencing the testimony of witnesses, potential witnesses or individuals who participated in such illegal entry and other illegal activities;

6. Endeavoring to misuse the Central Intelligence Agency, an agency of the United States;

7. Disseminating information received from officers of the Department of Justice of the United States to subjects of investigations conducted by lawfully authorized investigative officers and employees of the United States, for the purpose of aiding and assisting such subjects in their attempts to avoid criminal liability;

8. Making false or misleading public statements for the purpose of deceiving the people of the United States into believing that a thorough and complete investigation had been conducted with respect to allegations of misconduct on the part of personnel of the executive branch of the United States and personnel of the Committee for the Re-election of the President, and that there was no involvement of such personnel in such misconduct; or

9. Endeavoring to cause prospective defendants, and individuals duly tried and convicted, to expect favored treatment and consideration in return for their silence or false testimony, or rewarding individuals for their silence or false testimony.

In all of this, Richard M. Nixon has acted in a manner contrary to his trust as President and subversive of constitutional government, to the great prejudice of the cause of law and justice and to the manifest injury of the people of the United States.

Wherefore Richard M. Nixon, by such conduct, warrants impeachment and trial, and removal from office.

Article II

Using the powers of the office of president of the United States, Richard M. Nixon, in violation of his constitutional oath faithfully to execute the office of president of the United States and, to the best of his ability, preserve, protect and defend the Constitution of the United States, and in disregard of his constitutional duty to take care that the laws be faithfully executed, has repeatedly engaged in conduct violating the constitutional rights of citizens, impairing the due and proper administration of justice and the conduct of lawful inquiries, or contravening the laws governing agencies of the executive branch and the purposes of these agencies.

This conduct has included one or more of the following:

1. He has, acting personally and through his subordinates and agents, endeavored to obtain from the Internal Revenue Service, in violation of the constitutional rights of citizens, confidential information contained in income tax returns for purposes not authorized by law and to cause, in violation of the constitutional rights of citizens, income tax audits or other income tax investigations to be initiated or conducted in a discriminatory manner.

FIGURE 5-4 *(continued)*

2. He misused the Federal Bureau of Investigation, the Secret Service and other executive personnel in violation or disregard of the constitutional rights of citizens by directing or authorizing such agencies or personnel to conduct or continue electronic surveillance or other investigations for purposes unrelated to national security, the enforcement of laws or any other lawful function of his office; and he did direct the concealment of certain records made by the Federal Bureau of Investigation of electronic surveillance.

3. He has, acting personally and through his subordinates and agents, in violation or disregard of the constitutional rights of citizens, authorized and permitted to be maintained a secret investigative unit within the office of the president, financed in part with money derived from campaign contributions to him, which unlawfully utilized the resources of the Central Intelligence Agency, engaged in covert and unlawful activities and attempted to prejudice the constitutional right of an accused to a fair trial.

4. He has failed to take care that the laws were faithfully executed by failing to act when he knew or had reason to know that his close subordinates endeavored to impede and frustrate lawful inquiries by duly constituted executive, judicial and legislative entities concerning the unlawful entry into the headquarters of the Democratic National Committee and the cover-up thereof, and concerning other unlawful activities including those relating to the confirmation of Richard Kleindienst as attorney general of the United States, the electronic surveillance of private citizens, the break-in into the office of Dr. Lewis Fielding and the campaign financing practices of the Committee to Re-elect the President.

5. In disregard of the rule of law, he knowingly misused the executive power by interfering with agencies of the executive branch, including the Federal Bureau of Investigation, the Criminal Division and the Office of Watergate Special Prosecution Force, of the Department of Justice and the Central Intelligence Agency, in violation of his duty to take care that the laws be faithfully executed.

In all of this, Richard M. Nixon has acted in a manner contrary to his trust as president and subversive of constitutional government, to the great prejudice of the cause of law and justice and to the manifest injury of the people of the United States.

Wherefore Richard M. Nixon, by such conduct, warrants impeachment and trial and removal from office.

Article III

In his conduct of the office of president of the United States, Richard M. Nixon, contrary to his oath faithfully to execute the office of president of the United States and, to the best of his ability, preserve, protect and defend the Constitution of the United States, and in violation of his constitutional duty to take care that the laws be faithfully executed, has failed without lawful cause or excuse to produce papers and things as directed by duly authorized subpoenas issued by the Committee on the Judiciary of the House of Representatives on April 11,

FIGURE 5-4   *(continued)*

1974; May 15, 1974; May 30, 1974, and June 24, 1974, and willfully disobeyed such subpoenas.

The subpoenaed papers and things were deemed necessary by the committee in order to resolve by direct evidence fundamental, factual questions relating to presidential direction, knowledge or approval of actions demonstrated by other evidence to be substantial grounds for impeachment of the president.

In refusing to produce these papers and things Richard M. Nixon, substituting his judgment as to what materials were necessary for the inquiry, interposed the powers of the presidency against the lawful subpoenas of the House of Representatives, thereby assuming to himself functions and judgments necessary to the exercise of the sole power of impeachment vested by the Constitution in the House of Representatives.

In all of this, Richard M. Nixon has acted in a manner contrary to his trust as president and subversive of constitutional government, to the great prejudice of the cause of law and justice and to the manifest injury of the people of the United States.

Wherefore, Richard M. Nixon by such conduct, warrants impeachment and trial and removal from office.

* * *

FIGURE 5-4 *(continued)*

when it reconvened votes on the second and third articles were taken. Johnson was again acquitted. The impeachment was abandoned and votes were never held on the remaining articles.

These two impeachment trials stand as evidence that impeachment is intended, as the Constitution states, for high crimes and misdemeanors. The impeachments of both Chase and Johnson were politically motivated. Today, it is accepted, in part because of the failures in these cases, that public officials may not be impeached for political reasons. Rather, the political remedy lies in the ballot box.

Sources: William Rehnquist, *Grand Inquests* (William Morrow 1992); Gene Smith, *High Crimes and Misdemeanors* (William Morrow 1977).

Article II, § 4, provides that the "President, Vice-President and all civil Officers of the United States shall be removed from Office on Impeachment for, and Conviction of Treason, Bribery, or other high Crimes and Misdemeanors." In addition to the President and Vice President, any federal officer who undergoes the nomination and confirmation process may be impeached. This includes ambassadors, Cabinet officers, and judges. Members of Congress may not be impeached, as they are not "civil officers." They are subject to exclusion and expulsion, however, by their house.

What qualifies as a high crime or misdemeanor is not well defined. It is generally believed that this phrase includes more than violations of criminal law. Said another way, Congress decides what a high crime or misdemeanor is without any necessary reference to the criminal laws. Article II, § 2, clause 1, exempts impeachments from the pardon power of the President.

Article I, § 3, clause 7, limits the power of impeachment to removal from office. It further provides that "the Party convicted shall nevertheless be liable and subject to Indictment, Trial, Judgment, and Punishment, according to Law." Alcee Hastings, a federal judge, was acquitted of crimes before he was impeached. He appealed his conviction, claiming that the Constitution requires removal before criminal trial. His claim was rejected by the appellate court.[53] The two events may occur in any order and at any time.

Between the adoption of the Constitution and 1994, there were seventeen impeachments, including one President, one senator, a Supreme Court Justice, and twelve lower court judges.[54] Not all the impeached officials were convicted. President Andrew Johnson, for example, was impeached but not convicted. The same is true of the only justice impeached, Samuel Chase. President Richard Nixon resigned after articles of impeachment were introduced in the House but before they were acted upon. (See Figure 5-3.) Of the thirteen federal judges impeached, only seven were convicted.

Conviction of an official prior to removal creates interesting legal and political problems. District judge Harry Claiborne was convicted of tax fraud and sentenced to two years in prison. He refused to resign and was imprisoned for five months before Congress removed him from office. He was the first sitting federal judge to be imprisoned. The possible legal problems presented by having a federal judge incarcerated in a federal prison are obvious. On the political side, federal judges who are not removed, but are convicted of crimes and sentenced to prison, continue to receive their pay and benefits. Although constitutionally required, such circumstances engender public disrespect for the judiciary and government generally.

§ 5.11 Initiation of Constitutional Amendments

Article 5 of the Constitution states, in part:

The Congress, whenever two thirds of both Houses shall deem it necessary, shall propose Amendments to this Constitution, or, on the

Application of the Legislatures of two thirds of the several States, shall call a Convention for proposing Amendments, which, in either Case, shall be valid to all Intents and Purposes, as part of this Constitution, when ratified by the Legislatures of three fourths of the several States, or by Conventions in three fourths thereof, as the one or the other Mode of Ratification may be proposed by the Congress ... .

Accordingly, there are two methods of initiating a constitutional amendment. Congressional resolution is the first. Two-thirds majorities in both houses of Congress are required. The President does not play a role in this process. Second, with two-thirds of the state legislatures or more, a convention can be convened to propose amendments. To date, initiation by Congress is the only method that has been successfully used to initiate amendments.

Regardless of which method of proposal is employed, Congress is empowered to decide the method of ratification. There are two methods: by concurrence of three-fourths of the state legislatures or by conventions in three-fourths of the states.

Congress holds considerable authority in the amendment process. It may establish a time limit for ratification of a proposal, regardless of the method of proposal, and it is empowered to decide whether an amendment has been ratified.

There are twenty-seven amendments to the Constitution. The twenty-seventh, ratified in 1992, provides that Congress may increase its pay in future congressional terms, but not in the present term. This amendment was part of the original twelve amendments of 1789. It and one other were not ratified, but the remaining ten were and are known as the Bill of Rights. No time limit was placed on ratification and the twenty-seventh now holds the record for longest ratification waiting period, having been ratified 203 years after its proposal.

The preceding amendment, the twenty-sixth, holds the opposite record; that is, its ratification was the fastest ever. The Twenty-sixth Amendment lowered the voting age in federal and state elections to eighteen. The amendment was, in part, a response to World War II, the Korean conflict, and a Supreme Court decision. Many Americans, including President Eisenhower and Senator Randolph (who had urged a change in law since WW II), believed that eighteen-year-old men who could die for their nation should be empowered to vote for their leaders. In 1970, Congress enacted legislation lowering the voting age to eighteen for both federal and state elections. The Supreme Court held, in *Oregon v. Mitchell*,[55] that Congress could lower the voting age for federal elections, but not state and local elections. Within three months of the Court's decision in *Oregon v. Mitchell,* an amendment was introduced in Congress to change the law established in that case. Three months after the proposal was sent to the states, the needed three-fourths of the states ratified the proposal. So, on June 30, 1971, the franchise was extended to eighteen-year-old citizens.[56]

By the mid 1990s, over 10,000 proposals to amend the Constitution had been introduced in Congress. Individual states have called for constitutional conventions over 400 times.[57] Proposals have scanned the spectrum, including over fifty proposals to prohibit polygamy; hundreds to prohibit abortion or to declare that life begins at conception; to prohibit duels; to mandate a balanced budget; to prohibit child labor; to allow school prayer; to change the name of the United States of America to the United States of the World[58]; and to establish a Court of the Union, comprised of state supreme court justices, that would have the authority to review and reverse Supreme Court decisions.[59]

Four amendments have been adopted to reverse constitutional decisions of the Supreme Court:

1. The Eleventh Amendment, which provides for state immunity in federal court. Enacted in response to *Chisholm v. Georgia.*[60]

2. The Fourteenth Amendment, which provides for due process and equal protection in the states. Enacted, partly, in response to *Dred Scott v. Sandford.*[61]

3. The Sixteenth Amendment, which provides for the federal income tax. Enacted in response to *Pollock v. Farmer's Loan & Trust Co.,*[62] in which the Court ruled the federal income tax unconstitutional.

4. The Twenty-sixth Amendment, which provides that all individuals eighteen years of age and older possess the right to vote in state and national elections. Enacted in response to *Oregon v. Mitchell.*[63]

One amendment has been ratified to repeal another. The Eighteenth Amendment's prohibition of alcohol (1919) was repealed by the Twenty-first Amendment (1933).

Amendments may concern any subject, with one exception. The final clause of Article V states that "no State, without its consent, shall be deprived of its equal Suffrage in the Senate." This provision creates an interesting paradox: May the Constitution be amended to allow inequal suffrage amendments without individual state consent? On the one hand, a literal reading leads to the conclusion that under no circumstances can a state's suffrage be changed without its consent. On the other hand, it is possible to circumvent this amendment by amending it, permitting state suffrage to be changed pursuant to normal amendment procedures. If this is accepted, the state suffrage provision is rendered meaningless. There is no case law directly examining the meaning of this provision at this time.

§ 5.12 Power over Federal Courts

Article III grants Congress considerable authority over the federal judiciary. Section 1, for example, establishes the Supreme Court, but leaves the creation of all other courts to Congress. This power is first mentioned in Article I, § 8, clause 9. If Congress had wished, the Supreme Court would be the only federal court.

Section 2, clause 2, then grants Congress the authority to make exceptions to the appellate jurisdiction of the Supreme Court. The precise contours of this provision have not been defined. Recall from *Marbury v. Madison* that Congress may not extend or restrict the jurisdiction of a federal court beyond the limits of the Constitution. For example, Congress may not give the Supreme Court original jurisdiction where it has none under the Constitution. See Chapter 4 for a complete discussion of Congress's power over the judicial branch.

§ 5.13 Federal Property, Territories, and Native Americans

Congress may control, by appropriate legislation, the purchase and sale of property. It may also provide for the use of eminent domain; however, whenever the federal government takes property from a person, the Fifth Amendment demands just compensation.

Congress may regulate federal properties, including establishing criminal laws that apply on these properties. Some properties are held by the federal government exclusively; others are concurrently held with the states. In many instances, the federal government enters into agreements with states and localities that provide for the application of local laws, as well as for local law enforcement. Accordingly, local and state police agencies are responsible for enforcing federal, state, and local laws in many federal lands.

Article IV, § 3, clause 2, delegates to Congress the power to "dispose of and make all needful Rules and Regulations respecting the Territory or other Property belonging to the United States." This includes the power to acquire, dispose of, establish governments in, and tax territories.

There are many forms of affiliation with the United States. A people, or geographical area, may be a territory, commonwealth, or free association state. Territorial affiliation is the closest and most direct relationship. Washington, D.C., American Samoa, Puerto Rico, Guam, and the American Virgin Islands are territories. A *territory* is an area over which the United States has control, but it is not a state. Territories may be *unorganized,* that is, no specific statute establishes a territorial government. In such cases, the President of the United States possesses the authority to establish laws and institutions in the territory. A territory may also be *organized.* To be organized, Congress must establish and provide for territorial government by statute. Once this occurs, changes cannot be made by the President. Rather, congressional action is required. Because it is more difficult to obtain the necessary majority in Congress to enact laws than it is for the President to act unilaterally, organized territories are thought to enjoy greater independence than unorganized territories.

A commonwealth, in contrast, is created by a compact approved by both Congress and the people of the area. Commonwealth governments have a degree more autonomy than do territorial governments. The United States Constitution has greater applicability in territories than in commonwealths. American Samoa and the Commonwealth of the Northern Mariana Islands are commonwealths.

The most detached relationship is one of *free association.* The Federated States of Micronesia, the Republic of the Marshall Islands, and the Republic of Palau are examples of freely associated states. The power of Congress to regulate territories and commonwealths is greater than over freely associated states. Freely associated states are sovereign and self-governing, that is, free to develop and enforce their own domestic laws and policies. The United States Constitution is not applicable in freely associated states.

The United States provides monies and technical support to enhance the states' political and economic development. In addition, the United States provides military protection. In exchange, the free association state agrees to extend military rights to the United States, such as the right to establish and maintain bases and to exclude the military of other nations from the area. In most cases, the freely associated state is permitted to conduct its own foreign affairs, but it does so in consultation with the United States. Citizens of freely associated states normally also possess greater rights than other foreigners to travel to or live and work in the United States. Concurrently, the same is true of United States citizens who want to travel to the associated state. Either the United States or the freely associated state may terminate the agreement with notice (e.g., six months). The President may not terminate the agreement without the concurrence of Congress. A plebiscite is required for most freely associated states to terminate their affiliation with the United States.

Congress also has the authority to regulate the lands belonging to Native American tribes. Also, the commerce clause provides that Congress may regulate commerce with "Indian tribes."

§ 5.14 Enforcement of Civil Rights

Congressional jurisdiction over civil rights matters stems from several sources. The commerce clause, for example, has been relied upon by Congress when regulating the availability of public accommodations (such as hotels) to all people regardless of race or color.

The Thirteenth, Fourteenth, and Fifteenth Amendments all contain the following language: "Congress shall have the power to enforce this article by appropriate legislation." The three amendments are commonly referred to as the Civil War, Reconstruction, and Civil Rights Amendments. The Thirteenth (1865) abolishes slavery, the Fourteenth (1868) provides for due process and equal protection of laws, and the Fifteenth (1870) assures that all citizens may enjoy the franchise, regardless of race or color.

The courts have construed these provisions broadly, so that Congress has considerable authority and flexibility in remedying America's civil rights ills. Congress may regulate both private and civil associations. For example, Congress has prohibited racial discrimination in employment, regardless of whether it occurs in the private or public sector.

Several statutes have been enacted providing for equal treatment in housing, contract relationships, and employment. The "appropriate legislation" provision includes the power to create both civil and criminal remedies for violations. Because there is a specific constitutional grant of authority in this area, congressional regulation may extend to areas that have traditionally been regulated by the states and may apply against the states as well.

In addition, the Court has held that Congress's power under these amendments extends beyond fashioning remedies for strict constitutional violations. It may go further and create rights and remedies under these amendments. This is illustrated in *Katzenbach v. Morgan.*

As *Katzenbach* demonstrates, Congress may preempt state laws in this area. Also, it may extend rights under the Civil War Amendments further than they would otherwise reach. The purpose here is not to explain the state of civil rights law; rather, it is to demonstrate the authority Congress has in this area.

§ 5.15 Other Powers

Congress possesses many other powers. It exercises control over aliens and immigration. The power to establish a post office and postal roads is expressly delegated to Congress. Control of patents and copyrights also falls into Congress's domain. Bankruptcy law is exclusively

KATZENBACH v. MORGAN
384 U.S. 641 (1966)

[The Voting Rights Act of 1965 (§ 4) provided that Puerto Ricans who had completed at least the sixth grade shall be entitled to vote, regardless of English language skills. The statute was intended to preempt a New York state law that required voters to be English-literate. There were thousands of Puerto Ricans living in New York at the time. The Court had previously upheld the New York law, but now was addressing the issue of Congress's statute, which was intended to set aside New York's law.]

Mr. Justice Brennan delivered the opinion of the Court. ...

[We] hold that, in the application challenged in these cases, § 4(e) [of the Voting Rights Act] is a proper exercise of the powers granted to Congress by § 5 of the Fourteenth Amendment [allowing Congress to enforce that amendment with appropriate legislation] and that by force of the Supremacy Clause, Article VI, the New York English literacy requirement cannot be enforced to the extent that it is inconsistent with § 4(e).

Under the distribution of powers effected by the Constitution, the States establish qualifications for voting. [O]f course, the States have no power to grant or withhold franchise on conditions that are forbidden by the Fourteenth Amendment, or any other provision of the Constitution. Such exercises of state power are no more immune to the limitations of the Fourteenth Amendment than any other state action. The Equal Protection Clause itself has been held to forbid some state laws that restrict the right to vote.

The Attorney General of the State of New York argues that an exercise of congressional power under § 5 of the Fourteenth Amendment that prohibits the enforcement of state law can only be sustained if the judicial branch determines that the state law is prohibited by the provisions of the Amendment that Congress sought to enforce. More specifically, he urges that § 4(e) cannot be sustained as appropriate legislation to enforce the Equal Protection Clause unless the judiciary decides—even with the guidance of a congressional judgment—that the application of the English literacy requirement prohibited by § 4(e) is forbidden by the Equal Protection Clause itself. We disagree. Neither the language nor history of § 5 supports such a construction. As was said in regard to § 5 in *Ex Parte Virginia*, 100 U.S. 339, 345, "It is the power of Congress which has been enlarged. Congress is authorized to *enforce* the prohibitions by appropriate legislation. Some legislation is contemplated to make the amendments fully effective." ...

Thus our task in this case is not to determine whether the New York English literacy requirement as applied to deny the right to vote to a person who successfully completed the sixth grade in a Puerto Rican school violates the Equal Protection Clause. ... [Rather, the issue is] whether Congress [may] prohibit the enforcement of the state law by legislating under § 5 of the Fourteenth Amendment? In answering this question, our task is limited to determining whether such legislation is, as required by § 5, appropriate legislation to enforce the Equal Protection Clause.

By including § 5 the draftsmen sought to grant to Congress, by a specific provision applicable to the Fourteenth Amendment, the same broad powers expressed in the Necessary and Proper Clause ... .

There can be no doubt that § 4(e) may be regarded as an enactment to enforce the Equal Protection Clause. Congress explicitly declared that it enacted § 4(e) "to secure the rights under the fourteenth amendment of persons educated in American-flag schools in which the predominant classroom language was other than English." [Section] 4(e) may be viewed as a measure to secure for the Puerto Rican community residing in New York nondiscriminatory treatment by government—both in the imposition of voting qualifications and the provision or administration of governmental services, such as public schools, public housing and law enforcement.

Section 4(e) may be readily seen as "plainly adapted" to furthering these aims of the Equal Protection Clause. The practical effect of § 4(e) is to prohibit New York from denying the right to vote to large segments of its Puerto Rican community. ... It is well within congressional authority to say this need of the Puerto Rican minority for the vote warranted federal intrusion upon any state interests served by the English literacy requirement. It was for Congress, as the branch that made this judgment, to assess and weigh the various conflicting considerations—the risk or pervasiveness of the discrimination in governmental services, the effectiveness of eliminating the state restriction on the right to vote as a means of dealing with the evil, the adequacy or availability of alternative remedies, and the nature and significance of the state interests that would be affected by the nullification of the English literacy requirement as applied to residents who have successfully completed the sixth grade in a Puerto Rican school. It is not for us to review the congressional resolution of these factors. ...

We therefore conclude that § 4(e), in the application challenged in this case, is appropriate legislation to enforce the Equal Protection Clause and that the judgment of the District Court must be and hereby is reversed.

---

federal, and Congress has enacted an entire scheme of bankruptcy law and has created a system of bankruptcy courts to enforce those laws. Because of the importance of admiralty issues to the federal government, the framers delegated them to Congress. Congress may regulate national elections. The admission of new states to the union is a congressional responsibility, as is assuring each state a republican form of government.

In terms of the structure of the federal government, Congress controls where the Constitution does not. For example, Congress is responsible for creating and abolishing agencies and determining the organizational structure of America's bureaucracy.

In addition, Congress creates governmental and quasi-governmental corporations to accomplish governmental objectives. The first corporation chartered by Congress was the Bank of the United States in 1791. Since that time, Congress has created many corporations, such as the Federal Deposit Insurance Corporation (FDIC), which insures bank deposits, and the National Railroad Passenger Corporation (Amtrak), which was created to save passenger train travel from extinction. Congress normally provides for government selection of corporate officers, but may otherwise make these corporations independent. Even though a corporation may be declared independent, if it is created by Congress and serves a governmental purpose, and a majority of its board members and officers are appointed by governmental officials, its actions are considered governmental for purposes of constitutional analysis. Thus,

Amtrak's decision not to allow political messages on its billboards was subject to First Amendment free speech limitations.[64]

§ 5.16 Necessary and Proper Powers

One of the most important enumerations of authority in Article I is the necessary and proper clause of § 8, clause 18. Congress shall have the power to "make all Laws which shall be necessary and proper for carrying into Execution the foregoing Powers, and all other Powers vested by this Constitution in the Government of the United States, or in any Department or Officer thereof." This clause represents an exception to the concept of a limited federal government. It is an expression that there are implied, unenumerated federal powers.

The necessary and proper clause is attendant to Congress's enumerated powers. Therefore, it must first be determined that Congress or another federal department has power over a subject pursuant to a separate constitutional provision. Then the necessary and proper clause empowers Congress to undertake whatever actions are necessary to fully enforce the granted power. The necessary and proper clause has been used to significantly increase the power and size of the federal government.

Note that the clause applies to more than congressional power. Congress may enact legislation to expand any power delegated to the federal government or officer or department thereof. Therefore, Congress may enact laws that support presidential (or other executive officials') powers. For example, the President is responsible for diplomacy. Congress may therefore enact laws establishing the State Department, providing for the foreign service, or authorizing the expenditure of funds.

The necessary and proper clause was relied upon by Justice Marshall in *McCulloch v. Maryland,* wherein the Court upheld the power of the federal government to create a national bank. There is no express provision allowing the establishment of a national bank, but the Court reasoned that a national bank was a proper extension of Congress's fiscal powers to collect taxes and borrow money, which are expressly authorized by the Constitution. The Court stated, in *McCulloch v. Maryland,* that a law is valid under the necessary and proper clause if it supports a legitimate objective and is "plainly adapted to that end."

Combine the necessary and proper clause with the commerce clause, the Civil Rights Amendments, and general expansion of the other enumerated powers, and the result is a very powerful federal government moving into the twenty-first century.

Summary

The framers intended for two groups to be represented in Congress: the people (House of Representatives) and the states (Senate). Equal representation in the Senate assured that the larger states would not take advantage of the smaller states. Although originally selected by the states, today senators are popularly elected, as are members of the House of Representatives.

In recent decades, federal power had grown considerably. The growth appears to be the natural consequence of a nation (and world) that is becoming rapidly interconnected and interdependent. The commerce clause, the necessary and proper clause, the Civil Rights Amendments (13 to 15), and the supremacy clause have facilitated this increased power. The Supreme Court has been largely permissive of federal expansion and in contemporary times has read the Tenth Amendment as not establishing a distinct sphere of state power. Moving into the twenty-first century, it is reasonable to anticipate that federal power will continue to increase. In addition, the emerging globalization of the world's economies, cultures, and laws will present new constitutional issues to the judiciary of the twenty-first century.

Review Questions

1. Define the affectation doctrine.

2. What is the cumulative effects doctrine?

3. May the President declare war? May Congress?

4. Describe the process for removing the President, Vice President, Article III judge, and other public officials from office.

5. Does the Fifth Amendment freedom from self-incrimination apply in congressional hearings?

6. Is a member of Congress immune from criminal arrest during session? From a civil summons and complaint?

7. Describe the procedures to amend the Constitution.

8. What is the necessary and proper clause? Explain its significance.

9. Do the states or federal government have jurisidiction over post offices? Patents and copyrights? Murder? Education?

Review Problems

1. In your opinion, should Congress be permitted to regulate for the health, welfare, and morality of the people? Explain.

2. Other than impeachment, there is no constitutional mechanism to discipline judges. Congress has enacted a statute, however, that allows judges to discipline themselves. The Judicial Conduct and Disability Act of 1980, 28 U.S.C. § 372, provides that cases may be temporarily reassigned from judges, private or public sanctions may be issued, and in extreme cases, a file may be reported to Congress for consideration of impeachment.
   a. Is this law constitutional? Explain.
   b. What if a cases are repeatedly reassigned from an Article III judge? Explain.
   c. Would it be constitutional for Congress to delegate to the Supreme Court the authority to remove an Article III judge? Explain.
   d. Do you believe that federal judges should be appointed for life? Explain.

Notes

[1] Robert Byrne, comp. *1,911 Best Things Anybody Ever Said* (Fawcett Columbine 1988).

[2] Art. I, § 5, clause 3.

[3] Art. I, § 5, clause 2.

[4] Art. I, § 5, clause 1.

[5] Art. I, §§ 2 and 3.

[6] *United States v. Munoz-Flores*, 495 U.S. 385 (1990).

[7] Art. I, § 5.

[8] Art. I, § 6, clause 2.

[9] *United States Term Limits v. Thornton*, 514 U.S. ___ , 115 S. Ct. 1842 (1995).

[10] *McIntyre v. Fallahay*, 766 F.2d 1098 (7th Cir. 1985).

[11] 395 U.S. 486 (1969).

[12] *Kilbourn v. Thompson*, 103 U.S. 168, 189 (1881).

[13] *United States v. Johnson*, 383 U.S. 169 (1966).

[14] *Hutchinson v. Proxmire*, 443 U.S. 111 (1979).

[15] *Kilbourn*, 103 U.S. at 204.

[16] *United States v. Rostenkowski*, 59 F.3d 1291 (D.C. Cir. 1995).

[17] *Id.*

[18] *United States v. Gillock*, 445 U.S. 360 (1980).

[19] *Stafford v. Wallace*, 258 U.S. 495 (1922).

[20] 295 U.S. 330 (1935).

[21] 295 U.S. 495 (1935).

22 *See Carter v. Carter Coal Co.,* 298 U.S. 238 (1936).

23 *NLRB v. Jones & Laughlin Steel Corp.,* 301 U.S. 1 (1937).

24 17 U.S. 316 (1819).

25 *Heart of Atlanta Motel Inc. v. United States,* 379 U.S. 241, 257 (1964).

26 *Hodel v. Virginia Surface Mining & Reclamation Ass'n,* 452 U.S. 264 (1981).

27 *Heart of Atlanta Motel Inc. v. United States,* 379 U.S. 241 (1964).

28 *Katzenbach v. McClung,* 379 U.S. 294 (1964).

29 18 U.S.C. § 2421.

30 18 U.S.C. § 2261 *et seq.*

31 28 U.S.C. § 1073.

32 28 U.S.C. § 921 *et seq.*

33 28 U.S.C. § 2251 *et. seq.*

34 *Perez v. United States,* 402 U.S. 146 (1971).

35 The law was invalidated by a U.S. district court in *United States v. Cortner,* 834 F. Supp. 242 (M.D. Tenn. 1993), but the Sixth Circuit Court of Appeals has found to the contrary. *See United States v. Johnson,* 22 F.3d 106 (6th Cir. 1994); *United States v. Osteen,* 30 F.3d 135 (6th Cir. 1994).

36 *United States v. Oliver,* 60 F.3d 547 (9th Cir. 1995); *United States v. Carolina,* 61 F.3d 917 (10th Cir. 1995).

37 157 U.S. 429 (1895).

38 Art. I, § 2, clause 3.

39 Art. I, § 9, clause 5.

40 483 U.S. 203 (1987).

41 Art. I, § 8, clauses 5 and 6.

42 *McCulloch v. Maryland,* 17 U.S. (4 Wheat.) 316 (1819).

43 Art. I, § 8, clause 2.

44 Art. I, § 8, clause 4.

45 *Woods v. Cloyd W. Miller Co.,* 333 U.S. 138 (1948).

46 *Korematsu v. United States,* 323 U.S. 214 (1944).

47 Art. I, § 8, clauses 15 and 16.

48 *Perpich v. Department of Defense,* 496 U.S. 334 (1990).

49 323 U.S. 214 (1944).

50 *Watkins v. United States,* 354 U.S. 178, 200 (1957).

51 *Barenblatt v. United States,* 360 U.S. 109 (1959).

52 Art. II, § 2, clause 2.

53 *Hastings v. United States,* 681 F.2d 706 (11th Cir. 1982). *See also United States v. Claiborne,* 727 F.2d 842 (9th Cir. 1984).

54 Michael Broyde, "Expediting Impeachment: Removing Article III Federal Judges After Criminal Conviction," 17 *Harv. J. L. & Pub. Pol'y* 157 (1994).

55 400 U.S. 112 (1970).

56 Jerome Angel, *Amending America* 138–39 (Random House 1993). This book is recommended to those who are interested in the history of constitutional amendments.

57 Maggie McComas, "Amending the Constitution," *Constitution* 26 (Spring–Summer 1992).

58 This information was taken from *Amending America, supra* n. 57.

59 John Vile, "Proposals to Amend the Bill of Rights: Are Fundamental Rights in Jeopardy?" 75 *Judicature* 62 (Aug./Sept. 1991).

60 2 U.S. (2 Dall.) 419 (1793).

61 60 U.S. (19 How.) 393 (1856).

62 157 U.S. 429 (1895).

63 400 U.S. 112 (1970).

64 *Lebron v. National Railroad Passenger Corp.*, 513 U.S. ___ , 115 S. Ct. 961 (1995).

CHAPTER 6

THE PRESIDENCY

§ 6.1 Selection, Tenure, and Succession

One of the defects of the Articles of Confederation was the absence
of a strong executive with unified powers. The President of the Continental Congress served as the nation's highest executive, but held little
power. Even more, many functions that are today considered "executive"
were performed by legislative committees. This proved to be inefficient,
and many people believed the nation needed a strong, central figure.

Many proposals were considered at the Philadelphia Convention,
including installing a monarch and having multiple presidents. The framers finally agreed on what is now found in Article II. Section 1, clause 1,
states:

> The executive Power shall be vested in a President of the United States
> of America. He shall hold his Office during the Term of Four Years,
> and, together with the Vice President, chosen for the same Term, be
> elected ... .

This clause provides for one President and one Vice President, each
to serve four years. Not every American qualifies to be President. The
Constitution requires that a person be a natural-born citizen, thirty-five
years of age, and at least fourteen years a resident of the United States.[1]
Natural-born citizen has not been defined, but it appears to exclude
naturalized citizens, though not individuals born abroad on United
States soil.

The President is not elected by direct, popular vote. Rather, a system
of electors, known as the **electoral college**, chooses the President. Each
state has a group of electors equal to the number of representatives it
has in the House and Senate.[2] The Twenty-Third Amendment gives the
District of Columbia the number of electors it would have if a state.

TERMS

electoral college [†]   The body empowered by the Constitution to elect the
president and vice president of [the] United States, composed of presidential

However, that number may not exceed that of the smallest state. Today, the practice is for all electors to vote as a block in favor of the candidate who receives the greatest number of popular votes in the state. Under this system, it is possible for a candidate to lose the election, while garnishing the largest number of popular votes. This occurred in the 1888 election in which Benjamin Harrison defeated Grover Cleveland, even though Cleveland received the larger popular vote.

If no candidate receives a majority vote in the electoral college, the House of Representatives selects the victor. Thomas Jefferson and John Quincy Adams were elected in this manner.

The original Constitution did not limit the number of terms a President may serve. The Twenty-Second Amendment, ratified in 1951, limits Presidents to two terms. The Twenty-Fifth Amendment establishes rules of succession to the presidency. First, if the President dies, resigns, or is removed, the Vice President assumes the presidency. The new President is then empowered to nominate another Vice President, who must be confirmed by both houses of Congress.

If the President becomes unable to perform his or her responsibilities, the Vice President assumes the role of Acting President. Presidential disability may be declared either by the President or by the Vice President and other officers in letters to the Speaker of the House and President Pro Tempore of the Senate. Congress is empowered to resolve any dispute between the President and Vice President (together with other executive officials) concerning the President's ability to perform the functions of the office.[3] Although this issue has never been presented, there can be little question that Congress's decision is a nonjusticiable political question.

Further succession is provided for by statute.[4] After the Vice President, the following officials would be appointed, in this order: Speaker of the House, President Pro Tempore of the Senate, Secretary of State, Secretary of the Treasury, Secretary of Defense, Attorney General, Secretary of the Interior, Secretary of Agriculture, Secretary of Commerce, Secretary of Labor, Secretary of Health and Human Services, Secretary of Energy, Secretary of Education, and Secretary of Veterans Affairs. Of course, replacements must satisfy the constitutional qualifications, that is, be thirty-five years of age, a natural-born citizen, and fourteen years a resident of the United States.

TERMS

electors chosen by the voters at each presidential election. In practice, however, the electoral college votes in accordance with the popular vote.

Like federal judges, the President is shielded from financial coercion by Congress through Article II, § 1, clause 7, which prohibits the President's salary from being decreased during his or her term.

§ 6.2 Shared Powers

The framers included a thorough system of checks and balances between the executive and legislative branches, so most of the powers possessed by the President are shared with Congress. In most instances, the line between congressional authority and presidential authority is defined by practice.

Through the political question doctrine, the Court has managed to avoid many power conflicts between the President and Congress. When the Court has agreed to involve itself, it has taken two approaches. The first is a separations of functions approach. That is, in some cases the Court applies a strictly formal interpretation of the functions of the two branches. When looking at a case from this perspective, the Court asks the question, "To which branch is this function delegated?"

In most cases, however, the Court has taken a different approach to cases involving legislative-executive power conflicts. This second approach focuses more on check-and-balance principles than on strict separation principles. Functions are viewed as shared and cooperation is put at a premium. Look for these two views in the following discussions of domestic and foreign powers.

The result of practice and law has been favorable to the presidency. Most power conflicts between Congress and the President have concluded that power rests with the President. In a few particular instances, Congress has attempted to control the growth of presidential power. For example, through the War Powers Act, Congress attempted to limit the President's power to commit the nation to war. However, in other instances, Congress has attempted to increase presidential authority over lawmaking. Delegations of legislative authority to the executive branch are discussed at length in Chapter 7. For the moment, bear in mind that through legislation Congress controls, to some extent, executive power.

There is a reason the President often prevails in power struggles: the presidency is unified. Congress is collegial. Even more, it is fragmented. To resolve most matters, both houses must act. The President can act swiftly, often before Congress has had an opportunity to meet. As a result, even if a power is shared, the President tends to dominate. There is a positive correlation between the need for quick and efficient action and presidential dominance. That is, as the need for swift and efficient action increases, so does the likelihood that the President will make the decisions.

§ 6.3 Domestic Powers

The Constitution grants the President certain powers. Other powers are inherent and have been defined through practice. Recall that few powers are possessed exclusively by one branch. Most presidential powers are closely shared with Congress, especially in the foreign affairs and military areas. This discussion begins with an examination of domestic presidential authority and then turns to foreign affairs.

Legislation

True, Congress is the primary governmental authority empowered to make law. But the President plays a role in the lawmaking process, through two processes. First, he or she participates in congressional lawmaking. Second, the President actually creates law.

As to the former, the President affects congressional lawmaking both directly and indirectly. The President has a direct influence on congressional lawmaking through the veto power. Article I, § 7, clause 2, requires all bills that have passed the House and Senate to be submitted to the President. The President may then sign the bill, making it law, or veto it. Any bills not returned to Congress within ten days become law automatically, unless Congress is not in session. In such a case, the law dies as a consequence of the President's failure to return it. This is known as the **pocket veto**.

In the event of a veto, the Constitution requires the President to return the bill to the house where it originated. The President is required to attach "objections" to the bill for consideration by Congress. A two-thirds vote in both houses overrides a presidential veto.

TERMS

---

pocket veto [†]   The veto of a congressional bill by the president by retaining it until Congress is no longer in session, neither signing nor vetoing it. The effect of such inaction is to nullify the legislation without affirmatively vetoing it. The pocket veto is also available to governors under some state constitutions.

Amicus

William Howard Taft: President and Chief Justice

Most successful political figures hold several positions, elected and appointed, during their lives. Only one person, however, has served as both the nation's highest executive and its highest judicial officer.

William Howard Taft was born on September 15, 1857, in Cincinnati, Ohio. He was married in June 1886, and he remained married to the same woman until his death at age 72. He was a Republican and held many positions before being elected President, including local prosecutor, state judge, federal judge, law school dean, governor-general of the Philippines, and provisional governor of Cuba. He was elected President and served from 1909 to 1913. Taft lost his reelection bid to Woodrow Wilson and accepted a position as professor of law at Yale, which he held until June 30, 1921, the date he began his term as Chief Justice of the Supreme Court. He was nominated by President Warren Harding. He served as Chief Justice until February 3, 1930. ▥

Although not expressly stated in the Constitution, the President is de facto an initiator of legislation. By proposing a budget, returning bills with objections, and conferring with members of Congress concerning legislation, the President affects the development of legislation. In addition, the Vice President serves as the President of the Senate and is entitled to vote to break ties in that body.[5]

Executive Orders and Presidential Proclamations

No provision in the Constitution gives the President the power to directly make law. Regardless, all American presidents have made law through **executive orders** and *presidential proclamations*. Orders and proclamations are tools used by the President to perform executive functions. As such, they are not an independent source of presidential authority. A President only uses orders and proclamations to enforce otherwise lawful presidential power. If lawfully promulgated, orders and proclamations have the effect of statutes. To assure public notice, executive orders must be published in the *Federal Register*.

TERMS

executive order[†] An order issued by the chief executive officer of government, whether national, state, or local.

Federal Register[†] An official publication, printed daily, containing regulations and proposed regulations issued by administrative agencies, as well as

All the executive powers discussed so far have derived from the Constitution or act of Congress. Whether the President possesses additional power—inherent powers—has been the subject of intense debate since the formation of the Constitution. That question is at the heart of *Youngstown Sheet & Tube Co. v. Sawyer.*

The *Youngstown* Court followed a strictly formal approach to separation of powers. It could find no authorization in the Constitution (or legislation) for President Truman to seize property; therefore, the action was invalidated. The dissent followed a more functional, shared-powers approach. The President as chief executive and commander-in-chief has the implied power to act in response to emergencies, assuming there is no prohibitory statute.

It appears that there is no inherent domestic presidential power. Clearly, Congress may extend emergency powers to a President. Whether the President may temporarily act while awaiting congressional action is unknown. In *Youngstown,* the Court found that Congress has implicitly rejected the use of seizures before the President acted. If it had not, it is possible that Congress's nonaction following the seizure could have been perceived by the Court as implicit approval, and the outcome might have been different.

Justice Jackson's outline of presidential authority is generally accepted and provides a good framework for reference. The President has the greatest authority when acting pursuant to the Constitution. Presidential power is at its next highest status when the President is acting pursuant to a statute, and weakest when acting against Congress. There is a "twilight" zone in the middle where the extent of presidential authority is not well defined. Justice Jackson was referring to situations in which presidential action is neither expressly permitted nor prohibited by the Constitution. Clearly, presidential authority is truly at its peak when expressly authorized by the Constitution. Conversely, presidential authority is at its lowest when adverse to the Constitution.

Impoundment and Nonenforcement of Laws

Does presidential power include the power to not enforce laws? This issue arises in two contexts: refusal to spend congressionally appropriated funds and refusal to enforce law.

TERMS

other rulemaking and other official business of the executive branch of government. All regulations are ultimately published in the Code of Federal Regulations.

YOUNGSTOWN SHEET & TUBE CO.
v.
SAWYER
343 U.S. 579 (1952)

Mr. Justice Black delivered the opinion of the Court.

We are asked to decide whether President Truman was acting within his constitutional power when he issued an order directing the Secretary of Commerce to take possession of and operate most of the Nation's steel mills. The mill owners argue that the President's order amounts to lawmaking, a legislative function which the Constitution has expressly confided to the Congress and not the President. The Government's position is that the order was made on findings of the President that his action was necessary to avert a national catastrophe which would inevitably result from a stoppage of steel production, and that in meeting this grave emergency the President was acting within the aggregate of his constitutional powers as the Nation's Chief Executive and Commander in Chief of the Armed Forces of the United States. The issue emerges here from the following series of events:

[Steel company management and steel workers' unions had a dispute over wages and other conditions. As a result, they could not reach a collective bargaining agreement. The federal Mediation and Conciliation Service and Federal Wage Stabilization Board attempted unsuccessfully to settle the dispute. The workers' union gave notice of intent to strike.] The indispensability of steel as a component of substantially all weapons and other war materials led the President to believe that the proposed work stoppage would immediately jeopardize our national defense and that governmental seizure of the steel mills was necessary in order to assure the continued availability of steel. Reciting these considerations for his action, the President, a few hours before the strike was to begin, issued Executive Order 10340. [The] order directed the Secretary of Commerce to take possession of most of the steel mills and keep them running. The Secretary immediately issued his own orders, calling upon the presidents of the various seized companies to serve as operating managers for the United States ... . The next morning the President sent a message to Congress reporting his action ... . [Congress never took action. The companies complied, but filed suit in federal court seeking an injunction prohibiting the order from being enforced. The companies prevailed in the district court.]

The President's power, if any, to issue the order must stem either from an act of Congress or from the Constitution itself. There is no statute that expressly authorizes the President to take possession of property as he did here. Nor is there any act of Congress to which our attention has been directed from which such a power can fairly be implied ... .

Moreover, the use of the seizure technique to solve labor disputes in order to prevent work stoppages was not only unauthorized by any congressional enactment; prior to this controversy, Congress had refused to adopt that method of settling labor disputes. When the Taft-Hartley Act was under consideration in 1947, Congress rejected an amendment which would have authorized such governmental seizures in cases of emergency ... .

It is clear that if the President had authority to issue the order he did, it must be found in some provision of the Constitution ... . The contention is that presidential power should be implied from the aggregate of his powers under the Constitution. Particular reliance is placed on provisions in Article II which say that "The executive Power shall be vested in a President ... "; that "he shall take Care that the Laws be faithfully executed"; and that he "shall be Commander in Chief of the Army and Navy of the United States."

The order cannot properly be sustained as an exercise of the President's military power as Commander in Chief of the Armed Forces. The Government attempts to do so by citing a number of cases upholding broad powers in military commanders engaged in day-to-day fighting in a theater of war. Such cases need not concern us here. Even though "theater of war" be an expanding concept, we cannot with faithfulness to our constitutional system hold that the Commander and Chief of the Armed Forces has the ultimate power as such to take possession of private property in order to keep labor disputes from stopping production. This is a job for the Nation's lawmakers, not for its military authorities.

Nor can the seizure order be sustained because of the several constitutional provisions that grant executive power to the President. In the framework of our Constitution, the President's power to see that the laws are faithfully executed refutes the idea that he is to be lawmaker. The Constitution limits his functions in the lawmaking process to the recommending of laws ... and the vetoing of laws ... .

The Founders of this Nation entrusted the lawmaking power to the Congress alone in both good and bad times. It would do no good to recall the historical events, the fears of power and the hopes for freedom that lay behind their choice. Such a review would but confirm our holding that this seizure order cannot stand.

The judgment of the District Court is affirmed.

Mr. Justice Jackson, concurring in the judgment and opinion of the Court.

... Presidential powers are not fixed but fluctuate, depending upon their disjunction or conjunction with those of Congress ... .

1. When the President acts pursuant to an express or implied authorization of Congress, his authority is at its maximum, for it includes all that he possesses in his own right plus all that Congress can delegate ... . If his act is held unconstitutional under these circumstances, it usually means that the Federal Government as an undivided whole lacks power. A seizure executed by the President pursuant to an Act of Congress would be supported by the strongest of presumptions and the widest latitude of judicial interpretation, and the burden of persuasion would rest heavily upon any who might attack it.

2. When the President acts in absence of either a congressional grant or denial of authority, he can only rely upon his own independent powers, but there is a zone of twilight in which he and Congress may have concurrent authority,

or in which its distribution is uncertain. Therefore, congressional inertia, indifference or acquiescence may sometimes, at least in practical matters, enable, if not invite, [presidential] measures ... .

3. When the President takes measures incompatible with the expressed or implied will of Congress, his power is at its lowest ebb, for then he can rely only upon his own constitutional powers minus any constitutional powers of Congress over the matter ... . [Justice Jackson analyzed the seizure under the third category and found that the President had acted unlawfully].

Mr. Justice Burton, concurring.

... The present situation is not comparable to that of an imminent invasion or threatened attack. We do not face the issue of what might be the President's constitutional power to meet such catastrophic situations. Nor is it claimed that the current seizure is in the nature of a military command addressed by the President, as Commander-in-Chief, to a mobilized nation waging, or imminently threatened with, total war.

Mr. Justice Clark, concurring.

[The] Constitution does grant to the President extensive authority in times of grave and imperative national emergency. In fact, to my thinking, such a grant may well be necessary to the very existence of the Constitution itself. As Lincoln aptly said, "[is] it possible to lose the nation and yet preserve the Constitution?" ...

[Several] statutes furnish the guideposts for decision in this case. [N]either the Defense Production Act nor Taft-Hartley authorized the seizure challenged here, and the Government made no effort to comply with the procedures established by the Selective Service Act of 1948, a statute which expressly authorizes seizures when producers fail to supply necessary defense material ... .

Mr. Chief Justice Vinson, with whom Mr. Justice Reed and Mr. Justice Minton join, dissenting.

The President of the United States directed the Secretary of Commerce to take temporary possession of the Nation's steel mills during the existing emergency because "a work stoppage would immediately jeopardize and imperil our national defense and the defense of those joined with us in resisting aggression, and would add to the continuing danger of our soldiers, sailors, and airmen engaged in combat in the field." ...

Plaintiffs do not remotely suggest any basis for rejecting the President's finding that *any* stoppage of steel production would immediately place the Nation in peril. [According to the plaintiffs], the President is left powerless at the very moment when the need for action may be most pressing and when no one, other than he, is immediately capable of action. Under this view, he is left powerless [because the power belongs to Congress] ... .

A review of executive action demonstrates that our Presidents have on many occasions exhibited the leadership contemplated by the Framers when they made the President Commander in Chief, and imposed upon him the trust to "take Care that the Laws be faithfully executed." With or without explicit statutory authorization, Presidents have at such times dealt with national emergencies by acting promptly and resolutely to enforce legislative programs, at least to save those programs until Congress could act. Congress and the courts have responded to such executive intiative with consistent approval ... .

Our first President displayed at once the leadership contemplated by the Framers. When the national revenue laws were openly flouted in some sections of Pennsylvania, President Washington, without waiting for a call from the state government, summoned the militia and took decisive steps to secure the faithful execution of the laws. [Hamilton,] whose defense of the Proclamation [of Neutrality concerning the French Revolution] has endured the test of time, invoked the argument that the Executive has the duty to do that which will preserve the peace until Congress acts ... .

In an action furnishing a most apt precedent for this case, President Lincoln without statutory authority directed the seizure of rail and telegraph lines leading to Washington ... .

The broad executive power granted by Article II to an officer on duty 365 days a year cannot, it is said, be invoked to avert disaster. Instead, the President must confine himself to sending a message to Congress recommending action. Under this messenger-boy concept of the Office, the President cannot even act to preserve legislative programs from destruction so that Congress will have something left to act upon ... .

The President immediately informed Congress of his action and clearly stated his intention to abide by the legislative will. No basis for claims of arbitrary action, unlimited powers or dictatorial usurpation of congressional power appears from the facts of this case. On the contrary, judicial, legislative and executive precedents throughout our history demonstrate that in this case the President acted in full comformity with his duties under the Constitution ... .

[The Court's decision was issued on June 2 and then the union then struck for nearly two months. The war effort was not seriously affected by the strike.]

Impoundment

Impoundment refers to a President's refusal to expend congressionally appropriated funds. Presidents have long claimed impoundment power, usually for economic reasons, such as to combat inflation. Opponents of the power assert that Article II imposes an affirmative obligation on the President to execute all of the laws and that the President lacks the power to refuse enforcement of particular laws. Further, because the Constitution expressly delegates fiscal powers to Congress, as well as the general power to make the nation's laws, a refusal to spend appropriated funds is a usurpation of legislative power.

The application of impoundment to specific sections of a law with many appropriations is much like the **line-item veto**. The line-item veto is not provided for by Constitution or statute. Lower courts have rejected the theory of implied impoundment power, at least in the domestic arena. In the foreign affairs context, presidential power is likely greater. For example, Congress may not attempt to control diplomacy, which is an executive power, through appropriations. Thus, Congress could not appropriate funds to open an embassy in a nation where the executive has terminated relations.

Executive/Prosecutorial Discretion

In terms of civil and criminal law, the authority of the executive to exercise prosecutorial discretion is well established. Prosecutorial discretion includes the power to decide whether and when to investigate, prosecute, settle, and appeal individual cases. With the exception of decisions that are malicious, arbitrary, or premised upon some improper motive (such as race), courts do not interfere.

However, the authority of the executive to refuse to enforce a law altogether, or to refuse to enforce the law against an entire class of people covered by the law, is questionable. Recall that Article II provides that the President "shall take Care that the Laws be faithfully executed." This language appears to compel the executive to enforce all statutes, at least all that are facially valid. If a law has been declared unconstitutional or otherwise invalid by a court, the executive has the contrary obligation not to enforce that law. Similarly, a law that is facially or obviously invalid should not be enforced. For example, the Supreme Court decided in *Texas v. Johnson*[6] that First Amendment freedom of expression includes burning the nation's flag. In that case, a Texas statute criminalizing this conduct was invalidated. The United States Congress responded by enacting a federal law criminalizing the same conduct, in obvious contravention of the First Amendment.[7] In such a case, the President could have issued an order to the United States Attorneys, directing them not to enforce the law, without running afoul of his duty to enforce the laws.

TERMS

line item veto[†]   The right of a governor under most state constitutions to veto individual appropriations in an appropriation act rather than being compelled either to veto the act as a whole or to sign it into law. The president of the United States does not have a line item veto.

Appointment and Removal of Officials

Article II, § 2, clause 2, provides that the President shall nominate ambassadors, public ministers and consuls, judges of the Supreme Court, and other officers of the United States. As to ministers and officers, Cabinet officers such as the Secretary of State, Attorney General, and Surgeon General are examples.

Presidential Appointments of Supreme Court Justices   **SIDEBAR**

Although a President exercises no control over a Justice, once that Justice is confirmed, presidents do attempt to select individuals with whom they share a political philosophy. Even though superficial and often unsuccessful, presidents tend to look to such factors as political party affiliation, prior political positions held, and opinions rendered, if the candidate has had judicial experience. For example, 82 percent of the nominees of Republican presidents have been Republican and 95 percent of the nominees of Democratic presidents have been from the Democratic party.[8]

Another study indicates that a President's strength and popularity affect the likelihood of confirmation. For example, for presidents who would be re-elected, only 7.3 percent of their nominations were rejected. For presidents who were not re-elected, the rejection rate increased to 18.6 percent. Of presidents who could not be re-elected because they were in their second term, the rate was 26.3 percent. Finally, the rate of failure was the highest for those presidents who were not elected; it was 60 percent.[9]

As a check on this power, the Senate must confirm appointments. The President has plenary nomination power. He or she may nominate any person he or she wishes and eliminate a candidate for any reason. Similarly, it appears that the Senate possesses the same authority. It may deny confirmation for any reason. In fact, the Constitution does not require the Senate to explain itself. The presidential power of appointment is personal and may not be delegated to others.

The Constitution provides further that, for inferior officers, Congress may vest the appointment power in the President, courts of law, or heads of departments. Congress may rest the appointment power solely in one of these three; that is, no Senate confirmation is required. Congress may not delegate the appointment power to any other person or group. For example, a statute that delegated the appointment of the Federal Election Commission to the President Pro Tempore of the Senate and Speaker of the House was invalidated.[10]

Even though Congress may not appoint executive officials, it may establish qualifications for appointment. These qualifications must be related to the position; arbitrary qualifications are invalid. For example, a requirement that a candidate be of a particular political party would be invalid. However, requiring a nominee for Surgeon General to be a physician is reasonable.

The tricky question is what constitutes an inferior office. An examination of an officer's duties and responsibilities, as well as who the officer supervises and who he or she is supervised by, is necessary. Generally, all officers below Cabinet officials are "inferior." Under, assistant, and deputy secretaries are examples of inferior officers. The nomination power may be delegated to courts of law, as well as to the President. Under this authority, Congress delegated the power to appoint special judges (inferior officers) to the chief judge of the Tax Court. The fact that the Tax Court is not an Article III court is not dispositive. Legislatively established tribunals are "courts" under the appointments clause.[11]

Federal officials are mobile. Some change positions through promotion. Other officials change positions as requested by the President. In most circumstances, transferring officials must undergo the appointment process a second time. For example, a change from Secretary of Energy to Secretary of State could not occur without Senate confirmation to the new position. However, when the change in position does not bring with it a substantial change in responsibility, a second confirmation may be unnecessary. For example, all commissioned military officers are nominated by the President and confirmed by the Senate. A change in rank does not require a new confirmation, nor does a change of an officer from a line position to military judge. However, promoting an officer to Chair of the Joint Chiefs of Staff does require confirmation.[12]

The Constitution provides that the President may make temporary appointments to fill vacancies while the Senate is not in session. This applies to all positions for which the President holds the nomination power. The appointee must be confirmed by the Senate during its next session. If not, the appointment expires automatically.

Most of the work of the federal government is not performed by primary or inferior officers, but by federal employees. These persons may be appointed in whatever manner Congress wishes to impose, so long as the method comports with due process and equal protection. Most federal employees are hired through a civil service system. This system has been approved by the Supreme Court, even though it limits the presidential power over executive branch officials.

Once appointed, federal judges enjoy lifetime tenure. This is not true of executive officials. As part of the appointment power, as well as the power as chief executive, the President may remove executive branch officials who have undergone the nomination and confirmation process. The President's removal power over "purely executive" officials is nearly unlimited. Members of the President's Cabinet, such as the Secretary of State, are examples of purely executive officials.

As to executive branch officials who serve quasi-legislative or quasi-judicial functions, Congress may limit the President's removal power in certain circumstances. For example, because the role of the **independent counsel** is to investigate crime within the executive branch, Congress may limit removal of the independent counsel to good cause. Congress may not, however, completely exempt an independent counsel from executive control, even if the objective is to keep the executive branch in check.

In addition to presidential removal, Congress may remove officers through impeachment. The impeachment process is discussed in Chapter 5.

Reprieves and Pardons

Section 2, clause 1, of Article II states: "The President ... shall have Power to grant Reprieves and Pardons for offenses against the United States, except in cases of impeachment." The framers borrowed this concept from England, where the Crown held an absolute power to pardon and otherwise alter sentences.

A full **pardon** has the effect of totally cancelling both the conviction and the punishment. "[I]n the eyes of the law the offender is as innocent as if he had never committed the offense."[13] Therefore, a fully pardoned offender has all rights restored, and the pardoned offense may not be used to enhance sentences for later convictions. Accordingly, a lawyer-offender cannot be denied a license to practice law because of a pardoned offense.[14]

Pardons do not have to be complete. The President may **commute**, or lessen, a sentence. A term of imprisonment may be reduced or a lesser punishment may be substituted for a greater one, such as life imprisonment for death.

=== TERMS ===

independent counsel[†]   Under federal statute, counsel who may be specially appointed to investigate and prosecute high government officials for crimes committed in office.

pardon[†]   An act of grace by the chief executive of the government, ... relieving a person of the legal consequences of a crime of which he or she has been convicted. A pardon erases the conviction.

commutation of sentence[†]   The substitution of a less severe punishment for a more severe punishment.

The President may also impose conditions upon pardons. Conditions must be reasonable and not encroach upon constitutionally secured rights. Requiring restitution to victims or deportation of pardoned aliens is permissible. Prohibiting a pardoned offender from attending church or engaging in lawful political activities would not be valid. A condition may impose a disability that was not originally available, so long as the the pardon on the whole truly reduces the sentenced punishment. Pardons may not be used to enhance sentences. For example, in *Schick v. Reed,* the Court upheld a commutation of a death sentence to life imprisonment without the possibility of parole, even though the law under which the offender was sentenced did not provide for life without the possibility of parole.[15] The President may revoke a pardon if an offender violates the conditions imposed.

Amnesty to entire classes of offenders are within the pardon power. Hence, President Carter's amnesty of all the men who evaded military service in Vietnam was lawful under the pardons clause. Presidents may also issue **reprieves** that have the effect of delaying the imposition of a punishment.

Any offense against the United States may be pardoned, with the exception of impeachments. The underlying offenses that led to impeachment may be pardoned, but not the impeachment and removal from office by Congress.

SIDEBAR

Famous Pardons

Two of the best-known pardons of recent times were those of Richard Nixon and the men who evaded the draft during the Vietnam conflict.

In June 1972, the Watergate Building in Washington, D.C., which housed the Democratic National Headquarters, was burglarized. This event triggered two years of investigations by journalists, Congress, and prosecutors of the executive branch. President Nixon was implicated, a bill of impeachment was introduced in the House, and he resigned. On September 8, 1974, President Ford granted former President Nixon an unconditional pardon for any and all criminal acts committed while in office. A Michigan lawyer, Murphy, challenged the pardon. His primary allegation was that a pardon cannot be granted before an individual has been

---

TERMS

amnesty[†]   An act of the government granting a pardon for a past crime. Amnesty is rarely exercised in favor of individuals, but is usually applied to a group or class of persons who are accountable for crimes for which they have not yet been convicted.

reprieve[†]   The postponement of the carrying out of a sentence. A reprieve is not a commutation of sentence; it is merely a delay.

charged with a crime. The United States District Court for the Western District of Michigan rejected this claim.[16]

During the Vietnam conflict, many men fled abroad, primarily to Canada, to avoid the draft. Many others failed to register for the draft or deserted after induction. President Ford established a clemency program on September 17, 1974, through which draft evaders and military deserters could perform up to two years of civilian service in exchange for a full pardon. This program was announced through Proclamation No. 4313. Approximately 22,000 persons took advantage of this pardon. This was a small percentage of the total evaders and deserters.

On January 21, 1977, President Carter issued Proclamation No. 4483, which extended Ford's pardon to all men who had evaded the draft from August 4, 1964, to March 28, 1973. The pardon covered approximately 13,000 men, including 7 who were in prison for draft evasion convictions and another 2,500 who were under indictment. The pardon did not include those who had used force or violence, the 4,500 deserters who were at large, or the 88,700 men who had received general or dishonorable discharges for deserting or being absent without leave.

Even though Presidents Ford's and Carter's pardons were controversial, they were not the first of a kind. There have been several presidential pardons of evaders, deserters, and enemies:

- President Thomas Jefferson granted full pardons to all deserters from the United States army
- President James Madison proclaimed a full pardon for deserters during the War of 1812
- President Abraham Lincoln pardoned those who deserted during the Civil War
- President Andrew Johnson pardoned ex-Confederates
- President Theodore Roosevelt pardoned those individuals who had aided the insurrection in the Philippines.[17]

Pardons do not make an offender whole. The government does not compensate the pardoned individual for any losses sustained as a consequence of arrest, trial, conviction, or sentence served. The pardoned offender is not entitled to compensation for property seized and sold before the pardon was granted. However, if seized property remains in the possession of the government, it is returned to the pardoned individual. Once pardoned, an individual loses the privilege against self-incrimination and may be compelled to testify about the crime.

The pardon power is vested in the President and may not be interfered with by Congress or the courts. Statutes limiting the pardon power are unconstitutional and courts may not review the wisdom of granting or denying a pardon. The remedy for presidential indiscretion in the use of the pardon is at the polls, or, in the extreme, in removal from office through impeachment.

Chief Administrative Officer

The President sits at the apex of the federal bureaucracy. He or she is the chief administrative officer. This role includes the power to develop and declare federal policy, supervise lower executive officers, represent the nation in contract negotiations, manage federal properties, receive citizen complaints, recommend budgets for the government, issue executive orders, and promulgate administrative rules and regulations.

Many presidential functions may be delegated to lower federal officials. Some functions, however, may not be delegated. For example, the President must personally sign or veto bills, nominate officials, and sign pardons. Of course, the President may seek the advice of other officials when making these decisions.

Emergency Powers

Both the President and Congress may respond to emergencies with appropriate action. For example, President Lincoln declared martial law in the rebellious states. The Constitution does not specifically allow this, but it was justified as part of the power of the Commander-in-Chief. Again, recall that presidential power is at its peak when authorized by Congress and at its lowest when acting contrary to Congress. Hence, presidential declarations of martial law may be overturned by Congress.

During martial law, the military may be deployed within the United States and persons arrested may be tried under military law. However, there must be a genuine invasion or insurrection or an imminent threat of either. The Court stated in *Ex parte Milligan*[18] that "[m]artial law cannot arise from a threatened invasion. The necessity must be actual and present; the invasion real, such as effectively closes the courts and deposes the civil administration." Whether martial law is constitutional is a justiciable question.[19]

In times of emergency, the right of **habeas corpus** may be suspended. Habeas corpus existed in the common law and was brought by the founders to this nation. The framers provided, in Article I, § 9, clause 2, that "[t]he privilege of the Writ of Habeas Corpus shall not be suspended, unless when in Cases of Rebellion or Invasion the public

---

TERMS

habeas corpus [Latin for] "you have the body." A writ whose purpose is to obtain immediate relief from illegal imprisonment by having the "body" (that is, the prisoner) delivered from custody and brought before the court. A writ of habeas corpus is a means for attacking the constitutionality of the

Safety may require it." Contrary to the assertion of several presidents, this power does not belong to the President. The placement of it in Article I makes it unquestionable that the power belongs to Congress. Whether the power may be delegated to the President by Congress has not been answered. If Congress's ability to meet in the future were threatened, then such a delegation should be upheld. So long as Congress is able to meet, then the decision may be nondelegable.

Habeas corpus may be suspended only in times of invasion or rebellion. *Milligan* stresses that the threat must be both present and genuine. Even more, civilian government must be disabled. The purpose of martial law is to establish order while civilian government is inoperable. Milligan was a citizen of Indiana. He did not serve in the military during the Civil War, nor was he present in the rebel states during the war. He was charged with conspiracy to aid the Confederacy, tried in a military court, convicted, and sentenced to death. He sought habeas corpus, asserting that he had a right to be tried in a civilian court.

The Court invalidated his conviction and held that he should have been tried in a common-law court, not a military court. The facts that Indiana was never the site of insurrection or fighting, that the civil courts in Indiana continued in operation, and that Milligan was a continuous twenty-year resident who did not serve in the military on either side during the war was proof that there was no threat justifying suspension of his rights to habeas corpus and to be tried in a common-law court by a jury of his peers.

Even a war that has not reached American soil increases both presidential and congressional domestic powers. The combination of executive and legislative war powers proved significant in the *Korematsu* case.

In short, in *Korematsu* the Supreme Court decided that the exigencies of World War II (i.e., fear of a West Coast invasion, espionage, and sabotage) outweighed the civil liberties of the Japanese-Americans living on the West Coast. Note that Justice Black's description of racial discrimination analysis became the precursor of contemporary equal protection law. Racial classifications are "suspect." He stated that the government must have a "pressing" governmental reason to racially classify and that courts must review such classifications with "rigid scrunity." Today, *compelling* and *strict scrutiny* is the nomenclature. Pursuant to statute enacted in 1988, the United States tendered an apology and reparation of $20,000 to each surviving detainee.

TERMS

statute under which, or the proceedings in which, the original conviction was obtained. There are numerous writs of habeas corpus, each applicable in different procedural circumstances. The full name of the ordinary writ of habeas corpus is *habeas corpus ad subjiciendum.*

KOREMATSU
v.
UNITED STATES
323 U.S. 214 (1944)

[Congress enacted legislation in 1942 authorizing the President to restrict movement or residence within military areas and war zones. At the time, concern was building throughout the nation that the Japanese were going to invade the West Coast. This, matched with suspicions about the loyalty of citizens and aliens of Japanese ancestry, led President Roosevelt to issue an executive order authorizing military commanders to exclude persons from military areas and war zones. General DeWitt, commander of the Western Command, then issued several orders directed at Japanese persons. These included curfew, exclusion from certain areas, and internment in camps. When Korematsu failed to leave an area to be interned, he was prosecuted. The curfew order had been previously upheld in *Hirabayashi v. United States,* 320 U.S. 81 (1943).]

Mr. Justice Black delivered the opinion of the Court.

* * *

It should be noted, to begin with, that all legal restrictions which curtail the civil rights of a single racial group are immediately suspect. That is not to say that all such restrictions are unconstitutional. It is to say that courts must subject them to the most rigid scrutiny. Pressing public necessity may sometimes justify the existence of such restrictions; racial antagonism never can ... .

The 1942 Act was attacked in the *Hirabayashi* case as an unconstitutional delegation of power; it was contended that the curfew order and other orders on which it rested were beyond the war powers of the Congress, the military authorities and of the President, as Commander in Chief of the Army; and finally that to apply the curfew order against none but citizens of Japanese ancestry amounted to a constitutionally prohibited discrimination solely on account of race. To these questions, we gave the serious consideration which their importance justified. We upheld the curfew order as an exercise of the power of the government to take steps necessary to prevent espionage and sabotage in an area threatened by Japanese attack ... .

Here, as in the *Hirabayashi* case ... "we cannot reject as unfounded the judgment of the military authorities and of Congress that there were disloyal members of that population, whose number and strength could not be precisely and quickly ascertained. We cannot say that the war-making branches of the Government did not have ground for believing that in a critical hour such persons could not readily be isolated and separately dealt with, and constituted a menace to the national defense and safety, which demanded that prompt and adequate measures be taken to guard against it."

Like curfew, exclusion of those of Japanese origin was deemed necessary because of the presence of an unascertained number of disloyal members of the group, most of whom we have no doubt were loyal to this country. It was because we could not reject the finding of the military authorities that it was impossible to bring about an immediate segregation of the disloyal from the loyal that we sustained the validity of the curfew order as applying to the whole group. In the instant case, temporary exclusion of the entire group was rested by the military on the same ground. The judgment that exclusion of the entire group was for the same reason a military imperative answers the contention that the exclusion was in the nature of group punishment based on antagonism to those of Japanese origin. That there were members of the group who retained loyalties to Japan has been confirmed by investigations made subsequent to the exclusion. Approximately five thousand American citizens of Japanese ancestry refused to swear unqualified allegiance to the United States and to renounce allegiance to the Japanese Emperor, and several thousand evacuees requested repatriation to Japan.

We uphold the exclusion order as of the time it was made and when the petitioner violated it ... . In doing so, we are not unmindful of the hardships imposed by it upon a large group of American citizens ... . But hardships are part of war, and war is an aggregation of hardships. All citizens alike, both in and out of uniform, feel the impact of war in greater or lesser measure. Citizenship has its responsibilities as well as its privileges, and in time of war the burden is always heavier. Compulsory exclusion of large groups of citizens from their homes, except under circumstances of direst emergency and peril, is inconsistent with our basic governmental institutions. But when under conditions of modern warfare our shores are threatened by hostile forces, the power to protect must be commensurate with the threatened danger ... .

We are thus being asked to pass at this time upon the whole subsequent detention program in both assembly and relocation centers, although the only issues framed at the trial related to petitioner's remaining in the prohibited area in violation of the exclusion order ... .

Some of the members of the Court are of the view that evacuation and detention in an Assembly Center were inseparable. After May 3, 1942, the date of Exclusion Order No. 34, Korematsu was under compulsion to leave the area not as he would choose but via an Assembly Center. The Assembly Center was conceived as a part of the machinery for group evacuation. The power to exclude includes the power to do it by force if necessary. And any forcible measure must necessarily entail some degree of detention or restraint whatever method of removal is selected. But whichever view is taken, it results in holding that the order under which petitioner was convicted was valid.

It is said that we are dealing here with the case of imprisonment of a citizen in a concentration camp solely because of his ancestry, without evidence or inquiry concerning his loyalty and good disposition towards the United States. Our task would be simple, our duty clear, were this a case involving the imprisonment of a loyal citizen in a concentration camp because of racial prejudice. Regardless of the true nature of the assembly and relocation centers—and we deem it unjustifiable to call them concentration camps with all the ugly connotations that term implies—we are dealing specifically with nothing but an exclusion order. To cast this case into outlines of racial prejudice, without reference to the real military dangers which were presented, merely confuses the issue. Korematsu was not excluded from the Military Area because of hostility to him or his race. He was excluded because we are at war with the Japanese Empire, because the properly constituted military authorities feared an invasion of our West Coast and felt constrained to take proper security measures, because they decided that the military urgency of the situation demanded that all citizens of Japanese ancestry be segregated from the West Coast temporarily, and finally, because Congress, reposing its confidence in this time of war in our military leaders—as inevitably it must—determined that they should have the power to do just this. There was evidence of disloyalty on the part of some, the military authorities considered that the need for action was great, and time was short. We cannot—by availing ourselves of the calm perspective of hindsight—now say that at that time these actions were unjustified.

Mr. Justice Roberts, dissenting.

This is not a case of keeping people off the streets at night ... nor a case of temporary exclusion of a citizen from an area for his own safety or that of the community ... . On the contrary, it is the case of convicting a citizen as a punishment for not submitting to imprisonment in a concentration camp, based on his ancestry, and solely because of his ancestry, without evidence or inquiry concerning his loyalty ... .

Mr. Justice Murphy, dissenting.

This exclusion of "all persons of Japanese ancestry, both alien and nonalien," from the Pacific

Coast area on the plea of military necessity in the absence of martial law ought not to be approved. Such exclusion goes over "the very brink of constitutional power" and falls into the ugly abyss of racism … .

[W]e must accord great respect and consideration to the judgments of the military authorities who are on the scene and who have full knowledge of the military facts. The scope of their discretion must, as a matter of necessity and common sense, be wide. And their judgments ought not to be overruled lightly by those whose training and duties ill-equip them to deal intelligently with matters so vital to the physical security of the nation.

At the same time, however, it is essential that there be definite limits to military discretion, especially where martial law has not been declared. Individuals must not be left impoverished of their constitutional rights on a plea of military necessity that has neither substance nor support … .

The judicial test of whether the Government, on a plea of military necessity, can validly deprive an indivdual of any of his constitutional rights is whether the deprivation is reasonably related to a public danger that is so "immediate, imminent, and impending" as not to admit of delay and not to permit of ordinary constitutional processes … .

But to infer that examples of individual disloyalty prove a group's disloyalty and justify discriminatory action against the entire group is to deny that under our system of law individual guilt is the sole basis for deprivation of rights. Moreover, this inference, which is at the very heart of the evacuation orders, has been used in support of the abhorrent and despicable treatment of minority groups by the dictatorial tyrannies which this nation is now pledged to destroy. To give constitutional sanction to that inference in this case, however well-intentioned may have been the military command on the Pacific Coast, is to adopt one of the cruelest of the rationales used by our enemies to destroy the dignity of the

individual and to encourage and open the door to discriminatory actions against other minority groups in the passions of tomorrow.

Moreover, there was no adequate proof that the Federal Bureau of Investigation and the military and naval intelligence services did not have the espionage and sabotage situation well in hand … .

Mr. Justice Jackson, dissenting.

Korematsu was born on our soil, of parents born in Japan. The Constitution makes him a citizen of the United States by nativity and a citizen of California by residence. No claim is made that he is not loyal to this country … . Korematsu, however, has been convicted of an act not commonly a crime. It consists of merely being present in the state whereof he is a citizen, near the place where he was born, and where all his life he has lived … .

A citizen's presence in the locality, however, was made a crime only if his parents were of Japanese birth. Had Korematsu been one of four—the others being say, a German alien enemy, an Italian alien enemy, and a citizen of American-born ancestors, convicted of treason but out on parole—only Korematsu's presence would have violated the order. The difference between their innocence and his crime would result, not from anything he did, said, or thought, different than they, but only in that he was born of different racial stock.

Now, if any fundamental assumption underlies our system, it is that guilt is personal and not inheritable. Even if all of one's antecedents had been convicted of treason, the Constitution forbids its penalties to be visited upon him, for it provides that "no Attainder of Treason shall work Corruption of Blood, or Forfeiture except during the Life of the Person attainted." Article 3, § 3, cl. 2. But here is an example to make an otherwise innocent act a crime merely because this prisoner is the son of parents as to whom he had no choice, and belongs to a race from which there is no way to resign … .

§ 6.4 Foreign Affairs Powers

Foreign affairs are exclusively a national concern. By uniting into one nation, the states agreed that jurisdiction over foreign affairs would be vested in the federal government.

The foreign affairs power is shared between the President and Congress. The Constitution does not spell out the precise contours of these powers and, because of the political question doctrine, the Court has issued few opinions in this area. The largest source of information in this area is practice, that is, the roles that the President and Congress have historically accepted and performed. Through practice, the President has assumed most of the foreign affairs powers. Due to its unitary nature, the presidency has proven to operate more quickly and secretly than could Congress, both important features in the foreign affairs arena. (See Figure 6-1).

These principles were recognized by the Supreme Court in *United States v. Curtiss-Wright Export Corp.,* a 1936 Supreme Court decision that involved a presidential proclamation prohibiting the sale of arms to combatants in South America.[20] The proclamation had been approved by Congress. The defendants, who were convicted of selling arms to one of the prohibited parties, challenged the delegation to the President as an unlawful delegation of legislative authority. They prevailed in the lower court, but the Supreme Court reversed.

It found that federal power is different in foreign affairs than in the domestic sphere; specifically, the federal government possesses inherent

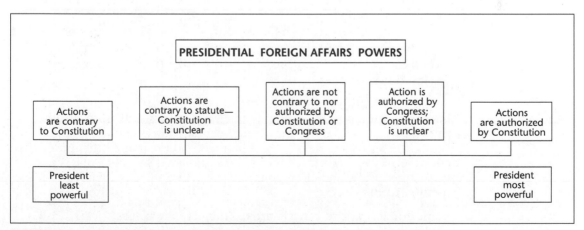

FIGURE 6-1 Presidential Powers Relating to Foreign Affairs

foreign affairs powers. In reaching this conclusion, the Court reasoned that one purpose of the 1789 Constitution was to carve out some of the powers held by the states and place them into a federal government. For example, domestic powers that had previously belonged to the states were transferred to the federal government. However, only limited powers were vested in the federal government, with the states possessing the remainder. The *Curtiss-Wright* Court determined that the states had never held foreign affairs powers; rather, such powers passed directly from the British Crown to the United States (colonies) collectively. Therefore, foreign affairs powers had never belonged to the states. There is no evidence that the framers intended to change this arrangement in the new Constitution. Accordingly,

> [i]t results that the investment of the federal government with the powers of external sovereignty did not depend upon the affirmative grants of the Constitution. The powers to declare and wage war, to conclude peace, to make treaties, to maintain diplomatic relations with other sovereignties, if they never had been mentioned in the Constitution, would have vested in the federal government as necessary concomitants of nationality.

The Court then concluded that the "President alone has the power to speak or listen as a representative of the nation ... . The President is the sole organ of the nation in its external relations, and its sole representative with foreign nations." The Court went further and concluded that the President could have issued the proclamation without congressional approval. Recall *Youngstown,* however. The President's power is at lowest ebb when acting contrary to Congress's intent. Although the President could have acted in the absence of congressional approval in *Curtiss-Wright,* he could not have acted if Congress had specifically disapproved of the action.

Why did the Court trust the President with such broad authority? It said that foreign relations require "caution and unity of design," objectives that the President is more likely to realize than is Congress. The Court stated further that

> [the President], not Congress, has the better opportunity of knowing the conditions which prevail in foreign countries, and especially is this true in time of war. He has his confidential sources of information. He has his agents in the form of diplomatic, consular and other officials. Secrecy in respect of information gathered by them may be highly necessary, and the premature disclosure of it productive of harmful results.

Some foreign affairs powers are exclusively, or at least nearly exclusively, held by the President. The President is the sole official of the United States responsible for communicating with foreign nations. Of course, the President may, and often does, delegate this power to subordinates. Through the Department of State and its Secretary, the President engages in continuous contact with other nations. At times members of Congress engage in dialogue with foreign powers, but this practice is of questionable constitutional and statutory validity.

The Supreme Court has recognized that it is the President who is responsible for recognizing foreign governments. This is a political question and nonreviewable by the courts.[21] The power to recognize governments includes the power to establish relations and develop foreign policy concerning recognized nations. Conversely, the President may order relations with a foreign power terminated and may withdraw the United States' diplomatic representatives from a nation.

So, through practice, federalism, congressional approval, and Supreme Court deference to the other two branches to determine the nature of their foreign affairs relationship, the President has dominated the foreign affairs arena. This has been largely true of the treaty and war powers as well.

§ 6.5 Treaties and Executive Agreements

Treaty Power

As previously mentioned, the Constitution empowers the President to "make Treaties, provided two thirds of the Senators present concur."[22] The treaty power is exclusively federal. Article I, § 10, clause 1, prohibits states from entering into treaties, alliances, or confederations, and from granting letters of marque and reprisal. Clause 3 of that section further prohibits states from making agreements or compacts with other states or nations, without the consent of Congress, except in times of extreme emergency. A two-thirds majority in the Senate is required to confirm a treaty. Only two-thirds of the Senators present is required, not two-thirds of the whole body.

Although treaty making is a shared federal power, the President alone is responsible for negotiating with other nations. The President also decides which nations should be negotiated with, what the subject matter of negotiations should be, and who will represent the nation. Presidents may appoint any person to represent the country in negotiations, without congressional approval. In addition to the members of the professional diplomatic corps (foreign service personnel), presidents have used members of Congress, prominent businesspersons, and past presidents as negotiators. Former President Jimmy Carter, for example, has been actively involved in diplomatic efforts since leaving the Oval Office.

The supremacy clause declares that the "Constitution, and the Laws of the United States which shall be made in Pursuance thereof; and all Treaties made, or which shall be made, under the Authority of the United States, shall be the supreme Law of the Land."[23] The language of this article permits two constructions. The first construction focuses on the placement of the semicolon. The "laws of the United States," which refers primarily to statutes, are treated differently than treaties under this construction. The laws are subject to constitutional limitations, namely, "Constitution, and the Laws ... which shall be made in Pursuance thereof," whereas treaties are not. Under this interpretation, treaties are made under the authority of the United States and are equal to the Constitution.

The second construction reads the Constitution as limiting both laws and treaties. This interpretation has been adopted by the Court. For example, *Reid v. Covert*[24] involved two cases with nearly identical facts. Two women, both civilians, were charged with murdering their servicemen husbands. Both murders occurred while the men were serving abroad (one in Japan and the other in Great Britain). The United States had entered into executive agreements with both nations providing that military personnel and their families would be tried by United States military courts in the nation where the crime was alleged to have been committed. Accordingly, the women were tried in Great Britain and Japan—but military law denied the women rights they would have enjoyed in United States courts. The Supreme Court stated that the women were protected by the Bill of Rights because "[t]he United States is entirely a creature of the Constitution. Its power and authority have no other source."[25] The Court continued, "[no] agreement with a foreign nation can confer power on the Congress, or on any branch of Government, which is free from the restraints of the Constitution."[26] Accordingly, a President may not negotiate away the civil liberties of American citizens through the treaty power. The Court held that the women were entitled to the protections of the Constitution.

This defines the relationship between the Constitution and treaties, but what about the relationship between statutes and treaties? Which prevails if there is a conflict? Both are the supreme law of the land. Accordingly, they are of equal legal weight or authority. If a treaty and statute both deal with the same topic, courts attempt to interpret them as consistent with one another. If this is not possible, then the latest of the two prevails. Thus, Congress may amend or repeal a treaty by statute. Similarly, statutes may be amended or repealed by treaties. However, because of the international consequences of amending or repealing treaties, congressional intent is not inferred. Congress must clearly express an intent to alter an existing treaty.[27]

Federalism issues also arise in the treaty context. What if a treaty conflicts with state law? Even more, does the Tenth Amendment restrict the treaty power? The answer to the first is that the state law is defeated, and to the second the answer is no. The supremacy clause is the foundation for both answers. There is, of course, no problem with matters that fall squarely within the jurisdiction of the federal government. For example, a state law that affects commerce with other nations is voided by a treaty with contrary provisions.

But the treaty power has proven much greater than that. The federal government may, through the treaty power, regulate matters that usually fall within the sphere of state authority. For example, in *Hauenstein v. Lynham*,[28] a state law that prohibited aliens from inheriting property was overridden by a treaty that provided otherwise.

Missouri v. Holland[29] also stands for the principle that the Tenth Amendment does not limit the treaty power. In addition, the Court announced that federal power could be expanded through the treaty power. In 1913, Congress enacted a statute to protect migratory birds. That law was invalidated by lower federal courts as exceeding federal power. Later, the United States and Britain entered into a treaty that required protection of the same birds. Missouri claimed that the federal government had again exceeded its authority and encroached upon state powers. The Court rejected those claims.

The Court reasoned that the Tenth Amendment does not create specific state powers; rather, it reserves to the states those powers not given to the federal government. The treaty power was delegated to the federal government, so the Tenth Amendment does not limit it. In further support of the decision, Justice Oliver Wendell Holmes, who wrote the majority opinion, noted that migratory birds are inherently a national concern and that the treaty did not encroach upon any constitutionally secured rights of citizens.

Executory and Self-Executing Treaties

Treaties are characterized as either **executory** or **self-executing**. An executory treaty is not immediately enforceable as domestic law. Congressional action is necessary to carry it into effect. An executory treaty is not, therefore, the supreme law of the land until Congress has enacted implementing legislation. A self-executing treaty, in contrast, requires no statute to implement its provisions. It is already in a form that courts can enforce.

─────────────────── TERMS ───────────────────

executory[†]   Not yet fully performed, completed, fulfilled, or carried out; to be performed, either wholly or in part; not yet executed.

self-executing[†]   Self-acting; going into effect without need of further action.

Executive Agreements

In addition to treaties, the President may enter into an **executive agreement** with a foreign power. Treaties and executive agreements may be similar in substance, but in procedure they are very different. Treaties must be approved by the Senate, whereas executive agreements are entered into unilaterally by the President. Executive agreements are known by many names, including *executive agreement, memorandum of understanding, memorandum of arrangement,* and *technical agreement,* among others. In recent years, for example, the State Department reported the creation of 300 executive agreements a year through its office. The Defense Department reported a similar number, and there are many more from other agencies.[30]

There is no explicit language in the Constitution approving of executive agreements, compacts, and accords. Regardless, they are an accepted presidential power. In fact, over 90 percent of all agreements with foreign nations are in the form of executive agreements, not treaties.

There are three types of executive agreements, each characterized by different sources of power.[31] The first is the *treaty-authorized executive agreement.* Of the three types of executive agreements, it most closely resembles a treaty, because the agreement is authorized by an existing treaty that has already been approved by the Senate. This is common, for example, for treaties that resolve large policy issues but not the details of implementation. The details are left to future negotiations and the treaty contains a provision authorizing the President to enter into agreements with the treaty's signatories for this purpose. Because the requisite two-thirds Senate vote approves of such agreements, they are seldom found to be invalid. Of course, an agreement that exceeds the treaty authorization is not on the same footing. It is treated as one of the other two forms of executive agreements.

The second type of executive agreement is the *congressionally authorized executive agreement.* This is different from the treaty-authorized executive agreement in two respects. First, congressional approval usually occurs by majority vote in both houses, often through joint resolution. Second, approval usually comes after the agreement has been concluded and executed. Even though this form of agreement need not go through the two-thirds Senate approval procedure, it is checked by Congress and is generally accepted.

TERMS

executive agreement [†]   An agreement with a foreign government, made by the president acting within his or her executive powers.

The third form of executive agreement is the *solely executive agreement*. It is not approved by Congress in any fashion and is founded upon presidential power alone. Generally, this form of agreement is valid only if its subject matter is exclusively executive. Because of the absence of congressional involvement, this form is most questionable. An example is an agreement to recongnize a foreign government. Because this is an executive, rather than congressional, power, the President may unilaterally enter into such an agreement. It has been estimated that only 7 percent of executive agreements are purely exective.[32]

All executive agreements that are premised entirely upon executive power may be altered by Congress. For purposes of analysis, Justice Jackson's three-part test of presidential power applies to executive agreements. If the President enters into a solely executive agreement concerning a subject that is exclusively executive, then Congress may not interfere. For example, Congress is without authority to amend an executive agreement recognizing a foreign power. The same would be true of armistice agreements, as the President possesses the power to end hostilities without congressional authorization. If the subject of an agreement is one over which the President and Congress share powers, however, then Congress may amend or abolish the agreement.

Because congressionally approved agreements are not approved by the Senate, as are treaties, they differ in their effect on existing legislation. Recall that a treaty may amend an existing statute. This appears reasonable because both Congress (the Senate) and the President are acting. But only the President acts in executive agreements. For this reason, unless the President is acting within the sphere of exclusive executive powers, an executive agreement may not alter existing legislation. Even more, if an executive agreement is wholly inconsistent with statutory law, then it is void.[33]

Executive Agreement or Treaty? Circular 175   **SIDEBAR**

When will the President rely on an executive agreement rather than a treaty to memorialize an agreement with a foreign nation? The State Department has issued guidelines concerning when executive agreements are appropriate. The following factors are considered, as announced in the State Department's Circular 175:

1. The extent to which the agreement affects the nation as a whole
2. The extent to which state laws will be affected
3. Whether congressional action is necessary
4. Domestic and foreign practice
5. Congressional preference
6. The degree of formality desired

7. The expected duration of the agreement and the need for prompt conclusion
8. Whether the Constitution delegates the subject matter to the President.[34]

These State Department guidelines are intended to assist its officials in the performance of their duties. Courts, however, may consider these factors, but need not rely on them. Rather, judicial review will center around federalism principles, particularly the nature of the executive agreement and whether Congress has approved or disapproved of it. If not, a reviewing court will determine whether the subject matter is inherently executive.

Like treaties, executive agreements are limited by the Constitution. Executive agreements are law of the United States under the supremacy clause and prevail over conflicting state laws. The case *Dames & Moore v. Regan* illustrates the use of an executive agreement by President James Carter to free Americans who were held captive in Iran.

Although the executive agreement at issue in *Dames & Moore* was of the solely executive type (that is, it was never expressly approved by Congress), the Court found that Congress had implicitly approved it. Because of inaction (failure to enact legislation disapproving of the agreement), a scheme of legislation that supported the power generally, a history of presidential authority in the area, and provisions in the agreement intended to protect the rights of interested individuals (claims tribunal), the agreement was upheld.

Congress has enacted several laws intended to control the presidential power to make executive agreements. In some instances, Congress disapproves of executive agreements on certain subjects in advance. In others, Congress disapproves of agreements after they have been enacted. Also, federal legislation requires presidents to report all executive agreements to Congress after execution. Figure 6-2 summarizes agreement creation and source.

The final issue in this area is termination power. May a President terminate a treaty? An executive agreement? May Congress terminate either? The Constitution does not express a termination method.

It is argued that because treaties are approved by a two-thirds vote of the Senate, they must be terminated in the same manner. Conversely, it is argued that the President possesses the inherent power to terminate treaties. This area of law is not well defined, in part because the Supreme Court has treated the issue as a nonjusticiable political question.[35] Recall Justice Jackson's tripartite analysis in *Youngstown* when considering this issue.

Though there are no concrete answers, a few conclusions can be drawn. First, treaties most assuredly can be terminated when the President and Senate concur. Second, terminations with congressional approval (majority votes in both houses) are likely valid. Third, solely executive terminations are the most vulnerable. The extent to which

FIGURE 6-2
Treaties
and Executive
Agreements

TREATIES AND EXECUTIVE AGREEMENTS

Type of Agreement	Description/ Method of Creation	Constitutional Source
Treaty —Executory —Self-executing	Presidential negotiation and drafting. ⅔ favorable vote in Senate (of senators present).	—Art. II, § 2, cl. 2 establishes federal power and method —Art. I, § 10 prohibits the states from making agreements with other nations, except in emergencies.
Treaty-authorized executive agreement	Existing treaty that has senatorial approval authorizes the President to unilaterally make an agreement with a nation. Usually done to allow signatory nations to a treaty to resolve issues of implementation more easily.	—Art. II, § 2, cl. 2
Congressionally authorized executive agreement	Presidential negotiation and agreement making are authorized by both houses of Congress, usually by joint resolution.	—Inherent executive power —Congressional authorization —Practice
Solely executive agreement	President unilaterally negotiates and executes an agreement. Congress does not participate either before or after execution.	—Inherent executive power —Practice

the treaty regulates a subject within the President's domain is relevant. Also, congressional attitude, whether express or implied, will also be considered.

§ 6.6 War Powers

Article II, § 2, clause 1, declares the President to be the Commander-in-Chief of the Army and Navy of the United States and of the state militias when called into national service. Only the Army and Navy are

DAMES & MOORE
v.
REGAN

453 U.S. 654 (1981)

Justice Rehnquist delivered the opinion of the Court.

* * *

On November 4, 1979, the American Embassy in Tehran was seized and our diplomatic personnel were captured and held hostage. In response to that crisis, President Carter, acting pursuant to the International Emergency Economic Powers Act, declared a national emergency on November 14, 1979, and blocked the removal or transfer of "all property and interests in property of the Government of Iran, its instrumentalities and controlled entities of the Central Bank of Iran which are or become subject to the jurisdiction of the United States ... ."

[On] November 14, 1979, the Treasury Department's Office of Foreign Assets Control issued a regulation providing that "[u]nless licensed or authorized ... any attachment, judgment, decree, lien, execution, garnishment, or other judicial process is null and void with respect to any property in which on or since [the date of the order] existed an interest of Iran." ...

On December 19, 1979, petitioner Dames and Moore filed suit in the United States District Court [against] the Government of Iran, the Atomic Energy Organization of Iran, and a number of Iranian banks. [Dames and Moore] alleged that its wholly owned subsidiary, Dames and Moore International, S.R.L., was a party to a written contract with the Atomic Energy Organization, and that the subsidiary's entire interest in the contract had been assigned to petitioner. [Dames and Moore] contended ... it was owed $3,436,694.30 plus interest for services performed under the contract prior to the date of termination. The District Court issued orders of attachment directed against property of the defendants, and the property of certain Iranian banks was then attached to secure any judgment that might be entered against them.

On January 20, 1981, the Americans held hostage were released by Iran pursuant to an Agreement entered into the day [before]. [This] agreement stated "[i]t is the purpose ... to terminate all litigation as between the Government of each party and the nationals of the other, and to bring about the settlement and termination of all such claims through binding arbitration." In furtherance of this goal, the Agreement called for the establishment of an Iran-United States Claims Tribunal which would arbitrate any claims not settled within six months. Awards of the Claims Tribunal are to be "final and binding" and "enforceable ... in the courts of any nation in accordance with its laws." Under the Agreement, the United States is obligated

> to terminate all legal proceedings in United States courts involving claims of United States persons and institutions against Iran and its state enterprises, to nullify all attachments and judgments obtained therein, to prohibit all further litigation based on such claims, and to bring about the termination of such claims through binding arbitration.

In addition, the United States must "act to bring about the transfer" by July 19, 1981 of all Iranian assets held in this country by American banks. One billion dollars of these assets will be deposited in a security account in the Bank of England, to the account of the Algerian Central Bank, and used to satisfy awards rendered against Iran by the Claims Tribunal.

On January 19, 1981, President Carter issued a series of Executive Orders implementing the terms of the agreement ... .

The parties and the lower court all agreed that much relevant analysis is contained in [*Youngstown*]. Justice Black's opinion for the Court in that case [stated that the] "President's power, if any, to issue the order must stem either from an act of Congress or from the Constitution itself." Justice Jackson's concurring opinion elaborated in a general way the consequences of different types of interaction between the two democratic branches in assessing Presidential authority to act in any given case.

Although we have in the past found and do today find Justice Jackson's classification of executive actions into three categories analytically useful, Jackson himself recognized that his three categories represented "a somewhat oversimplified grouping," and it is doubtless the case that executive action in any particular instance falls, not neatly in one of three pigeonholes [recall the three: the President acting pursuant to statute, in the absence of any statute, and against statute] ... . This is particularly true as respects cases such as the one before us, involving responses to international crises the nature of which Congress can hardly have been expected to anticipate in any detail.

[The] Government has principally relied on § 203 of the [International Emergency Economic Powers Act (IEEPA), which] provides in part:

> [The] President may [nullify], void, prevent or prohibit any acquisition, holding, withholding, use, transfer, withdrawal, transportation, importation or exportation of, or dealing in, or exercising any right, power, or privilege with respect to, or transactions involving, any property in which any foreign country or a national thereof has any interest; by any person, or with respect to any property, subject to the jurisdiction of the United States.

The Government contends that the acts of "nullifying" the attachments and ordering the "transfer" of the frozen assets are specifically authorized by the plain language of the above statute. ...

Because the President's action in nullifying the attachments and ordering the transfer of assets was taken pursuant to specific congressional authorization, it is "supported by the strongest of presumptions and the widest latitude of judicial interpretation, and the burden of persuasion would rest heavily upon any who might attack it." *Youngstown*, 343 U.S. at 637 (Jackson, J., concurring). Under the circumstances of this case, we cannot say that petitioner has sustained that heavy burden. A contrary ruling would mean that the Federal Government as a whole lacked

the power exercised by the President, and that we are not prepared to say.

Although we have concluded that the IEEPA constitutes specific congressional authorization to the President to nullify the attachments and order the transfer of Iranian assets, there remains the question of the President's authority to suspend claims pending in American courts. Such claims have, of course, an existence apart from the attachments which accompany them. In terminating these claims [the] President purported to act under authority of both the IEEPA and so-called "Hostage Act." We conclude that neither the IEEPA nor the Hostage Act constitutes specific authorization of the President's action suspending claims. This is not to say that these statutory provisions are entirely irrelevant to the question of the validity of the President's action. We think both statutes highly relevant in the looser sense of indicating congressional acceptance of a broad scope for executive action in circumstances such as those presented in this case. [The] IEEPA delegates broad authority to the President to act in times of national emergency with respect to property of a foreign country. The Hostage Act similarly indicates congressional willingness that the President have broad discretion when responding to the hostile acts of foreign sovereigns ... .

Although we have declined to conclude that the IEEPA or the Hostage Act directly authorizes the President's suspension of claims for the reasons noted, we cannot ignore the general tenor of Congress' legislation in this area in trying to determine whether the President is acting alone or at least with the acceptance of Congress. [Congress] cannot anticipate and legislate with regard to every possible action the President may find it necessary to take [for] every possible situation in which he might act. Such failure of Congress specifically to delegate authority does not, "especially ... in the areas of foreign policy and national security," imply "congressional disapproval" of action taken by the Executive. On the contrary, the enactment of legislation closely related to the question of the President's authority in a particular case which evinces legislative intent to accord the President broad discretion may be considered to "invite" "measures on independent presidential responsibility." At least this is so where there is no contrary indication of legislative intent and when, as here, there is a history of congressional acquiescence in conduct of the sort engaged in by the President ... .

In light of the foregoing—the inferences to be drawn from the character of the legislation Congress has enacted in the area such as the IEEPA and the Hostage Act, and from the history of acquiescence in executive claims settlement—we conclude that the President was authorized to suspend pending claims. Justice Frankfurter pointed out in *Youngstown*, "a systematic, unbroken, executive practice, long pursued to the knowledge of the Congress and never before questioned ... may be treated as a gloss on the 'Executive Power' vested in the President by § 1 of Art. II." Past practice does not, by itself, create power, but "long-continued pratice, known to

and acquiesced in by Congress, would raise a presumption that the [act] had been [committed] in pursuance of [Congress's] consent ... .

Our conclusion is buttressed by the fact that the means chosen by the President to settle the claims of American nationals provided an alternative forum, the Claims Tribunal, which is capable of providing meaningful relief ... .

Just as importantly, Congress has not disapproved of the action taken here. Though Congress has held hearings on the Iranian Agreement itself, Congress has not enacted legislation, or even passed a resolution, indicating its displeasure with the Agreement. Quite the contrary, the relevant Senate Committee has stated that the establishment of the Tribunal is "of vital importance to the United States." We are thus clearly not confronted with a situation in which Congress has in some way resisted the exercise of Presidential authority.

specifically mentioned because that was the whole of the military in 1789. It is not seriously questioned that the framers intended to include the entire military with the language. Therefore, the President is the Commander-in-Chief of all branches of the armed forces: Army, Navy, Marines, and Air Force. The framers specifically chose civilian command of the military to keep the military in check.

As Commander-in-Chief, the President sits at the top of the hierarchy. He or she is the chief general and chief admiral of the armed forces. The extent to which the President becomes involved in the daily operations of the armed forces is left to his or her discretion. Although the Constitution delegates the power to regulate the armed forces to Congress,[36] the President may issue regulations covering the same subject. Congress is the final authority and thus executive regulations, orders, and commands must be consistent with legislation to be valid. The power to promulgate regulations may be delegated to the secretaries of the armed forces.

The most controversial and discussed power of the President concerns the initiation of hostilities and the commitment of American military forces to ventures abroad. The power to declare war clearly rests with Congress. Other methods were considered by the framers. Hamilton initially suggested that the Senate alone should possess the power. He argued that the Senate would be best suited to make the decision, because of its familiarity with foreign affairs through the treaty and related powers. (He later changed his opinion and advocated that it be a shared presidential and Senate power.) Randolph believed the power should lie with the House of Representatives, the true voice of the people. Butler argued that the power was by its nature executive and should be delegated exclusively to the President. The delegates finally settled on excluding the President, but involving the entire Congress in the decision.[37] A simple majority vote in each house is required to declare war.

Even though the framers rejected presidential power to declare war, presidents have de facto exercised the power since the beginning. The first controversy actually involved a presidential decision not to use force. In 1798, George Washington issued a proclamation declaring the neutrality of the United States in a war between Great Britain and France. Alexander Hamilton defended the President's action, while James Madison argued that it was an invasion of Congress's authority to declare war. Madison reasoned that the power to declare war necessarily includes the power to declare peace. Since that time, presidents have on hundreds of occasions involved the United States in conflicts without congressional approval. Some presidents have openly resisted congressional involvement in the decision to commit troops. President Bush remarked, "I didn't have to get permission from some old goat in the United States Congress to kick Saddam Hussein out of Kuwait."[38] Of the hundreds of military ventures in which the United States has been involved, only five were accompanied by a declaration of war.

There have been more than 200 instances of military action without declarations of war or other congressional authorization. The first occurred in 1798 when the United States and France had the first of several military conflicts over a two-year period. Such actions continue into the present day. Both the Korean and Vietnam "wars" fall into this category.

The source of presidential authority to make war is primarily the Commander-in-Chief power, but it is also custom. Clearly, presidents have often made "war" without congressional authorization. However, it is not likely that presidential authority can overcome adverse congressional resolution. If Congress prohibits, or requires a cessation of, military action, the President must comply. To do otherwise would not be faithful execution of the laws.

Presidents have justified their unilateral decisions to use the military for several reasons: to defend national economic interests abroad, to defend United States citizens abroad, to assist foreign persons from abuse, and to honor treaty obligations. Clearly, presidential authority would be at its highest point if the United States were invaded. Unilateral presidential power to repel invasions cannot be questioned.

Congress has attempted to control presidential war-making authority through the War Powers Resolution of 1973.[39] Section 2 of the Resolution announces Congress's objective:

It is the purpose of this joint resolution to fulfill the intent of the framers of the Constitution of the United States and to insure that the collective judgment of both the Congress and the President will apply to the introduction of United States Armed Forces into hostilities, or into situations where imminent involvement in hostilities is clearly indicated by the circumstances, and to the continued use of such forces in hostilities or in such situations.

The resolution (which is reprinted in Appendix G) provides that the President must notify Congress of any introduction of the United States military into hostilities, or situations where hostilities are imminent, within forty-eight hours. With few exceptions, Congress then has sixty days to act. If it cannot meet during this time, the President is authorized to continue the military action. If Congress does meet, it may declare war, authorize the action, require a termination of hostilities, or not act. If Congress does not act, the President is required to terminate the military action. The President has no veto power.[40]

The constitutionality of the War Powers Resolution is questionable. One objection that has been voiced by several presidents is that it interferes with an inherent presidential power. Another objection concerns the absence of a presidential veto. The Supreme Court has invalidated the use of the **legislative veto** and the War Powers Resolution appears to be just that. See Chapter 7 for a further discussion of the legislative veto. Finally, the Resolution may represent an unlawful delegation of Congress's war-making power to the President.

The precise relationship between Congress and the President in the war powers area is unknown. The federal judiciary has been reluctant to become involved in this area, usually ruling that these cases are nonjusticiable political questions. Instead, History, cooperation between the two branches, and public opinion shape this area of law.

Once war has been initiated, the President is responsible for deciding military strategy and technique. These are command decisions with which Congress may not interfere. The President supervises the war and its participants. His or her power is more limited in terms of military discipline, which Congress may regulate. The President alone executes congressional regulations of the military, and he or she may

---

TERMS

legislative veto   An act of a legislature invalidating executive action in a particular instance. Generally, legislative vetos are unconstitutional. Once power is delegated by Congress to the President, it is generally prohibited from interfering with the President's enforcement.

establish rules that do not conflict with congressional regulations. The President's largest limitation as to the conduct of wars is money. Congress alone may appropriate funds.

The powers of the federal government, at least of the political branches, are generally increased during times of war. The government's war power is most potent when Congress and the President join forces. The federal government may enact economic regulations (such as price and rental controls and rationing of food and supplies), draft servicepersons, and the like. Also, as previously discussed, the internment of Americans of the same ancestry as a war enemy was permitted during World War II, in spite of the absence of conflict on American soil, in the *Korematsu* case. Although presidential authority is enhanced during wartime, alone it is not as powerful as when accompanied by congressional support. This is evinced by the Court's invalidation of President Truman's seizure of steel mills (*Youngstown*) during the Korean conflict.

Presidents may call state militias into active national service when necessary. By a statute, which was upheld by the Court, the President may now order state militias into service abroad without the consent of state officials. During domestic emergencies, such as invasion, the President may declare martial law. If Congress is unable to meet and has preapproved the action, the President may suspend habeas corpus. So long as Congress is unable to meet due to domestic hostility, the presidential authority to both legislate and execute laws will be increased.

§ 6.7   Presidential Privilege

At common law, several confidentiality privileges developed to preserve the integrity of special relationships. Many of these continue today. For example, communications between attorneys and clients are confidential. Attorneys have an ethical obligation not to disclose the content of these communications and courts may not compel their disclosure (with few exceptions). Physician-patient, clergy-parishioner, and therapist-patient are other examples. The privilege is intended to create an atmosphere of openness and freedom of communication.

The Constitution does not expressly provide for confidentiality between the President and his or her staff. However, presidents and their subordinates have long claimed that a privilege is inherent in the separation of powers. The privilege, it has been asserted, prohibits courts from ordering executive branch officials from disclosing internal communications or documents. The issue was first addressed by a federal court in the 1807 treason prosecution of Aaron Burr. At issue in *United*

States v. Burr[41] was the production of a letter Aaron Burr had sent to President Thomas Jefferson. Chief Justice John Marshall, who sat as trial judge, ruled that the President was subject to the order of the court and could be ordered to produce the letter.[42] The issue remained dormant thereafter for many years. It surfaced again, with vigor, during and following the Nixon presidency. Consider *United States v. Nixon*,[43] an excerpt of which appears in Chapter 3.

President Richard Nixon claimed that his tape recordings of Oval Office conversations and documents relating to the Watergate investigation were privileged from disclosure to a grand jury. The Court agreed that there should be an executive privilege if there were to be frank and open discussions in the White House, but it would not extend the privilege as far as President Nixon urged.

The Court held that presidential communications are presumed to be privileged. By asserting executive privilege, a President establishes a prima facie case of nondisclosure. However, the presumption may be overcome. In this particular case, the Court held that the President's generalized privilege was defeated by "demonstrated, specific need for evidence in a pending criminal trial."[44] However, the Court also concluded that the trial court should first conduct an in camera inspection of the records to determine if disclosure was appropriate. Records not material to the Watergate investigation were ordered to remain confidential.

The Supreme Court has not had an opportunity to deal with the privilege in the context of national security, military, or diplomatic records. It is likely that the courts would find national security records to be privileged. Nor has the Court had to deal with the issue in the context of civil litigation. The need for information is more critical in criminal cases, in which both the public and the accused have more at stake than during civil litigation. For this reason, it will be more difficult to overcome the executive privilege in a civil case.[45] Of course, the precise nature and facts of each case, civil or criminal, must be considered.

After President Nixon resigned, he entered into an agreement with the General Services Administration (GSA) for the storage of over 2 million documents and 880 tape recordings relating to his presidency. In response, Congress passed a bill requiring the GSA to screen the materials and return private ones to President Nixon, preserve materials of historical value, make the materials available in judicial proceedings, and establish rules concerning public access to the materials. President Ford signed the bill into law and Jimmy Carter, the newly elected President, supported the legislation.

President Nixon challenged the law as violative of separation of powers principles and the executive privilege. The Court rejected those claims in *Nixon v. Administrator of General Services Administration*.[46] In President Nixon's favor, the Court held that a former President may assert the executive privilege. However, in this particular case, the fact that neither President Ford nor Carter supported Nixon's contentions made his position weaker. In further support of its rejection of the separations claim, the Court noted that the executive branch had been delegated the authority to maintain, screen, and determine public access to the materials.

As to his claim of privilege, the Court found that the standards set out in *United States v. Nixon* applied. However, instead of judicial in camera inspection, Congress had delegated the review to the administrator of the General Services Administration. The Court found this acceptable, as this person was an executive branch official and would be sensitive to executive concerns. The privilege was further overcome by the public need to preserve and reconstruct its history and the absence of support by Presidents Ford or Carter for Nixon's claim.

In summary, a President enjoys a limited privilege against being compelled to disclose records and other materials created in the course of executive duties. The Supreme Court has determined that issues relating to the presidential privilege are justiciable. (As announced in *Marbury v. Madison*,[47] it is the Court's duty to say what the law is.) A presidential assertion of privilege creates a presumption of nondisclosure that must be overcome by the party seeking the information. If the information sought concerns purely executive powers, such as diplomacy and national security, then the privilege may be absolute, or, at least, nearly impossible to overcome. If the matter is not as sensitive, then a generalized claim of privilege may be overcome by the need for information in a particular criminal case. To a lesser degree, this is also true in civil cases.

§ 6.8 Presidential Immunity

In addition to a privilege against disclosure of executive materials, presidents and their subordinates may also be immune from civil liability for actions committed in furtherance of their duties. Generally, the President is absolutely immune from suit and liability for official acts.[48] The scope of the immunity is broad—acts within the *outer perimeter* of official function are covered. This absolute immunity stems from the doctrine of separation of powers, common-law history, and the desire not to divert the attention of the President from his or her duties. Both sitting and past presidents enjoy this immunity. (See Figure 6-3.)

Lower executive officials are also entitled to immunity, but in most circumstances it is not absolute. Rather, it is characterized as *qualified*. An executive official is entitled to absolute immunity only when performing

PRESIDENTIAL PRIVILEGE AND IMMUNITY—IMPORTANT CASES

Privilege

United States v. Burr 25 F. Cas. 30 (C.C.D.Va. 1807)	John Marshall, sitting as a trial judge, decided that President Thomas Jefferson could be ordered to produce a letter written by Aaron Burr as part of Burr's treason trial.
United States v. Nixon 418 U.S. 904 (1974)	The Supreme Court ruled that although a presidential privilege exists, and is presumed to exist if asserted, it may be overcome by a specific need for evidence in a criminal case.
Nixon v. Administrator of General Services Administration, 433 U.S. 425 (1977)	Established that former Presidents may assert the privilege. Also, a congressional delegation of authority to review a previous President's documents for privilege was approved.

Immunity

Nixon v. Fitzgerald, 457 U.S. 800 (1982)	Presidents are absolutely immune for official acts. Immunity extends to the outer perimeter of official function.
Harlow v. Fitzgerald, 457 U.S. 800 (1982)	Lower federal officials are shielded by absolute immunity when performing a purely executive function. Otherwise, lower officials are shielded by a qualified immunity.
Jones v. Clinton, 72 F.3d 1354 (8th Cir. 1996) (on appeal at the time of publication of this text)	Presidents are not immune from civil litigation unrelated to the performance of official duties.

FIGURE 6-3 Important Cases on Presidential Privilege and Immunity

a near-presidential function; that is, the official is performing a function that is inherently executive and is closely tied to the presidency itself. It is likely that, to satisfy this test, an officer must have been acting under a direct delegation from the President. Military, national security, and diplomatic functions are most likely to fall into this category.

In most instances an officer will be protected by a qualified immunity. Under the qualified immunity, an officer may be liable for acts that violate *clearly established law.* If the law is not clearly established, the officer is not liable for any injuries caused. The test is objective, not subjective. Thus, the question is whether a reasonably competent official would have known the law, not whether the officer-defendant knew the law.[49] To protect officials from pernicious litigation, courts are instructed to consider the state of the law in pretrial proceedings and to dismiss cases in which the law was not clearly established. Therefore, in the end, the official acting properly is immune from liability, but not from suit. Presidents are, in contrast, immune from both suit and liability.

As previously indicated, presidents and their subordinates are not immune from equitable relief (e.g., injunctions). Executive acts that are justiciable and unconstitutional may be enjoined by courts. Core executive functions, however, will not be reviewed under the nonjusticiability doctrine.

As of the printing of this text, it appears that the President does not enjoy a privilege against civil actions unrelated to the peformance of official duties. President William Clinton was sued by Paula Jones for sexual harassment, assault, and state tort claims in federal district court. President Clinton asserted that the action should be dismissed pending his departure from office. The district court accepted this position in part. The court ordered the President to respond to discovery, but further held that separations principles shielded the President from trial until he had vacated the presidency. On appeal in 1996, the United States Court of Appeals for the Eighth Circuit reversed the trial court's decision. The court of appeals stated that the presidency is not a monarchy and that liability for unofficial acts does not threaten presidential performance. Accordingly, sitting presidents are subject to liability for "unofficial acts." The court did emphasize that trial courts must be sensitive to a President's schedule and time demands so as to avoid interfering with presidential functions.[50]

JONES v. CLINTON

72 F.3d 1354 (8th Cir. 1996)

Bowman, Circuit Judge.

We have before us in this appeal the novel question whether the person currently serving as President of the United States is entitled to immunity from civil liability for his unofficial acts, i.e. for acts committed by him in his personal capacity rather than in his capacity as President. William Jefferson Clinton, who here is sued personally, and not as President, appeals from the District Court's decision staying trial proceedings, for the duration of his presidency, on claims brought against him by Paula Corbin Jones. He argues that the court instead should have dismissed Mrs. Jones' suit without prejudice to the refiling of her suit when he no longer is President. Mr. Clinton also challenges the District Court's decision to allow discovery to proceed in the case during the stay in the trial. Mrs. Jones cross-appeals, seeking to have the stays entered by the District Court lifted, so that she might proceed to trial on her claims ... .

On May 6, 1994, Mrs. Jones filed suit in the District Court against Mr. Clinton and Danny Ferguson, an Arkansas State Trooper who was assigned to Mr. Clinton's security detail ... . Mrs. Jones alleges that Mr. Clinton, under color of state law, violated her constitutional rights to equal protection and due process by sexually harassing and assaulting her. She further alleges that Mr. Clinton and Trooper Ferguson conspired to violate those rights ... .

Mr. Clinton argues that this suit should be dismissed solely because of his status as President. The immunity he seeks would protect him for as long as he is President, but would expire when his presidency has been completed ... .

We start with the truism that Article II of the Constitution, which vests the executive power of the federal government in the President, did not create a monarchy. The President is cloaked with none of the attributes of sovereign immunity. To the contrary, the President, like all other government officials, is subject to the same laws that apply to all other members of society ... . Nevertheless, mindful that for the sake of the nation's general good the Constitution empowers officials to act within the scope of their official responsibilities, the Supreme Court has recognized "that there are some officials whose special functions require a full exemption from liability" for their performance of official acts. The list of those entitled to absolute immunity from civil liability includes the President of the United States for his official acts ... members of Congress for their legislative acts, regardless of motive ... judges of general jurisdiction for judicial acts ... prosecutors for prosecutorial functions ... and certain executive officials performing certain judicial and prosecutorial functions ... . In addition, witnesses are entitled to absolute immunity from civil suit for testimony given in judicial proceedings ... . We are unaware, however, of any case in which any public official ever has been granted immunity from suit for his unofficial acts [and this case appears to present an issue of first impression for federal courts] ... .

There is no suggestion in this case that federal legislation is the source of [presidential immunity] ... . Nor is presidential immunity of any kind explicit in the text of the Constitution. Instead, whatever immunity the President enjoys flows by implication from the separation of powers doctrine ... .

Mrs. Jones is constitutionally entitled to access to the courts and to the equal protection of the laws ... .

Mr. Clinton argues that, if he is presently amenable to suit for his private acts, the proceedings against him inevitably will intrude upon the office of President ... . [The Supreme Court in an earlier case] was troubled by the potential impact of private civil suits arising out of the President's performance of his official duties on the future performance of those duties ... .

Mrs. Jones' claims, except for her defamation claim, concern actions by Mr. Clinton that, beyond cavil, are unrelated to his duties as President. This lawsuit does not implicate presidential decision-making. If this suit goes forward, the President still will be able to carry out his duties without any concern that he might be sued for damages by a constituent aggrieved by some official presidential act. Though amenable to suit for his private acts, the President retains the absolute immunity [for official acts].

Mr. Clinton argues that denying his claim to immunity will give the judiciary carte blanche to intrude unconstitutionally upon the Executive Branch and in fact will disrupt the performance of his presidential duties and responsibilities ... .

The Constitution by no means contemplates total separation of each of the three branches of government ... . But under the Constitution ... no one branch may [overly intrude upon another] ... .

The discretion of the courts in suits such as this one comes into play ... by controlling the scheduling of the case as necessary to avoid interference with specific, particularized, clearly articulated presidential duties. If the trial preliminaries or the trial itself become barriers to the effective performance of his official duties, Mr. Clinton's remedy is to pursue motions for rescheduling, additional time, or continuances. Again, we have every confidence that the District Court will discharge its responsibility to protect the President's role as our government's chief executive officer, without impeding Mrs. Jones' right to have her claims heard without undue delay ... .

To sum up, we hold that the Constitution does not confer upon an incumbent President any immunity from civil actions that arise from his unofficial acts... .

[At the time of this writing, this case had not been appealed, but the time for appeal had not lapsed.]

Summary

The American presidency is unique. Instead of a monarch, we have an elected official as the head of our government. Unlike in many nations, executive power is not divided between two positions, a president and prime minister. Instead, Article II vests all executive power in one person.

In terms of domestic power, the President is responsible for the enforcement of laws. This includes statutes and court orders. Presidential power in this context is largely defined by the other two branches. As to foreign affairs, Justice Jackson established a paradigm for understanding presidential authority. Presidential power is the greatest when authorized by the Constitution. After that, presidential power is greatest when authorized by Congress. The President, of course, acts without authority if the action is contrary to the Constitution. Presidential authority is weakest when contrary to an express statement of Congress. The cases in the middle—what Justice Jackson referred to as the twilight area—are the most complex to resolve.

To protect the integrity of the presidency, the law recongizes that a President must feel free to consult with advisors. Accordingly, presidential communications are privileged. The Supreme Court has held that a presidential assertion of privilege is prima facie proof of its applicability. This may be overcome, however, if a party can demonstrate a specific need for the evidence in a pending criminal trial.

Similarly, the President is immune from damages liability for the performance of presidential functions. The scope of presidential functions is drawn broadly in favor of the President. This rule prevents a disabling of the presidency by civil litigation and the fear of litigation. As this book went to press, the lower courts had ruled that President Clinton may be liable for acts unrelated to the performance of his duties, even while sitting as President. President Clinton's petition for *certiorari* had not been decided when this book was printed.

Review Questions

1. What are the basic qualifications to be President, as established by Article II of the Constitution?

2. Identify the ways in which the President plays a role in lawmaking.

3. Justice Jackson's tripartite analysis of presidential power, announced in *Youngstown,* has been referred to by members of the Court on many occasions since that decision was rendered. Describe that analysis.

4. What is executive impoundment?

5. What is an executive order?

6. What is the presidential and congressional role in appointments (Supreme Court justices, etc.)?

7. Presidents may grant pardons and reprieves. Distinguish the two.

8. Distinguish treaties from executive agreements.

9. Does the Constitution provide that the President may suspend habeas corpus?

10. Distinguish presidential privilege from presidential immunity.

Review Problems

1. Consider whether the President should possess an inherent power to respond to emergencies. Make your best argument in favor of and opposing such a power.

2. Assume that the President does possess an inherent power to respond to emergencies, such as in *Youngstown.* Should the judiciary be empowered to review the President's determination that an emergency exists? Explain.

3. The President enjoys absolute immunity for all official actions. This does not mean that no remedy exists for misbehavior. Identify possible remedies against a President for official actions that are harmful.

4. In an interview of President Nixon by David Frost on May 20, 1977, the following occurred.

   Frost. So what in a sense, you're saying is that there are certain situations, and the Huston Plan or that part of it was one of them, where the President can decide that it's in the best interests of the nation or something, and do something illegal.

   Nixon. Well, when the President does it, that means it is not illegal.

Do you agree with President Nixon that if a President commits an act in the best interest of the country, that act is by nature lawful? Is his position supported by the judicially created doctrine of absolute immunity? Explain.

5. Article I states that Congress possesses the legislative powers "herein granted." There is no such language in Article II. It has been contended that this language indicates that the framers did not intend to limit the President to the powers enumerated in Article II. Do you agree? Also, note that a congressional privilege is expressed in the Constitution, but no similar presidential privilege is mentioned. What is the import of this ommission?

Notes

[1] Art. I, § 1, cl. 5.

[2] Amendment XII.

[3] Amendment XXV, §§ 3 and 4.

[4] 3 U.S.C. § 19.

[5] Art. I, § 3, cl. 4.

[6] 491 U.S. 397 (1989).

[7] The statute was declared unconstitutional in *United States v. Eichman,* 496 U.S. 310 (1990).

[8] Thomas Halper, "Supreme Court Appointments: Criteria and Consequences," 21 *N.Y.L. Forum* 563 (1976).

[9] Thomas Halper, "Senate Rejection of Supreme Court Nominees," 22 *Drake L. Rev.* 102 (1972).

[10] *Buckley v. Valeo,* 424 U.S. 1 (1976).

[11] *Freytag v. Commissioner of Internal Revenue,* 501 U.S. 868 (1991).

[12] *Weiss v. United States,* 114 S. Ct. 752 (1994).

[13] *Ex parte Garland,* 71 U.S. 333, 380 (1867).

[14] *Id.*

[15] *Schick v. Reed,* 419 U.S. 256 (1974).

[16] *Murphy v. Ford,* 390 F. Supp. 1372 (W.D. Mich. 1995).

[17] *See* "Keeping His First Promise," *Time,* Jan. 31, 1977; "Carter's First Act Touches Off a Storm," *U.S. News & World Report,* Jan. 31, 1977; "Carter Pardons Draft Evaders, Orders a Study of Deserters," *New York Times,* Jan. 22, 1977.

[18] 71 U.S. (4 Wall.) 2 (1866).

[19] *Sterling v. Constantin,* 287 U.S. 378 (1932).

[20] 299 U.S. 304 (1936).

[21] *United States v. Pink,* 315 U.S. 203 (1942).

[22] Article II, § 2, clause 2.

[23] Article VI, clause 2.

24 354 U.S. 1 (1957).

25 *Id.* at 5–6.

26 *Id.* at 16.

27 *Cook v. United States,* 288 U.S. 102 (1933).

28 100 U.S. 483 (1879).

29 252 U.S. 416 (1920).

30 Richard Erikson, "The Making of Executive Agreements by the United States Department of Defense: An Agenda for Progress," 13 *B.U. Int'l L.J.* 45, 46 (1995).

31 *See* Kenneth Randall, "The Treaty Power," 51 *Ohio St. L.J.* 1089 (1990) and Jack Weiss, "The Approval of Arms Control Agreements as Congressional-Executive Agreements," 38 *U.C.L.A. L. Rev.* 1533 (1991) for further discussion of this topic.

32 Erikson, *supra* n.30, at 46.

33 *United States v. Capps, Inc.,* 204 F.2d 655 (4th Cir. 1953).

34 Kenneth Randall, "The Treaty Power," 51 *Ohio St. L.J.* 1089 (1990).

35 *Goldwater v. Carter,* 444 U.S. 996 (1979).

36 Article I, § 8, clause 14.

37 Thomas and Thomas, *The War-Making Powers of the President* 7 (SMU Press 1982).

38 Jane Stromseth, "Rethinking War Powers: Congress, The President, and the United Nations," 81 *Georgetown L.J.* 597, 597 (1993), citing 28 *Weekly Comp. Pres. Doc.* 1119, 1120–21 (June 20, 1992).

39 50 U.S.C. § 1541 *et seq.*

40 *Id.*

41 25 F. Cas. 30, 35 (C.C. D. Va. 1807).

42 Aaron Burr had previously killed his political nemesis Alexander Hamilton in a duel. Burr was charged with treason in this case because he allegedly stated in the letter to Jefferson that he intended to move to the southwest (Mexico) and establish a new government. Burr was acquitted, but the trial proved to be the last chapter of his political career.

43 418 U.S. 904 (1974).

44 *Id.* at 713.

45 Since the *Nixon* case, several presidents have appeared in civil matters, either voluntarily or under subpoena. *See* Nowak and Rotunda, *Constitutional Law* § 7.1, n.28 (West Hornbook 1991), for a list.

46 433 U.S. 425 (1977).

47 5 U.S. 137 (1803).

48 *Nixon v. Fitzgerald,* 457 U.S. 800 (1982).

49 *Harlow v. Fitzgerald,* 457 U.S. 800 (1982).

50 *Jones v. Clinton,* 72 F.3d 1354 (8th Cir. 1996), 1996 WL 5658.

CHAPTER 7

ADMINISTRATIVE AGENCIES IN THE CONSTITUTIONAL SCHEME

§ 7.1 Introduction

Since the beginning of this nation, administrative agencies have continuously increased in number, size, and power. The daily lives of all citizens are affected by administrative agencies. Consider these examples: the processing, manufacturing, packing, labeling, advertising, and sale of nearly all products in the United States is regulated by agencies such as the Food and Drug Administration and the Department of Agriculture; the Internal Revenue Service oversees the collection of taxes from all citizens; the Federal Aviation Administration regulates commercial air transportation; the distribution of public welfare benefits (Aid to Dependent Children and food stamps) is regulated by the Department of Health and Human Services and the Department of Agriculture. These are only a few illustrations of the extent to which federal administrative agencies play a role in the daily lives of citizens. To get a complete picture, it is necessary to add state and local agencies. State departments of motor vehicles issue drivers' licenses, register cars, and issue automobile tags; doctors, lawyers, barbers, plumbers, and electricians are among the many whose professions and trades are regulated by state agencies; state departments of revenue collect taxes; state and local governments regulate building and construction; and federal, state, and local agencies regulate the environment.

Why do we need agencies at all? Why have they become so numerous and powerful? The answer to both questions is twofold. First, the job of governing has become too large for Congress, the courts, and the President to handle. There were 4 million citizens when the Constitution was adopted (1789). There are now over 260 million people in the United States. People are more mobile, technology is changing at unprecedented speed, and other social changes have increased the demands on government. Congress does not have the time to make all the laws, the President to enforce all the laws, or the courts to adjudicate all the cases.

Second, agencies possess expertise. Every year Congress must deal with a large and diverse number of issues. Discrimination, environmental concerns, military and national security matters, and funding for science and art are but a few examples. Congress is too small to be expert in every subject. Agencies, however, specialize and, as a result, they possess technical knowledge and experience in their subject areas. They can hire specialists and benefit from continuous contact with the same subjects.

Where do administrative agencies fit into the United States constitutional scheme? What powers may they possess and who oversees them? These topics are explored in this chapter.

§ 7.2 Agencies and Separation of Powers Principles

There is no constitutional provision establishing administrative agencies, nor is the role of agencies in the United States governmental structure defined. Regardless, agencies have been part of the federal government since the beginning. Agencies have been analogized to a "fourth branch" of government. This is not accurate, as the Constitution establishes only three branches and does not permit the creation of a fourth. Even more, as you will learn, agencies are accountable to the three constitutional branches. Regardless, agencies are vital components of government. They are also unique. Though they are not a branch of government, they do perform the functions of all three branches of government, creating separation of powers problems. In fact, many, if not most, contemporary separation of powers cases decided by the Supreme Court arise in the administrative context. Accordingly, much of separations jurisprudence has arisen in the administrative context.

§ 7.3 Appointment and Control of Federal Officers

Nearly every agency is created by Congress through its lawmaking power. Congress, the President, and constitutional courts are not "agencies." Legislation that creates an agency and defines its powers is known as **enabling legislation**. Once created, agencies fall into the executive branch.

Many agencies are headed by one of the President's Cabinet officers. In some cases, a lower federal official heads an agency. Agencies may be headed by an individual or a group (collegial agencies).

Many agency heads undergo the presidential nomination and senatorial confirmation process. Pursuant to Article II, § 2, clause 2, Congress may delegate the appointment of lower federal officials to either the President, the courts, or department heads. *Department heads,* as used in this clause, refers to Secretary-level executive officials. Hence, members of the President's Cabinet may be empowered to appoint lower officials. Congress may not vest the appointment power in its own officers because they are neither courts nor department heads. Consequently, a statute that vested the power of appointment of the voting members of the Federal Election Commission in the President Pro Tem of the Senate and Speaker of the House was invalidated.[1] As to inferior officers, the appointment power may rest solely with the President, the courts, or an agency head. If Congress chooses this procedure, Senate approval is bypassed. This option exists only as to inferior officers; judges and superior officers *must* receive presidential nomination and senatorial approval.

Most federal employees are neither superior nor inferior officers. Rather, they comprise a third group that is not covered by the appointments clause. Today, the civil service system governs their selection and tenure.

Other than impeachment, the Constitution does not establish a method of removal of federal officers. Yet presidents have long held that they may remove federal officers (see Figure 7-1). Removal, it has been contended, is part of the President's executive power. Through the years, however, Congress has found it desirable to limit the presidential power to terminate federal officials. The primary reason to limit presidential termination power is to improve the quality of the agency by reducing the degree to which its head is influenced by political concerns. An agency whose head cannot be terminated by the President

---

TERMS

enabling act (enabling legislation)[†]   1. A statute that grants new powers or authority to persons or corporations. 2. A statute that gives the government the power to enforce other legislation or that carries out a provision of a constitution. The term also applies to a clause in a statute granting the government the power to enforce or carry out that statute. Such a provision is called an enabling clause.

PRESIDENTIAL CONTROL OF OFFICERS AND JUDGES AFTER APPOINTMENT

Officer	Appointment Method	Control
Judges	Nomination by President and confirmation by Senate	None
Superior officers	Nomination by President and confirmation by Senate	Removal at will, so long as duties are executive in nature
Inferior officers	Nomination by President or courts or heads of department, as decided by Congress. Confirmation by Senate is an optional requirement that Congress decides	Removal at will if duties are purely executive in nature. Otherwise, Congress may limit removal to good cause
Other federal employees	Civil service system	Marginal (civil service system procedures)

FIGURE 7-1   Presidential Control of Officers and Judges after Appointment

without cause is known as an **independent agency**. The Interstate Commerce Commission, established in 1887, was the nation's first independent agency. An agency whose head serves at the pleasure of the President is known as an **executive agency**. There are many executive and independent agencies. (See Figure 7-2.)

Some jurists have contended that Congress may not interfere with presidential removal of federal officers. Nevertheless, the presidential power to terminate an independent agency's head is normally limited to "good cause." Disagreements over policy and politics are not good cause, whereas corruption and incompetence are. There are three theories concerning the relationship between the President and Congress concerning independent agencies: (1) the President possesses complete control over federal officials as part of the executive function and

TERMS

independent agency   An agency whose head may be terminated by the President only for good cause.

executive agency   An agency whose head serves at the pleasure of the President.

Amicus

Two Eminent Justices: Holmes and Cardozo

Oliver Wendell Holmes, Jr., was born March 8, 1841, in Boston, Massachusetts. The son of a physician and author, he earned an undergraduate education at Harvard and served in the military during the Civil War. After the war, he returned to Harvard to study law. He graduated from law school in 1866. For the next fifteen years, Holmes managed a private practice. In addition, he periodically taught constitutional law at Harvard, and was editor of the *American Law Review.* From 1882 to 1899 he served as a justice on the Massachusetts Supreme Court and then, from 1899 to 1902, as chief justice of that court. President Theodore Roosevelt nominated Holmes, who was subsequently confirmed, to the Supreme Court of the United States in 1902. Holmes was an active Justice and author. *The Common Law* (1881), *The Path of the Law* (1897), *Law in Science and Science in Law* (1899), and *Natural Law* (1918) are some of his best-known works. He resigned from the Court in 1932, at age 91. He died at 93. Due to philosophical differences between himself and his brethren, Holmes was often in the minority. Accordingly, he earned the nickname "the Great Dissenter."

Benjamin Nathan Cardozo was born May 24, 1870, in New York City, New York. He was a Columbia University graduate. He was the son of a New York trial judge who resigned in the wake of allegations that he was involved with Boss Tweed's corrupt Tammany Hall administration. Benjamin served six weeks as a trial judge before he was appointed to serve on the New York Court of Appeals, the highest court of the state, in 1913. In 1927 he was appointed chief judge of the court. President Hoover nominated him, and he was confirmed, as an Associate Justice of the United States Supreme Court in 1932. He succeeded Oliver Wendell Holmes, Jr.

Like Holmes, Cardozo played many roles. He was a justice, educator, and author. His text, *The Nature of the Judicial Process* (1921) continues to be required reading in many law schools today. He also penned *The Growth of the Law* (1924) and *The Paradoxes of Legal Science* (1928).

Both Holmes and Cardozo greatly influenced the development of American law through their writings, teachings, and judicial contributions. ▐▐

Congress may not limit the President's authority to terminate federal officials; (2) Congress may regulate administrative agencies so long as it does not interfere with the President's ability to faithfully execute the laws; (3) Congress possesses nearly plenary authority over the federal bureaucracy and the President is relegated to simply enforcing and executing the laws Congress creates. As you will learn, the second theory has prevailed.

In *Myers v. United States,* the constitutionality of limiting the President's power to remove the postmaster of the United States was considered by the Supreme Court. *Myers* leaves the impression that Congress may not limit the presidential removal power whatsoever. Time would prove otherwise.

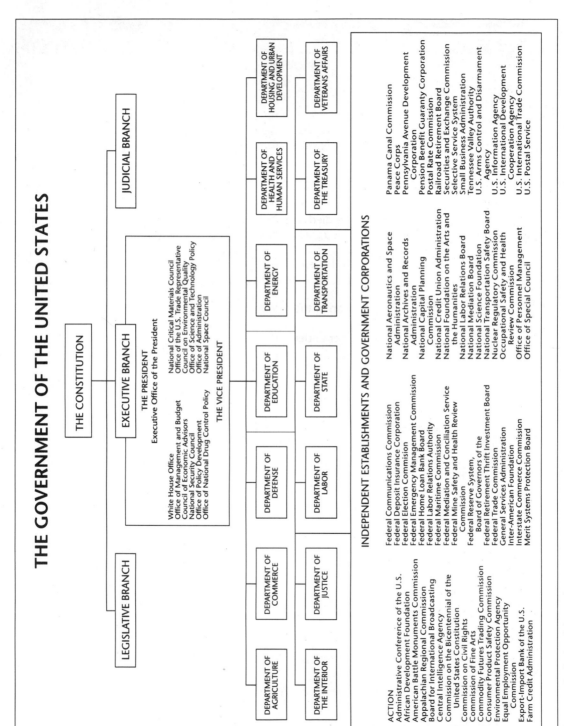

THE GOVERNMENT OF THE UNITED STATES

THE CONSTITUTION

LEGISLATIVE BRANCH | EXECUTIVE BRANCH | JUDICIAL BRANCH

THE PRESIDENT
Executive Office of the President

White House Office
Office of Management and Budget
Council of Economic Advisors
National Security Council
Office of Policy Development
Office of National Drug Control Policy

National Critical Materials Council
Office of the U.S. Trade Representative
Council on Environmental Quality
Office of Science and Technology Policy
Office of Administration
National Space Council

THE VICE PRESIDENT

DEPARTMENT OF AGRICULTURE
DEPARTMENT OF COMMERCE
DEPARTMENT OF DEFENSE
DEPARTMENT OF EDUCATION
DEPARTMENT OF ENERGY
DEPARTMENT OF HEALTH AND HUMAN SERVICES
DEPARTMENT OF HOUSING AND URBAN DEVELOPMENT

DEPARTMENT OF THE INTERIOR
DEPARTMENT OF JUSTICE
DEPARTMENT OF LABOR
DEPARTMENT OF STATE
DEPARTMENT OF TRANSPORTATION
DEPARTMENT OF THE TREASURY
DEPARTMENT OF VETERANS AFFAIRS

INDEPENDENT ESTABLISHMENTS AND GOVERNMENT CORPORATIONS

ACTION
Administrative Conference of the U.S.
African Development Foundation
American Battle Monuments Commission
Appalachian Regional Commission
Board for International Broadcasting
Central Intelligence Agency
Commission on the Bicentennial of the
    United States Constitution
Commission on Civil Rights
Commission of Fine Arts
Commodity Futures Trading Commission
Consumer Product Safety Commission
Environmental Protection Agency
Equal Employment Opportunity
    Commission
Export-Import Bank of the U.S.
Farm Credit Administration

Federal Communications Commission
Federal Deposit Insurance Corporation
Federal Election Commission
Federal Emergency Management Commission
Federal Home Loan Bank Board
Federal Labor Relations Authority
Federal Maritime Commission
Federal Mediation and Conciliation Service
Federal Mine Safety and Health Review
    Commission
Federal Reserve System,
    Board of Governors of the
Federal Retirement Thrift Investment Board
Federal Trade Commission
General Services Administration
Inter-American Foundation
Interstate Commerce Commission
Merit Systems Protection Board

National Aeronautics and Space
    Administration
National Archives and Records
    Administration
National Capital Planning
    Commission
National Credit Union Administration
National Foundation on the Arts and
    the Humanities
National Labor Relations Board
National Mediation Board
National Science Foundation
National Transportation Safety Board
Nuclear Regulatory Commission
Occupational Safety and Health
    Review Commission
Office of Personnel Management
Office of Special Council

Panama Canal Commission
Peace Corps
Pennsylvania Avenue Development
    Corporation
Pension Benefit Guaranty Corporation
Postal Rate Commission
Railroad Retirement Board
Securities and Exchange Commission
Selective Service System
Small Business Administration
Tennessee Valley Authority
U.S. Arms Control and Disarmament
    Agency
U.S. Information Agency
U.S. International Development
    Cooperation Agency
U.S. International Trade Commission
U.S. Postal Service

FIGURE 7-2 Federal Agencies

MYERS
v.
UNITED STATES
272 U.S. 52 (1926)

[A federal statute (1863) provided that postmasters could be removed by the President only with Senate approval. Contrary to the law, a postmaster from Oregon, Myers, was removed by the Postmaster General under orders from the President. Myers sued to recover his lost salary in the Court of Claims. He did not prevail. He died in the interim, but his estate brought an appeal to the Supreme Court alleging that the President was without the authority to terminate his employment.]

Mr. Chief Justice Taft delivered the opinion of the Court.

This case presents the question whether under the Constitution the President has the exclusive power of removing executive officers of the United States whom he has appointed by and with the advice and consent of the Senate. ...

Made responsible under the Constitution for the effective enforcement of the law, the President needs as an indispensable aid to meet it the disciplinary influence upon those who act under him of a reserve power of removal. But it is contended that executive officers appointed by the President with the consent of the Senate are bound by the statutory law, and are not his servants to do his will, and that his obligation to care for the faithful execution of the law does not authorize him to treat them as such. The degree of guidance in the discharge of their duties that the President may exercise over executive officers varies with the character of their service as prescribed in the law under which they act. The highest and most important duties which his subordinates perform are those in which they act for him. In such cases they are exercising not their own but his discretion. This field is a very large one. It is sometimes described as political. ... Each head of a department is and must be the President's alter ego in the matters of that department where the President is required by law to exercise authority. ...

The imperative reasons requiring an unrestricted power to remove the most important of his subordinates in their most important duties must therefore control the interpretation of the Constitution as to all appointed by him.

... [T]he President should have a like power to remove his appointees charged with other duties than those above described. The ordinary duties of officers prescribed by statute come under the general administrative control of the President by virtue of the general grant to him of the executive power, and he may properly supervise and guide their construction of the statute under which they act in order to secure that unitary and uniform execution of the laws which article 2 of the Constitution evidently contemplated in vesting general executive power in the President alone. Laws are often passed with specific provision for the adoption of regulations by a department or bureau head to make the law workable and effective. The ability and judgment manifested by the official thus empowered, as well as his energy and stimulation of his subordinates, are subjects which the President must consider and supervise in his administrative control. Finding such officers to be negligent and inefficient, the President should have the power to remove them. Of course there may be duties so peculiarly and specifically committed to the discretion of a particular officer as to raise a question whether the President may overrule or revise the officer's interpretation of his statutory duty in a particular instance. Then there may be duties of a quasi judicial character imposed on executive officers and members of executive tribunals whose decisions after hearing affect interests of individuals, the discharge of which the President cannot in a particular case properly influence or control. But even in such a case he may consider the decision after its rendition as a reason for removing the officer, on the ground that the discretion regularly entrusted to that officer by statute has not been on the whole intelligently or wisely exercised. Otherwise he does not discharge his own constitutional duty of seeing that the laws be faithfully executed. ...

[The Court then noted that the First Congress created three executive departments, War, State, and Treasury, and that the Secretaries of all three were removable by the President solely. The Court considered this evidence that the framers considered removal an executive power.]

Summing up ... the facts as to acquiescence by all branches of the government in the legislative decision of 1789 as to executive officers, whether superior or inferior, we find that from 1789 to 1863 [when the statute at issue was adopted], a period of 74 years, there was no act of Congress, no executive act, and no decision of this court at variance with the declaration of the First Congress; but there was, as we have seen, clear affirmative recognition of it by each branch of government.

Our conclusion on the merits, sustained by the arguments before stated, is that article 2 grants to the President the executive power of the government,—i.e. the general administrative control of those executing the laws, including the power of appointment and removal of executive officers—a conclusion confirmed by his obligation to take care that the laws be faithfully executed; that article 2 excludes the exercise of legislative power by Congress to provide for ap-pointments and removals, except only as granted therein to Congress in the matter of inferior offices; that Congress is only given power to provide for appointments and removals of inferior officers after it has vested, and on condition that it does vest, their appointment in other authority than the President with the Senate's consent; that the provisions of the second section of article 2, which blend action by the legislative branch, or by part of it, in the work of the executive, are limitations to be strictly construed, and not to be extended by implication; that the President's power of removal is further established as an incident to his specifically enumerated function of appointment by and with the advice of the Senate, but that such incident does not by implication extend to removals the Senate's power of checking appointments; and, finally, that to hold otherwise would make it impossible for the President, in case of political or other difference with the Senate or Congress, to take care that the laws be faithfully executed. ...

For the reasons given, we must therefore hold that the provision of the law of 1876 by which the unrestricted power of removal of first-class postmasters is denied the President is in violation of the Constitution and invalid. This leads to the affirmance of the judgment of the Court of Claims.

The Federal Trade Commission, which is the subject of the *Humphrey's Executor* case, was structured as an independent agency. Unlike the statute in *Myers,* however, Congress did not require Senate approval or removal; rather, it limited the reasons for which the President could remove an officer to cause. Compare the decision in *Humphrey's* to the *Myers* opinion.

Thus, it is clear that congressional ability to control the President's removal of federal officers hinges upon the character of the officer's responsibilities. If a position is purely executive, the person who fills it serves at the pleasure of the President, and Congress may not provide otherwise. Primary offices, such as Cabinet offices, are purely executive. Others are as well—United States Attorneys, for example. They are not temporary employees, they perform purely executive functions

HUMPHREY'S EXECUTOR
v.
UNITED STATES
295 U.S. 602 (1935)

[Humphrey had been appointed to sit on the Federal Trade Commission (FTC). Statute established that FTC commissioners were to serve seven years and, further, that a commissioner could be removed by the President for inefficiency, neglect of duty, or malfeasance in office. President Roosevelt asked Humphrey to resign. He refused. Humphrey subsequently died, but his estate prosecuted an action against the United States in the Court of Claims for his lost pay. The Court of Claims certified two questions to the Supreme Court: 1. Does the Federal Trade Claims Act limit the removal of commissions by the President to the causes listed in the statute?; and 2. If so, is such a limitation constitutional?]

Mr. Justice Sutherland delivered the opinion of the Court.

First. The question first to be considered is whether, by the provisions of § 1 of the Federal Trade Act ... the President's power is limited to removal for the specific causes enumerated therein. ...

The commission is to be non-partisan; and it must, from the very nature of its duties, act with entire impartiality. It is charged with the enforcement of no policy except the policy of the law. Its duties are neither political nor executive, but predominately quasi-judicial and quasi-legislative. Like the Interstate Commerce Commission, its members are called upon to exercise the trained judgment of a body of experts "appointed by law and informed by experience." ...

The legislative reports in both houses of Congress clearly reflect the view that a fixed term was necessary to the effective and fair administration of the law. ...

The debates in both houses demonstrate that the prevailing view was that the commission was not to be "subject to anybody in the government but ... only the people of the United States"; free from "political domination or control" or the "probability or possibility of such a thing"; to be "separate and apart from any existing department of government—not subject to the orders of the President." ...

Thus, the language of the act, the legislative reports, and the general purposes of the legislation as reflected by the debates, all combine to demonstrate the Congressional intent to create a body of experts who shall gain expertise by length of service—a body which shall be independent of executive authority, *except in its selection,* and free to exercise its judgment without the leave or hindrance of any other official or any department of the government. To the accomplishment of these purposes, it is clear that Congress was of the opinion that length and certainty of tenure would vitally contribute. And to hold that, nevertheless, the members of the commission continue in office at the mere will of the President, might be to thwart, in large measure, the very ends which Congress sought to realize by definitely fixing the term of office.

We conclude that the intent of the act is to limit the executive power of removal to the causes enumerated, the existence of none of which is claimed here; and we pass to the second question.

Second. To support its contention that the removal provision of § 1, as we have just construed it, is an unconstitutional interference with the executive power of the President, the government's chief reliance [is] on *Myers v. United States,* 272 U.S. 52, 47 S. Ct 21. ... [T]he narrow point actually decided [in *Myers*] was only that the President had power to remove a postmaster of the first class, without the advice and consent of the Senate as required by act of Congress. ...

The office of postmaster is so essentially unlike the office now involved that the decision in the *Myers* case cannot be accepted as controlling our decision here. A postmaster is an executive officer restricted to the performance of executive functions. He is charged with no duty at all related to either the legislative or judicial power. The actual decision in the *Myers* case finds support in the theory that such an officer is merely one of the units in the executive department and, hence, inherently subject to the exclusive and illimitable power of removal by the Chief Executive, whose subordinate and aid he is. Putting aside *dicta,* which may be followed if sufficiently persuasive but which are not controlling, the necessary reach of the decision goes far enough to include all purely executive officers. It goes no farther;—much less does it include an officer who occupies no place in the executive department and who exercises no part of the executive power vested by the Constitution in the President.

The Federal Trade Commission is an administrative body created by Congress to carry into effect legislative policies embodied in the statute in accordance with the legislative standard therein prescribed, and to perform other specified duties as a legislative or as a judicial aid. Such a body cannot in any proper sense be characterized as an arm or an eye of the executive. Its duties are performed without executive leave and, in the contemplation of the statute, must be free from executive control. In administering the provisions of the statute in respect of "unfair methods of competition"—that is to say in filling in and administering the details embodied by that general standard—the commission acts in part quasi-legislatively and in part quasi-judicially. In making investigations and reports thereon for the information of Congress under § 6, in aid of the legislative power, it acts as a legislative agency. Under § 7, which authorizes the commission to act as a master in chancery under rules prescribed by the court, it acts as an agency of the judiciary. To the extent that it exercises any executive function—as distinguished from executive power in the constitutional sense—it does so in the discharge and effectuation of its quasi-legislative or quasi-judicial powers, or as an agency of the legislative or judicial departments of the government. ...

We think it plain under the Constitution that illimitable power of removal is not possessed by the President in respect of officers of the character of those just named. The authority of Congress, in creating quasi-legislative or quasi-judicial agencies, to require them to act in discharge of their duties independently of executive control cannot well be doubted; and that authority includes, as an appropriate incident, power to fix the period during which they shall continue in office, and to forbid their removal except for cause in the meantime. For this is quite evident that one who holds office only during the pleasure of another, cannot be depended upon to maintain an attitude of independence against the latter's will.

The fundamental necessity of maintaining each of the three general departments of government entirely free from the control or coercive influence, direct or indirect, of either of the others, has often been stressed and is hardly open to serious question. ...

The result of what we now have said is this: Whether the power of the President to remove an officer shall prevail over the authority of Congress to condition the power by fixing a definite term and precluding a removal except for cause, will depend upon the character of the office; the *Myers* decision, affirming the power of the President alone to make the removal, is confined to purely executive officers; and as to officers of the kind here under consideration, we hold that no removal can be made during the prescribed term for which the officer is appointed, except for one or more of the causes named in the applicable statute.

To the extent that, between the decision in the *Myers* case, which sustains the unrestricted power of the President to remove purely executive officers, and our present decision that such power does not extend to an office such as that here involved, there shall remain a field of doubt, we leave such cases as may fall within it for future consideration and determination as they may arise.

In accordance with the foregoing, the questions submitted are answered.
Question No. 1, Yes.
Question No. 2, Yes.

(e.g., prosecution of cases), they possess administrative authority, and they render policy decisions.

If an officer performs quasi-legislative or quasi-judicial functions, then Congress may control her tenure. Note that even when Congress may dictate the terms of an official's tenure, it may never control that tenure. For example, in a 1986 Supreme Court decision, *Bowsher v. Synar,*[2] a statute that empowered Congress to remove the Comptroller General, an executive official, was invalidated because it violated the separation of powers. The Court found the statute to be a dangerous usurpation of executive power.

The issue concerning the power of Congress to limit presidential removal power surfaced again in 1988. To combat crime in government, Congress enacted the Ethics in Government Act in 1978. Pursuant to that statute, an independent counsel (also known as a *special prosecutor*) may be appointed to investigate and prosecute cases. The Attorney General is required to request appointment under the statute after finding reasonable grounds to believe that a crime was committed, but the selection and appointment are made by a special panel of three federal judges. Once appointed, the independent counsel's judgment may not be interfered with by the Attorney General or anyone else. An independent counsel may be removed by the Attorney General only for good cause. The law was carefully tailored to provide the independent counsel with as much independence as possible without violating separations principles.

In *Morrison v. Olson,*[3] the constitutionality of the independent counsel law was considered. The issue was particularly challenging because the objective of the law is to shield the independent counsel from political pressures, although the prosecution function appears to be a "purely executive function" over which the President has plenary authority.

The Court upheld the independent counsel law in *Morrison* for the following reasons:

1. Unlike the situation in *Bowsher v. Synar,* the independent counsel law does not represent an attempt by Congress to control an executive function. The decision to have counsel appointed and removed is left to the Attorney General.

2. An independent counsel is an inferior officer in terms of the appointments clause. The independent counsel's appointment is temporary; she does not exercise any policy-making authority, nor does she possess significant administrative authority. This being the case, it is proper for Congress to limit removal to good cause.

3. The use of federal judges to select the independent counsel is appropriate. They may not review the Attorney General's decision to request appointment and the statute does not empower them

to supervise the investigation or prosecution of the case. Thus, there is no encroachment of the judiciary on executive turf. Nor does the role endanger the integrity of the judiciary. Further, the appointments clause specifically states that inferior officers may be appointed by courts.

4. The President's ability to perform his or her constitutionally assigned functions is not disturbed by this process, especially as the decision to appoint and the power to remove are vested in the executive (Attorney General).

It can be reasonably argued that *Morrison* altered the test from "nature of function" to "is the President's ability to perform the constitutionally assigned functions impaired?" More likely, both standards continue to be viable and must be considered by a reviewing court.

§ 7.4 Delegation

As executive branch entities, administrative agencies perform executive functions. The preceding discussion of control of administrative officials mentioned that agencies may perform **quasi-legislative** and **quasi-judicial** functions. For example, administrative agencies are empowered to create rules (a quasi-legislative function) and to adjudicate cases (a quasi-judicial function). Agencies are given this power so that they may fulfill their mandate and unburden the constitutional branches from some of the ever-increasing burdens. From where do agencies receive these powers? From Congress. The act of granting quasi-judicial and quasi-legislative authority to an agency is referred to as **delegation**.

Separation of powers problems are created by delegations to agencies. How can Congress transfer its powers, or the powers of the judiciary, to an agency? Does this not violate the separation of powers? The assertion that all delegations are unconstitutional has been rejected.

TERMS

quasi-legislative [†] A term applied to the legislative functions of an administrative agency, [such as] rulemaking.

quasi-judicial [†] A term applied to the adjudicatory functions of an administrative agency, i.e., taking evidence and making findings of fact and findings of law.

delegation of powers [†] … 3. The transfer of power from the president to an administrative agency.

There are, however, limits to the congressional delegation power. These limits are known as the *nondelegation doctrine.*

§ 7.5 Nondelegation Doctrine

The Supreme Court has developed a nondelegation doctrine (also called the *delegation doctrine*) to preserve the integrity of the separation of powers. A delegation may be unlawful in two different ways, one quantitative and the other qualitative. A delegation may be unconstitutional if:

1. It is excessive *or*
2. It places control over an essential function of one branch in another branch.

A delegation may be "excessive" if Congress delegates too much of its or the judiciary's power to an administrative agency or if an essential function of one of the two branches is transferred. For example, Congress may not abdicate its authority by establishing an agency responsible for lawmaking generally. Nor may it delegate certain essential functions, such as impeachment. This power is given to the House of Representatives and may not be delegated to another.

A delegation may also be violative of the Constitution if it places control over an essential function of one branch in another branch. For example, placing the power to finally decide constitutional issues in an administrative agency would encroach upon an essential judicial function. See Figure 7-3 for a summary of cases that have shaped this area of law.

Quasi-Legislative Powers

Before 1934, delegations of legislative powers were routinely approved by the courts.[4] However, during Roosevelt's New Deal, the Supreme Court invalidated several laws as either exceeding federal power under the commerce clause (discussed in Chapter 5) or as excessive delegations of legislative powers.

Schechter Poultry Corp. v. United States, a 1935 Supreme Court decision,[5] was such a case. Congress had delegated to the President the authority to approve "codes of fair competition" for the poultry industry. The defendant corporation was convicted of violating the code established by an agency (acting through subdelegation from the President), over its objection that the delegation to the President was unlawful.

FIGURE 7-3
Selected Cases
on Delegation

DELEGATION: SUMMARY OF SELECTED CASES

Case	Holding and Effect of Decision
Schechter Poultry Corp. v. United States, 295 U.S. 495 (1935); *Paramount Refining Co. v. Ryan,* 293 U.S. 388 (1935)	The only Supreme Court invalidations of delegations based upon nondelegation doctrine.
J.W. Hampton, Jr. & Co. v. United States, 276 U.S. 394 (1928)	Congress must provide an intelligible principle to guide agencies.
Lichter v. United States, 334 U.S. 546 (1948)	Delegation to recover excessive profits in governmental contracts was upheld.
Arizona v. California, 373 U.S. 546 (1963)	Delegation to Secretary of Interior to decide water apportionment was upheld.
Mistretta v. United States, 488 U.S. 361 (1989)	Delegation of authority to administrative commission to establish sentencing guidelines was upheld.
NLRB v. Jones & Laughlin Steel Corp., 301 U.S. 1 (1937)	Under public rights doctrine, NLRB may be delegated the authority to hear unfair labor practice cases.
Atlas Roofing Co. v. Occupational Safety & Health Review Commission, 430 U.S. 442 (1977)	Under public rights doctrine, OSHA may be delegated the authority to impose penalties on employers.
Northern Pipeline Construction Co. v. Marathon Pipeline Co., 458 U.S. 50 (1932); *Granfinanciera, S.A. v. Nordberg,* 492 U.S. 33 (1989)	Under public rights doctrine, public issues may be decided by bankruptcy judges, but not private ones.
Gomez v. United States, 490 U.S. 858 (1989); *Peretz v. United States,* 501 U.S. 923 (1991)	U.S. magistrate judges may preside over criminal pretrial proceedings. Consent of the parties is required to have a magistrate judge preside over a criminal trial.
Touby v. United States, 500 U.S. 160 (1991)	Delegation to Attorney General to temporarily schedule drugs was approved. Question of whether more than an intelligible principle is required in penal cases raised but not decided.

The Supreme Court reversed the conviction because it found no solid policy statement to guide the agency when it created the code. In fact, the Court found that the policy statement issued by Congress had conflicting goals. For example, Congress wanted the code to discourage monopolies, but also to encourage cooperative actions among competitors.

In *Panama Refining Co. v. Ryan*,[6] Congress authorized the President to prohibit the transportation of certain oil products in interstate commerce. The Supreme Court found the delegation unlawful because Congress granted too much legislative authority to the President, in particular the decision as to whether a product should be allowed into interstate commerce. The Court reasoned that the executive is charged with enforcing such prohibitions, not creating them.

By the late 1930s the Court had changed direction, and its scrutiny of legislation for delegation violations (and commerce clause excesses) lessened. Today, nearly all challenged delegations are validated. However, the Court requires that receiving agencies be provided with standards or an **intelligible principle** to guide them in the performance of the delegated responsibilities.[7] To satisfy the intelligible principle test, Congress must establish the overarching policy in an area and must provide basic guidelines concerning how the delegation is to be performed. The test is not rigorous. General policies and standards are adequate.

The intelligible principle test is designed to protect the integrity of the separation of powers and to keep agencies within the limits established by elected representatives. An intelligible principle facilitates congressional control and gives reviewing courts standards by which to judge the lawfulness of agency actions. The Supreme Court stated it this way: "A congressional delegation of power ... must be accompanied by discernible standards, so that the delegatee's actions may be measured by its fidelity to the legislative will."[8]

There is no precise definition of "intelligible principle." To understand what is required by the test, it is best to examine specific cases.

Arizona v. California[9] represents a valid delegation. The Secretary of Interior was delegated considerable authority over the apportionment of water from the Colorado River by the Boulder Canyon Project Act. The delegation was upheld because the statute ordered the Secretary to consider various factors when deciding priority for water use. For example, he was ordered to consider river regulation, flood control, irrigation, domestic water consumption, and power production needs.

TERMS

intelligible principle test   The test used to determine if Congress has provided an agency with sufficient guidance in the performance of a delegated duty.

The Court found that this provided the Secretary with sufficient standards from which to work. If Congress had simply left the decision to the Secretary's discretion, without listing the factors to be considered, the delegation would have failed.

In *Lichter v. United States*,[10] the Supreme Court upheld a delegation to administrative officers to recover "excessive profits" when renegotiating contracts involving war goods. Those who challenged the statute claimed that the phrase "excessive profits" was too vague and broad a delegation. The Court disagreed, holding that the phrase provided sufficient guidance and that the delegation was a proper exercise of congressional war powers.

An important case was handed down by the Supreme Court in 1989, *Mistretta v. United States*.[11] *Mistretta* involved a delegation to the United States Sentencing Commission. Congress established the commission to research sentencing in the federal courts and to draft a set of sentencing guidelines for use by federal judges. The enabling statute was challenged as an unlawful delegation of a legislative function, namely, determining what punishment should be imposed for criminal behavior.

The delegation was upheld because: (1) the commission was mandated to use current sentencing averages as a "starting point"; (2) the purposes and goals of sentencing (the policy issues) were established by Congress; and (3) the commission had to work within statutorily prescribed minimums and maximums when setting the guideline ranges (that is, the guidelines could not be used to sentence an individual to more or less time than Congress had set out by statute). The Court held that Congress had provided the commission with an intelligible principle by which it could perform its duties.

In practice, the intelligible principle test has proven ineffective in controlling broad delegations. Justice Blackmun commented that when reviewing delegations, the Court "has been driven by a practical understanding that in our increasingly complex society, replete with ever changing and more technical problems, Congress simply cannot do its job absent an ability to delegate power under broad general directives."[12] In fact, the last statute to have been invalidated under the nondelegation doctrine was *Schechter Poultry*. Many commentators have called for more meaningful review of statutes for excessive delegations of legislative authority.

Quasi-Adjudicative Powers

In addition to delegating quasi-legislative powers to agencies, Congress may also empower agencies to perform quasi-adjudicative functions. For example, agency tribunals discipline license holders, fine violators, and resolve disputes between companies and consumers. In some instances, the agencies employ powers that have historically been exercised by courts of law. In fact, the transfer of cases from courts of law to administrative tribunals is increasing. The separation of powers issue is obvious when Congress transfers the power to adjudicate a case from an Article III court to an administrative body. The purpose of Article III is twofold: to protect the integrity of the judiciary in the constitutional scheme and to assure that individuals will have their rights litigated before judges who are free from the domination of the political branches of government. Does this means that all claims must be heard by Article III judges?

The Supreme Court addressed this issue as early as 1932 in *Crowell v. Benson*,[13] in which it held that claims for damages resulting from work-related maritime injuries could be heard by an administrative official. The Court recognized in this case, however, that only certain cases can be transferred out of courts of law to Article I courts or officials.

The determination of whether a congressional delegation of judicial authority to an administrative agency is constitutional hinges upon the degree to which the delegation threatens the institutional integrity of the judicial branch. In 1986, the Court recognized four factors to be considered in this vein:

1. The extent to which the essential attributes of judicial power are reserved to Article III judges
2. The extent to which the non-Article III tribunals exercise what are normally Article III powers
3. The origins and importance of the right(s) to be adjudicated
4. The reasons Congress chose to vest the adjudicatory power in an administrative officer or tribunal.[14]

All of these factors must be considered, and no one is in itself dispositive. The third factor has proven critical, however. Under what is known as the **public rights doctrine**, the Supreme Court treats the adjudication of public rights different from private rights. So-called "public rights" may be adjudicated by administrative officials, whereas private rights must be tried by Article III judges. Generally, when a case involves determining the liability between two private parties, it is a private-right case. But some apparent private rights may be adjudicated by administrative courts if they did not exist at the common law. A public rights case is one in which:

TERMS

---

public rights doctrine   Rule providing that if a claim is public in nature and not private, Congress may delegate its adjudication to a non-Article III tribunal.

1. The government is a party or
2. Congress has created a regulatory scheme and a private right is integrated into that scheme.

The first category does not refer to criminal cases, even though the government is always a party in such cases.[15] A public right was found in *Atlas Roofing Co. v. Occupational Safety & Health Review Commission.*[16] The Occupational Safety and Health Act (OSHA) empowered the commission to impose civil penalties on employers for maintaining unsafe and unhealthy working conditions. The Court rejected the claims of punished employers that the nature of the claims covered by the act were private. On the contrary, no such remedy existed at the common law. The claim was a creation of Congress. Accordingly, it is public and may be adjudicated by an administrative agency.

Note that the right to have a claim heard by an Article III judge usually parallels the right to have a jury. The Seventh Amendment assures a jury trial in "[s]uits at common law, where the value in controversy shall exceed twenty dollars." As a consequence, if a claim can be placed with an agency for adjudication, there is probably no right to a jury trial.

Similar decisions have been reached in other cases. For example, an administrative tribunal may be charged with the responsibility of adjudicating unfair labor practice cases and awarding damages (back pay),[17] and the Commodity Futures Exchange Commission may entertain state-law counterclaims when customers of commodities brokers could seek money damages, even though these cases involve what appear to be private rights.[18] However, the availability of review by an Article III judge is important and may even be required for such a delegation to be valid.[19]

The use of United States Bankruptcy judges has also been challenged. Bankruptcy judges are legislative, non-Article III judges. In *Northern Pipeline Construction Co. v. Marathon Pipe Line Co.*,[20] the Supreme Court invalidated a portion of the Bankruptcy Act that permitted bankruptcy judges to hear contract claims. Then, in 1989, the Supreme Court handed down *Granfinanciera, S.A. v. Nordberg,*[21] wherein it held that the act of a trustee in bankruptcy in recovering fraudulently conveyed property was private in nature, not public. Accordingly, the law that delegated the factual decision making in such cases to bankruptcy judges was invalidated. The Court did not answer the question of whether an Article I bankruptcy judge may preside over a jury trial that arises during a bankruptcy proceeding.

Interesting delegation issues have also arisen in the context of use of United States magistrate-judges. District judges (trial-level federal judges) are empowered under Article III of the Constitution. Article III judges undergo presidential nomination and Senate confirmation; magistrates do not. The positions of Article III judges are established under the Constitution; those of magistrates are not. Article II judges are insulated from political concerns by life tenure; magistrates are not. Article III judges may be removed only by Congress, through impeachment; magistrates may be removed by Article III judges.

Magistrate positions came into being through the Federal Magistrates Act (Act), and are therefore creations not of the Constitution but of Congress. The Act delegates certain responsibilities to magistrates and allows Article III judges to delegate additional duties so long as the delegations are consistent with the Constitution and other laws of the United States.

Because magistrates are not Article III judges, only certain responsibilities may be delegated to them. For example, in *Gomez v. United States*,[22] it was determined that without the parties' consent, a magistrate may not be delegated the responsibility of conducting voir dire in a felony criminal case. The Court held that voir dire is a critical stage in the proceeding and so must be supervised by a constitutionally empowered judge. A later case, *Peretz v. United States*,[23] affirmed *Gomez,* but further explained that magistrate-judges may preside over criminal trials if the parties consent. If any party objects, then a district judge must preside over the critical stages of the case. The Court rejected the defendant's claim that conducting the voir dire is an inherently judicial function that cannot be delegated even with the consent of the parties (the defendant consented to have the magistrate-judge preside and then complained on appeal).

> The Court stated that the ultimate decision whether to invoke the magistrate's assistance is made by the district court, subject to veto by the parties. The decision whether to empanel the jury the selection of which a magistrate has supervised also remains entirely with the district court. Because the entire process takes place under the district court's total control and jurisdiction, there is no danger that use of the magistrate involves a congressional attempt to transfer jurisdiction to non-Article III tribunals for the purpose of emasculating constitutional courts [citations omitted].

Because there was no separation of powers violation, the issue was whether a party may waive the right to have an Article III judge preside. The Court answered this affirmatively.

Gomez and *Peretz* stress the importance of agency accountability. When examining delegations of adjudicative power, courts look to whether the agency remains accountable to the judiciary. Whether the officer herself, such as with magistrate-judges, remains accountable to constitutional judges and whether the particular function is reviewed by constitutional judges are critical.

Because the Act was drafted to keep magistrate-judges accountable to Article III judges, rather than to Congress or the President, most such delegations have been upheld. Under the Act, all decisions made by magistrates are reviewed de novo by district judges; magistrates may be removed by Article III judges; and magistrate-judges may not suffer a reduction in pay during their appointment. For these reasons, the Court has generally upheld the Act.

Criminal Law Powers

Special rules govern when agencies are delegated penal powers, that is, the power to establish what acts are criminal, what punishment should be meted out, and to try criminal charges. Because of the threat to civil liberties, agencies have limited authority in these areas.

In 1991 the Supreme Court issued a decision sustaining a delegation in the criminal law context. *Touby v. United States*[24] involved a statute that authorized the Attorney General to temporarily declare a drug as Schedule I controlled under the Controlled Substances Act. Possession, distribution, or use of controlled substances are criminal under that statute, and therefore the Attorney General was delegated the responsibility of declaring penal law.

Congress delegated this power because it normally takes six months to a year to permanently schedule new drugs. Drug dealers took advantage of this gap in time by developing new "designer drugs" that were similar in effect to existing drugs but different in chemical composition. Until permanently scheduled, designer drugs could be possessed, distributed, or used lawfully. To resolve this problem, Congress delegated the authority to the Attorney General to temporarily add, remove, or move drugs between schedules. The defendant raised two delegation issues: first, he claimed that the delegation to the Attorney General was excessive; second, that more than an intelligible principle must be provided when Congress delegates penal rulemaking authority and that such was not done.

Accordingly, it is unknown whether Congress must provide more than an intelligible principle when delegating penal rulemaking authority. It is likely that a future case may declare a higher standard. Whatever that standard proves to be, the Court stated that the statute at issue in *Touby* satisfies it.

Although Congress may delegate penal rulemaking to an agency, it may not delegate the power to establish penalties, with the possible exception of small fines. Congress may provide a range from which an agency establishes the penalty for a rule violation.

TOUBY
v.
UNITED STATES
500 U.S. 160 (1991)

Justice O'Connor wrote the opinion of the Court.

Petitioners were convicted of manufacturing and conspiring to manufacture "Euphoria," a drug temporarily designated as a schedule I controlled substance pursuant to § 201(h) of the Controlled Substances Act ... . We consider whether § 201(h) unconstitutionally delegates legislative power to the Attorney General and whether the Attorney General's subdelegation to the Drug Enforcement Administration (DEA) was authorized by statute.

I

In 1970, Congress enacted the Controlled Substances Act (Act) ... . The Act establishes five categories or "schedules" of controlled substances, the manufacture, possession, and distribution of which the Act regulates or prohibits. Violations involving schedule I substances carry the most severe penalties, as these substances are believed to pose the most serious threat to public safety. Relevant here, § 201(a) of the Act authorizes the Attorney General to add or remove substances, or to move a substance from one schedule to another. ...

When adding a substance to a schedule, the Attorney General must follow specified procedures. First, the Attorney General must request a scientific and medical evaluation from the Secretary of Health and Human Services (HHS), together with a recommendation as to whether the substance should be controlled. A substance cannot be scheduled if the Secretary recommends against it. ... Second, the Attorney General must consider eight factors with respect to the substance, including its potential for abuse, scientific evidence of its pharmacological effect, its psychic or physiological dependence liability, and whether the substance is an immediate precursor of a substance already controlled. ... Third, the Attorney General must comply with the notice-and-hearing

procedures of the Administrative Procedure Act ... which permit comment by interested parties. ... In addition, the Act permits any aggrieved person to challenge the scheduling of a substance by the Attorney General in a court of appeals. ...

It takes time to comply with these procedural requirements. From the time when law enforcement officials identify a dangerous new drug, it typically takes 6 to 12 months to add it to one of the schedules. ... Drug traffickers were able to take advantage of this time gap by designing drugs that were similar in pharmacological effect to scheduled substances but differing slightly in chemical composition, so that existing schedules did not apply to them. These "designer drugs" were developed and widely marketed long before the Government was able to schedule them and initiate prosecutions. ...

To combat the "designer drug" problem, Congress in 1984 amended the Act to create an expedited procedure by which the Attorney General can schedule a substance on a temporary basis when doing so is "necessary to avoid an imminent hazard to the public safety." § 201(h) ... . Temporary scheduling under § 201(h) allows the Attorney General to bypass, for a limited time, several of the requirements for permanent scheduling. The Attorney General need consider only three of the eight factors required for permanent scheduling. ... Rather than comply with the APA notice-and-hearing provisions, the Attorney General need provide only a 30-day notice of the proposed scheduling in the *Federal Register*. ... Notice also must be transmitted to the Secretary of the HHS, but the Secretary's prior approval of a proposed scheduling order is not required. ... Finally, § 201(h) ... provides that an order to schedule a substance temporarily "is not subject to judicial review."

Because it has fewer procedural requirements, temporary scheduling enables the government to respond more quickly to the threat posed by dangerous new drugs. A temporary scheduling order can be issued 30 days after a new drug is identified, and the order remains valid for one year. During this 1-year period, the Attorney

General presumably will initiate the permanent scheduling process, in which case the temporary scheduling order remains valid for an additional six months. ...

The Attorney General promulgated regulations delegating to the DEA his powers under the Act, including the power to schedule controlled substances on a temporary basis. Pursuant to that delegation, the DEA Administrator issued an order scheduling temporarily 4-methylaminorex, known more commonly as "Euphoria," as a schedule I controlled substance. The Administrator subsequently initiated formal rulemaking procedures, following which Euphoria was added permanently to schedule I.

While the temporary scheduling order was in effect, DEA agents, executing a valid search warrant, discovered a fully operational drug laboratory in Daniel and Lyrissa Touby's home. The Toubys were indicted for manufacturing and conspiring to manufacture Euphoria. They moved to dismiss the indictment on the grounds that § 201(h) unconstitutionally delegates legislative power to the Attorney General, and that the Attorney General improperly delegated his temporary scheduling authority to the DEA. The United States District Court for the District of New Jersey denied the motion ... and the Court of Appeals for the Third Circuit affirmed petitioner's subsequent convictions ... and [we] now affirm.

II

The Constitution provides that "[a]ll legislative Powers herein granted shall be vested in a Congress of the United States. From this language the Court has derived the nondelegation doctrine: that Congress may not constitutionally delegate its legislative power to another Branch of government. "The nondelegation doctrine is rooted in the principle of separation of powers that underlies our tripartite system of government." ...

We have long recognized that the nondelegation doctrine does not prevent Congress from seeking assistance, within proper limits, from its coordinate branches. ...

Petitioners wisely concede that Congress has set forth in § 201(h) an "intelligible principle" to constrain the Attorney General's discretion to schedule controlled substances on a temporary basis. ...

Petitioners suggest, however, that something more than an "intelligible principle" is required when Congress authorizes another Branch to promulgate regulations that contemplate criminal sanctions. They contend that regulations of this sort pose a heightened risk to individual liberty and that Congress must therefore provide more specific guidance. Our cases are not entirely clear as to whether or not more specific guidance is in fact required. ... We need not resolve the issue today. We conclude that § 201(h) passes muster even if greater congressional specificity is required in the criminal context.

Although it features fewer procedural requirements than the permanent scheduling statute, § 201(h) meaningfully constrains the Attorney General's discretion to define criminal conduct. To schedule a drug temporarily, the Attorney General must find that doing so is "necessary to avoid an imminent hazard to the public safety." ... In making this determination, he is "required to consider" three factors: the drug's "history and current pattern of abuse"; "[t]he scope, duration, and significance of abuse"; and "[w]hat, if any, risk there is to the public health." ... Included within these factors are three other factors on which the statute places a special emphasis; "actual abuse, diversion from legitimate channels, and clandestine importation, manufacture, or distribution." ... The Attorney General also must publish 30-day notice of the proposed scheduling in the *Federal Register*, transmit notice to the Secretary of HHS, and "take into consideration any comments submitted by the Secretary in response." ...

In addition to satisfying the numerous requirements of § 201(h), the Attorney General must satisfy the requirements of § 202(b) ... . Thus, apart from the "imminent hazard" determination required by § 201(h), the Attorney General, if he wishes to add temporarily a drug to schedule I, must find it "has a high potential for abuse," that it "has no currently accepted medical use in treatment in the United States," and that "[t]here is a lack of accepted safety for use of the drug ... under medical supervision." ...

It is clear that in §§ 201 (h) and 202(b) Congress has placed multiple specific restrictions on the Attorney General's discretion to define criminal conduct. These restrictions satisfy the constitutional requirements of the nondelegation doctrine.

Petitioners point to two other aspects of the temporary scheduling statute that allegedly render it unconstitutional. They argue first that it concentrates too much power in the Attorney General. Petitioners concede that Congress may legitimately authorize someone in the Executive Branch to schedule drugs temporarily, but argue that it must be someone other than the Attorney General because he wields the power to prosecute crimes. They insist that allowing the Attorney General both to schedule a particular drug and to prosecute those who manufacture that drug violates the principle of separation of powers. ...

This argument has no basis in our separation-of-powers jurisprudence. The principle of separation of powers focuses on the distribution of power among the three coequal Branches ... it does not speak to the manner in which authority is parceled out within a single Branch. The Constitution vests all executive power in the President ... and it is the President to whom both the Secretary and the Attorney General report. Petitioners' argument that temporary scheduling authority should not be vested in one executive officer rather than another does not implicate separation-of-powers concerns; it merely challenges the wisdom of a legitimate policy judgment made by Congress.

[The Court also concluded that the Attorney General's subdelegation was lawful.]

Agencies may also act in a quasi-adjudicative role in criminal cases, although this power is very limited. Most administrative judges are not sufficiently connected to the judiciary to hear criminal cases. As discussed earlier, United States magistrates may hear criminal cases, although they may not preside over the voir dire (jury selection) in felony cases without the consent of both parties. United States Magistrates may be delegated greater authority than administrative law judges because they are not officers of the executive branch, serve at the pleasure of constitutionally selected judges, and are otherwise insulated from the political branches.

Administrative Procedure Act

To govern the procedures used by administrative agencies, Congress enacted the Administrative Procedure Act (APA) in 1946.[25] The APA was intended to curb the growing power of agencies.

Among the many subjects the APA regulates are rulemaking and adjudication. Rulemaking is the administrative equivalent of lawmaking. The power to create substantive rules is not inherent; rather, it must be delegated to an agency by Congress. That delegation must be supported by an intelligible principle to confine the agency's authority.

The APA provides two rulemaking methods, formal and informal. In both the public is given an opportunity to comment on proposed rulemaking. Public participation is greater in **formal rulemaking**, during which interested persons are allowed to participate orally in a hearing. Public participation in **informal rulemaking** is limited to written comment. A new rule must be published and an explanation of the agency's rationale in creating the rule must accompany the publication. An agency is required to explain its decision more thoroughly in formal rulemaking than in informal rulemaking. A properly promulgated rule has the effect of a statute.

The APA also governs agency adjudications, including agency notice to parties, participation requirements, and general procedures. Most agency hearings are presided over by administrative law judges (ALJs). ALJs are not Article III judges, but Congress has attempted to assure their independence by limiting their removal to good cause and placing their selection and compensation within the civil service system. Agency decisions are reviewable by courts.[26]

§ 7.6 Legislative Veto

One method that Congress used for many years to control agency behavior was the **legislative veto**. The term *legislative veto* refers to any process whereby Congress may review and reverse an agency decision. It is an attempt to control the implementation of delegated powers. Knowing that review was available, Congress was more comfortable

---

TERMS

formal rulemaking A process used by administrative agencies to create rules and regulations. The Administrative Procedure Act provides that formal rulemaking is required only when mandated by statute. Otherwise, informal rulemaking may be used by an agency. Formal rulemaking involves formal hearings and is more expensive and time-consuming than informal rulemaking. This process is also known as *rulemaking on the record.*

informal rulemaking A process used by administrative agencies to create rules and regulations. The Administrative Procedure Act provides that agencies may use this procedure unless formal rulemaking is required by statute. Informal rulemaking is less costly and less time-consuming than its formal counterpart. This process is also known as *notice-and-comment rulemaking.*

legislative veto An act of a legislature invalidating executive action in a particular instance. Generally, legislative vetos are unconstitutional. Once power is delegated by Congress to the President, it is generally prohibited from interfering with the President's enforcement.

IMMIGRATION &
NATURALIZATION SERVICE
v.
CHADHA
462 U.S. 919 (1983)

[Chadha was an alien who had been residing in the United States under a student visa. His visa expired and he applied to remain in the United States under a hardship provision of the Immigration Nationality Act (INA). The Attorney General granted his request for suspension of deportation, but the House of Representatives, pursuant to a legislative veto provision of the INA, invalidated the Attorney General's decision. That provision allowed either house of Congress to invalidate executive decisions concerning deportation. Chadha appealed the House's decision to the court of appeals, which invalidated the veto provision of the INA.]

Chief Justice Burger delivered the opinion of the Court.

We granted certiorari ... [to review] a challenge to the constitutionality of a provision in § 244(c)(2) of the Immigration and Nationality Act ... authorizing one House of Congress, by resolution, to invalidate the decision of the Executive Branch ... to allow a particular deportable alien to remain in the United States. ...

We turn now to the question whether action of one House of Congress under § 244(c)(2) violates strictures of the Constitution. We begin, of course, with the presumption that the challenged statute is valid. ...

Our inquiry is sharpened rather than blunted by the fact that Congressional veto provisions are appearing with increasing frequency in statutes which delegate authority to executive and independent agencies:

> Since 1932, when the first veto provision was enacted into law, 295 congressional veto-type procedures have been inserted in 196 different statutes ... .

Justice White undertakes to make a case for the proposition that the one House veto is a useful "political invention," and we need not challenge that assertion. ... But policy arguments supporting even useful "political inventions" are subject to the demands of the Constitution which defines powers and, with respect to this subject, sets out just how those powers are to be exercised. ...

THE PRESENTMENT CLAUSES

The records of the Constitutional Convention reveal that the requirement that all legislation be presented to the President before becoming law was uniformly accepted by the Framers. Presentment to the President and the Presidential veto were considered so imperative that the draftsmen took special pains to assure that these requirements could not be circumvented. During the final debate on Art. I, § 7, cl. 2, James Madison expressed concern that it might easily be evaded by the simple expedient of calling a proposed law a "resolution" or "vote" rather than a "bill." As a consequence, Art I., § 7, cl. 3 [requiring bills, resolutions, and vote that require concurrence of both Houses to be presented to the President] ... was added.

The decision to provide the President with a limited and qualified power to nullify proposed legislation by veto was based on the profound conviction of the Framers that the powers conferred on Congress were the powers to be most carefully circumscribed. It is beyond doubt that lawmaking was a power to be shared by both Houses and the President. ...

BICAMERALISM

The bicameral requirement of Art. I, §§ 1, 7 was of scarcely less concern to the Framers than was the Presidential veto and indeed the two concepts are interdependent. By providing that no law could take effect without the concurrence of the prescribed majority of the Members of both Houses, the Framers reemphasized their belief, already remarked upon in connection with the Presentment Clauses, that legislation should not be enacted unless it has been carefully and fully considered by the Nation's elected officials. In the Constitutional Convention debates on the need for a bicameral legislature, James Wilson, later to become a Justice of this Court, commented:

> Despotism comes on mankind in different shapes. Sometimes in an Executive, sometimes in a military, one. Is there danger of a Legislative despotism? Theory and practice both proclaim it. If the legislative authority be not restrained, there can be neither liberty nor stability; and it can only be restrained by dividing it within itself, into distinct and independent branches. In a single house there is no check, but the inadequate one, of the virtue and good sense of those who compose it. ...

We see therefore that the Framers were acutely conscious that the bicameral requirement and the Presentment Clauses would serve essential constitutional functions. The President's participation in the legislative process was to protect the Executive Branch from Congress and to protect the whole people from improvident laws. ... It emerges clearly that the prescription for legislative action in Art. I, §§ 1, 7 represents the Framers' decision that the legislative power of the Federal government be exercised in accord with a single, finely wrought and exhaustively considered, procedure.

The Constitution sought to divide the delegated powers of the new federal government into three defined categories, legislative, executive and judicial, to assure, as nearly as possible, that each Branch of government would confine itself to its assigned responsibility. ...

Although not "hermetically" sealed from one another, the powers delegated to the three Branches are functionally identifiable. When any Branch acts, it is presumptively exercising the power the Constitution has delegated to it. When the Executive acts, it presumptively acts in an executive or administrative capacity as defined in Art. II. And when, as here, one House of Congress purports to act, it is presumptively acting within its assigned sphere.

Beginning with this presumption, we must nevertheless establish that the challenged action ... is of the kind to which the procedural requirements of Art. I, § 7 apply. Not every action taken by either House is subject to the bicameralism

and presentment requirements of Art. I. Whether actions taken by either House are, in law and fact, an exercise of legislative power depends not on their form but upon "whether they contain matter which is properly to be regarded as legislative in its character and effect." ...

Examination of the action taken here by one House pursuant to § 244(c)(2) reveals that it was essentially legislative in purpose and effect. In purporting to exercise power defined in Art. I, § 8, cl. 4, to "establish uniform Rule of Naturalization," the House took action that had the purpose and effect of altering the legal rights, duties and relations of persons, including the Attorney General, Executive Branch officials and Chadha, all outside the legislative branch. Section 244(c)(2) purports to authorize one House of Congress to require the Attorney General to deport an individual alien whose deportation otherwise would be cancelled under § 244. The one-House veto operated in this case to overrule the Attorney General and mandate Chadha's deportation; absent the House action, Chadha would remain in the United States. Congress had *acted* and its action has altered Chadha's status. ...

Finally, we see that the Framers intended to authorize either House of Congress to act alone and outside of its prescribed bicameral legislative role; they narrowly and precisely defined the procedure for such action. There are but four provisions in the Constitution, explicit and unambiguous, by which one House may act alone with the unreviewable force of law, not subject to the President's veto:

(a) The House of Representatives alone was given the power to initiate impeachments. Art. I, § 2, cl. 6;

(b) The Senate alone was given the power to conduct trials following impeachment on charges initiated by the House and convict following trial. Art. I, § 3, cl. 5;

(c) The Senate alone was given final unreviewable power to approve or to disapprove presidential appointments. Art. II, § 2, cl. 2;

(d) The Senate alone was given final unreviewable power to ratify treaties negotiated by the President. Art. II, § 2, cl. 2.

Clearly, when the Draftsmen sought to confer special powers on one House independent of the other House, or of the President, they did so in explicit, unambiguous terms. ...

Since it is clear that the action by the House under § 244(c)(2) was not within any of the express constitutional exceptions authorizing one House to act alone, and equally clear that it was an exercise of legislative power, that action was subject to standards prescribed in Article I. ...

V

We hold that the Congressional veto provision in § 244(c)(2) is severable from the Act and that it is unconstitutional. Accordingly, the judgment of the Court of Appeals is Affirmed.

[Justice Powell concurred with the judgment, but on different grounds. He concluded that "when Congress finds that a particular person does not satisfy the statutory criteria for permanent residence in this country it has assumed a judicial function in violation of the principle of separation of powers."

Justice White dissented. He concluded that the legislative veto is a good tool for keeping administrative agencies in check by elected representatives.]

delegating broad powers to agencies. The veto mechanism varied, but it was common for one house to be empowered to veto agency actions.

Chadha specifically dealt with a one-House veto. But the Court's reasoning in that case requires both bicameral action and presentment of bills or resolutions to the President. This was confirmed in another decision in which the Court invalidated the provision of a statute that permitted both Houses to veto agency action without presentment to the President.[27] That same case extended the prohibition against legislative vetoes to independent agencies.

Even though the Court could have decided *Chadha* on narrow grounds, (e.g., that Congress had attempted to render a judicial decision in violation of the separation of powers), it chose to invalidate the legislative veto generally. Before this decision, Congress had placed veto provisions in many laws, including the War Powers Resolution. That law allows the President to commit United States armed forces to combat situations without congressional approval, but also requires the President to report such actions to Congress. Congress may then end American involvement by joint resolution without presentment to the President. *Chadha* appears to render this provision of the War Powers Resolution unconstitutional, as well as similar provisions in other laws.

The invalidation of the legislative veto has not left Congress with recourse. Of course, Congress may veto agency decisions through resolutions that pass both Houses and are signed by the President (or override presidential veto by two-thirds votes in both Houses). Congress added a new program to its calendar in 1995 that is intended to increase its review of agency-created rules. **Corrections Day**, which occurs twice monthly, is an opportunity for members to introduce legislation to change or repeal agency rules.

Congress also attempts to control agency decision making through oversight hearings. Informal methods, such as calls from individual members of Congress to agency officials, are also used to persuade agency officials to follow (or dissuade them from) a particular course of action.

Summary

Although not specifically provided for in the Constitution, the administrative state is now an integral part of government in the United States. The number of agencies continually increases, as does the authority they possess. Although increasing, this power is checked. With the exception of independent agencies, the President acts as the chief of the administrative state. He controls the functioning of the agencies through control of agency heads, through the creation of rules governing their existence and functioning, and by collaboration with Congress in the creation of applicable statutes. Congress also wields a considerable amount of authority over agencies. It has the authority to create, reorganize, and disband them. In many instances, Congress must confirm presidential nominations of agency heads. Finally, Congress holds the purse strings.

The judiciary has not been silent on the rise of the administrative state. It has developed rules concerning delegations of authority and the procedures agencies must follow when performing their functions. Although outside the scope of this book, the courts have also been active in defining the rights of citizens when dealing with agencies.

This is not to say that all people are pleased with the state of administrative law. In spite of the checks previously discussed, Congress and the President appear unable to control the administrative machine at times. The Supreme Court's rejection of the legislative veto added another obstacle to Congress's desire to increase its oversight of agencies. Congress and the President are likely to seek new ways to control and oversee the nation's agencies as they move into the twenty-first century.

TERMS

Corrections Day   Part of Congress's schedule; occurs twice a month. A time specially set aside for legislation intended to amend or repeal administrative rules.

Review Questions

1. Why are administrative agencies necessary in the contemporary United States?

2. What clause of the Constitution establishes administrative agencies?

3. What test is used to determine whether a delegation of power to an agency by Congress is lawful, that is, that Congress has not delegated too much power?

4. Distinguish independent agencies from executive agencies.

5. State the two ways a delegation may violate the Constitution.

6. Must Congress provide an agency with more than an intelligible principle when delegating criminal rulemaking authority?

7. What is a legislative veto? Is it constitutional?

8. What is the Administrative Procedure Act?

Review Problems

1. Justice White stated, in his dissent in *Immigration & Naturalization Service v. Chadha,* that the Court's decision left Congress with a "Hobson's choice: either to refrain from delegating the necessary authority, leaving itself with a hopeless task of writing laws with the requisite specificity to cover endless special circumstances across the entire policy landscape, or in the alternative, to abdicate its lawmaking function to the executive branch and independent agencies. To choose the former leaves major national problems unresolved; to opt for the latter risks unaccountability [in] policymaking by those not elected to fill that role." Why, he asks, is it permissible to empower unelected officials in administrative agencies to make laws, but not to empower Congress, the true lawmaker, to check this power?

2. Do you agree with Justice Powell's conclusion in *Chadha,* that is, that a congressional decision to deport specific individuals is a judicial function? What are the characteristics of adjudication as opposed to legislation?

3. Assume that more than an intelligible principle is required for delegations of penal rulemaking authority. Create and defend a standard you believe is appropriate.

4. Draft two bills creating two different independent agencies. The bills should be only a few paragraphs each. Both should have a single agency

head and identical removal provisions. However, you are to draft one so that the subject matter is properly independent and the other not. So, one bill should be lawful and the other invalid. Have your instructor or a classmate review your work.

Notes

[1] *Buckley v. Valeo,* 424 U.S. 1 (1976).

[2] 478 U.S. 714 (1986).

[3] 487 U.S. 654 (1988).

[4] *See,* for example, *United States v. Gramaud,* 220 U.S. 506 (1911).

[5] 295 U.S. 495 (1935).

[6] 293 U.S. 388 (1935).

[7] *J.W. Hampton, Jr. & Co. v. United States,* 276 U.S. 394 (1928).

[8] *Eastlake v. Forest City Enterprises,* 426 U.S. 668 (1976).

[9] 373 U.S. 546 (1963).

[10] 334 U.S. 546 (1948).

[11] 488 U.S. 361 (1989).

[12] *Mistretta v. United States,* 488 U.S. 361, 372 (1989).

[13] 285 U.S. 22 (1932).

[14] *Commodity Futures Trading Commission v. Schor,* 478 U.S. 833 (1986).

[15] *Northern Pipeline Construction Co. v. Marathon Pipe Line Co.,* 458 U.S. 50, n.24 (1982).

[16] 430 U.S. 442 (1977).

[17] *NLRB v. Jones & Laughlin Steel Corp.,* 301 U.S. 1 (1937).

[18] *Commodity Futures Trading Commission v. Schor,* 478 U.S. 833 (1986).

[19] *Atlas Roofing,* 430 U.S. 442 (1977).

[20] 458 U.S. 50 (1982).

[21] 492 U.S. 33 (1989).

[22] 490 U.S. 858 (1989).

[23] 501 U.S. 923 (1991).

[24] 500 U.S. 160 (1991).

[25] 5 U.S.C. § 551 *et seq.*

[26] For a more thorough discussion of the APA and rulemaking and adjudication, *see* Daniel Hall, *Administrative Law* chs. 3, 7 (Delmar/Lawyers Cooperative Publishing 1994).

[27] *Process Gas Consumers Group v. Consumers Energy Council,* 463 U.S. 1216, *reh'g denied,* 463 U.S. 1250 (1983).

CHAPTER 8

CONTEMPORARY FEDERALISM: THE STATE AND FEDERAL RELATIONSHIP

Preoccupation by our people with the constitutionality, instead of with the wisdom of legislation or of executive action is preoccupation with false value. ... Focusing attention on constitutionality tends to make constitutionality synonomous with wisdom.

Justice Frankfurter[1]

In the compound republic of America, the power surrendered by the people is first divided between two distinct governments, and then the portion allotted to each subdivided among distinct and separate departments. Hence a double security arises to the rights of the people. The different governments will control each other, at the same time each will be controlled by itself.

— *James Madison*

§ 8.1 State Powers

As you have previously learned, the framers intended to establish a stronger national government than existed under the Articles of Confederation. They did not intend, however, to abolish the states. Rather, they created a limited federal government, carving out specific powers for it. The remainder of the powers were intended to belong either to the states or to the people. The federal government and states govern together—they are dual sovereigns. These principles are enshrined in the Ninth and Tenth Amendments.

Amendment IX

The enumeration in the Constitution, of certain rights, shall not be construed to deny or disparage others retained by the people.

Amendment X

The powers not delegated to the United States by the Constitution, nor prohibited by it to the States, are reserved to the States respectively, or to the people.

The reserved powers of the states are commonly known as *police powers*. It is the police power that a state invokes when it performs the many functions people are accustomed to, such as declaring conduct criminal, providing education, licensing professionals, issuing construction and building permits, and regulating product safety. The states have power over their physical boundaries; Article IV, § 3, clause 1, prohibits Congress from establishing a state within the boundary of an existing state, joining states into one, or taking a portion of one state and making it a part of another without the consent of all the states involved.

As we have seen, the federal government has many powers as well. Some powers are exclusively federal—that is, a state may not simultaneously exercise them—such as coining money, conducting diplomacy with foreign nations, and declaring war. The converse is also true. Some subjects are purely local in nature and Congress may not regulate them. This is true of regulating guns in and around schools, the subject of *United States v. Lopez* (see Chapter 5). Power over many policy areas, however, is concurrently held. Interstate commerce is such a subject. It is possible for both a state and the federal government to regulate interstate commerce. That legislation may be consistent, overlapping, conflicting, or complementary. Problems arise when state and federal regulations clash. This chapter examines the body of law governing these conflicts and other subject areas where federal and state powers intersect.

§ 8.2 Congressional Action: Preemption and Validation

If concurrent jurisdiction over a subject exists, and both the state and federal governments have enacted legislation, the federal law prevails, under the supremacy clause. Even more, in some circumstances the federal government is deemed to have preempted state action. The **preemption** doctrine holds that in three instances state regulation is precluded or invalidated by federal regulation:

1. When Congress expressly states that it intends to preempt state regulation

2. When a state law is inconsistent with federal law, even though no express preemption statement has been made by Congress

3. When Congress has enacted a legislative scheme that comprehensively regulates a field.

═══════════════ **TERMS** ═══════════════

preemption[†] The doctrine that once Congress has enacted legislation in a given field, a state may not enact a law inconsistent with the federal statute. ... A similar doctrine also governs the relationship between the state government and local government.

Amicus

George Washington: Slave Owner to Abolitionist

When George Washington was born in 1732, slavery was largely unchallenged. The slavery institution was particularly entrenched in the southern states and Washington was a Virginian. He inherited slaves and bought others during his lifetime. In 1766, Washington sold a slave named Tom to individuals in the West Indies as punishment for being a runaway. Washington instructed the transporting captain to keep Tom handcuffed during the voyage and further commented that Tom "was exceedingly healthy and good at the hoe" and that if he was kept "clean and trimmed up" he would sell for a good price. Eight years later, Washington's change in philosophy began to be apparent when he assisted in the drafting of the Fairfax Resolutions, which in part, denounced the importation of slaves into the colonies. He referred to the slave trade as "wicked, cruel, and unnatural."

During the Revolutionary War, Washington was exposed to other regions of the nation that were not economically dependent upon slavery. Even more, he developed relationships with abolitionists whom he respected. As a result, he began to seriously question the propriety of the institution during this period. In a transitional period between slave owner and abolitionist, Washington discontinued selling his slaves. In addition, he would move a slave only with the slave's permission.

By 1793, Washington had decided that he wanted to free his slaves. He knew this was an expensive decision. He held hundreds of slaves and they were each worth a considerable amount of money. He held many estates and would no longer have help to manage these properties. There was another problem—the slaves were not prepared for freedom. Washington was concerned, especially for the older slaves, that without property or employment, his freed slaves would not survive. Accordingly, he initially decided to rent all his properties, except the main house at Mount Vernon, Virginia. The rent would provide him with an income. He expected the farmers who leased his land to hire the freed slaves. This would provide a transitional period for the slaves to adjust to freedom. There were other problems. Unlike many owners, Washington encouraged slaves to marry. Many of the slaves on Washington's property were owned by his wife's, Martha Washington, previous husband. As a result, freedom would have separated many families. In the end, his leasing plan did not bloom. Instead, he freed his slaves on a piecemeal basis. He did not pursue some that ran away. When he left public life, he left many slaves in Pennsylvania. This had the effect of freeing them, as Pennsylvania law provided for the freedom of slaves that were alone for a period of time. Finally, he set the date for the manumission of the remainder of his slaves at Martha's death. Martha, however, freed the slaves before she died. She continued to care for the elderly and infirm slaves until her death.

Source: James Flexner, "Washington and Slavery," *Constitution* (No. 2, Spring-Summer 1991).

The first of the three is self-explanatory; Congress preempts if it expressly states such through public law. As to the second and third types of preemption, several factors are considered by courts, including whether the subject has historically been state or federal, the need for uniformity, the likelihood of conflicts in administration of state and federal programs, and the pervasiveness of the federal regulatory scheme. As to the third type, Congress has sufficiently occupied a field whenever it is possible to reasonably infer that it left no room for the states to supplement federal law.

If it is determined that Congress has preempted a policy area, all state laws, even if consistent with federal law, are void. The Court does not lightly infer preemption, and when a policy area is one that touches the states' police powers, preemption will not be found unless there is a "clear and manifest" intent by Congress.[2] Similarly, because preemption of an entire field totally divests the states of power over a policy area, it is found only in extreme cases.

Also, if Congress has expressed its attitude toward preemption, then courts are not to consider implicit preemption. This occurs in situations in which Congress has preempted some specific state regulations, but not all. That is, express preemption of one aspect of a subject precludes the possibility of a court finding implicit preemption of the entire subject. For example, the fact that Congress expressly preempts state licensing of interstate shipping indicates that it did not intend to preempt the entire field. Accordingly, state regulations that do not excessively burden interstate commerce are presumably valid.

Note that lawfully promulgated federal regulations may also preempt state law. Of course, Congress may specifically allow for concurrent state regulation, and often does. See Figure 8-1 for instances in which the Supreme Court found that federal law preempted state law.

Congress may also announce the opposite of preemption: it may validate state legislation of interstate commerce. This is sometimes done before a state has regulated and sometimes after. In some instances, Congress requires federal approval of state laws and objectives before validation. For example, the Federal Occupational Safety and Health Act regulated the training, testing, and licensing of hazardous waste site employees (among other things). Congress provided that federal law shall govern unless a state receives approval for its own plan from the United States Department of Labor. Illinois regulated the area without obtaining federal approval, leading the Court to conclude that the Illinois law was preempted by the federal government.[3]

§ 8.3 Congressional Inaction: The Dormant Commerce Clause

The discussion so far has been concerned with situations in which Congress has chosen to regulate. Difficult problems also arise when Congress does not act. Does the commerce clause preclude state action

PREEMPTION CASES

Gade v. National Solid Wastes Management Ass'n, 505 U.S. 88 (1992)	Illinois regulation of the training, testing, and licensing of hazardous waste site workers preempted by federal Occupational Safety and Health Act.	*Form of Preemption:* Express and Inconsistency. Congress provided that federal law shall govern unless a state receives approval for its own plan from the U.S. Department of Labor.
Morales v. Trans World Airlines, Inc., 504 U.S. 374 (1992)	Language in the federal Airline Deregulation Act, stating that states shall not enforce laws "relating to rates, routes, or services," preempted state deceptive practices law against airlines for deceptive fares.	*Form of Preemption:* Express.
City of Burbank v. Lockhead Air Terminal, 411 U.S. 624 (1973)	City ordinance regulating aircraft noise by prohibiting flights during certain hours was preempted by Federal Aviation Act and the Noise Control Act.	*Form of Preemption:* Express.
McDermott v. Wisconsin, 228 U.S. 115 (1913)	Wisconsin food labeling laws were invalidated because compliance with federal food labeling laws required violation of Wisconsin's laws.	*Form of Preemption:* Inconsistency.
Pennsylvania v. Nelson, 350 U.S. 497 (1956)	Pennsylvania criminal sedition act preempted by federal sedition laws.	*Form of Preemption:* Inconsistency and field occupation.

FIGURE 8-1   Selected Preemption Cases

in some circumtances, even in the absence of federal legislation? The answer is yes—and when it does, it is referred to as the **dormant commerce clause**.

TERMS

dormant commerce clause   Judicial doctrine providing that even if federal power to regulate interstate and international commerce is not exercised, state power to regulate these areas is sometimes precluded.

Cooley v. Board of Wardens[4] is an early dormant commerce clause case. Decided in 1851, its central holding has become known as the *Cooley* **doctrine**. If a subject in interstate commerce is by nature national in character or needs uniformity of law to be effective, then its regulation is exclusively federal. If not federal, then it falls within the state sphere. Largely premised upon dual federalism principles, *Cooley* has limited application in an era of cooperative federalism.

Discriminatory State Laws

Cooley does not address what is to be done with state laws that discriminate against interstate commerce. A state law is discriminatory and an invalid exercise of the police power when it favors local interests over out-of-state interests or intends to reduce the competitive advantage an out-of-state participant may have over locals. After all, one of the purposes of federal jurisdiction over interstate and international commerce was to bring an end to the local rivalries that existed under the Articles of Confederation. The commerce clause is premised upon a national market, and the states may not enact barriers to the interstate sale of products or services.

Discriminatory state laws are perceived as particularly pernicious by the Court and are scrutinized closely. State laws that are facially discriminatory are "virtually per se invalid."[5] Laws that place a state in economic isolation or favor its residents over out-of-state persons are per se unconstitutional. The Court will examine both the state's reason for regulating and the effect of the regulation on interstate commerce. If the state's objectives cannot be achieved in a less burdensome manner *and* outweigh the harm to interstate commerce, the law will be upheld. This is a rigorous standard for a state to meet.

Accordingly, a New York statute that prohibited the sale of milk purchased out of state at a lower price than that obtainable in state was invalidated.[6] The commerce clause does not tolerate a state's attempt to discourage out-of-state products. A state statute that prohibited the sale of certain fish out of the state of Oklahoma, while allowing sale within the state, was void as violating the dormant commerce clause.[7]

Attempts by a state to conserve its resources may also violate the dormant commerce clause if the effect of these regulations is discrimination

---

TERMS

***Cooley* doctrine**   Named for the case in which it was announced, *Cooley v. Board of Wardens*, 53 U.S. 299 (1851); provides that if a subject of interstate commerce is national in character, then regulation of that subject is exclusively federal.

against out-of-state users or sellers. Although the Court has recognized that states have an interest in regulating water use, it has also determined that water is a commodity in interstate commerce subject to dormant commerce clause jurisprudence. In *Sporhase v. Nebraska*,[8] the Court invalidated the reciprocity provision of a statute that prohibited the export of water to a state that does not permit water to be imported to Nebraska. The Court approved of other regulations that were intended to conserve water but found the reciprocity provision unlawfully discriminatory. As an aside, the Court noted that a state may create a limited preference for its own citizens when regulating vital natural resources. The reciprocity provision examined, however, excessively obstructed interstate commerce.

Waste disposal laws have also been the subject of dormant commerce clause jurisprudence. Increasingly, the disposal of human and hazardous wastes is becoming a problem for all cities and towns. In an effort to combat disposal problems, states and localities have enacted a multitude of laws concerning disposal areas, methods, access, and the like. Philadelphia, as well as other cities, attacked the problem of limited landfill space directly. It prohibited the importation of out-of-state solid and liquid wastes. The Court invalidated this law in the 1978 case of *City of Philadelphia v. New Jersey*.[9] Philadelphia could take action to curb its problem, such as prohibiting the disposal of wastes altogether or limiting disposal to certain types of wastes, but it could not discriminate against persons wanting to bring waste in from out of state.

A locality may not indirectly accomplish what it is prohibited from accomplishing directly. *Philadelphia* involved a direct discrimination, but *C&A Carbone v. Clarkstown*[10] involved a processing requirement that had the indirect effect of discriminating against out-of-state dumpers. Clarkstown had entered into a contract with a local solid waste processor, which agreed that the town would provide a certain amount of waste and the processor would process it (i.e., separate recyclable from nonrecyclable waste). A town ordinance then required all nonrecyclable wastes from all sources to be deposited with the private contractor to be processed and disposed. The ordinance was held unlawful because it prevented out-of-state processors from competing and because it increased the cost of depositing out-of-state waste in Clarkstown. Less restrictive alternatives existed for the town. If the town was genuinely concerned about the quality of processing, it could enact quality standards that would apply to all. Instead, it chose to discriminate against nonlocal processors and waste dumpers.

State laws requiring reciprocal action by other states have been closely scrutinized by the Court. In *Great Atlantic & Pacific Tea Co. v. Cottrell*,[11] a Mississippi law that permitted milk to enter the state from another state only if the other state had entered into a reciprocal inspection standards agreement was invalidated. The Court rejected

Mississippi's contention that the law was necessary to protect the health of its citizens. Further, the Court found that the health rationale was a pretext and that it was Mississippi's intention to favor local vendors. Also, in *Sporhase v. Nebraska*,[12] the Court struck down the reciprocity provision of a Nebraska law that restricted the exportation of water to states that permitted the importation of their water to Nebraska. Again, the Court found this to be unnecessarily discriminatory.

Not all discriminatory laws have failed. Maine's prohibition on the importation of certain baitfish, to prevent the introduction of certain parasites not common to Maine, was upheld. The Court held that Maine's interest in protecting local fisheries was significant and that there was no alternative method of achieving this objective that was less burdensome to interstate commerce.[13]

Burdensome State Laws

It is possible for state regulation to be nondiscriminatory, yet burdensome to interstate commerce. Again, the Court weighs the state's interest against the burden on interstate commerce to determine whether the dormant commerce clause has been violated. However, the test is not as rigorous as in the facially discriminatory cases discussed earlier. Accordingly, local regulation is more likely to be valid when challenged as burdensome than when challenged as facially discriminatory. In most of these cases, the state asserts that the regulation is necessary to protect the health and welfare of its citizens.

Many dormant commerce clause cases have arisen in the context of state regulation of interstate transportation. Most state laws regulating transportation safety are validated by the Court. However, some overburden interstate commerce. For example, an Arizona law that prohibited trains with more than seventy freight cars or fourteen passenger cars was held unconstitutional. The Court noted that long trains were common throughout the United States and that company compliance with the law would be very burdensome to interstate commerce. A company would have to either change its practice nationwide or stop at the border of Arizona and reduce the length of its trains. If allowed, then every state could regulate train transportation and trains would be forced to stop at every border and make adjustments to comply with local law. Further, Arizona's evidence that shorter trains are safer was marginal. Thus, the burden on interstate commerce outweighed Arizona's interest in protecting its citizens.[14]

Similarly, an Illinois law requiring a certain mud flap on trucks was invalidated. The law would have prevented trucks from using a mud flap that was legal in nearly every other state. Again, the safety advantages were minimal; the burden on interstate commerce high.[15] For nearly identical reasons, an Iowa law that forbade trucks longer than sixty-five feet from using its roads was held unconstitutional.[16] The Court concluded that to comply, a truck would either have to avoid the state or stop at the border, detach the trailer that caused the vehicle to exceed the limit, and ship it separately. The burden on interstate commerce in both cases was significant. Further, the state's asserted safety concern was negated by the increased danger caused by the second alternative.

Some state laws that burden interstate commerce have been upheld. For example, state laws requiring railroads to have full crews on trains have been upheld. Also, a state law that prohibited the sale of milk in nonrecyclable plastic containers, but permitted the use of other nonrecyclable materials such as paperboard, was upheld because (1) its impact on interstate commerce was minimal, (2) it treated in-state and out-of-state retailers identically, and (3) the state had a legitimate conservation and waste disposal interest.[17]

Liquor Laws

State regulation of liquor requires special constitutional analysis due to the Twenty-First Amendment, § 1. Section 2, which repealed Prohibition, reads:

> The transportation or importation into any State, Territory, or possession of the United States for delivery or use therein of intoxicating liquors, in violation of the laws thereof, is hereby prohibited.

Pursuant to this amendment, the states possess greater power over the interstate aspects of liquor than they do over other items. In particular, the dormant commerce clause has limited application in the liquor arena. A state may tax, or otherwise discourage, the importation of liquor without violating the dormant commerce clause.

Broad state powers over liquor are not absolute, though. First, Congress regulates foreign trade and a state may not interfere with this authority, even when the trade subject is liquor. Second, extreme interferences with interstate commerce will be invalidated. For example, a New York law that required distillers to sell their products in New York at the lowest price in the United States violated the commerce clause.[18]

Note that even though the federal government does not have the power to establish the drinking age, it may coerce the states into setting a minimum age. Hence, withholding of federal highway funds from states that did not enact and enforce a twenty-one-years-of-age drinking limit was deemed constitutional.[19]

State Taxation as Discriminatory and Burdensome

State taxes may also discriminate against or burden interstate commerce and, accordingly, violate the dormant commerce clause. Yet tax revenues are needed by state and local governments to pay for the services they provide. It would be unfair to allow out-of-state market participants to avail themselves of local services but not to contribute revenues. For example, an out-of-state market participant may use the courts of a state to enforce a contract, the police to investigate fraud, and administrative agencies to file business claims of many varieties. In regard to discriminatory taxing, the Supreme Court applies the strict scrutiny test, as with other allegedly discriminatory laws. That is, the law is valid only if a government can show a compelling interest. The Court has held that laws intended to equalize the tax burdens between in-state and out-of-state participants are valid. Thus, if in-state market participants are shouldering most or all of a tax burden, the state may act. The Court established the following test:

1. If a state has identified an intrastate tax for which it is attempting to equalize the burden between in-state and out-of state participants, and

2. The taxing scheme leaves both sets of participants with approximately equal tax burdens, and

3. Approximately the same events are taxed.[20]

If all these criteria are met, the law will most probably pass the test.

The Supreme Court also developed a test concerning burdensome tax laws. It permits states and localities to extract a fair tax, yet prevents them from overburdening interstate commerce. The test was announced in *Complete Auto Transit, Inc. v. Brady*,[21] a 1977 case. Pursuant to this test, a state or local tax on a product or service in interstate commerce is valid if the tax:

1. Is applied to an activity with a substantial nexus to the taxing state; and

2. Is fairly apportioned; and

3. Does not discriminate against interstate commerce; and

4. Is fairly related to the services provided by the state.

Two interstate passenger bus transportation cases can be used to illustrate the application of this test. First, *Central Greyhound Line, Inc. v. Mealey*[22] involved an unapportioned tax on gross receipts from interstate bus tickets. The tax was based upon the total number of miles traveled. The law did not distinguish between intrastate and interstate miles. Applying the *Complete Auto Transit* test, it is clear that the activity was related to the taxing state. However, the second and third elements were not satisfied.

The second element has two aspects: internal and external consistency. To know whether internal consistency is satisfied, one must ask whether, if every state enacted an identical law, intrastate commerce would be favored. External consistency focuses on whether a state is taking more than its share of an interstate transaction. The tax in *Central Greyhound* failed these elements because the possibility of duplicative taxes on interstate travel was presented. The state in which the ticket was purchased and the states through which a passenger traveled could all tax the trip. Because the tax on travel out of the state in which the ticket was purchased would be greater, the law unfairly discriminated against interstate commerce.

In a similar case decided in 1995, *Oklahoma Tax Commission v. Jefferson Lines*,[23] the Court examined a sales tax imposed on intrastate and interstate bus tickets. Jefferson paid the tax on the intrastate tickets it sold, but refused to pay the tax on interstate tickets. It relied on the *Central Greyhound* case in support of its position.

Again, the first element of the *Complete Auto Transit* test was satisfied. The tax was imposed by the state in which the ticket was sold. The Court rejected Jefferson's argument that *Central Greyhound* applied, finding that the sales tax in *Jefferson* was different from the gross receipts tax in *Central Greyhound*. The sales tax was identical for both instate and out-of-state purchases (4.5 percent of the ticket price). Recall that the problem in *Central Greyhound* was the possibility of successive and duplicative taxes on interstate commerce. *Jefferson,* however, involved a transactional tax. The tax was imposed on the sale and delivery of the ticket. No other state could tax that activity. As to the fourth element, the Court found that the amount (first 4 percent, later 4.5 percent) was reasonably related to the services provided by the state. As to this element, a state does not have to prove that a taxpayer receives a direct benefit from a tax. Rather, it is enough that the tax reasonably relate to the types of services that benefit the taxpayer. The dissent in *Jefferson* argued that there is no meaningful difference between the two cases and that *Central Greyhound* should apply.

The Fourteenth Amendment's due process clause also restricts a state's power to tax out-of-state individuals. There must be a **minimum contact** between a state and the person taxed.[24] State citizenship may establish the requisite contact. Contact with a transaction may

minimum contacts test †   A doctrine under which a state court is permitted to acquire personal jurisdiction over a nonresident, although he or she also satisfy due process. For example, the sale of goods in a state or the execution and performance of a contract in a state by out-of-state parties create minimum contacts.

State taxation of the federal government may also be unconstitutional. This topic is discussed in § 8.4.

State as Market Participant

States not only regulate commerce, but also participate in commerce, as buyers and, less often, as sellers. When a state is a participant in, as opposed to a regulator of, the market, the dormant commerce clause does not apply. The Court has determined that although the commerce clause was intended to limit the states' power to regulate commerce, it was not intended to limit their ability to participate in the market.

A state may purchase exclusively from local vendors and provide goods and services exclusively to local vendors, even though it may not require the same from local businesses. Accordingly, a state decision to sell cement produced at a state-owned plant to state residents only was validated by the Supreme Court.[25] A state may also charge higher prices to out-of-state purchasers when it is engaged in manufacturing or selling a product or service. States have taken advantage of this exception to the dormant commerce clause and have solved problems that they could not remedy as regulators by becoming participants. For example, consider the nationwide waste disposal problem discussed earlier. Pursuant to the dormant commerce clause, a state may not establish a regulatory scheme that discriminates against out-of-state disposers. This caused local and state governments to purchase landfills and disposal sites. By 1989, 81 percent of the nation's landfills were owned by a government.[26] As owners, local governments may limit disposal to residents.

In some instances, it is difficult to determine whether to treat a state as a market participant or as a regulator, because it may be both. If a state is a participant, but uses its regulatory power to interfere with the free market, then dormant commerce clause analysis should be applied.[27] If state regulation is only incidental to its participation, then the state should not be limited by the dormant commerce clause.

See Figure 8-2 for a summary of commerce clause cases.

TERMS

is not personally served with process within the state, if he or she has had such a substantial connection with that state that due process is not offended by the court's exercise of jurisdiction over him or her.

DORMANT COMMERCE CLAUSE (DCC): SELECTED CASES

Cooley v. Board of Wardens, 53 U.S. 299 (1851)	Early DCC case; little application today.
Baldwin v. G.A.F. Seelig, Inc., 294 U.S. 511 (1935)	State statute prohibiting the sale of milk out of state at lower price than within state was invalidated.
Sporhase v. Nebraska, 458 U.S. 941 (1982)	State statute prohibiting the export of water to a state that did not permit water to flow the other direction was invalidated.
City of Philadelphia v. New Jersey, 437 U.S. 617 (1978)	City ordinance prohibiting the import of wastes to city's disposal sites was invalidated.
C&A Carbone v. Clarkstown, 114 S. Ct. 1677 (1994)	An ordinance that indirectly benefited local processors was invalidated.
Maine v. Taylor, 477 U.S. 131 (1986)	State statute prohibiting the importation of certain fish (to protect the state's fisheries) was upheld.
Bibb v. Navajo Freight Lines, Inc., 359 U.S. 520 (1959)	State law mandating particular mud flaps was invalidated as overburdening and interfering with interstate commerce.
Minnesota v. Clover Leaf Creamery Co., 449 U.S. 456 (1981)	State prohibition on the sale of milk in nonrecyclable plastic containers was upheld.
Oregon Waste Systems, Inc. v. Department of Environmental Quality, 114 S. Ct. 1345 (1995); *Fulton Corp. v. Faulkner,* 116 S. Ct. 848 (1996); *United Food & Commercial Workers Union v. Brown Group,* 116 S. Ct. 1529 (1996)	State laws that are facially discriminatory are tested under the strict scrutiny test. In tax cases, such a law survives only if it can be shown that the state is attempting to equalize the tax burdens between in- and out-of-state participants.

FIGURE 8-2   Selected Dormant Commerce Clause Cases

Privileges and Immunities

There are two privileges and immunities clauses in the Constitution. One is located in the Fourteenth Amendment. The other, which is the subject of this discussion, is found in Article IV, § 2, clause 1, and states that "[t]he citizens of each State shall be entitled to all Privilege and Immunities of Citizens in the several States."

There is an intersection between some commerce clause cases and some privileges and immunities cases. When a state regulates to advance a local market over the interstate market, it simultaneously discriminates against interstate commerce and deprives the residents of other states of the privileges it extends to its own.

The clause is not absolute, however. A state may grant greater benefits to its own residents if *substantial cause* to do so exists. Further, the clause protects only fundamental rights. *Fundamental* in this context differs from other areas of constitutional law, such as in due process analysis. Here, *fundamental* refers to those rights that are important to the preservation of the union—those that contribute to making this a federation as opposed to a confederation.

There is no bright line of demarcation between fundamental and nonfundamental rights. The right to practice law is fundamental and a state law restricting that right to state residents is unconstitutional.[28] The right to earn a living as a commercial fisher is fundamental as well.[29] Sport hunting for elk is not fundamental, and, as such, not protected by the privileges and immunities clause.[30]

There is no way to know whether a court will analyze a case in terms of the privileges and immunities clause or the commerce clause. However, the commerce clause has been the subject of more litigation and interpretation than has the privileges and immunities clause, and appears to be a favored application. One important distinction between commerce clause and privileges and immunities clause rulings can be made. Congress can legitimize state behavior under the commerce clause. Privileges and immunities jurisprudence, in contrast, transcends statutory law and cannot be altered by Congress.

§ 8.4 Intergovernmental Immunity

This section examines the power of the national government to regulate the states and vice versa. To begin with the latter, states are generally prohibited from regulating the federal government. Congress may consent to state regulation but rarely does. Thus, a state may not enact minimum wages that apply to federal employees or regulate the safety of federal employees while at work; since the 1819 decision in *McCulloch v. Maryland*,[31] it has been clear that states may not tax the federal government or its subunits.

In the nation's early years, the states enjoyed immunity from the federal government as well. The Tenth Amendment was construed as a state shield from federal regulation. Today, the states enjoy only limited immunity from the federal government. Two cases decided since 1976 are important in this regard, one asserting state sovereignty and the other denying it.

In 1976 the Supreme Court handed down *National League of Cities v. Usery*.[32] That case was concerned with whether the federal Fair Labor Standards Act, which mandates the minimum wage and maximum work hours, could be applied to state employees. Initially, Congress exempted all public employees from the Act, but later amended the law to include employees of hospitals, institutions, and schools.

The Supreme Court invalidated the law insofar as it reached public employees because "[o]ne undoubted attribute of state sovereignty is the States' power to determine the wages which shall be paid to those whom they employ in order to carry out their governmental functions." The Court stated further that application of the Act to the states "impermissibly interfere[s] with the integral governmental functions of these bodies," and threatens their "separate and independent existence." In short, "Congress may not exercise [its] power so as to force directly upon the States its choices as to how essential decisions regarding the conduct of integral governmental functions are to be made." (The essential functions the Court referred to are providing hospitals, schools, and fire and police protection.)

The *Usery* majority opinion was written by Justice Rehnquist and the vote count was five to four. Justice Blackmun concurred, although he stated that he was "not untroubled by certain possible implications" of the decision. Nine years later, the Court reversed *Usery* in *Garcia v. San Antonio Metropolitan Transit Authority*. The vote was again five to four, but Justice Blackmun had crossed over to the other side.

Garcia inflicted a serious, but not fatal, wound to state sovereignty. The Court stated that "constitutional structure might impose" limits on the federal authority to regulate the states under the commerce clause. Through its quotation of Justice Frankfurter, it appeared to indicate that the limitation would prevent only "horrible" encroachments on state power.

Just such an encroachment was found in the 1992 case of *New York v. United States*.[33] Faced with a shortage of disposal sites for low-level radioactive waste throughout the United States, Congress enacted the Low-Level Radioactive Waste Policy Amendments Act. This statute imposed upon the states an obligation to provide for the disposal of waste generated within their borders. This could be done solely or in compact with other states. Congress established three incentives to bring the states into compliance:

1. *Financial:* States with disposal sites were authorized to impose a surcharge on waste received from states that did not establish their own disposal sites. One-fourth of the surcharge was to be collected by the federal government and then distributed to compliant

GARCIA
v.
SAN ANTONIO METROPOLITAN
TRANSIT AUTHORITY
469 U.S. 528 (1985)

Justice Blackmun delivered the opinion of the Court.

We revisit in these cases an issue raised in *National League of Cities v. Usery.* In that litigation, this Court, by a sharply divided vote, ruled that the Commerce Clause does not empower Congress to enforce the minimum-wage and overtime provisions of the Fair Labor Standards Act (FLSA) against the States "in areas of traditional governmental functions." Although *National League of Cities* supplies some examples of "traditional governmental functions," it did not offer a general explanation of how a "traditional" function is to be distinguished from a "nontraditional" one. Since then, federal and state courts have struggled with the task, thus imposed, of identifying a traditional function for purposes of state immunity under the Commerce Clause.

In the present cases, a Federal District Court concluded that municipal ownership and operation of a mass-transit system is a traditional governmental function and thus, under *National League of Cities,* is exempt from the obligation of the FLSA. Faced with the identical question, three Federal Courts of Appeals and one state appellate court have reached the opposite conclusion.

Our examination of this "function" standard applied in these and other cases over the last eight years now persuades us that the attempt to draw boundaries of state regulatory immunity in terms of "traditional governmental function" is not only unworkable but is also inconsistent with the established principles of federalism and, indeed, with those very federalism principles on which *National League of Cities* purported to rest. That case, accordingly, is overruled. ...

[The Court then discussed the difficulty in distinguishing traditional from nontraditional functions.]

We therefore now reject, as unsound in principle and unworkable in practice, a rule of state immunity from federal regulation that turns on a judicial appraisal of whether a particular governmental function is "integral" or "traditional." Any such rule leads to inconsistent results at the same time that it disserves principles of democratic self-governance, and it breeds inconsistency precisely because it is divorced from those principles. If there are to be limits on the Federal Government's power to interfere with state functions—as undoubtably there are—we must look elsewhere to find them. We accordingly return to the underlying issue that confronted this Court in *National League of Cities*—the manner in which the Constitution insulates States from the reach of Congress' power under the Commerce Clause. ...

The States unquestionably do "retai[n] a significant measure of sovereign authority." They do so, however, only to the extent that the Constitution has not divested them of their original powers and transferred those powers to the Federal Government. ...

With rare exceptions, like the guarantee, in Article IV, § 3, of state territorial integrity, the Constitution does not carve out express elements of state sovereignty that Congress may not employ its delegated powers to displace. ...

Apart from the limitation on federal authority inherent in the delegated nature of Congress' Article I powers, the principal means chosen by the Framers to ensure the role of the States in the federal system lies in the structure of the Federal Government itself. It is no novelty to observe that the composition of the Federal Government was designed in large part to protect the States from overreaching by Congress. The Framers thus gave the States a role in the selection both of the Executive and Legislative Branches of the Federal Government. The States were vested with indirect influence over the House of Representatives and the Presidency by their control of electoral qualifications and their role in presidential elections. ... They were given more direct influence in the Senate, where each State received equal representation and each Senator was to be selected by the legislature of his State. ... The significance attached to the States' equal representation in the Senate is underscored by the prohibition of any constitutional amendment divesting a State of equal representation without the State's consent. Art. V. ...

We realize that changes in the structure of the Federal Government have taken place since 1789, not the least of which has been the substitution of popular election of Senators by the adoption of the Seventeenth Amendment in 1913, and that these changes may work to alter the influence of the States in the federal political process. Nonetheless, against this background, we are convinced that the fundamental limitation that the constitutional scheme imposes on the Commerce Clause to protect the "States as States" is one of process rather than one of result. ...

Of course, we continue to recognize that the States occupy a special and specific position in our constitutional system and that the scope of Congress' authority under the Commerce Clause must reflect that position. ...

These cases do not require us to identify or define what affirmative limits the constitutional structure might impose on federal action affecting the States under the Commerce Clause. We note and accept Justice Frankfurter's observation in *New York v. United States,* 326 U.S. 572 (1946):

> "The process of Constitutional adjudication does not thrive on conjuring up horrible possibilities that never happen in the real world and devising doctrines sufficiently comprehensive in detail to cover the remotest contingency. Nor need we go beyond what is required for a reasoned disposition of the kind of controversy now before the Court." ...

We do not lightly overrule recent precedent. We have not hesitated, however, when it has become apparent that a prior decision has departed from a proper understanding of congressional power under the Commerce Clause. Due respect for the reach of congressional power within the federal system mandates that we do so now. ...

Justice Powell, with whom The Chief Justice [Burger], Justice Rehnquist, and Justice O'Connor join, dissenting.

... Despite some genuflecting in the Court's opinion to the concept of federalism, today's decision effectively reduces the Tenth Amendment to meaningless rhetoric when Congress acts pursuant to the Commerce Clause. ...

Today's opinion does not explain how the States' role in the electoral process guarantees that particular exercises of the Commerce Clause power will not infringe on residual State sovereignty. Members of Congress are elected from the various States, but once in office they are Members of the Federal Government. ...

More troubling than the local infirmities in the Court's reasoning is the result of its holding, i.e., that federal political officials, invoking the Commerce Clause, are the sole judges of the limits of their own power. This result is inconsistent with the fundamental principles of our constitutional system. At least since *Marbury v. Madison* it has been the settled province of the federal judiciary "to say what the law is" with respect to the constitutionality of acts of Congress. ...

In our federal system, the States have a major role that cannot be preempted by the National Government. As contemporaneous writings and the debates at the ratifying conventions make clear, the States' ratification of the Constitution was predicated on this understanding of federalism. Indeed, the Tenth Amendment was adopted specifically to ensure that the important role promised the States by the proponents of the Constitution was realized. ...

By usurping functions traditionally performed by the State, federal overreaching under the Commerce Clause undermines the constitutionally mandated balance of power between the States and the Federal Government, a balance designed to protect our fundamental liberties. ...

[The Tenth] Amendment states explicitly that "[t]he powers not delegated to the United States ... are reserved to the States." The Court recasts this language to say that the States retain their sovereign powers "only to the extent that the Constitution has not divested them of their original powers and transferred those powers to the Federal Government." This rephrasing is not a distinction without a difference; rather, it reflects the Court's unprecedented view that Congress is free under the Commerce Clause to assume a State's traditional sovereign power, and to do so without judicial review of its action. ...

Justice O'Connor, with whom Justice Powell and Justice Rehnquist join, dissenting.
... [T]he Federal Government has, with this Court's blessing, undertaken to tell the States the age at which they can retire their law enforcement officers, and the regulatory standards, procedures, and even the agenda which their utilities commissions must consider and follow. ... The political process has not protected against these encroachments on state activities, even though they directly impinge on a State's ability to make and enforce its laws. With the abandonment of essentials of state sovereignty and Congress is the latter's underdeveloped capacity for self-restraint. ...

states. The receiving state was authorized to keep the remaining three-quarters of the surcharge.

2. *Access:* Eventually, a state could refuse to receive waste from a state without its own disposal site.

3. *Take Title:* If a state had not provided for disposal of the waste by 1996, it would required to take title to the waste from the private producer, be responsible for disposal, and be responsible for all damages incurred by the waste's producer resulting from the state not timely taking possession of the waste.

The parties agreed that the federal government has the authority under the commerce clause to regulate the disposal of radioactive waste. The state of New York objected, however, to the manner of regulation. It asserted that Congress may regulate the private producers of the waste—individuals—but not the states. The Supreme Court agreed.

The first two incentives were upheld as consonant with Congress's power under the commerce and spending clauses. The Court reaffirmed the long-held rule that the federal government can attach conditions to the receipt of federal funds. Requiring a state to regulate in a particular manner is a permissible condition. Accordingly, it was lawful for the federal government to withhold federal highway funds from states that refused to adopt maximum speed or minimum drinking age laws. It is also permissible, when Congress has the power to regulate a private activity directly, to give the states a choice to regulate the activity according to federal standards or have their laws preempted by federal laws. The Court decided, however, that these incentives possessed a characteristic not present in the third: state freedom of choice.

> By either of these two methods, as by any other permissible method of encouraging a State to conform to federal policy choices, the residents of the State retain the ultimate decision as to whether or not the State will comply. If a State's citizens view federal policy as sufficiently contrary to local interests, they may elect to decline a federal grant. If state

residents would prefer their government to devote its attention and resources to problems other than those deemed important by Congress, they may choose to have the Federal Government rather than the State bear the expense of a federally mandated regulatory program.

But the third provision, the take-title provision, is different. It directs that states either regulate as directed or take title to privately owned waste. There is no true choice, because Congress cannot compel either. It does not have the power to order a state to enact laws, nor does it have the power to require a state to subsidize a private business. Congress, therefore, "has crossed the line distinguishing encouragement from coercion," because the take-title provision amounts to a commandeering of state legislative power. "Whether one views the take title provision as lying outside Congress' enumerated powers, or as infringing upon the core of state sovereignty reserved by the Tenth Amendment, the provision is inconsistent with the federal structure of our Government established by the Constitution."

Accordingly, pursuant to *Garcia*, the federal government may regulate state activity, but *New York* prohibits Congress from directly compelling a state to regulate. Financial incentives are acceptable and this is the method Congress uses to impose federal policy on the states. Hence, the federal government may withhold funds from states that do not regulate radioactive wastes, but it cannot require them to regulate the area. Some commentators have criticized this as a distinction without a difference.

Although it prohibited the federal government from mandating state regulation, the Court has softened the effect of *Garcia* by narrowly construing statutes that regulate states. In *Gregory v. Ashcroft*,[34] the Court refused to subject state judges to the federal Age Discrimination in Employment Act (ADEA), because they are "policy-making" officials. The Court concluded that Congress must clearly express an intent to include policy-making officials within the grasp of such a law. Because Congress had not, the officials were exempt. However, the impact of the decision is limited because the Court did not go so far as to say that Congress may not regulate state policy makers.

§ 8.5 Compacts and Interstate Comity

Article I, § 10, clause 1, prohibits states from entering into treaties, alliances, or confederations with foreign nations. Clause 3 of this section further states that "[n]o State shall, without the Consent of Congress … enter into any Agreement or Compact with another State, or with a foreign Power."

Through these provisions, the framers granted exclusive federal jurisdiction in making treaties and a strong federal role in interstate compacts and agreements. There is no significant difference between a compact and an agreement, except that the former appears to refer to written agreements and the latter to oral agreements.

The purpose of requiring congressional approval of compacts is to protect the integrity of the nation. Congress, which will be mindful of concerns of national unity and cooperation, must consent to agreements between states that may change the character of the nation. Not all agreements or cooperative efforts between states need federal approval. Only those agreements that tend to change the power relationships of the states, threaten the integrity of the Union, or diminish the power of the federal government are subject to the consent clause. For example, an interstate cooperative effort to combat drug trafficking does not require congressional approval. However, an agreement between neighboring states to alter their borders or to combine into one state would.

Cooperation, or *comity,* between the states is constitutionally mandated in some circumstances. Article IV, § 1, demands that each state give its sister states' laws, records, and judicial proceedings **full faith and credit**. This means, with a few exceptions, that a judgment entered in one state can be enforced in another state. For example, suppose Nazarene obtains a judgment for $50,000 against Ronald in a Nebraska state court. Ronald moves to Montana immediately following the conclusion of the litigation. Nazarene is empowered under the full faith and credit clause to register her judgment in Montana and enforce it there, even though it was rendered in Nebraska.

In some circumstances, the law of one state must be applied in the courts of another state. Assume that Nazarene and Ronald enter into a contract in Wyoming. That contract provides that all disputes arising under it shall be governed by the law of Wyoming, regardless of where litigated. So the law of Wyoming would apply, even if the case is filed in Nebraska. These are only a few examples of the application of the full faith and credit clause.

The interstate rendition clause, found in Article IV, § 2, clause 2, provides that

> [a] Person charged in any State with Treason, Felony, or other Crime, who shall flee from Justice, and be found in another State, shall on demand

---

TERMS

full faith and credit [†]   A reference to the requirement of Article IV of the Constitution that each state give "full faith and credit" to the "public acts, records, and judicial proceedings" of every other state. This means that a state's judicial acts must be given the same effect by the courts of all other states as they receive at home.

of the executive Authority of the State from which he fled, be delivered up, to be removed to the State having Jurisdiction of the Crime.

In spite of the clause's plain language, until 1987 it was interpreted as not creating a binding obligation on state officials to extradite fugitives. However, the Supreme Court re-examined the clause in *Puerto Rico v. Branstad*[35] and held that the clause creates a mandatory duty to extradite fugitives properly demanded. A state may not examine the nature of the pending charges or make an independent determination of whether the fugitive will be treated fairly. The state may only satisfy itself that the extradition documents are proper, that the individual sought has been charged with a crime, and that the detainee is the person charged. If these are answered in the affirmative, then the state must extradite the fugitive to the demanding state. Failure or refusal to extradite are is reviewable and a federal court may order the extradition.

Finally, the privileges and immunities clause of Article IV also promotes interstate comity. See the discussion of this clause earlier in this chapter.

§ 8.6 Guarantee and Militia Clauses

The guarantee clause, Article IV, § 4, states:

The United States shall guarantee to every State in this Union a Republican Form of Government, and shall protect each of them against Invasion; and on Application of the Legislature, or of the Executive (when the Legislature cannot be convened) against domestic Violence.

This clause has not been invoked very often and there are few cases defining its precise meaning. Congress relied on the guarantee clause to support its reconstruction efforts in the South following the Civil War. For example, Congress required the southern states to enact new constitutions respecting a republican form of government. Similarly, Congress has reviewed the constitutions of territories that have applied for statehood to determine whether they should be admitted into the Union. Although it has never happened, Congress could nullify any state attempt to change to an nonrepublican form of government.

A precise definition of "republican form of govenment" has been rendered. Generally, it refers to a form of government that respects individual and property rights. Certainly, the electoral process is also an element of a republican form of government. Therefore, it would not be republican for a state to establish a government in which officials obtain their positions through inheritance.

The requirement of a republican form of government does not mean that a state must establish a governmental structure identical to that of the United States. The states are generally free to design their governments in any manner they wish, so long as they remain republican in nature. For example, a state may choose to have a unicameral legislature, as Nebraska has, even though the United States has chosen the bicameral model. Generally, Congress's decisions under the guarantee clause are nonjusticiable political questions. As such, federal courts will not interfere with Congress when it acts under the guarantee clause.

The guarantee clause also empowers the United States to protect the states from invasions and domestic violence. Even though the clause appears to limit federal intervention to quell domestic violence to occasions when state authorities have requested assistance, presidents have on many occasions, pursuant to congressional authorization, acted without such a request.[36]

Article I, § 8, delegates to Congress the power to provide for the national defense, establish a military, regulate the armed forces, and to declare war.

Congress also possesses power over the state militias. Article I, § 8, clause 15, extends to Congress the power to call "forth the militia to execute the Laws of the Union, suppress Insurrections and repel Invasions." The Supreme Court upheld a statute that delegated the power to call state militias into national service without the consent of state officials.[37] The President may call on state militias to serve abroad, as well as domestically. Clause 16 of the same section gives Congress the power to organize, arm, and discipline the state militias (National Guard). However, the states retain the power to appoint officers and train the militias under the rules established by Congress. The power of the states to maintain militias under the original Constitution was questionable. Article I, § 10, clause 3, states that "[n]o State shall, without the Consent of Congress ... keep Troops, or Ships of War in time of Peace." However, the Second Amendment provides that the power of the states to maintain well-regulated militias shall not be infringed.

§ 8.7 State Constitutionalism and the New Federalism

Every state has its own constitution. Like the federal Constitution, state constitutions contain declarations or bills of individual rights. In fact, many clauses in state bills of rights are worded identically, or nearly so, to the federal Constitution.

For the first 150 years of the nation, these bills were the foundation of civil rights, especially in criminal cases. This was true because the federal Bill of Rights was construed as limiting the power of the federal government only. Thus, the Fourth Amendment's prohibition of unreasonable searches and seizures, the Eighth Amendment's prohibition of cruel and unusual punishments, and the Fifth Amendment's privilege against self-incrimination did not apply in state criminal proceedings.

This has changed. During the Warren Court era, almost the entire Bill of Rights was **incorporated**. A right is incorporated, through the Fourteenth Amendment's due process clause, if it is "fundamental and essential to an ordered liberty." As one of the post-Civil War amendments, the Fourteenth Amendment was written with the intention of limiting the states. Although it did not happen for many years after adoption, the Supreme Court eventually concluded that the Fourteenth Amendment incorporated all the rights that are fundamental to an ordered liberty. Today, only the Seventh Amendment's right to a jury trial in civil cases, the Fifth Amendment's right to grand jury indictment, and the Eighth Amendment's right to reasonable bail have not been incorporated. Therefore, federal constitutional law is now a significant factor in all criminal proceedings.

Note that there was a gap in time between the ratification of the Fourteenth Amendment (1868) and the Court's recognition of its incorporation of fundamental rights (1960s). During that period, state constitutional law played a larger role in protecting civil liberties. For example, the Illinois Supreme Court ruled in 1882 that racial segregation was illegal.[38] The United States Supreme Court did not reach this conclusion until 1954.[39]

Once it occurred, the effect of incorporation was the displacement of state constitutional law for many years. In recent years, however, there has been a rebirth in state constitutional law. This is often referred to as the *New Federalism.*

State constitutional law may not decrease or limit federally secured rights, but a state may extend civil rights beyond what the federal Constitution secures. In some cases, this may occur expressly. For example, both the Florida and Alaska constitutions expressly protect privacy, whereas the federal constitution does not. Rather, a national right to privacy was only recently declared by the Supreme Court (as a *penumbra* or implied protection), and it is somewhat controversial because of the

---

TERMS

selective incorporation doctrine   Under the Due Process Clause of the Fourteenth Amendment, those rights in the federal Bill of Rights that are fundamental and necessary to an ordered liberty are applied against the states. Other incorporation theories exist.

absence of express language in the Constitution establishing the right. The Washington state constitution protects "private affairs," which has been interpreted more broadly than *privacy* under the Fourth Amendment. Many states provide for education through their constitutions, although the federal Constitution does not contain a right to education. In addition to protecting freedom of religion, as does the First Amendment of the federal Constitution, Georgia's constitution protects freedom of "conscience."[40]

In some instances, a state constitution may expressly provide a protection that is implicit in the federal Constitution. For example, Florida's bill of rights protects "expression," whereas the national Constitution protects "speech." As you will learn later, however, the term *speech* has been interpreted as meaning "expression."

Also, many state constitutions protect individuals from one another. For example, the Illinois free speech clause prohibits both public and private actors from encroaching upon an individual's freedom of expression; the federal Constitution restricts only government actors. Similarly, the Montana constitution's equal rights amendment prohibits gender-based discrimination by the state, persons, and corporations.

In other instances, the language of a state constitution may not expressly provide greater protection than the federal Constitution. Regardless, the courts of the state may interpret it as providing greater individual rights. This may be happen even if the state constitutional provision uses language identical to its federal counterpart. Historically, this has not been so, however. Many state courts, if not most, interpreted their constitutional provisions as parallelling counterpart federal constitutional provisions. In rare cases this is required by the state constitution.

Increasingly, however, this is not occurring. During the past two decades, commentators, judges, and attorneys have exhibited a renewed interest in state constitutional law. State constitutions are now viewed as an independent source of individual liberties. See Figure 8-3 for a comparison between selected state constitutions and the federal Constitution.

Approaches to Dual Constitutionalism

One scholar (John Shaw) has identified three approaches (models) to the relationship between federal and state constitutionalism (dual constitutionalism): **primacy**; **interstitial**; and **dual sovereignty**.[41]

───────────────────────── TERMS ─────────────────────────

primacy   An approach to constitutional interpretation that requires state judges to apply their state's constitution before turning to the federal Constitution.

STATE CONSTITUTIONALISM

What follows are a few examples of differences between state constitutions and the United States Constitution. The list is not exhaustive; the particular states and rights chosen are intended only as illustrations.

Rights Expressed in State Constitutions But Not in the Federal Constitution

- EDUCATION—Texas (art. 7); Utah (art. X, § 1)
- VICTIM RIGHTS—Arizona (art. 2, § 2.1)
- RIGHT OF REVOLUTION—New Hampshire (art. I, § 10)
- WATER RIGHTS—Utah (art. XVII, § 1)
- CARE FOR THE NEEDY—New York (art. XVII, § 1)
- FREEDOM FROM PRIVATE DISCRIMINATION BASED UPON GENDER, RACE, ETHNICITY, CULTURE, POLITICAL BELIEFS, AND RELIGION—Montana (art. II, § 4)

Rights Implicitly Secured by the Federal Constitution and Expressly Protected by State Constitutions

- EXPRESSION (other than speech)—Implicitly protected by U.S. Constitution's First Amendment free speech clause; expressly protected by Florida's constitution (art. I, § 4)
- PRIVACY—Implicitly protected by several amendments to the U.S. Constitution, including the Fourth, Fifth, Ninth, and Fourteenth; expressly protected by Florida (art. I, § 23) and Alaska (art. I, § 22).

Rights Expressed in Both State and Federal Constitutions But Interpreted More Broadly under State Law

- FREEDOM FROM UNREASONABLE SEARCHES AND SEIZURES—Pennsylvania rejected the U.S. Supreme Court's *Leon* (good faith exception to warrant requirement) decision. *Commonwealth v. Edmunds*, 586 A.2d 887 (Pa. 1991).
- FREEDOM FROM UNREASONABLE SEARCHES AND SEIZURES—Pennsylvania rejected the Supreme Court's standing requirements for defendants in possession cases. *Commonwealth v. Sell*, 470 A.2d 457 (Pa. 1983).
- FREEDOM FROM SELF-INCRIMINATION—Hawaii's courts have interpreted Hawaii's counterpart clause as providing greater protection to the accused. *Hawaii v. Bowe*, 881 P.2d 538 (Haw. 1994).

FIGURE 8-3 Comparison of State Constitutions with the Federal Constitution

TERMS

interstitial An approach to constitutional interpretation that requires state judges to apply the federal Constitution before turning to their state's constitution.

dual sovereignty An approach to constitutional interpretation that requires state judges to apply both the federal and state constitutions simultaneously.

- FREEDOM FROM SELF-INCRIMINATION—Hawaii, California, and Pennsylvania have rejected the Supreme Court's decisions permitting statements of defendants made in violation of *Miranda* to be used to impeach the defendant. *Hawaii v. Santiago*, 492 P.2d 657 (Haw. 1971); *California v. Disbrow*, 545 P.2d 272 (1976); *Commonwealth v. Triplett*, 341 A.2d 62 (Pa. 1975).

Unusual Provisions in State Constitutions

- DUELING—Any person who duels is ineligible to hold public office in West Virginia (art. IV, § 10).

FIGURE 8-3   *(continued)*

The primacy approach treats state constitutions as the primary source of individuals' rights, with the federal Constitution acting as a backup or safety net. Under this theory, courts have an obligation to examine claims under the state constitution before turning to the federal constitution. At least three states (New Hampshire, Oregon, and Maine) have adopted this approach.

An interstitial approach, in contrast, views the federal Constitution as the fundamental source of individual rights, with the state constitutions as supplements. Using such an approach, courts look first to the federal Constitution and then to the appropriate state constitution. This is the most common approach.

The third approach, dual sovereignty, has been adopted by at least one state (Vermont). Under this approach, the federal and state constitutions are examined simultaneously. Then, rather than basing its decision on one or the other, a reviewing court will, if possible, decide the case using both, providing two independent sources to support its decision.

Bear in mind that most states have not identified which approach they follow. Nevertheless, a reading of state constitutional decisions often leads to the conclusion that a state follows, at least generally, one of these three models.

The primacy approach is growing in popularity, and there are now a number of instances in which state courts have determined that their constitutions protect criminal defendants to a greater extent than does the national constitution. Between 1977 and 1986, there were 200 state constitutional decisions affording greater individual liberties than the federal Constitution. Only two years later there were 400 such decisions.[42] The Supreme Court of Pennsylvania has strongly asserted that its state's constitution has its own meaning, separate and independent from the federal Constitution. In a 1991 case, that Court stated:

> [T]he decisions of the [U.S. Supreme] Court are not, and should not be, dispositive of questions regarding rights guaranteed by counter-part

provisions of State Law. Accordingly, such decisions are not mechanically applicable to state law issues, and state court judges and members of the bar seriously err if they so treat them. Rather, state court judges, and also practitioners, do well to scrutinize constitutional decisions by federal courts, for only if they are found to be logically persuasive and well-reasoned, paying due regard to precedent and the policies underlying specific constitutional guarantees, may they properly claim persuasive weight as guide posts when interpreting counter-part state guarantees.[43]

The California courts have taken a similar approach. Even if a provision's interpretation has paralleled that of national law, the courts favor citing state law over federal law.

Whether a state court depends upon state or federal law when defining a right determines what court has the final word on the subject. If a right is founded upon federal law, the Supreme Court of the United States is the final arbiter. If a right is founded upon state law, the highest court of the state is the final arbiter—again assuming that no federal right is encroached upon by the state decision. For example, if a state court were to find that a fetus has a right to life in every instance, the decision would be void as violative of the federally secured right to privacy held by the mothers in some circumstances.

If a state court relies upon federal law when defining a right, the possibility of reversal by a federal court, usually the Supreme Court, exists. This is what occurred in California concerning the use of peyote, a drug made from cactus, by Native Americans. The Supreme Court of California decided in 1965 that the use of peyote by Native Americans during religious ceremonies was protected by the United States Constitution's First Amendment free exercise of religion clause.[44] That decision was not disturbed until 1990, when the Supreme Court of the United States decided that regulation of peyote as a drug was a reasonable burden upon the First Amendment[45] and, therefore, reversed the 1965 California decision. Although the defendant asserted both the federal and state free exercise guarantees, the California Supreme Court relied entirely upon federal law in making its decision. Whether that court will later find the activity to be protected by the California constitution remains to be seen.

Some state courts have established tests to determine whether their state constitutions are parallel to, or more expansive than, the federal constitution in securing individual liberties. The Supreme Court of Washington identified six factors to be taken into consideration:

1. Language of the state constitutional text
2. Differences between the state and federal texts
3. Constitutional history
4. Preexisting state law

5. Structural differences between Washington state and the United States

6. Local concerns.[46]

The two case excerpts accompanying this section concern the *exclusionary rule,* a judicially created rule that requires the exclusion of evidence that was illegally obtained by the government from criminal trials. For example, if the police search a home without probable cause or a warrant, cocaine found in the home may not be used to convict the homeowner of possession of a controlled substance. The Constitution does not expressly provide for the exclusionary rule; rather, the Supreme Court has found it to be implicit in several amendments (e.g. the Fourth Amendment's protection from unreasonable searches and seizures). Several exceptions to the exclusionary rule have been made by the Court since it first announced the rule's existence. Some state courts have refused to adopt these exceptions into their own jurisprudence. This is the subject of the *Leon* and *Edmunds* cases, one issued by the Supreme Court of the United States, wherein it recognized a good-faith exception to the exclusionary rule; and the other by the Supreme Court of Pennsylvania, expressly rejecting the good-faith exception in state prosecutions.

UNITED STATES
v.
LEON
468 U.S. 897 (1984)

[Facially valid warrants were issued by a state judge. The searches conducted under the warrants produced narcotics and other evidence of narcotics violations.]

The respondents ... filed motions to suppress the evidence seized pursuant to the warrant. The District Court held an evidentiary hearing and, while recognizing that the case was a close one, ... granted the motions to suppress in part. It concluded that the affidavit was insufficient to establish probable cause. ... In response to a request from the Government, the court made clear that Officer Rombach had acted in good faith. ... [This decision was affirmed on appeal before the Court of Appeals.]

The Government's petition for certiorari expressly declined to seek review of the lower courts' determinations that the search warrant was unsupported by probable cause and presented only the question "[w]hether the Fourth Amendment exclusionary rule should be modified so as not to bar the admission of evidence seized in reasonable, good-faith reliance on a search warrant that is subsequently held to be defective." ...

[T]he exclusionary rule is designed to deter police misconduct rather than to punish the errors of judges and magistrates. ...

If exclusion of evidence obtained pursuant to a subsequently invalidated warrant is to have any deterrent effect, therefore, it must alter the behavior of the individual law enforcement officers or the policies of their departments. One could argue that applying the exclusionary rule in cases where the police failed to demonstrate probable cause in the warrant application deters future inadequate presentations or "magistrate shopping" and thus promotes the ends of the Fourth Amendment. Suppressing evidence obtained pursuant to a technically defective warrant supported by probable cause also might encourage officers to scrutinize more closely the form of the warrant and to point out suspected judicial errors. We find such arguments speculative and conclude that suppression of evidence obtained pursuant to a warrant should be ordered only on a case-by-case basis and only in those unusual cases in which exclusion will further the purposes of the exclusionary rule.

We conclude that the marginal or nonexistent benefits produced by suppressing evidence obtained in objectively reasonable reliance on a subsequently invalidated search warrant cannot justify the substantial costs of exclusion. We do not suggest, however, that exclusion is always inappropriate in cases where an officer has obtained a warrant and abided by its terms. ... [A]n officer's reliance on the magistrate's probable-cause determination and on the technical sufficiency of the warrant he issues must be objectively reasonable ... and it is clear that in some circumstances the officer will have no reasonable grounds for believing that the warrant was properly issued.

COMMONWEALTH
v.
EDMUNDS
526 Pa. 374 (1991)

[The defendant was convicted in the Court of Common Pleas, Criminal Division, of possession of marijuana and related offenses, and the defendant appealed. The Superior Court affirmed the conviction.]

The issue presented to this court is whether Pennsylvania should adopt the "good faith" exception to the exclusionary rule as articulated by the United States Supreme Court in the case of *United States v. Leon,* 468 U.S. 897, 104 S. Ct. 3405, 82 L. Ed. 2d 677 (1984). We conclude that a "good faith" exception to the exclusionary rule would frustrate the guarantees embodied in Article I, Section 8, of the Pennsylvania Constitution. Accordingly, the decision of the Superior Court is reversed. ...

The trial court held that the search warrant failed to establish probable cause that the marijuana would be at the location to be searched on the date it was issued. The trial court found that the warrant failed to set forth with specificity the date upon which the anonymous informants observed the marijuana. ... However, the trial court went on to deny the defendant's motion to suppress the marijuana. Applying the rationale of *Leon,* the trial court looked beyond the four corners of the affidavit, in order to establish that the officers executing the warrant acted in "good faith" in relying upon the warrant to conduct the search. ...

We must now determine whether the good-faith exception to the exclusionary rule is properly part of the jurisprudence of this Commonwealth, by virtue of Article 1, Section 8 of the Pennsylvania Constitution. In concluding that it is not, we set forth a methodology to be followed in analyzing future state constitutional issues which arise under our own Constitution. ...

This Court has long emphasized that, in interpreting a provision of the Pennsylvania Constitution, we are not bound by the decisions of the United States Supreme Court which interpret similar (yet distinct) federal constitutional provisions. ... [T]he federal constitution establishes certain minimum levels which are "equally applicable to the [analogous] state constitutional provision." ... However, each state has the power to provide broader standards, and go beyond the minimum floor which is established by the federal Constitution. ...

Here in Pennsylvania, we have stated with increasing frequency that it is both important and necessary that we undertake an independent analysis of the Pennsylvania Constitution, each time a provision of that fundamental document is implicated. ...

The recent focus on the "New Federalism" has emphasized the importance of state constitutions with respect to individual rights and criminal procedure. As such, we find it important to set forth certain factors to be briefed and analyzed by litigants in each case hereafter implicating a provision of the Pennsylvania constitution. The decision of the United States Supreme Court in *Michigan v. Long,* 463 U.S. 1032, 103 S. Ct. 3469, 77 L. Ed. 2d 1201 (1983), now requires us to make a "plain statement" of the adequate and independent state grounds upon which we rely, in order to avoid any doubt that we have rested our decision squarely upon Pennsylvania jurisprudence. Accordingly, as a general rule it is important that litigants brief and analyze at least the following four factors:

1. text of the Pennsylvania constitutional provision;
2. history of the provision, including Pennsylvania case-law;
3. related case-law from other states;
4. policy considerations, including unique issues of state and local concern, and applicability within modern Pennsylvania jurisprudence.

Depending upon the particular issue presented, an examination of related federal precedent may be useful as part of the state constitutional analysis, not as binding authority, but as one form of guidance. ... Utilizing the above four factors, and having reviewed *Leon,* we conclude that a "good-faith" exception to the exclusionary rule would frustrate the guarantees embodied in Article I, Section 8 of our Commonwealth's Constitution. ...

The United States Supreme Court in *Leon* made clear that, in its view, the sole purpose for the exclusionary rule under the 4th Amendment [to the Constitution of the United States] was to deter police misconduct. ... The *Leon* majority also made clear that, under the Federal Constitution, the exclusionary rule operated as "a judicially created remedy designed to safeguard Fourth Amendment rights generally through its deterrent effect, rather than a personal constitutional right of the party aggrieved ... ."

[T]he exclusionary rule in Pennsylvania has consistently served to bolster the twin aims of Article I, Section 8, to wit, the safeguarding of privacy and the fundamental requirement that warrants shall only be issued upon probable cause. ...

The linch-pin that has been developed to determine whether it is appropriate to issue a search warrant is the test of probable cause. ... It is designed to protect us from unwarranted and even vindictive incursions upon our privacy. It insulates from dictatorial and tyrannical rule by the state, and preserves the concept of democracy that assures the freedom of citizens. This concept is second to none in its importance in delineating the dignity of the individual living in a free society. ...

Whether the United States Supreme Court has determined that the exclusionary rule does not advance the 4th Amendment purpose of deterring police conduct is irrelevant. Indeed, we disagree with the Court's suggestion in *Leon* that we in Pennsylvania have been employing the exclusionary rule all these years to deter police corruption. We flatly reject this notion. ... What is significant, however, is that our Constitution has historically been interpreted to incorporate a strong right to privacy, and an equally strong adherence to the requirement of probable cause under Article I, Section 8. Citizens in this Commonwealth possess such rights, even where a police officer in "good faith" carrying out his or her duties inadvertently invades the privacy or circumvents the strictures of probable cause. To adopt a "good faith" exception to the exclusionary rule, we believe, would virtually emasculate those clear safeguards which have been carefully developed under the Pennsylvania Constitution over the past 200 years. ...

As another example, several states (including California, Hawaii, and Pennsylvania) have not followed the Supreme Court's lead in allowing statements made in violation of *Miranda* to be used by the prosecution in impeachment of a defendant.[47]

State constitutionalism has reached beyond criminal law. Several states guarantee a right to primary and secondary education through their constitutions. In New York, the state owes a duty to provide shelters to homeless families under a constitutional provision that requires the legislature to provide for the "[a]id, care, and support of the needy."[48] Even though the Supreme Court has held that indigent women have no right to have abortions funded by the federal government, the New Jersey Supreme Court has held otherwise concerning state funds.[49] These are but a few of the many instances in which a right has received greater protection under state law than under federal law.[50]

When a state court decides a case on **adequate and independent state grounds**, federal judicial review of any federal issues is unnecessary. Of course, the state-law basis for the decision must be consistent with the United States Constitution for this rule to apply.

State law is adequate in these cases if it logically resolves the issue without the support of federal constitutional law. The more troubling issue concerns the second prong, independence. Often, the issue is whether a state court decided a case upon state or federal constitutional principles. It is common for a state court to cite both state and federal constitutional provisions in support of a decision. In such cases, whether the state court relied upon federal or state case law, state or federal constitutional history, and the like must be considered. Generally, it must be plain that a decision is made upon state grounds to avoid review of federal legal issues.

Summary

Few would disagree that the framers were successful in constructing a stronger national government through the new Constitution. The contemporary issue is whether the federal government has become too large and powerful.

TERMS

adequate and independent state grounds doctrine   Federal judicial review of a state decision in a case that included both state and federal claims will not occur if the lower court's decision rested upon adequate and independent state law.

The states are empowered to regulate intrastate commerce and the federal government is empowered to regulate interstate commerce. In 1789, intrastate and interstate commerce did not meet as often as they do in the contemporary highly mobile and technologically advanced world. The effect is that today, nearly all commerce has an interstate, if not international, aspect. Because state laws that burden, discriminate, or otherwise interfere with interstate commerce are invalid (via dormant commerce clause theories), as well as those that conflict with federal law (via preemption), the authority of the state has greatly diminished. This remains controversial today.

Even more controversial, however, is the status of intergovernmental immunity. Today, the federal government has the authority to regulate the states. For example, state employees are entitled to the protections of federal minimum wage and hour, occupational safety, and discrimination laws. A similar state law does not apply to federal employees working within the state.

A few policy areas remain within the jurisdiction of the states: the police powers, for example. In addition, the preservation of civil liberties by state constitutions, beyond that secured by the federal Constitution, has received considerable attention by state courts in recent years.

Review Questions

1. Define preemption and identify its three forms.

2. Define "dormant commerce clause."

3. Discuss the significance of *Garcia v. San Antonio Metropolitan Transit Authority* to state–federal relations.

4. What role does Congress play in the creation of interstate compacts, if any?

5. What does the full faith and credit clause require of the states?

6. What does the interstate rendition clause require of the states?

7. Does Congress possess the authority to regulate state militias?

8. To what does New Federalism refer?

Review Problems

1. North Carolina has an emerging apple-growing industry. To reduce fraud and protect consumers, its legislature enacts the following statute:

   > All apples imported into the State shall be inspected and approved by the United States Department of Agriculture (USDA). All containers in which apples are contained, and all advertisements for the sale of apples, shall bear or display the USDA approval label, but no other.

   The State of Washington has the largest and most refined apple industry in the nation. As a result of its experience, Washington has developed a higher grade of apples and a higher standard of rating than the USDA. Apples, Inc., a Washington company, shipped apples to North Carolina bearing the Washington state standard stamp. The apples were rejected at the border and Apples, Inc. brought suit to enjoin enforcement of the North Carolina law. What should the outcome be? Explain.

2. The majority in *Garcia* stressed that the states are protected by political structures, not law. To what was the majority referring? Is this argument as strong today as it would have been 100 years ago?

3. In 1997, the Supreme Court of the United States hands down an opinion upholding a state law providing for life imprisonment with no possibility of parole for possession of 650 grams of cocaine. The offender's claim that the punishment was out of proportion to his crime, and therefore violative of the Eighth Amendment's prohibition of cruel and unusual punishments, was rejected. In another Supreme Court decision, rendered years earlier, the Court held that defendants have a Sixth Amendment right to counsel at sentencing hearings.

   In 1998, Katrina is arrested and convicted for possession of the 650 grams of cocaine. At sentencing, she asserts that life without parole violates the state constitution's prohibition of cruel or unusual punishments. She also asserts the right to have counsel at sentencing. The state contends that both issues have been decided: the sentence is constitutional, and it concedes that she is entitled to counsel at the hearing. However, the state also contends that if the court decides that the sentence is unconstitutional, as urged by Katrina, it should also reconsider the counsel issue, as the state constitution only assures counsel at "criminal trials." Discuss the state's position.

Notes

1 *Dennis v. United States*, 341 U.S. 494, 555 (1951) (concurring opinion).

2 *Cipollone v. Liggett Group, Inc.*, 112 S. Ct. 2608 (1992).

3 *Gade v. National Solid Wastes Management Ass'n*, 505 U.S. 88 (1992).

4 53 U.S. 299 (1851).

5 *United Food & Commercial Workers Union v. Brown Group,* 116 S. Ct. 1529 (1996); *Oregon Waste Systems, Inc. v. Department of Environmental Quality,* 114 S. Ct. 1345 (1995).

6 *Baldwin v. G.A.F. Seelig, Inc.,* 294 U.S. 511 (1935).

7 *Hughes v. Oklahoma,* 441 U.S. 322 (1979).

8 458 U.S. 941 (1982).

9 437 U.S. 617 (1978).

10 114 S. Ct. 1677 (1994).

11 424 U.S. 366 (1976).

12 458 U.S. 941 (1982).

13 *Maine v. Taylor,* 477 U.S. 131 (1986).

14 *Southern Pacific Co. v. Arizona,* 325 U.S. 761 (1945).

15 *Bibb v. Navajo Freight Lines, Inc.,* 359 U.S. 520 (1959).

16 *Kassel v. Consolidated Freightways Corp.,* 450 U.S. 622 (1981).

17 *Minnesota v. Clover Leaf Creamery Co.,* 449 U.S. 456 (1981).

18 *Brown-Forman Distillers Corp. v. New York State Liquor Authority,* 476 U.S. 573 (1986).

19 *South Dakota v. Dole,* 483 U.S. 203 (1987).

20 *Oregon Waste Systems, Inc. v. Department of Environmental Quality,* 114 S. Ct. 1345 (1995); *Fulton Corp. v. Faulkner,* 116 S. Ct. 848 (1996).

21 430 U.S. 274 (1977).

22 334 U.S. 653 (1948).

23 115 S. Ct. 1331 (1995).

24 *International Shoe v. Washington,* 326 U.S. 310 (1945).

25 *Reeves, Inc. v. State,* 447 U.S. 429 (1980).

26 David Pomper, "Recycling *Philadelphia v. New Jersey*: The Dormant Commerce Clause, Postindustrial "Natural" Resources, and the Solid Waste Crisis," 137 *U. Pa. L. Rev.* 1309, 1311 (1989).

27 *See South-Central Timber Development, Inc. v. Wunnicke,* 467 U.S. 82 (1984).

28 *Supreme Court of Virginia v. Friedman,* 487 U.S. 59 (1988).

29 *Toomer v. Witsell,* 334 U.S. 385 (1948).

30 *Hicklin v. Orbeck,* 437 U.S. 518 (1978).

31 17 U.S. 316 (1819).

32 426 U.S. 833 (1976).

33 112 S. Ct. 2408 (1992).

34 501 U.S. 452 (1991).

35 483 U.S. 219 (1987).

36 *See* Chester Antieau, 2 *Modern Constitutional Law* § 14:6 (Lawyers Cooperative Publishing 1969).

37 *Perpich v. Department of Defense,* 110 S. Ct. 2418 (1990).

38 *Longress v. Board of Education,* 101 Ill. 308 (1882).

39 *Brown v. Board of Education,* 347 U.S. 483 (1954).

40 *See* Dorothy Beasley, "Federalism and the Protection of Individual Rights: The American State Constitutional Perspective" 11 *Ga. St. U. L. Rev.* 681 (1995).

41 This model was adopted from John Shaw, "Principled Interpretations of State Constitutional Law—Why Don't the 'Primacy' States Practice What They Preach?," 54 *U. Pitt. L. Rev. 1019 (1993).*

42 Helen Hershkoff, "State Constitutions: A National Perspective," 3 *Widener J. Pub. L.* 7 (1993).

43 *Commonwealth v. Ludwig,* 527 Pa. 472, 478 (1991).

44 *People v. Woody,* 61 Cal. 2d 716, 394 P.2d 813 (1965).

45 *Department of Human Resources v. Smith,* 494 U.S. 872 (1990).

46 *State v. Gunwall,* 106 Wash. 2d 54, 58 (1986).

47 *See People v. Disbrow,* 16 Cal. 3d 101, 545 P.2d 272 (1976) (California); *State v. Santiago,* 53 Haw. 254, 492 P.2d 657 (1971) (Hawaii); *Commonwealth v. Triplett,* 462 Pa. 244, 341 A.2d 62 (1975) (Pennsylvania).

48 *McCain v. Koch,* 502 N.Y.2d 720 (1987).

49 *Right to Choose v. Byrne,* 450 A.2d 925 (N.J. 1982).

50 *See* Joseph Cook, *Constitutional Rights of the Accused, 2d Ed.* § 1:8, n. 16 (Lawyers Cooperative Publishing 1989) for a more thorough list.

APPENDIX A

THE CONSTITUTION OF THE UNITED STATES OF AMERICA

We the People of the United States, in Order to form a more perfect Union, establish Justice, insure domestic Tranquility, provide for the common defence, promote the general Welfare, and secure the Blessings of Liberty to ourselves and our Posterity, do ordain and establish this Constitution for the United States of America.

ARTICLE I

Section 1 All legislative Powers herein granted shall be vested in a Congress of the United States, which shall consist of a Senate and House of Representatives.

Section 2 (1) The House of Representatives shall be composed of Members chosen every second Year by the People of the several States, and the Electors in each State shall have the Qualifications requisite for Electors of the most numerous Branch of the State Legislature.

(2) No Person shall be a Representative who shall not have attained to the age of twenty-five Years, and been seven Years a Citizen of the United States, and who shall not, when elected, be an Inhabitant of that State in which he shall be chosen.

(3) Representatives and direct Taxes shall be apportioned among the several States which may be included within this Union, according to their respective Numbers, which shall be determined by adding to the whole Number of free Persons, including those bound to Service for a Term of Years, and excluding Indians not taxed, three fifths of all other Persons. The actual Enumeration shall be made within three Years after the first Meeting of the Congress of the United States, and within every subsequent Term of ten Years, in such Manner as they shall by Law direct. The Number of Representatives shall not exceed one for every thirty Thousand, but each State shall have at Least one Representative; and until such enumeration shall be made, the State of New Hampshire shall be entitled to chuse three, Massachusetts eight, Rhode Island and Providence Plantations one, Connecticut five, New York six, New Jersey four, Pennsylvania eight, Delaware one, Maryland six, Virginia ten, North Carolina five, South Carolina five, and Georgia three.

(4) When vacancies happen in the Representation from any State, the Executive Authority thereof shall issue Writs of Election to fill such Vacancies.

(5) The House of Representatives shall chuse their Speaker and other Officers; and shall have the sole Power of Impeachment.

Section 3 (1) The Senate of the United States shall be composed of two Senators from each State, chosen by the Legislature thereof, for six Years; and each Senator shall have one Vote.

(2) Immediately after they shall be assembled in Consequence of the first Election, they shall be divided as equally as may be into three Classes. The Seats of the Senators of the first Class shall be vacated at the Expiration of the second Year, of the second Class at the Expiration of the fourth Year, and of the third Class at the Expiration of the sixth Year, so that one third may be chosen every second Year; and if Vacancies happen by Resignation, or otherwise, during the Recess of the Legislature of any State, the Executive thereof may make temporary Appointments until the next Meeting of the Legislature, which shall then fill such Vacancies.

(3) No Person shall be a Senator who shall not have attained to the Age of thirty Years, and been nine Years a Citizen of the United States, and who shall not, when elected, be an Inhabitant of that State for which he shall be chosen.

(4) The Vice President of the United States shall be President of the Senate, but shall have no Vote, unless they be equally divided.

(5) The Senate shall chuse their other Officers, and also a President pro tempore, in the Absence of the Vice President, or when he shall exercise the Office of the President of the United States.

(6) The Senate shall have the sole Power to try all Impeachments. When sitting for that Purpose, they shall be on Oath or Affirmation. When the President of the United States is tried, the Chief Justice shall preside: And no Person shall be convicted without the Concurrence of two thirds of the Members present.

(7) Judgment in Cases of Impeachment shall not extend further than to removal from Office, and disqualification to hold and enjoy any Office of honor, Trust or Profit under the United States: but the Party convicted shall nevertheless be liable and subject to Indictment, Trial, Judgment and Punishment, according to Law.

Section 4   (1) The Times, Places and Manner of holding Elections for Senators and Representatives, shall be prescribed in each State by the Legislature thereof; but the Congress may at any time by Law make or alter such Regulations, except as to the Places of chusing Senators.

(2) The Congress shall assemble at least once in every Year, and such Meeting shall be on the first Monday in December, unless they shall by Law appoint a different Day.

Section 5   (1) Each House shall be the Judge of the Elections, Returns and Qualifications of its own Members, and a Majority of each shall constitute a Quorum to do Business; but a smaller Number may adjourn from day to day, and may be authorized to compel the Attendance of absent Members, in such Manner, and under such Penalties as each House may provide.

(2) Each House may determine the Rules of its Proceedings, punish its Members for disorderly Behaviour, and, with the Concurrence of two thirds, expel a Member.

(3) Each House shall keep a Journal of its Proceedings, and from time to time publish the same, excepting such Parts as may in their Judgment require Secrecy; and the Yeas and Nays of the Members of either House on any question shall, at the Desire of one fifth of those Present, be entered on the Journal.

(4) Neither House, during the Session of Congress, shall, without the Consent of the other, adjourn for more than three days, nor to any other Place than that in which the two Houses shall be sitting.

Section 6   (1) The Senators and Representatives shall receive a Compensation for their Services, to be ascertained by Law, and paid out of the Treasury of the United States. They shall in all Cases, except Treason, Felony and Breach of the Peace, be privileged from Arrest during their Attendance at the Session of their respective Houses, and in going to and returning from the same; and for any Speech or Debate in either House, they shall not be questioned in any other Place.

(2) No Senator or Representative shall, during the Time for which he was elected, be appointed to any civil Office under the Authority of the United States, which shall have been created, or the Emoluments whereof shall have been encreased during such time; and no Person holding any Office under the United States, shall be a Member of either House during his Continuance in Office.

Section 7   (1) All Bills for raising Revenue shall originate in the House of Representatives; but the Senate may propose or concur with Amendments as on other Bills.

(2) Every Bill which shall have passed the House of Representatives and the Senate, shall, before it become a Law, be presented to the President of the United States; If he approve he

shall sign it, but if not he shall return it, with his Objections to that House in which it shall have originated, who shall enter the Objections at large on their Journal, and proceed to reconsider it. If after such Reconsideration two thirds of that House shall agree to pass the Bill, it shall be sent, together with the Objections, to the other House, by which it shall likewise be reconsidered, and if approved by two thirds of that House, it shall become a law. But in all such Cases the Votes of both Houses shall be determined by Yeas and Nays, and the Names of the Persons voting for and against the Bill shall be entered on the Journal of each House respectively. If any Bill shall not be returned by the President within ten Days (Sunday excepted) after it shall have been presented to him, the Same shall be a Law, in like Manner as if he had signed it, unless the Congress by their Adjournment prevent its Return, in which Case it shall not be a Law.

(3) Every Order, Resolution, or Vote to which the Concurrence of the Senate and House of Representatives may be necessary (except on a question of Adjournment) shall be presented to the President of the United States; and before the Same shall take Effect, shall be approved by him, or being disapproved by him, shall be repassed by two thirds of the Senate and House of Representatives, according to the Rules and Limitations prescribed in the Case of a Bill.

Section 8 (1) The Congress shall have Power To lay and collect Taxes, Duties, Imposts and Excises, to pay the Debts and provide for the common Defence and general Welfare of the United States; but all Duties, Imposts and Excises shall be uniform throughout the United States;

(2) To borrow Money on the credit of the United States;

(3) To regulate Commerce with foreign Nations, and among the several States, and with the Indian Tribes;

(4) To establish an uniform Rule of Naturalization, and uniform Laws on the subject of Bankruptcies throughout the United States;

(5) To coin Money, regulate the Value thereof, and of foreign Coin, and to fix the Standard of Weights and Measures;

(6) To provide for the Punishment of counterfeiting the Securities and current Coin of the United States;

(7) To establish Post Offices and post Roads;

(8) To promote the Progress of Science and useful Arts, by securing for limited Times to Authors and Inventors the exclusive Right to their respective Writings and Discoveries;

(9) To constitute Tribunals inferior to the supreme Court;

(10) To define and punish Piracies and Felonies committed on the high Seas, and Offenses against the Law of Nations;

(11) To declare War, grant Letters of Marque and Reprisal, and make Rules concerning Captures on Land and Water;

(12) To raise and support Armies, but no Appropriation of Money to that Use shall be for a longer Term than two Years;

(13) To provide and maintain a Navy;

(14) To make Rules for the Government and Regulation of the land and naval Forces;

(15) To provide for calling forth the Militia to execute the Laws of the Union, suppress Insurrections and repel Invasions;

(16) To provide for organizing, arming, and disciplining, the Militia, and for governing such Part of them as may be employed in the Service of the United States, reserving to the States respectively, the Appointment of the Officers, and the Authority of training the Militia according to the discipline prescribed by Congress;

(17) To exercise exclusive Legislation in all Cases whatsoever, over such District (not exceeding ten Miles square) as may, by Cession of particular States, and the Acceptance of Congress, become the Seat of the Government of the United States, and to exercise like Authority over all Places purchased by the Consent of the Legislature of the State in which the Same shall be, for the Erection of Forts, Magazines,

Arsenals, dock-Yards, and other needful Buildings;—And

(18) To make all Laws which shall be necessary and proper for carrying into Execution the foregoing Powers, and all other Powers vested by this Constitution in the Government of the United States, or in any Department or Officer thereof.

Section 9   (1) The Migration or Importation of such Persons as any of the States now existing shall think proper to admit, shall not be prohibited by the Congress prior to the Year one thousand eight hundred and eight, but a Tax or Duty may be imposed on such Importation, not exceeding ten dollars for each Person.

(2) The Privilege of the Writ of Habeas Corpus shall not be suspended unless when in Cases of Rebellion or Invasion the public Safety may require it.

(3) No Bill of Attainder or ex post facto Law shall be passed.

(4) No Capitation, or other direct, Tax shall be laid, unless in Proportion to the Census or Enumeration herein before directed to be taken.

(5) No Tax or Duty shall be laid on Articles exported from any State.

(6) No Preference shall be given by any Regulation of Commerce or Revenue to the Ports of one State over those of another; nor shall Vessels bound to, or from, one State, be obliged to enter, clear or pay Duties in another.

(7) No Money shall be drawn from the Treasury, but in Consequence of Appropriations made by Law; and a regular Statement and Account of the Receipts and Expenditures of all public Money shall be published from time to time.

(8) No Title of Nobility shall be granted by the United States: And no Person holding any Office of Profit or Trust under them, shall, without the Consent of the Congress, accept of any present, Emolument, Office, or Title, of any kind whatever, from any King, Prince or foreign State.

Section 10   (1) No State shall enter into any Treaty, Alliance, or Confederation; grant Letters of Marque and Reprisal; coin Money; emit Bills of Credit; make any Thing but gold and silver Coin a Tender in Payment of Debts; pass any Bill of Attainder, ex post facto Law, or Law impairing the Obligation of Contracts, or grant any Title of Nobility.

(2) No State shall, without the Consent of Congress, lay any Imposts or Duties on Imports or Exports, except what may be absolutely necessary for executing its inspection Laws: and the net Produce of all Duties and Imposts, laid by any State on Imports or Exports, shall be for the Use of the Treasury of the United States; and all such Laws shall be subject to the Revision and Controul of the Congress.

(3) No State shall, without the Consent of Congress, lay any Duty of Tonnage, keep Troops, or Ships of War in time of Peace, enter into any Agreement or Compact with another State, or with a foreign Power, or engage in War, unless actually invaded, or in such imminent Danger as will not admit of Delay.

ARTICLE II

Section 1   (1) The executive Power shall be vested in a President of the United States of America. He shall hold his Office during the Term of four Years, and, together with the Vice President, chosen for the same Term, be elected, as follows:

(2) Each State shall appoint, in such Manner as the Legislature thereof may direct, a Number of Electors, equal to the whole Number of Senators and Representatives to which the State may be entitled in the Congress: but no Senator or Representative, or Person holding an Office of Trust or Profit under the United States, shall be appointed an Elector.

The Electors shall meet in their respective States, and vote by Ballot for two Persons, of whom one at least shall not be an Inhabitant of the same State with themselves. And they shall make a List of all the Persons voted for, and of the Number of Votes for each; which List they shall sign and certify, and transmit sealed to the Seat of the Government of the

United States, directed to the President of the Senate. The President of the Senate shall, in the presence of the Senate and House of Representatives, open all the Certificates, and the Votes shall then be counted. The Person having the greatest Number of Votes shall be the President, if such Number be a Majority of the whole Number of Electors appointed; and if there be more than one who have such Majority, and have an equal Number of Votes, then the House of Representatives shall immediately chuse by Ballot one of them for President; and if no Person have a Majority, then from the five highest on the List the said House shall in like Manner chuse the President. But in chusing the President, the Votes shall be taken by States, the Representation from each State having one Vote; a quorum for this Purpose shall consist of a Member or Members from two thirds of the States, and a Majority of all the States shall be necessary to a Choice. In every Case, after the Choice of the President, the Person having the greatest Number of Votes of the Electors shall be the Vice President. But if there should remain two or more who have equal Votes, the Senate shall chuse from them by Ballot the Vice President.

(3) The Congress may determine the Time of chusing the Electors, and the Day on which they shall give their Votes; which Day shall be the same throughout the United States.

(4) No Person except a natural born Citizen, or a Citizen of the United States, at the time of the Adoption of this Constitution, shall be eligible to the Office of President; neither shall any Person be eligible to that Office who shall not have attained to the Age of thirty five Years, and been fourteen Years a Resident within the United States.

(5) In Case of the Removal of the President from Office, or of his Death, Resignation, or Inability to discharge the Powers and Duties of the said Office, the Same shall devolve on the Vice President, and the Congress may by Law provide for the Case of Removal, Death, Resignation or Inability, both of the President and Vice President, declaring what Officer shall then act as President, and such Officer shall act

accordingly, until the Disability be removed, or a President shall be elected.

(6) The President shall, at stated Times, receive for his Services, a Compensation, which shall neither be increased nor diminished during the Period for which he shall have been elected, and he shall not receive within that Period any other Emolument from the United States, or any of them.

(7) Before he enter on the Execution of his Office, he shall take the following Oath or Affirmation:—"I do solemnly swear (or affirm) that I will faithfully execute the Office of President of the United States, and will to the best of my Ability, preserve, protect and defend the Constitution of the United States."

Section 2 (1) The President shall be Commander in Chief of the Army and Navy of the United States, and of the Militia of the several States, when called into the actual Service of the United States; he may require the Opinion, in writing, of the principal Officer in each of the executive Departments, upon any Subject relating to the Duties of their respective Offices, and he shall have Power to grant Reprieves and Pardons for Offenses against the United States, except in Cases of Impeachment.

(2) He shall have Power, by and with the Advice and Consent of the Senate, to make Treaties, provided two thirds of the Senators present concur; and he shall nominate, and by and with the Advice and Consent of the Senate, shall appoint Ambassadors, other public Ministers and Consuls, Judges of the supreme Court, and all other Officers of the United States, whose Appointments are not herein otherwise provided for, and which shall be established by Law: but the Congress may by Law vest the Appointment of such inferior Officers, as they think proper, in the President alone, in the Courts of Law, or in the Heads of Departments.

(3) The President shall have Power to fill up all Vacancies that may happen during the Recess of the Senate, by granting Commissions which shall expire at the End of their next Session.

Section 3 He shall from time to time give to the Congress Information of the State of the Union, and recommend to their Consideration such Measures as he shall judge necessary and expedient; he may, on extraordinary Occasions, convene both Houses, or either of them, and in Case of Disagreement between them, with Respect to the Time of Adjournment, he may adjourn them to such Time as he shall think proper; he shall receive Ambassadors and other public Ministers; he shall take Care that the Laws be faithfully executed, and shall Commission all the Officers of the United States.

Section 4 The President, Vice President and all Civil Officers of the United States, shall be removed from Office on Impeachment for, and Conviction of, Treason, Bribery, or other high Crimes and Misdemeanors.

ARTICLE III

Section 1 The judicial Power of the United States, shall be vested in one supreme Court, and in such inferior Courts as the Congress may from time to time ordain and establish. The Judges, both of the supreme and inferior Courts, shall hold their Offices during good Behaviour, and shall, at stated Times, receive for their Services, a Compensation, which shall not be diminished during their Continuance in Office.

Section 2 (1) The judicial Power shall extend to all Cases, in Law and Equity, arising under this Constitution, the Laws of the United States, and Treaties made, or which shall be made, under their Authority;—to all Cases affecting Ambassadors, other public Ministers and Consuls;—to all Cases of admiralty and maritime Jurisdiction;—to Controversies to which the United States shall be a party— to Controversies between two or more States;— between a State and Citizens of another State;—between Citizens of different States;— between Citizens of the same State claiming Lands under Grants of different States, and between a State, or the Citizens thereof, and foreign States, Citizens or Subjects.

(2) In all Cases affecting Ambassadors, other public Ministers and Consuls, and those in which a State shall be Party, the supreme Court shall have original Jurisdiction. In all the other Cases before mentioned, the supreme Court shall have appellate Jurisdiction, both as to Law and Fact, with such Exceptions, and under such Regulations as the Congress shall make.

(3) The Trial of all Crimes, except in Cases of Impeachment, shall be by Jury; and such Trial shall be held in the State where the said Crimes shall have been committed; but when not committed within any State, the Trial shall be at such Place or Places as the Congress may by Law have directed.

Section 3 (1) Treason against the United States, shall consist only in levying War against them, or in adhering to their Enemies, giving them Aid and Comfort. No Person shall be convicted of Treason unless on the Testimony of two Witnesses to the same overt Act, or on Confession in open Court.

(2) The Congress shall have Power to declare the Punishment of Treason, but no Attainder of Treason shall work Corruption of Blood, or Forfeiture except during the Life of the Person attainted.

ARTICLE IV

Section 1 Full Faith and Credit shall be given in each State to the public Acts, Records, and judicial Proceedings of every other State. And the Congress may by general Laws prescribe the Manner in which such Acts, Records and Proceedings shall be proved, and the Effect thereof.

Section 2 (1) The Citizens of each State shall be entitled to all privileges and Immunities of Citizens in the several States.

(2) A Person charged in any State with Treason, Felony, or other Crime, who shall flee from Justice, and be found in another State, shall on Demand of the executive Authority of the State from which he fled, be delivered up, to be removed to the State having Jurisdiction of the Crime.

(3) No Person held to Service of Labour in one State, under the Laws thereof, escaping into another, shall, in Consequence of any Law or Regulation therein, be discharged from such Service or Labour, but shall be delivered up on Claim of the Party to whom such Service or Labour may be due.

Section 3 (1) New States may be admitted by the Congress into this Union; but no new State shall be formed or erected within the Jurisdiction of any other State; nor any State be formed by the Junction of two or more States, or Parts of States, without the Consent of the Legislatures of the States concerned as well as of the Congress.

(2) The Congress shall have power to dispose of and make all needful Rules and Regulations respecting the Territory or other Property belonging to the United States; and nothing in this Constitution shall be so construed as to Prejudice any Claims of the United States, or of any particular State.

Section 4 The United States shall guarantee to every State in this Union a Republican Form of Government, and shall protect each of them against Invasion; and on Application of the Legislature, or of the Executive (when the Legislature cannot be convened) against domestic Violence.

ARTICLE V

The Congress, whenever two thirds of both Houses shall deem it necessary, shall propose Amendments to this Constitution, or, on the Application of the Legislatures of two thirds of the several States, shall call a Convention for proposing Amendments, which, in either Case, shall be valid to all Intents and Purposes, as Part of this Constitution, when ratified by the Legislatures of three fourths of the several States, or by Conventions in three fourths thereof, as the one or the other Mode of Ratification may be proposed by the Congress; Provided that no Amendment which may be made prior to the Year One thousand eight hundred and eight shall in any Manner affect the first and fourth Clauses in the Ninth Section of the first Article; and that no State, without its Consent, shall be deprived of its equal Suffrage in the Senate.

ARTICLE VI

(1) All Debts contracted and Engagements entered into, before the Adoption of this Constitution, shall be as valid against the United States under this Constitution, as under the Confederation.

(2) This Constitution, and the Laws of the United States which shall be made in Pursuance thereof; and all Treaties made, or which shall be made, under the Authority of the United States, shall be the supreme Law of the Land; and the Judges in every State shall be bound thereby, any Thing in the Constitution or Laws of any State to the Contrary notwithstanding.

(3) The Senators and Representatives before mentioned, and the Members of the several State Legislatures, and all executive and judicial Officers, both of the United States and of the several States, shall be bound by Oath or Affirmation, to support this Constitution; but no religious Test shall ever be required as a Qualification to any Office or public Trust under the United States.

ARTICLE VII

The Ratification of the Conventions of nine States, shall be sufficient for the Establishment of this Constitution between the States so ratifying the Same.

ARTICLES IN ADDITION TO, AND AMENDMENT OF, THE CONSTITUTION OF THE UNITED STATES OF AMERICA, PROPOSED BY CONGRESS, AND RATIFIED BY THE SEVERAL STATES, PURSUANT TO THE FIFTH ARTICLE OF THE ORIGINAL CONSTITUTION

AMENDMENT I (1791)

Congress shall make no law respecting an establishment of religion, or prohibiting the free exercise thereof; or abridging the freedom of speech, or of the press; or the right of the people peaceably to assemble, and to petition the Government for a redress of grievances.

AMENDMENT II (1791)

A well regulated Militia, being necessary to the security of a free state, the right of the people to keep and bear Arms, shall not be infringed.

AMENDMENT III (1791)

No Soldier shall, in time of peace be quartered in any house, without the consent of the Owner, nor in time of war, but in a manner to be prescribed by law.

AMENDMENT IV (1791)

The right of the people to be secure in their persons, houses, papers, and effects, against unreasonable searches and seizures, shall not be violated, and no Warrants shall issue, but upon probable cause, supported by Oath or affirmation, and particularly describing the place to be searched, and the persons or things to be seized.

AMENDMENT V (1791)

No person shall be held to answer for a capital, or otherwise infamous crime, unless on a presentment or indictment of a Grand Jury, except in cases arising in the land or naval forces, or in the Militia, when in actual service in time of War or public danger; nor shall any person be subject for the same offence to be twice put in jeopardy of life or limb; nor shall be compelled in any criminal case to be a witness against himself, nor be deprived of life, liberty, or property, without due process of law; nor shall private property be taken for public use, without just compensation.

AMENDMENT VI (1791)

In all criminal prosecutions, the accused shall enjoy the right to a speedy and public trial, by an impartial jury of the State and district wherein the crime shall have been committed, which district shall have been previously ascertained by law, and to be informed of the nature and cause of the accusation; to be confronted with the witnesses against him; to have compulsory process for obtaining witnesses in his favor, and to have the Assistance of Counsel for his defence.

AMENDMENT VII (1791)

In Suits at common law, where the value in controversy shall exceed twenty dollars, the right of trial by jury shall be preserved, and no fact tried by a jury, shall be otherwise reexamined in any Court of the United States, than according to the rules of the common law.

AMENDMENT VIII (1791)

Excessive bail shall not be required, nor excessive fines imposed, nor cruel and unusual punishments inflicted.

AMENDMENT IX (1791)

The enumeration in the Constitution, of certain rights, shall not be construed to deny or disparage others retained by the people.

AMENDMENT X (1791)

The powers not delegated to the United States by the Constitution, nor prohibited by it to the States, are reserved to the States respectively, or to the people.

AMENDMENT XI (1798)

The Judicial power of the United States shall not be construed to extend to any suit in law or equity, commenced or prosecuted against one of the United States by Citizens of another

State, or by Citizens or Subjects of any Foreign State.

AMENDMENT XII (1804)

The Electors shall meet in their respective states and vote by ballot for President and Vice-President, one of whom, at least, shall not be an inhabitant of the same state with themselves; they shall name in their ballots the person voted for as President, and in distinct ballots the person voted for as Vice-President, and they shall make distinct lists of all persons voted for as President, and of all persons voted for as Vice-President, and of the number of votes for each, which lists they shall sign and certify, and transmit sealed to the seat of the government of the United States, directed to the President of the Senate;—The President of the Senate shall, in the presence of the Senate and House of Representatives, open all the certificates and the votes shall then be counted;—The person having the greatest number of votes for President, shall be the President, if such number be a majority of the whole number of Electors appointed; and if no person have such majority, then from the persons having the highest numbers not exceeding three on the list of those voted for as President, the House of Representatives shall choose immediately, by ballot, the President. But in choosing the President, the votes shall be taken by states, the representation from each state having one vote; a quorum for this purpose shall consist of a member or members from two-thirds of the states, and a majority of all the states shall be necessary to a choice. And if the House of Representatives shall not choose a President whenever the right of choice shall devolve upon them, before the fourth day of March next following, then the Vice-President shall act as President, as in the case of the death or other constitutional disability of the President—The person having the greatest number of votes as Vice-President, shall be the Vice-President, if such number be a majority of the whole number of Electors appointed, and if no person have a majority, then from the two highest numbers on the list, the Senate shall choose the Vice-President; A quorum for the purpose shall consist of two-thirds of the whole number of Senators, and a majority of the whole number shall be necessary to a choice. But no person constitutionally ineligible to the office of President shall be eligible to that of Vice-President of the United States.

AMENDMENT XIII (1865)

Section 1 Neither slavery nor involuntary servitude, except as a punishment for crime whereof the party shall have been duly convicted, shall exist within the United States, or any place subject to their jurisdiction.

Section 2 Congress shall have power to enforce this article by appropriate legislation.

AMENDMENT XIV (1868)

Section 1 All persons born or naturalized in the United States and subject to the jurisdiction thereof, are citizens of the United States and of the State wherein they reside. No State shall make or enforce any law which shall abridge the privileges or immunities of citizens of the United States; nor shall any State deprive any person of life, liberty, or property, without due process of law; nor deny to any person within its jurisdiction the equal protection of the laws.

Section 2 Representatives shall be apportioned among the several States according to their respective numbers, counting the whole number of persons in each State, excluding Indians not taxed. But when the right to vote at any election for the choice of electors for President and Vice-President of the United States, Representatives in Congress, the Executive and Judicial officers of a State, or the members of the Legislature thereof, is denied to any of the male inhabitants of such State, being twenty-one years of age, and citizens of the United States, or in any way abridged, except for participation in rebellion, or other crime, the basis of representation therein shall be reduced in the proportion which the number of such male citizens shall bear to the whole number of male citizens twenty-one years of age in such State.

Section 3 No person shall be a Senator or Representative in Congress, or elector of President and Vice-President, or hold any office, civil or military, under the United States, or under any State, who, having previously taken an oath, as a member of Congress, or as an officer of the United States, or as a member of any State legislature, or as an executive or judicial officer of any State, to support the Constitution of the United States, shall have engaged in insurrection or rebellion against the same, or given aid or comfort to the enemies thereof. But Congress may by a vote of two-thirds of each House, remove such disability.

Section 4 The validity of the public debt of the United States, authorized by law, including debts incurred for payment of pensions and bounties for services in suppressing insurrection or rebellion, shall not be questioned. But neither the United States nor any State shall assume or pay any debt or obligation incurred in aid of insurrection or rebellion against the United States, or any claim for the loss or emancipation of any slave; but all such debts, obligations and claims shall be held illegal and void.

Section 5 The Congress shall have power to enforce, by appropriate legislation, the provisions of this article.

AMENDMENT XV (1870)

Section 1 The right of citizens of the United States to vote shall not be denied or abridged by the United States or by any State on account of race, color, or previous condition of servitude.

Section 2 The Congress shall have power to enforce this article by appropriate legislation.

AMENDMENT XVI (1913)

The Congress shall have power to lay and collect taxes on incomes, from whatever source derived, without apportionment among the several States, and without regard to any census or enumeration.

AMENDMENT XVII (1913)

The Senate of the United States shall be composed of two Senators from each State, elected by the people thereof, for six years; and each Senator shall have one vote. The electors in each State shall have the qualifications requisite for electors of the most numerous branch of the State legislatures.

When vacancies happen in the representation of any State in the Senate, the executive authority of such State shall issue writs of election to fill such vacancies: *Provided,* That the legislature of any State may empower the executive thereof to make temporary appointments until the people fill the vacancies by election as the legislature may direct.

This amendment shall not be so construed as to affect the election or term of any Senator chosen before it becomes valid as part of the Constitution.

AMENDMENT XVIII (1919)

Section 1 After one year from the ratification of this article the manufacture, sale, or transportation of intoxicating liquors within, the importation thereof into, or the exportation thereof from the United States and all territory subject to the jurisdiction thereof for beverage purposes is hereby prohibited.

Section 2 The Congress and the several States shall have concurrent power to enforce this article by appropriate legislation.

Section 3 This article shall be inoperative unless it shall have been ratified as an amendment to the Constitution by the legislatures of the several States, as provided in the Constitution, within seven years from the date of the submission hereof to the States by the Congress.

AMENDMENT XIX (1920)

The right of citizens of the United States to vote shall not be denied or abridged by the United States or by any State on account of sex.

Congress shall have power to enforce this article by appropriate legislation.

AMENDMENT XX (1933)

Section 1   The terms of the President and Vice President shall end at noon on the 20th day of January, and the terms of Senators and Representatives at noon on the 3d day of January, of the years in which such terms would have ended if this article had not been ratified; and the terms of their successors shall then begin.

Section 2   The Congress shall assemble at least once in every year, and such meeting shall begin at noon on the 3d day of January, unless they shall by law appoint a different day.

Section 3   If, at the time fixed for the beginning of the term of the President, the President elect shall have died, the Vice President elect shall become President. If a President shall not have been chosen before the time fixed for the beginning of his term, or if the President elect shall have failed to qualify, then the Vice President elect shall act as President until a President shall have qualified; and the Congress may by law provide for the case wherein neither a President elect nor a Vice President elect shall have qualified, declaring who shall then act as President, or the manner in which one who is to act shall be selected, and such person shall act accordingly until a President or Vice President shall have qualified.

Section 4   The Congress may by law provide for the case of the death of any of the persons from whom the House of Representatives may choose a President whenever the right of choice shall have devolved upon them, and for the case of the death of any of the persons from whom the Senate may choose a Vice President whenever the right of choice shall have devolved upon them.

Section 5   Sections 1 and 2 shall take effect on the 15th day of October following the ratification of this article.

Section 6   This article shall be inoperative unless it shall have been ratified as an amendment to the Constitution by the legislatures of three-fourths of the several States within seven years from the date of its submission.

AMENDMENT XXI (1933)

Section 1   The eighteenth article of amendment to the Constitution of the United States is hereby repealed.

Section 2   The transportation or importation into any State, Territory or possession of the United States for delivery or use therein of intoxicating liquors, in violation of the laws thereof, is hereby prohibited.

Section 3   This article shall be inoperative unless it shall have been ratified as an amendment to the Constitution by conventions in the several States, as provided in the Constitution, within seven years from the date of the submission hereof to the States by the Congress.

AMENDMENT XXII (1951)

Section 1   No person shall be elected to the office of the President more than twice, and no person who has held the office of President, or acted as President, for more than two years of a term to which some other person was elected President shall be elected to the office of the President more than once. But this Article shall not apply to any person holding the office of President when this Article was proposed by the Congress, and shall not prevent any person who may be holding the office of President, or acting as President, during the term within which this Article becomes operative from holding the office of President or acting as President during the remainder of such term.

Section 2   This Article shall be inoperative unless it shall have been ratified as an amendment to the Constitution by the legislatures of three-fourths of the several States within seven years from the date of its submission to the States by the Congress.

AMENDMENT XXIII (1961)

Section 1   The District constituting the seat of Government of the United States shall appoint in such manner as the Congress may direct:

A number of electors of President and Vice President equal to the whole number of Senators and Representatives in Congress to which the District would be entitled if it were a State, but in no event more than the least populous State; they shall be in addition to those appointed by the States, but they shall be considered, for the purposes of the election of President and Vice President, to be electors appointed by a State; and they shall meet in the District and perform such duties as provided by the twelfth article of amendment.

Section 2   The Congress shall have power to enforce this article by appropriate legislation.

AMENDMENT XXIV (1964)

Section 1   The right of citizens of the United States to vote in any primary or other election for President or Vice President, for electors for President or Vice President, or for Senator or Representative in Congress, shall not be denied or abridged by the United States or any State by reason of failure to pay any poll tax or other tax.

Section 2   The Congress shall have power to enforce this article by appropriate legislation.

AMENDMENT XXV (1967)

Section 1   In case of the removal of the President from office or of his death or resignation, the Vice President shall become President.

Section 2   Whenever there is a vacancy in the office of the Vice President, the President shall nominate a Vice President who shall take office upon confirmation by a majority vote of both Houses of Congress.

Section 3   Whenever the President transmits to the President pro tempore of the Senate and the Speaker of the House of Representatives his written declaration that he is unable to discharge the powers and duties of his office, and until he transmits to them a written declaration to the contrary, such powers and duties shall be discharged by the Vice President as Acting President.

Section 4   Whenever the Vice President and a majority of either the principal officers of the executive departments or of such other body as Congress may by law provide, transmit to the President pro tempore of the Senate and the Speaker of the House of Representatives their written declaration that the President is unable to discharge the powers and duties of his office, the Vice President shall immediately assume the powers and duties of the office as Acting President.

Thereafter, when the President transmits to the President pro tempore of the Senate and the Speaker of the House of Representatives his written declaration that no inability exists, he shall resume the powers and duties of his office unless the Vice President and a majority of either the principal officers of the executive department or of such other body as Congress may by law provide, transmit within four days to the President pro tempore of the Senate and the Speaker of the House of Representatives their written declaration that the President is unable to discharge the powers and duties of his office. Thereupon Congress shall decide the issue, assembling within forty-eight hours for that purpose if not in session. If the Congress, within twenty-one days after receipt of the latter written declaration, or, if Congress is not in session, within twenty-one days after Congress is required to assemble, determines by two-thirds vote of both Houses that the President is unable to discharge the powers and duties of his office, the Vice President shall continue to discharge the same as Acting President; otherwise, the President shall resume the powers and duties of his office.

AMENDMENT XXVI (1971)

Section 1   The right of citizens of the United States, who are eighteen years of age or older, to vote shall not be denied or abridged by the United States or by any State on account of age.

Section 2   The Congress shall have power to enforce this article by appropriate legislation.

AMENDMENT XXVII (1992)

No law varying the compensation for the services of the senators and representatives shall take effect, until an election of representatives shall have intervened.

APPENDIX B

HOW TO READ AND BRIEF A CASE

Adapted from Ransford Pyle, *Foundations of Law: Cases, Commentary, and Ethics* (2d ed.) (Delmar Publishers/Lawyers Cooperative Publishing 1996).

Introduction

Reported judicial decisions have a style and format all their own. This discussion is designed to acquaint readers with the form and the nature of judicial decisions. Although judges have considerable freedom in how they write opinions, some uniformity of pattern comes from the similarity of purpose for decisions, especially decisions of appellate courts, which frequently serve as authority for later cases.

Similarity is also a product of custom. The influence of West Publishing Company, which publishes the regional reporter series as well as the federal reporters, has been great.

Which Court?

Knowing which court issued the opinion is extremely important. As a general rule, the higher the court, the more compelling its authority. The binding force of precedent depends on the relationship between the court which issues it and the court applying it. A decision of the Iowa Supreme Court has no precedential power over courts in Tennessee because each state has its own laws and legal system. Iowa courts may not dictate to Tennessee what Tennessee law is or should be. However, decisions of the Supreme Court of Tennessee, the highest court of that state, are binding precedent on other state courts in Tennessee—lower courts must follow the law as stated by a higher court in their jurisdiction.

Federal and State Courts

The United States has two parallel legal structures. Each state has its own set of laws and courts. In addition, the federal government has a separate legal authority through courts located in every state. Federal courts are not superior to state courts but parallel to them, having authority over different types of cases. For example, the U.S. Constitution restricts authority over patents and copyrights to the federal government. Thus, a patent case will be heard in federal court but not in a state court. In contrast, there are both federal and state civil rights laws, so a particular case might be filed in one or the other. When federal and state courts have concurrent jurisdiction of this sort, exercise of authority is governed by custom or law; but when state and federal law overlap and conflict, state law must yield to federal law.

Trial and Appellate Courts

State and federal courts are divided into trial and appellate courts. Most cases originate in trial courts, where evidence is presented, witnesses are questioned, and a judgment determining the rights of the parties is entered. If one of the parties to the case is dissatisfied with the result, the case may be appealed; an appellate court is petitioned to review the proceedings of the lower, or trial, court to determine if errors were made that would justify changing the outcome of the case.

The federal system provides a model followed in general terms by a majority of state systems. The U.S. District Court is the primary federal trial court. The next higher federal court is the United States Court of Appeals. It is called an intermediate appellate court because it is subordinate to the highest court, the U.S. Supreme Court.

Most states name their highest court Supreme Court; New York, a notable exception, calls its highest court the Court of Appeals and uses the designation Supreme Court for lower courts. Some states do not have intermediate appellate courts. There is also considerable variety in state trial courts and the names applied to them.

The careful researcher always takes note of the court issuing a decision because the higher the court, the greater the force of its decision. The decision of a court is binding on lower courts within its jurisdiction, meaning that the rules it lays down must be followed by lower courts faced with the same issue.

For Whom Are Judicial Opinions Written?

In evaluating any written material, the reader should assess the audience the writer is addressing and the writer's goals. Judges write decisions for two reasons. The first is to inform the parties to the dispute who won and who lost, giving the rules and reasoning the judge applied to the facts. The second is to inform the legal profession, attorneys and judges, of the rules applied to a given set of facts and the reasons for the decision.

Attorneys and Judges Read Judicial Opinions

Very few laypersons ever enter a law library to find and read cases. The people found in the county law library are usually lawyers, paralegals, and judges. Cases are rarely intended to be entertaining, and judges are not motivated to make their cases "reader-friendly." Their tasks are quite specific. Because any case may serve as precedent, or at least form a basis for subsequent legal arguments, judges are especially concerned with conveying a precise meaning by carefully framing the rules and providing the reasoning behind them. The higher the court, the greater this concern will be. Imagine writing an opinion for a highly skilled, highly intelligent readership that critically analyzes every word and phrase, an opinion that may well affect important rights of citizens in the future.

Judicial writing is different from most other kinds of writing in that its goal is neither simply to pass on information nor to persuade the reader of the author's point of view. The judge is stating the law, making a final judgment, but must do so with caution so that the statements are not misinterpreted or misused. An appreciation of the judge's dilemma is essential to critical evaluation of cases.

The Effect of Setting Precedent

The cost of litigation is great, and appeal of a decision incurs significant additional cost. It makes sense to appeal if the losing party reasonably concludes that the lower court was incorrect in its application of the law. It would be quite foolish to spend large sums of money to go to the higher court if the chances of winning were slim and the stakes were small. This means that the cases we read from appellate courts, and especially from the highest courts, generally involve questions with strong arguments on both sides. The judges of these courts are faced with difficult decisions and must respect the reasonable arguments of both sides in deciding which side will prevail.

Clarity versus Confusion

Judicial writing is often difficult and obscure, but such criticism of judicial writing often neglects to recognize that not only are the issues difficult to present with clarity, but also that often the importance of narrowing the application of the decision encourages tortuous reasoning. For example, when faced with a landmark case of reverse discrimination (a white applicant for medical school was denied admission, while less-qualified minority students were admitted), the U.S. Supreme Court was expected to lay down a rule concerning the constitutionality of such admissions programs. Those expectations were disappointed. The Justices wrote divergent opinions that made it very difficult to discover exactly what the rule was. At the time the issue was quite controversial, and the decision potentially could have affected efforts by the Administration and Congress to help the position of disadvantaged minorities. Any precedent of the court would have far-reaching consequences. Although the plaintiff won and subsequently entered medical school, there was some confusion as to why he won. The effect of the decision was to stifle future efforts to pursue reverse discrimination cases. Each Justice of the court viewed the problem in a different light, and the result was a resolution of the dispute without a clear picture of the rule to be applied in such cases.

Thus, the reader of cases should be aware that the complex reasoning of a judge's writing is not always due to the complexity of the issues, but may also be caused by the judge's desire to narrow the effect of the precedent.

Most appellate decisions are the product of three or more judges. A unanimous or majority opinion is not the reasoning of a single person. The author of an opinion must take into consideration the views of the judges who join in the opinion. In some cases, especially with the nine Justices of the U.S. Supreme Court, achieving a majority involves negotiation—one Justice may vote with the majority only if a key point in his or her reasoning is included or only if the rule is narrowed to cover a limited number of situations. The author of the opinion may thus be stating someone else's reasoning or opinion, or may be stating the argument to appease a Justice who is reluctant to join in the opinion. The politics of decision making may make it quite difficult to write a cohesive opinion that makes everyone happy.

Doing Justice to the Parties

It is a mistake to assume that judges are dispassionate, totally rational, and objective interpreters of the law. The notion that judges reason directly from the facts to the law in a rather mechanical fashion neglects the obvious fact that judges are human beings doing their best to dispense justice. We must suspect that in any given case, the judge or judges form an opinion as to which side should win and then select rules and arguments to support that side. (If justice clearly favors one side, it is usually not difficult to frame a convincing legal argument for that side to win.)

Sometimes a strict application of the law causes a very undesirable result. The Kentucky Court of Appeals was faced with such circumstances in *Strunk v. Strunk,* 445 S.W.2d 145, in which a man was dying of a kidney problem and his brother was the only appropriate donor for a life-saving kidney transplant. The problem was that the brother with the healthy kidneys was severely mentally retarded and therefore legally incompetent to consent to the operation. The issue facing the court was whether the mother of the two brothers could consent to the operation, acting as the guardian of the retarded brother. Kentucky precedents (cited by the dissenting judges, but ignored by the majority) seemed to show clearly that a guardian's authority did not extend to making such a decision. Faced with a heart-rending life-or-death decision, four of seven judges deciding the case ignored prior precedents. Three of the judges disagreed, and one wrote a vigorous dissenting opinion. The reasoning of the majority opinion was weak, but it is difficult to fault the judges under the circumstances.

The Format for a Reported Decision

The cases found in the reporters generally follow a uniform format with which researchers must become familiar. The first part of the case has no official authority. Authoritative statements begin with the actual text of the opinion.

Format Preceding the Opinion

West Publishing Company publishes the reporter series for which it has established a uniform format. The first page of *United States v. National Lead Co.*, 438 F.2d 935 (8th Cir. 1971) (Figure B-1) illustrates all the elements.

The Citation

The heading of the page indicates the citation "**UNITED STATES v. NATIONAL LEAD COMPANY**" and "Cite as 438 F.2d 935 (1971)." This is the name of the case and where it can be found, namely, on page 935 in Volume 438 of the Federal Reporter, Second Series. Note that this differs from the official citation, *United States v. National Lead Co.*, 438 F.2d 935 (8th Cir. 1971), that would be used in legal texts and opinions. The official citation indicates that the case was decided by the U.S. Court of Appeals for the Eighth Circuit.

The Caption

Figure B-2 shows the caption of the case, which names the parties. Note that the citation names only one party for each side, whereas the caption includes a codefendant, a union local of the AFL-CIO. The caption also indicates the status of the parties with regard to the suit as "Plaintiff-Appellant"

UNITED STATES v. NATIONAL LEAD COMPANY
Cite as 438 F.2d 935 (1971)

UNITED STATES of America,
Plaintiff-Appellant,
v.
NATIONAL LEAD COMPANY, a
Corporation, and Chemical
Workers' Basic Union Local 1744,
AFL-CIO , Defendants-Appellees.
No. 20427.
United States Court of Appeals,
Eighth Circuit. Feb. 26, 1971.

Action by government against company and union for alleged violations of Civil Rights Act of 1964. The United States District Court for the Eastern District of Missouri, Roy W. Harper, Senior District Judge, 315 F.Supp. 912, denied government's motion for preliminary injunction, and government appealed. The Court of Appeals, Bright, Circuit Judge, held that although, under facts, some of vestiges of employer's past discrimination seemed preserved in employer's transfer and promotion procedures, in view of fact that actual impact of this discrimination upon black employees possessing seniority dating back prior to end of discrimination was unclear, and in view of fact that an appropriate solution was not readily apparent from partial development of facts, denial of relief by way of a preliminary injunction was not error.

Affirmed and remanded.

1. Civil Rights 3

Employment policies which appear racially neutral but build upon bias that existed prior to enactment of 1964 Civil Rights Act to produce present discrimination are actionable. Civil Rights Act of 1964, § 701 et seq., 42 U.S.C.A. § 2000e et seq.

2. Civil Rights 3

Policy of 1964 Civil Rights Act is not fulfilled by a showing that black employees may enjoy substantially equal pay with others in similar capacities; the test is whether all employees possess an equal opportunity to fully enjoy all employment rights. Civil Rights Act of 1964, §§ 703(h), 706(g), 42 U.S.C.A. §§ 2000e-2(h), 2000e-5(g).

3. Injunction 137(4)

Although, under facts, some of vestiges of employer's past discrimination seemed preserved in employer's transfer and promotion procedures, in view of fact that actual impact of this discrimination upon black employees possessing seniority dating back prior to end of discrimination was unclear, and in view of fact that an appropriate solution was not readily apparent from partial development of facts, denial of relief by way of a preliminary injunction was not error. Civil Rights Act of 1964, §§ 701 et seq., 707(a) 42 U.S.C.A. §§ 2000e et seq., 2000e-6(a).

4. Injunction 147

In view of evidence disclosing that in recent years blacks had filled three of six vacancies for guard positions and that employer planned no immediate expansion of present guard force or filling of any existing vacancies, no need for preliminary injunction was shown with respect to guard force. Civil Rights Act of 1964, §§ 701 et seq., 707(a), 42 U.S.C.A. §§ 2000e et seq., 2000e-6(a).

◆

Jerris Leonard, Asst. Atty. Gen., Daniel Bartlett, Jr., U. S. Atty., David L. Rose, Stuart P. Herman, Attys., Dept. of Justice, Washington, D. C., for plaintiff-appellant.

Edward Weakley, Howard Elliott, Boyle, Priest, Elliott & Weakley, St. Louis, Mo., for National Lead Co.

Harry Moline, Jr., Thomas, Busse, Cullen, Clooney, Weil & King, St. Louis,

FIGURE B-1

Mo., for Chemical Workers' Basic Union, Local 1744, AFL-CIO.

Before GIBSON and BRIGHT, Circuit Judges, and McMANUS, Chief District Judge.

BRIGHT, Circuit Judge.

The United States by its Attorney General brings this action seeking in-

FIGURE B-1 *(continued)*

UNITED STATES of America
Plaintiff-Appellant,
v.
NATIONAL LEAD COMPANY,
a Corporation, and Chemical Workers'
Basic Union Local 1744, AFL-CIO,
Defendants-Appellees.

No. 20427.
United States Court of Appeals
Eighth Circuit.
Feb. 26, 1971.

FIGURE B-2

---

and "Defendants-Appellees." We can surmise from this that the United States brought the original suit as plaintiff and then also the appeal, apparently having lost the original suit.

Commonly the caption simply states "appellant" and "appellee," and the reader must discover from the text who brought the suit originally. It is important to note who is appellant and who is appellee because many opinions refer to the parties by those terms. In *National Lead,* Judge Bright refers to "the government" and "National Lead," which makes reading much less confusing.

Below the parties we find "No. 20427," the docket number, which is a number assigned to the case upon initial filing with the clerk of the court and by which it is identified prior to assigning it a volume and page number in the reporter series. This number is important when attempting to research the case prior to its official publication. Below the docket number is the name of the court issuing the decision and the date of the decision.

The Syllabus

Following the caption is a brief summary of the case called the *syllabus* (Figure B-3). Although this is sometimes written by the court or a reporter

Action by government against company and union for alleged violations of Civil Rights Act of 1964. The United States District Court for the Eastern District of Missouri, Roy W. Harper, Senior District Judge, 315 F.Supp. 912, denied government's motion for preliminary injunction, and government appealed. The Court of Appeals, Bright, Circuit Judge, held that although, under facts, some of vestiges of employer's past discrimination seemed preserved in employer's transfer and promotion procedures, in view of fact that actual impact of this discrimination upon black employees possessing seniority dating back prior to end of discrimination was unclear, and in view of fact that an appropriate solution was not readily apparent from partial development of facts, denial of relief by way of a preliminary injunction was not error.

Affirmed and remanded.

FIGURE B-3

appointed by the court, it is a narrow condensation of the court's ruling and cannot be relied upon as the precise holding of the court. The syllabus can be useful in obtaining a quick idea of what the case concerns—a summary of the issue and the holding of the court. Frequently legal researchers follow leads to cases, which upon reading prove to be unrelated to the issue being researched. Reading the syllabus may make reading the entire opinion unnecessary. However, if the syllabus suggests that the case may be important, a careful reading of the entire text of the opinion is usually necessary.

Headnotes

Figure B-4 illustrates the *headnotes,* which are statements of the major points of law discussed in the case. With limited editing, the headnotes tend to be nearly verbatim statements lifted from the opinion. The headnotes are listed in numerical order, starting at the beginning of the opinion, so that the reader may look quickly for the context of a point expressed by a headnote. For example, the part of the text that deals with a particular point made in the headnote will have the number of the headnote in brackets, e.g., [4], at the beginning of the paragraph or section in which it is discussed. This is very helpful when researching lengthy cases in which only one issue is of concern to the researcher.

To the right of the headnote number is a generic heading, such as "Civil Rights," and a *key number*. Because this reporter is published by West Publishing Company, it uses an indexing title and number that can be used throughout the many West indexes, reporters, and encyclopedias.

Although syllabi and headnotes are useful, they are not authoritative.

3. Injunction 137(4)

Although, under facts, some of vestiges of employer's past discrimination seemed preserved in employer's transfer and promotion procedures, in view of fact that actual impact of this discrimination upon black employees possessing seniority dating back prior to end of discrimination was unclear, and in view of fact that an appropriate solution was not readily apparent from partial development of facts, denial of relief by way of a preliminary injunction was not error. Civil Rights Act of 1964, §§ 701 et seq., 707(a) 42 U.S.C.A. §§ 2000e et seq., 2000e-6(a).

4. Injunction 147

In view of evidence disclosing that in recent years blacks had filled three of six vacancies for guard positions and that employer planned no immediate expansion of present guard force or filling of any existing vacancies, no need for preliminary injunction was shown with respect to guard force. Civil Rights Act of 1964, §§ 701 et seq., 707(a), 42 U.S.C.A. §§ 2000e et seq., 2000e-6(a).

FIGURE B-4

Attorneys for the Parties

Figure B-5 shows the *attorneys for the parties* as well as the judges sitting on the case. These are listed just above the beginning of the opinion, shown in Figure B-6.

Jerris Leonard, Asst. Atty. Gen., Daniel Bartlett, Jr., U.S. Atty., David L. Rose, Stuart P. Herman, Attys., Dept. of Justice, Washington, D.C., for plaintiff-appellant.

Edward Weakley, Howard Elliott, Boyle, Priest, Elliott & Weakley, St. Louis, Mo., for National Lead Co.

Harry Moline, Jr., Thomas, Busse, Cullen, Clooney, Weil & King, St. Louis, Mo., for Chemical Workers' Basic Union, Local 1744, AFL-CIO.

Before GIBSON and BRIGHT, Circuit Judges, and McMANUS, Chief District Judge.

FIGURE B-5

BRIGHT, Circuit Judge.
The United States by its Attorney
General brings this action seeking in-

FIGURE B-6

Format of the Opinion

Following the names of the attorneys and a list of the judges sitting on the case, the formal opinion (that is, the official discussion of the case) begins with the name of the judge writing the opinion, for example, "Bright, Circuit Judge," in *National Lead*. The author of the opinion has considerable freedom in presentation. Some opinions are written mechanically; a few are almost poetic. The peculiarities of any particular case may dictate a special logical order of its own. Nevertheless, the majority of opinions follow a standard format. When this format is followed, reading and understanding are simplified, but no judge is required to make an opinion easy reading. The following format is the one most frequently used.

Procedure

Most opinions begin with some reference to the outcome of the trial in the lower court and the basis for appeal. In a criminal case, for example, the opinion may state that the defendant was found guilty of aggravated assault and is appealing the judge's ruling to admit certain evidence over the defendant's objections that the evidence was prejudicial to the defendant's case. Often the remarks about procedure are brief and confusing, especially if the reader is not familiar with procedural rules. If the procedure is important to the opinion, a more elaborate discussion is usually found in the body of the opinion. Many things in the opinion become clear only upon further reading, and many opinions must be read at least twice for a full understanding. An opinion is like a jigsaw puzzle—the reader must put the parts together to see the full picture.

The Facts

Most of the text of an opinion in appellate decisions is concerned with a discussion of the law, but because a case revolves around a dispute concerning events that occurred between the parties, no opinion is complete without some discussion of the events that led to the trial. Trials generally explore these events in great detail and judge or jury settle the facts, so appellate opinions usually narrow the fact statement to the most relevant facts. In an interesting case, the reader is often left wanting to know more about what happened, but the judge is not writing a story. The important element in the opinion is the application of law.

The Issue

Following a summary of relevant facts, many writers describe the questions of law that must be decided. Rarely, this is made quite clear: "The only issue presented to the court is … " Unfortunately, few writers pinpoint the issue in this fashion, so the reader must search the text for the issue. At this point it is appropriate to introduce a favorite term used by attorneys: caveat. This means "warning" or, literally, "Let him beware."

Caveat: The issue is the most important element in an opinion. If the issue is not understood, the significance of the rule laid down by the court can easily be misunderstood. This point cannot be emphasized too strongly. Law students study cases for three years with one primary goal: "Identify the issues." Anyone can fill out forms, but a competently trained person can go right to the heart of a case and recognize its strengths and weaknesses.

The Discussion

The main body of the text of an opinion, often 90 percent of it, discusses the meaning of the issue(s) and offers a line of reasoning that leads to a disposition of the case and explains why a certain rule or rules must apply to the dispute. This part of the opinion is the most difficult to follow. The writer has a goal, but the goal is often not clear to the reader until the end. For this reason, it is usually helpful to look at the final paragraph in the case to see whether the appellate court affirmed (agreed with the lower court) or reversed (disagreed with the lower court). Many judges seem to like to hold the reader in suspense, but the reader need not play this game. By finding out the outcome of the decision, the reader can see how the writer of an opinion is building the conclusion. By recognizing the issue and knowing the rule applied, the reader can see the structure of the argument. The discussion section is the writer's justification of the holding.

The Holding

The holding states the *rule of the case,* that is, the rule the court applies to conclude whether the lower court was correct. The rule is *the law,* meaning that it determines the rights of the parties unless reversed by a higher court. It binds lower courts faced with a similar dispute in future cases. It is best to think of the holding as an answer to the issue.

Let us give a real-life example. A woman is suing for wrongful death. Her husband was killed in an auto accident, and she is attempting to collect damages based on the income her husband would have received had he lived, in which income she would have shared. Since the death, however, she has married an affluent man, and her lifestyle has not diminished. The issue is whether the jury can be informed of her remarriage. The court holds that the fact of her remarriage may not be kept from the jury. The court also holds that evidence of her new husband's earnings may *not* be presented to the jury. In this instance the holding goes a bit beyond the issue and clarifies it. (This particular issue has been answered quite differently in different states.) The reasoning for the holding is as follows: There is no justification for deliberately deceiving the jury about the woman's marital status. However, her current husband's earnings are irrelevant to the damage she suffered in losing her former husband. Fairness on this issue is difficult.

Evaluating Cases

Once the purpose, style, and structure of appellate decisions are grasped, mastering the content is a matter of concentration and experience. Researching cases generally has one or more of the following three goals:

1. Finding statements of the law.
2. Assessing the law in relation to the client's case.
3. Building an argument.

Finding the Law

Research of cases is done for a number of reasons. The principles that apply to a dispute may be unknown, unfamiliar, or forgotten. With experience, legal professionals come to develop a knack for guessing how a dispute will be decided and can even predict what rules will be applied. Once the issues of a case are recognized, a reasonable prediction of a fair outcome can be made. This is, however, merely tentative; the researchers must check their knowledge and memory against definitive statements of the law. In some instances a statute clearly defines the rights and duties that pertain to the case at hand; in others the elaboration of the law in the cases leaves little room for doubt. Frequently, however, the issue in a client's case is complex or unique, and no case can be found that is directly "on point." Ideally, research will result in finding a case that contains a fact situation so similar to that of the client that an assumption can be made that the same rule will apply. A case with a factual background identical to that of the client is said to be *on point,* as illustrated in the following example.

Suppose Laura Lee, while waiting for a bus, was hit and injured by an automobile. The driver had lost control because of a defective steering mechanism. Laura was seriously injured and the driver has minimal insurance (and may not have been at fault). The issue is whether the manufacturer of the automobile is liable. The owner could sue the automobile manufacturer, but can a bystander sue as well? A search reveals several cases involving bystanders who were injured by defective brakes and were able to sue the manufacturer for products liability. Although the facts are not identical, these cases are on point, because the issue is not what kind of defect caused the accident but whether a bystander can sue.

Distinguishing Cases

In some instances the facts of a dispute are used to *distinguish* it from similar cases. For example, in researching Laura Lee's case, a case is encountered in which a bystander was injured by an automobile with a defective steering mechanism. In that case, the bystander did not collect damages from the manufacturer. The case was distinguishable because the driver was intoxicated. The driver's negligence was not merely passive, such as procrastinating in obtaining repairs, but was actively caused by his intoxication. The intoxication was the true cause of the injury, so it would have been unfair to place liability on the manufacturer. (The manufacturer would probably be sued anyway simply because it has the resources to compensate for the injury.)

Only experience and knowledge of the law will develop the keen sense it takes to separate cases that are on point from those that are distinguishable. It is often the advocate's job to persuade on the basis of threading a way through a host of seemingly conflicting cases.

Briefing Cases

During your legal education, you may be instructed to "brief" cases. Even if your instructor does not require you to brief, you may want to, as briefing may increase your understanding of the material. There is no one correct method of briefing. What follows are the author's suggestions for briefing.

1. Read the case. On your first reading, do not take notes; simply get a "feel" for the case. Then read the case again and do the following.
2. State the relevant facts. Cases often read like little stories. You need to weed out the facts that have no bearing on the subject you are studying.
3. Identify the issues. *Issues* are legal questions raised by the facts of the case. Many issues may be addressed in a single opinion. Keep in mind your context and concentrate on the issues that are important to the subject your are studying.
4. State the applicable rules, standards, or other law.
5. Summarize the court's decision, analysis, and orders. Note whether the court affirmed, reversed, or remanded the case. You may want to add your own comments concerning the court's analysis, such as trends you discover (e.g., ideological bent of judges) or whether the court's analysis follows any particular method (e.g., originalism).

Summary

Judicial opinions are unique as a literary form in that their statements of law as defined by the court become precedent for future legal arguments and decisions. Judges must not only do justice to the parties but also must remain aware that their decisions determine rights of other parties in the future. Complex issues often result in opinions that are difficult to follow. Controversial issues may cause judges to be evasive in their conclusions.

A standard publishing format is followed in reported judicial decisions. In addition, custom has dictated a format for the text of the opinion itself. Judges are under no requirement to follow this format, and it is up to the reader to ferret out the issues and follow the reasoning.

APPENDIX C

RESEARCHING THE UNITED STATES CONSTITUTION*

Introduction

The United States Constitution is the document setting forth the fundamental principles of governance of this country. It is unique in that it was adopted in 1787 and has been the fundamental document of American governance ever since. There are twenty-six amendments to it, the first ten of which are known as the *Bill of Rights*. The language of the United States Constitution is very broad, setting up a framework of government, often without much detail. If you just want to read the United States Constitution, consult Appendix A.

The Constitution begins with a preamble. A *preamble*, according to *Ballentine's Legal Dictionary*, is a paragraph or clause explaining the reason for the enactment of the constitution and the object or objects it seeks to accomplish. The body of the document is divided into various parts, called *articles*, corresponding to the various subjects dealt with in the Constitution. The parts are further subdivided into subparts called *sections* and *clauses*. Article 5 of the Constitution is a provision describing the procedure for amending it. Any amendments to the Constitution are printed at the end of the Constitution.

Some people differentiate between the written and the "living" Constitution. The written United States Constitution, including all amendments, is relatively short in written form. The living Constitution includes those pages *and* all case law interpretations of the Constitution. When printed, the living Constitution requires numerous volumes. Scholars and laypersons alike have hotly debated constitutional interpretation. Some believe that all interpretation should be based on the plain language of the Constitution and should not stray far from it. Others believe that the broad language of the Constitution should be interpreted as needed to deal with legal questions never dreamed of when the Constitution was first enacted.

At some point you may need to locate and read a recent opinion of the United States Supreme Court or an appellate-level case involving a constitutional issue or research a problem concerning the Constitution. This appendix

---

* Carol M. Bast, who wrote this appendix, is the author of *Legal Research and Writing* (Lawyers Cooperative Publishing/Delmar Publishers, 1995). Portions of that book have been incorporated in this appendix. Courtesy of Delmar Publishers.

is designed to help you locate recent United States Supreme Court opinions and to provide basic information on researching the United States Constitution. It begins with a description of the various sources of law found in the law library, followed by information on locating recent opinions and some information on computer-assisted legal research (CALR). It then gives an overview of the research process.

Sources of Law

Your first trip through the law library may seem overwhelming. The law library contains all kinds of sources you need to consult when researching the United States Constitution. Primary sources, secondary sources, and finding tools are all sources of law, but they are used in different ways. Their use depends on the information they contain and how authoritative they are. *Primary sources*, including the Constitution and case law interpretations of the Constitution, contain the law itself; *secondary sources* contain commentary on the law; *finding tools*, as the name implies, are used to find primary and secondary sources. Primary sources are given the most weight, but secondary sources may be used if no primary sources are available. Finding tools are not authoritative and may not be quoted or cited. Nevertheless, finding tools are an important part of legal research. You may be able to locate relevant primary and secondary sources only by using finding tools.

Table C-1 lists common and frequently used primary and secondary sources and finding tools. As shown, the Constitution and state constitutions, cases, statutes, and administrative regulations are all primary sources. Secondary sources include treatises, legal periodicals, law review articles, legal encyclopedias, American Law Reports annotations, law dictionaries, legal thesauruses, continuing legal education publications, Restatements, and hornbooks. Finding tools include American Law Reports annotations, legal encyclopedias, digests, Shepard's Citators, and the *Index to Legal Periodicals*. Some sources are listed more than once. For example, American Law Reports annotations and legal encyclopedias are secondary sources, because of their commentary on law, but they are also used to find primary and secondary sources.

Table C-2 shows the judicial, legislative, and executive branches of the federal government and gives the names of the various entities within those branches and the reference materials containing the law made by each entity.

Locating Recent United States Supreme Court Opinions

Table C-2 names the three reporters containing decisions of the United States Supreme Court: United States Reports, Supreme Court Reporter, and

TABLE C-1 LEGAL SOURCES AND FINDING TOOLS

Primary Sources	Secondary Sources	Finding Tools
constitutions	treatises	American Law Reports
statutes	law review articles	
		legal encyclopedias
court rulings	legal periodicals	
		digests
administrative regulations	law dictionaries	
		Shepard's Citators
	legal thesauruses	
reporters		loose-leaf services
	continuing legal education publications	
loose-leaf services		Index to Legal Periodicals
	Restatements	
	hornbooks	
	American Law Reports annotations	
	legal encyclopedias	
	loose-leaf services	

United States Supreme Court Reports, Lawyers Edition. With a case citation, you can locate the case in one of these reporters and read its full text. In a case citation, the number preceding the abbreviation for the reporter is the volume number and the number following the abbreviation is the first page of the case. The paper-bound volumes at the end of a set of reporters are *advance sheets*. Advance sheets for Supreme Court Reporter and United States Supreme Court Reports, Lawyers Edition are available within a few weeks after decisions are announced. Later, the cases in the advance sheets are reprinted in the hardbound volumes.

If you want to read a recent United States Supreme Court case before the advance sheets appear, you can consult United States Law Week, WESTLAW, or LEXIS. WESTLAW and LEXIS are discussed in the following section. United States Law Week is a looseleaf pamphlet service housed in the law library in gray ring binders (two binders for each year). One volume contains the full text of the opinions as well as summaries of cases docketed, information concerning the Court's calendar, and summaries of oral arguments. The other volume contains information concerning important state court and lower court opinions, legislation, and administrative developments.

TABLE C-2 FEDERAL GOVERNMENT

Judicial Branch	Legislative Branch	Executive Branch
United States Supreme Court (9 Justices)	**Senate** **House of Representatives**	**President** *Presidential Documents*
slip opinions	*slip laws*	
loose-leaf service United States Law Week	*session laws* United States Statutes at Large	
reporters United States Reports Supreme Court Reporter United States Supreme Court Reports, Lawyers Edition	*code* United States Code *annotated codes* United States Code Annotated	
United States Circuit Courts of Appeal	United States Code Service	**Administrative Agencies**
reporter Federal Reporter		Federal Register
United States District Courts		*code* Code of Federal Regulations
reporter Federal Supplement		

Computer-Assisted Legal Research

Computer-assisted legal research (CALR) includes on-line services, such as WESTLAW and LEXIS, services contained on CD-ROM (compact disc-read only memory), and services accessible through the Internet, the worldwide computer network. With on-line services such as WESTLAW and LEXIS, the researcher is connected with the main computer by modem. The on-line service generally charges a subscription fee to give the researcher access to the service, and also charges for the amount of computer time used during research. If your educational institution has an on-line service, it may pay a special low educational price that allows unlimited research for a set fee.

WESTLAW and LEXIS, each more than twenty years old, are similar in that they contain the full text of federal and state primary sources as well as secondary and other related sources. Data on WESTLAW and LEXIS is found within "libraries." There is a library for United States Supreme Court decisions, a library for federal case law, a library for state case law, a library for federal statutes, a library for state statutes, and so on. You can locate a recent United States Supreme Court case by searching in the Supreme Court library and using information concerning the case, such as date of the case, name of the case, and subject matter of the case.

Valuable information may also be found on CD-ROM and the Internet. A researcher using a CD-ROM usually pays a fixed cost for the CD-ROM and updates during a given period of time. The CD-ROM allows unlimited research time without having to pay for on-line time. The CD-ROM is updated periodically by the publisher, which sends the researcher a replacement CD. The new CD contains all the information on the old CD and any information that has become available since the last CD. The Internet allows the user to access information and communicate worldwide. With the Internet, the legal researcher can access countless sources—from library holding catalogs to government agency information to legal bulletin boards to law-related mailing lists. The user can log on to the Internet free through many universities, or the user can pay for access through on-line commercial service providers.

Overview of Constitutional Research

The first step in researching a particular provision of the Constitution would likely be to consult an annotated version of the Constitution. (Such annotated versions are found both in United States Code Service and United States Code Annotated.) For example, if you are researching how the Fourth Amendment to the Constitution has been interpreted, you would look up the Fourth Amendment in either United States Code Service or United States Code Annotated, read the wording of the amendment, and consult the material following the amendment. The materials may refer you to related constitutional provisions, statutes, and administrative regulations, as well as digest topics, legal encyclopedia topics, law review articles, and case summaries. If a reference or case summary involves the same question you are researching, make a note of the citation, pull the authority, and read it. Often annotated codes contain a separate index located at the end of the Constitution. The index is designed to help you locate a particular provision within the Constitution.

Do not forget to update your research. Hardbound volumes of the annotated codes are updated by pocket parts. The pocket parts are updated by quarterly supplements. Because of the lag time between the announcement of an important United States Supreme Court decision interpreting the Constitution and the printing of the annual pocket part to the annotated code, the annotated code may be as much as two years behind current case law. Update your research by shepardizing and using computer-assisted legal research.

When researching, you may find it helpful to consult one or more of the various treatises dealing with constitutional law, in addition to reading the annotations in the annotated codes.

If you know little or nothing about the area of law involved in the problem you are researching, a good beginning point in your research is to read a textual explanation of that area of the law. Legal encyclopedias and American Law Reports are the two most widely available sources of this type of information. Check to see whether your library has any loose-leaf services that cover the area you are researching. Use key words you have identified to locate relevant topics in the legal encyclopedias, relevant annotations in American Law Reports, and relevant materials in loose-leaf services.

Law review and legal periodical articles may give you even more specific information. The *Index to Legal Periodicals* is a good source to use to locate these articles either by subject or by author. Familiarize yourself with other resources available in your library, including treatises and hornbooks. A legal textbook, such as this one, covering the area of law you are researching may be another good place to start.

Consult a digest to find relevant cases. You can find cases in the digest either by consulting the Descriptive-Word Indexes (located at the end of the digest set) or reviewing a topic outline (printed at the beginning of each topic). When you locate a primary source, use the primary source to locate other primary sources.

When are you finished with your research? You are probably finished when you have checked each of the main primary and secondary sources and you keep coming up with the same authorities. Table C-3 provides an overview of the research process. Before you stop, double-check to make sure you have shepardized any authorities you intend to use and follow any other avenues of research suggested by the information you obtain from shepardizing.

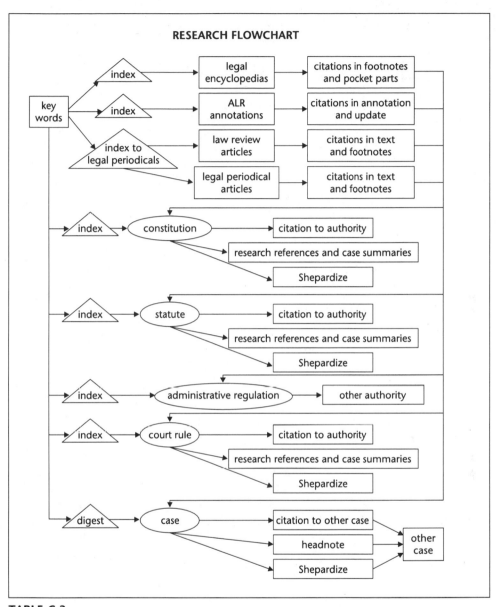

TABLE C-3

APPENDIX D

SELECTED FEDERAL STATUTES

28 U.S.C. § 1251

Supreme Court: Original Jurisdiction

(a) The Supreme Court shall have original and exclusive jurisdiction of all controversies between two or more States.

(b) The Supreme Court shall have original but not exclusive jurisdiction of:

(1) All actions or proceedings to which ambassadors, other public ministers, consuls, or vice consuls of foreign states are parties;

(2) All controversies between the United States and a State;

(3) All actions or proceedings by a State against the citizens of another State or against aliens.

28 U.S.C. § 1253

Supreme Court: Appeals from Three-Judge Courts

Except as otherwise provided by law, any party may appeal to the Supreme Court from an order granting or denying, after notice and hearing, an interlocutory or permanent injunction in any civil action, suit or proceeding required by any Act of Congress to be heard and determined by a district court of three judges.

28 U.S.C. § 1254

Supreme Court: Appeals from Courts of Appeals

Cases in the courts of appeals may be reviewed by the Supreme Court by the following methods:

(1) By writ of certiorari granted upon the petition of any party to any civil or criminal case, before or after rendition of judgment or decree;

(2) By certification at any time by a court of appeals of any question of law in any civil or criminal case as to which instructions are desired, and upon such certification the Supreme Court may give binding instructions or require the entire record to be sent up for decision of the entire matter in controversy.

28 U.S.C. § 1257

Supreme Court: Appeals from State Courts

(a) Final judgments or decrees rendered by the highest court of a State in which a decision could be had, may be reviewed by the Supreme Court by writ of certiorari where the validity of a treaty or statute of the United States is drawn in question or where the validity of a statute of any State is drawn in question on the ground of its being repugnant to the Constitution, treaties, or laws of the United States, or where any title, right, privilege, or immunity is specially set up or claimed under the Constitution or the treaties or statutes of, or any commission held or authority exercised under, the United States.

(b) For the purposes of this section, the term "highest court of a State" includes the District of Columbia Court of Appeals.

28 U.S.C. § 1331

District Courts: Federal Question Jurisdiction

The district courts shall have original jurisdiction of all civil actions arising under the Constitution, laws, or treaties of the United States.

28 U.S.C. § 1332

District Courts: Diversity Jurisdiction

(a) The district courts shall have original jurisdiction of all civil actions where the matter in controversy exceeds the sum or value of $50,000, exclusive of interest and costs, and is between—

(1) citizens of different States;

(2) citizens of a State and citizens or subjects of a foreign state;

(3) citizens of different States and in which citizens or subjects of a foreign state are additional parties; and

(4) a foreign state, defined in section 1603(a) of this title, as plaintiff and citizens of a State or of different States.

For the purposes of this section, section 1335, and section 1441, an alien admitted to the United States for permanent residence shall be deemed a citizen of the State in which such alien is domiciled.

(b) Except when express provision therefor is otherwise made in a statute of the United States, where the plaintiff who files the case originally in the Federal courts is finally adjudged to be entitled to recover less than the sum or value of $50,000, computed without regard to any setoff or counterclaim to which the defendant may be adjudged to be entitled, and exclusive or interest and costs, the district court may deny costs to the plaintiff and, in addition, may impose costs on the plaintiff.

(c) For the purposes of this section and section 1441 of this title—

(1) a corporation shall be deemed to be a citizen of any State by which it has been incorporated and of the State where it has its principal place of business, except that in any direct action against the insurer of a policy or contract of liability insurance, whether incorporated or unincorporated, to which action the insured is not joined as a party-defendant, such insurer shall be deemed a citizen of the State of which the insured is a citizen, as well as of any State by which the insurer has been incorporated and of the State where it has its principal place of business; and

(2) the legal representative of the estate of a decedent shall be deemed to be a citizen only of the same State as the decedent, and the legal representative of an infant or incompetent shall be deemed to be a citizen only of the same State as the infant or incompetent.

(d) The word "States", as used in this section, includes the Territories, the District of Columbia, and the Commonwealth of Puerto Rico.

28 U.S.C. § 1441

District Courts: Removal of Cases from State Courts

(a) Except as otherwise expressly provided by Act of Congress, any civil action brought in a State court of which the district courts of the United States have original jurisdiction, may be removed by the defendant or the defendants, to the district court of the United States for the district and division embracing the place where such action is pending. For purposes of removal under this chapter, the citizenship of defendants sued under fictitious names shall be disregarded.

(b) Any civil action of which the district courts have original jurisdiction founded on a claim or right arising under the Constitution, treaties or laws of the United States shall be removable without regard to the citizenship or residence of the parties. Any other such action shall be removable only if none of the parties in interest properly joined and served as defendants is a citizen of the State in which such action is brought.

(c) Whenever a separate and independent claim or cause of action within the jurisdiction conferred by section 1331 of this title is joined with one or more otherwise non-removable claims or causes of action, the entire case may be removed and the district court may determine all issues therein, or, in its discretion, may remand all matters in which State law predominates.

(d) Any civil action brought in a State court against a foreign state as defined in section 1603(a) of this title may be removed by the foreign state to the district court of the United States for the district and division embracing the place where such action is pending. Upon removal the action shall be tried by the court without jury. Where removal is based upon this subsection, the time limitations of section 1446(b) of this chapter may be enlarged at any time for cause shown.

(e) The court to which such civil action is removed is not precluded from hearing and determining any claim in such civil action because the State court from which such civil action is removed did not have jurisdiction over that claim.

APPENDIX E

JUSTICES OF THE UNITED STATES SUPREME COURT BY SEAT

Chief Justice

John Jay	1789–95
John Rutledge	1795 (unconfirmed)
Oliver Ellsworth	1796–1800
John Marshall	1801–35
Roger B. Taney	1836–64
Salmon P. Chase	1864–73
Morrison R. Waite	1874–88
Melville W. Fuller	1888–1910
Edward D. White	1910–21
William H. Taft	1921–30
Charles E. Hughes	1930–41
Harlan F. Stone	1941–46
Fred M. Vinson	1946–53
Earl Warren	1953–69
Warren Burger	1969–86
William H. Rehnquist	1986–

Seat Two

John Rutledge	1789–91
Thomas Johnson	1791–93
William Paterson	1793–1806
Henry B. Livingston	1806–23
Smith Thompson	1823–43
Samuel Nelson	1845–72
Ward Hunt	1872–82
Samuel Blatchford	1882–93
Edward D. White	1894–1910
Willis Van Devanter	1910–37
Hugo L. Black	1937–71
Lewis F. Powell, Jr.	1972–87
Anthony Kennedy	1988–

Seat Three

William Cushing	1789–1810
Joseph Story	1811–45
Levi Woodbury	1845–51
Benjamin Curtis	1851–57
Nathan Clifford	1858–81
Horace Gray	1881–1902
Oliver Wendell Holmes	1902–32
Benjamin N. Cardozo	1932–38
Felix Frankfurter	1939–62
Arthur Goldberg	1962–65

Seat Three *(continued)*

Abe Fortas	1965–70
Harry Blackmun	1970–94
Steven Breyer	1994–

Seat Four

James Wilson	1789–98
Bushrod Washington	1798–1829
Henry Baldwin	1830–44
Robert C. Grier	1846–70
William Strong	1870–80
William B. Woods	1880–87
Lucias Q. C. Lamar	1888–93
Howell E. Jackson	1893–95
Rufus W. Peckham	1895–1909
Horace H. Lurton	1909–14
James C. McReynolds	1914–41
James F. Byrnes	1941–42
Wiley B. Rutledge	1943–49
Sherman Minton	1949–56
William Brennan, Jr.	1956–90
David H. Souter	1990–

Seat Five

John Blair	1789–96
Samuel Chase	1796–1811
Gabriel Duval	1811–35
Phillip P. Barbour	1836–41
Peter V. Daniel	1841–60
Samuel F. Miller	1862–90
Henry B. Brown	1890–1906
William H. Moody	1906–10
Joseph R. Lamar	1910–16
Louis D. Brandeis	1916–39
William O. Douglas	1939–75
John Paul Stevens	1975–

Seat Six

James Iredell	1790–99
Alfred Moore	1799–1804
William Johnson	1804–34
James M. Wayne	1835–67
Joseph Bradley	1870–92
George Shiras, Jr.	1892–1903
William R. Day	1903–22

Seat Six *(continued)*
Pierce Butler   1922–39
Frank Murphy   1940–49
Tom C. Clark   1949–67
Thurgood Marshall   1967–91
Clarence Thomas   1991–

Seat Seven
Thomas Todd   1807–26
Robert Trimble   1826–28
John McLean   1829–61
Noah H. Swayne   1862–81
Stanley Matthews   1881–89
David J. Brewer   1889–1910
Charles E. Hughes   1910–16
John H. Clarke   1916–22
George Sutherland   1922–38
Stanley F. Reed   1938–57
Charles E. Whittaker   1957–62
Byron R. White   1962–93
Ruth Bader Ginsburg   1993–

Seat Eight
John Catron   1837–65
Harlan F. Stone   1925–41

Seat Eight *(continued)*
Robert H. Jackson   1941–54
John M. Harlan II   1955–71
William H. Rehnquist   1972–86
Antonin Scalia   1986–

Seat Nine
John McKinley   1837–52
John Campbell   1853–61
David Davis   1862–77
John M. Harlan I   1877–1911
Mahlon Pitney   1912–22
Edward T. Sanford   1923–30
Owen Roberts   1930–45
Harold H. Burton   1945–58
Potter Stewart   1958–81
Sandra Day O'Connor   1981–

Seat Ten
Stephen J. Field   1863–97
Joseph McKenna   1898–1925

APPENDIX F

SUPREME COURT TIMETABLE

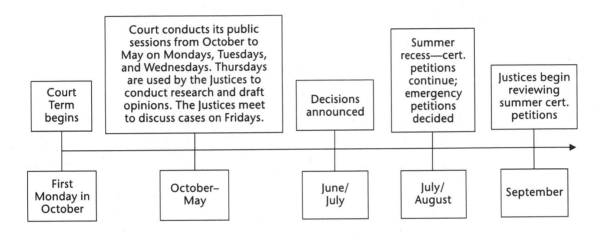

Court Term begins — First Monday in October

Court conducts its public sessions from October to May on Mondays, Tuesdays, and Wednesdays. Thursdays are used by the Justices to conduct research and draft opinions. The Justices meet to discuss cases on Fridays. — October–May

Decisions announced — June/July

Summer recess—cert. petitions continue; emergency petitions decided — July/August

Justices begin reviewing summer cert. petitions — September

APPENDIX G

WAR POWERS RESOLUTION

87 Stat. 555 (1973)

Resolved by the Senate and House of Representatives of the United States of America in Congress assembled. That:

Section 1. This joint resolution may be cited as the "War Powers Resolution."

Sec. 2. (a) It is the purpose of this joint resolution to fulfill the intent of the framers of the Constitution of the United States and insure that the collective judgment of both the Congress and the President will apply to the introduction of United States Armed Forces into hostilities, or into situations where imminent involvement in hostilities is clearly indicated by the circumstances, and to the continued use of such forces in hostilities or in such situations.

(b) Under article I, section 8, of the Constitution, it is specifically provided that the Congress shall have the power to make all laws necessary and proper for carrying into execution, not only its own powers but also all other powers vested by the Constitution in the Government of the United States, or in any department or officer thereof.

(c) The constitutional powers of the President as Commander-in-Chief to introduce United States Armed Forces into hostilities, or into situations where imminent involvement in hostilities is clearly indicated by the circumstances, are exercised only pursuant to (1) a declaration of war, (2) specific statutory authorization, or (3) a national emergency created by attack upon the United States, its territories or possessions, or its armed forces.

Sec. 3. The President in every possible instance shall consult with Congress before introducing United States Armed Forces into hostilities or into situations where imminent involvement in hostilities is clearly indicated by the circumstances, and after every such introduction shall consult regularly with the Congress until United States Armed Forces are no longer engaged in hostilities or have been removed from such situations.

Sec. 4. (a) In the absence of a declaration of war, in any case in which United States Forces are introduced—

(1) into hostilities or into situations where imminent involvement in hostilities is clearly indicated by the circumstances.

(2) into the territory, airspace or waters of a foreign nation, while equipped for combat, except for deployments which relate solely to supply, replacement, repair, or training of such forces; or

(3) in numbers which substantially enlarge United States Armed Forces equipped for combat already located in a foreign nation; the President shall submit within 48 hours to the Speaker of the House of Representatives and to the President pro tempore of the Senate a report, in writing, setting forth—

(A) the circumstances necessitating the introduction of United States Armed Forces;

(B) the constitutional and legislative authority under which such introduction took place; and

(C) the estimated scope and duration of the hostilities or involvement.

(b) The President shall provide such other information as the Congress may request in the fulfillment of its constitutional responsibilities with respect to committing the Nation to war and to the use of United States Armed Forces abroad.

(c) Whenever United States Armed Forces are introduced into hostilities or into any situation described in subsection (a) of this section, the President shall, so long as such armed forces continue to be engaged in such hostilities or situation, report to the Congress periodically on the status of such hostilities or situation as well as on the scope and duration of such hostilities or situation, but in no event shall he report to the Congress less often than once every six months.

Sec. 5. (a) Each report submitted pursuant to section 4(a)(1) shall be transmitted to the Speaker of the House of Representatives and to the President pro tempore of the Senate on the same calendar day. Each report so transmitted shall be referred to the Committee on Foreign Affairs of the House of Representatives and to the Committee on Foreign Relations of the Senate for appropriate action. If, when the report is transmitted, the Congress has adjourned sine die or has adjourned for any period in excess of three calendar days, the Speaker of the House of Representatives and the President pro tempore of the Senate, if they deem it advisable (or if petitioned by at least 30 percent of the membership of their respective Houses) shall jointly request the President to convene Congress in order that it may consider the report and take appropriate action pursuant to this section.

(b) Within sixty calendar days after a report is submitted or is required to be submitted pursuant to section 4(a)(1), whichever is earlier, the President shall terminate any use of United States Armed Forces with respect to which such report was submitted (or required to be submitted), unless the Congress (1) has declared war or has enacted a specific authorization for such use of United States Armed Forces, (2) has extended by law such sixty-day period, or (3) is physically unable to meet as a result of an armed attack upon the United States. Such sixty-day period shall be extended for not more than an additional thirty days if the President determines and certifies to the Congress in writing that unavoidable military necessity respecting the safety of United States Armed Forces requires the continued use of such armed forces in the course of bringing about a prompt removal of such forces.

(c) Notwithstanding subsection (b), at any time that United States Armed Forces are engaged in hostilities outside the territory of the United States, its possessions and territories without a declaration of war or specific statutory authorization, such forces shall be removed by the President if the Congress so directs by concurrent resolution.

Sec. 6. (a) Any joint resolution or bill introduced pursuant to section 5(b) at least thirty calendar days before the expiration of the sixty-day period specified in such section shall be referred to the Committee on Foreign Affairs of the House of Representatives or the Committee on Foreign Relations of the Senate, as the case may be, and such committee shall report one such joint resolution or bill, together with its recommendations, not later than twenty-four calendar days before the expiration of the sixty-day period specified in such section, unless such House shall otherwise determine by the yeas and nays.

(b) Any joint resolution or bill so reported shall become the pending business of the House in question (in the case of the Senate the time for debate shall be equally divided between the proponents and the opponents), and shall be voted on within three calendar days thereafter, unless such House shall otherwise determine by yeas and nays.

(c) Such a joint resolution or bill passed by one House shall be referred to the committee of the other House named in subsection (a) and shall be reported out not later than fourteen calendar days before the expiration of the sixty-day period specified in section 5(b). The joint resolution or bill so reported shall become the pending business of the House in question and shall be voted on within three calendar days after it has been reported, unless such House shall otherwise determine by yeas and nays.

(d) In the case of any disagreement between the two Houses of Congress with respect to a joint resolution or bill passed by both Houses, conferees shall be promptly appointed and the committee of conference shall make and file a report with respect to such resolution or bill not later than four calendar days before the expiration of the sixty-day period specified in section 5(b). In the event the conferees are unable to agree within 48 hours, they shall report back to their respective Houses in disagreement. Notwithstanding any rule in either House concerning the printing of conference reports in the Record or concerning any delay in the consideration of such reports, such report shall be acted on by both Houses not later than the expiration of such sixty-day period.

Sec. 7. (a) Any concurrent resolution introduced pursuant to section 5(c) shall be referred to the Committee on Foreign Affairs of the House of Representatives or the Committee on Foreign Relations of the Senate, as the case may be, and one such concurrent resolution shall be reported out by such committee together with its recommendations within fifteen calendar days, unless such House shall otherwise determine by the yeas and nays.

(b) Any concurrent resolution so reported shall become the pending business of the House in question (in the case of the Senate the time for debate shall be equally divided between the proponents and the opponents) and shall be voted on within three calendar days thereafter, unless such House shall otherwise determine by yeas and nays.

(c) Such a concurrent resolution passed by one House shall be referred to the committee of the other House named in subsection (a) and shall be reported out by such committee together with its recommendations within fifteen calendar days and shall thereupon become the pending business of such House and shall be voted upon within three calendar days, unless such House shall otherwise determine by yeas and nays.

(d) In the case of any disagreement between the two Houses of Congress with respect to a concurrent resolution passed by both Houses, conferees shall be promptly appointed and the committee of conference shall make and file a report with respect to such concurrent resolution within six calendar days after the legislation is referred to the committee of conference.

Notwithstanding any rule in either House concerning the printing of conference reports in the Record or concerning any delay in the consideration of such reports, such report shall be acted on by both Houses not later than six calendar days after the conference report is filed. In the event the conferees are unable to agree within 48 hours, they shall report back to their respective Houses in disagreement.

Sec. 8. (a) Authority to introduce United States Armed Forces into hostilities or into situations wherein involvement in hostilities is clearly indicated by the circumstances shall not be inferred—

(1) from any provision of law (whether or not in effect before the date of the enactment of this joint resolution), including any provision contained in any appropriation Act, unless such provision specifically authorizes the introduction of United States Armed Forces into hostilities or into such situations and states that it is intended to constitute specific statutory authorization within the meaning of this joint resolution; or

(2) from any treaty heretofore or hereafter ratified unless such treaty is implemented by legislation specifically authorizing the introduction of United States Armed Forces into hostilities or into such situations and stating that it is intended to constitute specific statutory authorization within the meaning of this joint resolution.

(b) Nothing in this joint resolution shall be construed to require any further specific statutory authorization to permit members of United States Armed Forces to participate jointly with members of the armed forces of one or more foreign countries in the headquarters operations of high-level military commands which were established prior to the date of enactment of this joint resolution and pursuant to the United Nations Charter or any treaty ratified by the United States prior to such date.

(c) For purposes of this joint resolution, the term "introduction of United States Armed Forces" includes the assignment of members of such armed forces to command, coordinate, participate in the movement of, or accompany the regular or irregular military forces of any foreign country or government when such military forces are engaged, or there exists an imminent threat that such forces will become engaged, in hostilities.

(d) Nothing in this joint resolution—

(1) is intended to alter the constitutional authority of the Congress or of the President, or the provisions of existing treaties; or

(2) shall be construed as granting any authority to the President with respect to the introduction of United States Armed Forces into hostilities or into situations wherein involvement in hostilities is clearly indicated by the circumstances which authority he would not have had in the absence of this joint resolution.

Sec. 9. If any provision of this joint resolution or the application thereof to any person or circumstance is held invalid, the remainder of the joint resolution and the application of such provision to any other person or circumstance shall not be affected thereby.

Sec. 10. This joint resolution shall take effect on the date of its enactment.

[Passed over Presidential veto November 7, 1973.]

GLOSSARY

adequate and independent state grounds doctrine Federal judicial review of a state decision in a case that included both state and federal claims will not occur if the lower court's decision rested upon adequate and independent state law.

advisory opinion [†] A judicial interpretation of a legal question requested by the legislative or executive branch of government. Typically, courts prefer not to give advisory opinions.

advisory opinion A judicial opinion concerning a legal issue over which no dispute or controversy exists. Federal courts are generally prohibited from rendering advisory opinions.

affectation doctrine Rule that provides Congress with authority to regulate intrastate activities that affect interstate commerce. Even though individual activity may not affect interstate commerce, the total effect of all individuals who engage in the activity may affect interstate commerce and provide Congress with the jurisdiction to regulate the activity.

amnesty [†] An act of the government granting a pardon for a past crime. Amnesty is rarely exercised in favor of individuals, but is usually applied to a group or class of persons who are accountable for crimes for which they have not yet been convicted.

antifederalist 1. A person who opposes establishment of a strong, centralized government in favor of local control. 2. A party that opposes establishment of a strong, centralized government in favor of local control.

appellate jurisdiction [†] The authority of one court to review the proceedings of another court or of an administrative agency.

avoidance The Supreme Court's practice of avoiding constitutional issues by deciding cases upon nonconstitutional grounds.

bicameral [†] Two-chambered, referring to the customary division of a legislature into two houses (a Senate and a House of Representatives).

bill [†] A proposed law, presented to the legislature for enactment; i.e., a legislative bill.

bill of attainder [†] A legislative act that inflicts capital punishment upon named persons without a judicial trial. Congress and the state legislatures are prohibited from issuing bills of attainder by the Constitution.

canons of construction and interpretation A set of judicially created rules that govern the interpretation of written law, such as statutes, regulations, and constitutions.

capable of repetition yet evading review An exception to the mootness doctrine, which provides that if an alleged harm may be repeated, but by its nature cannot be judicially determined in the normal legal process, that harm may become the basis of jurisdiction.

class action [†] An action brought by one or several plaintiffs on behalf of a class of persons. A class action may be appropriate when there has been injury to so many people that their voluntarily and unanimously joining in a lawsuit is improbable and impracticable. In such a situation, injured parties who wish to do so may, with the court's permission, sue on behalf of all. A class action is sometimes referred to as a representative action.

code [†] 1. The published statutes of a jurisdiction, arranged in systematic form. 2. A portion of the statutes of a jurisdiction, especially the statutes relating to a particular subject.

codification [†]   1. The process of arranging laws in a systematic form covering the entire law of a jurisdiction or a particular area of the law; the process of creating a code. 2. The process of turning a common law rule into a statute.

collateral consequences   An exception to the mootness doctrine, which provides for jurisdiction in cases in which the primary issue is moot, but secondary—*collateral*—issues remain.

commerce clause [†]   The clause in Article I, § 8, of the Constitution that gives Congress the power to regulate commerce between the states and between the United States and foreign countries. Federal statutes that regulate business and labor ... are based upon this power.

commutation of sentence [†]   The substitution of a less severe punishment for a more severe punishment.

***Cooley* doctrine**   Named for the case in which it was announced, *Cooley v. Board of Wardens*, 53 U.S. 299 (1851); provides that if a subject of interstate commerce is national in character, then regulation of that subject is exclusively federal.

cooperative federalism   The theory that the national government is supreme to the state governments. The powers of the national government are read broadly and the Tenth Amendment is read as not granting any specific powers to the states.

Corrections Day   Part of Congress's schedule; occurs twice a month. A time specially set aside for legislation intended to amend or repeal administrative rules.

countermajoritarian institution   Because its members are not elected by the people, are not accountable to the people, and are not required to consider public opinion in their decision making, the Supreme Court is considered by most to be a countermajoritarian institution. This does not mean, however, that the Court has historically been countermajoritarian in its decision making.

court of general jurisdiction [†]   Generally, another term for trial court; that is, a court having jurisdiction to try all classes of civil and criminal cases except those which can be heard only by a court of limited jurisdiction.

court of limited jurisdiction [†]   A court whose jurisdiction is limited to civil cases of a certain type or which involve a limited amount of money, or whose jurisdiction in criminal cases is confined to petty offenses and preliminary hearings. A court of limited jurisdiction is sometimes called a *court of special jurisdiction*.

de novo [†]   Anew; over again; a second time.

declaratory judgment (declaratory relief) [†]   A judgment that specifies the rights of the parties but orders no relief. Nonetheless, it is a binding judgment and the appropriate remedy for the determination of an actionable dispute when the plaintiff is in doubt as to his or her legal rights.

delegation of powers [†]   ... 3. The transfer of power from the president to an administrative agency.

dictum (obiter dictum) [†]   [E]xpressions or comments in a court opinion that are not necessary to support the decision made by the court; they are not binding authority and have no value as precedent. If nothing else can be found on point, an advocate may wish to attempt to persuade by citing cases that contain dicta.

distinguish [†]   To explain why a particular case is not precedent or authority with respect to the matter in controversy.

distinguishing on the facts   Choosing not to apply a rule from a previous case because its facts differ from the case sub judice.

diversity jurisdiction [†]   The jurisdiction of a federal court arising from diversity of citizenship, when the jurisdictional amount has been met.

diversity of citizenship [†]   A ground for invoking the original jurisdiction of a federal district court, the basis of jurisdiction being the existence of a controversy between citizens of different states.

dormant commerce clause Judicial doctrine providing that even if federal power to regulate interstate and international commerce is not exercised, state power to regulate these areas is sometimes precluded.

dormant commerce clause doctrine The idea that state laws that unduly burden interstate commerce, even if the subject is unregulated by the national government, are invalid under federalism principles, because the regulation of interstate and foreign commerce belongs exclusively to the federal government.

dual federalism The theory that the national government and the state governments are co-equal sovereigns. The national government is supreme only when its jurisdiction is explicitly granted by the Constitution.

dual sovereignty An approach to constitutional interpretation that requires state judges to apply both the federal and state constitutions simultaneously.

electoral college † The body empowered by the Constitution to elect the president and vice president of [the] United States, composed of presidential electors chosen by the voters at each presidential election. In practice, however, the electoral college votes in accordance with the popular vote.

en banc † [French for] "on the bench." A court, particularly an appellate court, with all the judges sitting together (sitting en banc) in a case.

enabling act (enabling legislation) † 1. A statute that grants new powers or authority to persons or corporations. 2. A statute that gives the government the power to enforce other legislation or that carries out a provision of a constitution. The term also applies to a clause in a statute granting the government the power to enforce or carry out that statute. Such a provision is called an enabling clause.

ex post facto law † A law making a person criminally liable for an act that was not criminal at the time it was committed. The Constitution prohibits both Congress and the states from enacting such laws.

executive agency An agency whose head serves at the pleasure of the President.

executive agreement † An agreement with a foreign government, made by the president acting within his or her executive powers.

executive order † An order issued by the chief executive officer of government, whether national, state, or local.

executory † Not yet fully performed, completed, fulfilled, or carried out; to be performed, either wholly or in part; not yet executed.

federal jurisdiction † The jurisdiction of the federal courts. Such jurisdiction is based upon the judicial powers granted by Article III of the Constitution and by federal statutes.

Federal Register † An official publication, printed daily, containing regulations and proposed regulations issued by administrative agencies, as well as other rulemaking and other official business of the executive branch of government. All regulations are ultimately published in the Code of Federal Regulations.

federalism † 1. Pertaining to a system of government that is federal in nature. 2. The system by which the states of the United States relate to each other and to the federal government.

federalism A governmental structure in which two or more levels of government operate concurrently with jurisdiction over the same citizens, and in which each governmental entity has some autonomy over specific policy areas. This is opposed to a *unitary system,* where there is one centralized government; and a *confederation,* where two or more governments combine to create a confederation government that has no direct authority over the citizens of each of its members.

federalist 1. A person who supports a strong, centralized government. 2. A political party that advocates a strong, centralized government.

formal rulemaking A process used by administrative agencies to create rules and regulations. The Administrative Procedure Act provides that formal rulemaking is required only when mandated by statute. Otherwise, informal rulemaking may be used by an agency. Formal rulemaking involves formal hearings and is more expensive and time-consuming than informal rulemaking. This process is also known as *rulemaking on the record.*

full faith and credit † A reference to the requirement of Article IV of the Constitution that each state give "full faith and credit" to the "public acts, records, and judicial proceedings" of every other state. This means that a state's judicial acts must be given the same effect by the courts of all other states as they receive at home.

gerrymandering † Manipulating the boundary lines of a political district to give an unfair advantage to one political party or to dilute the political strength of voters of a particular race, color, or national origin.

habeas corpus † [Latin for] "you have the body." A writ whose purpose is to obtain immediate relief from illegal imprisonment by having the "body" (that is, the prisoner) delivered from custody and brought before the court. A writ of habeas corpus is a means for attacking the constitutionality of the statute under which, or the proceedings in which, the original conviction was obtained. There are numerous writs of habeas corpus, each applicable in different procedural circumstances. The full name of the ordinary writ of habeas corpus is *habeas corpus ad subjiciendum.*

impeachment † The constitutional process by which high elected officers of the United States, including the president, may be removed from office. The accusation (articles of impeachment) is made by the House of Representatives and tried by the Senate, which sits as an impeachment court. Under the Constitution, the grounds for impeachment are "treason, bribery, or other high crimes and misdemeanors."

incorporation The Bill of Rights was intended to be applied only against the national government. However, the Supreme Court determined that most of the rights contained therein were "incorporated" by the due process clause of the Fourteenth Amendment. A right is *incorporated* if it is fundamental and necessary to an ordered liberty. Once incorporated, the right applies against the states.

independent agency An agency whose head may be terminated by the President only for good cause.

independent counsel † Under federal statute, counsel who may be specially appointed to investigate and prosecute high government officials for crimes committed in office.

informal rulemaking A process used by administrative agencies to create rules and regulations. The Administrative Procedure Act provides that agencies may use this procedure unless formal rulemaking is required by statute. Informal rulemaking is less costly and less time-consuming than its formal counterpart. This process is also known as *notice-and-comment rulemaking.*

intelligible principle test The test used to determine if Congress has provided an agency with sufficient guidance in the performance of a delegated duty.

intergovernmental immunity doctrine The doctrine that both the states and the national government possess some immunity from the regulation of the other under federalism principles. Generally, the federal government enjoys greater immunity than do the states.

interstitial An approach to constitutional interpretation that requires state judges to apply the federal Constitution before turning to their state's constitution.

joint resolution † A resolution adopted by both houses of a state legislature or of Congress. In most jurisdictions, a joint resolution is not a law, although a congressional resolution has the effect of law if it is signed by the president.

judicial activism   1. Use of judicial decisions to engage in social engineering. 2. A judicial philosophy that gives little deference to precedent and, therefore, commonly results in the abrogation of prior decisions.

judicial review   The power of the judiciary, as the final interpreter of the law, to declare an act of a coordinate governmental branch or state unconstitutional. The power is not expressly stated in the Constitution, but the Supreme Court announced that the judiciary possesses this power in *Marbury v. Madison,* 5 U.S. (1 Cranch) 137 (1803).

jurisdiction †   A term used in several senses: 1. In a general sense, the right of a court to adjudicate lawsuits of a certain kind. 2. In a specific sense, the right of a court to determine a particular case; in other words, the power of the court over the subject matter of, or the property involved in, the case at bar. 3. In a geographical sense, the power of a court to hear cases only within a specific territorial area.

justiciability doctrine   Rules that limit the authority of federal courts to hear cases, such as ripeness, mootness, political question, and standing.

legislative veto   An act of a legislature invalidating executive action in a particular instance. Generally, legislative vetos are unconstitutional. Once power is delegated by Congress to the President, it is generally prohibited from interfering with the President's enforcement.

line item veto †   The right of a governor under most state constitutions to veto individual appropriations in an appropriation act rather than being compelled either to veto the act as a whole or to sign it into law. The president of the United States does not have a line item veto.

literalism   An approach to interpreting the Constitution that focuses on the literal meanings of its words, rather than on other factors, such as the original intent of the framers. There are two forms of literalism, historical and contemporary. *Historical literalism* defines terms in the context of when the particular provision being considered was ratified. *Contemporary literalism* uses contemporary definitions.

marking up †   The detailed revision of a bill by a legislative committee.

minimum contacts test †   A doctrine under which a state court is permitted to acquire personal jurisdiction over a nonresident, although he or she is not personally served with process within the state, if he or she has had such a substantial connection with that state that due process is not offended by the court's exercise of jurisdiction over him or her.

modernism   An approach to interpreting the Constitution that allows courts to consider changes in social, economic, and political forces.

natural law †   A term referring to the concept that there exists, independent of manmade law, a law laid down (depending upon one's beliefs) by God or by nature, which human society must observe in order to be happy and at peace.

natural right †   A right existing under natural law, independent of manmade law.

necessary and proper clause †   Article I of the Constitution grants to Congress the power to make all laws "necessary and proper" for carrying out its constitutional responsibilities. The Supreme Court has long interpreted this provision to mean that Congress has the right not only to enact laws that are absolutely indispensable, but any laws that are reasonably related to effectuating the powers expressly granted to it by the Constitution.

original intent †   A term applied to the view of some scholars and jurists that judicial interpretation of the Constitution should be based on the words of the Constitution itself and the framers' "original intent," not on a contemporary understanding of the Constitution in the context of current realities. Adherents of this doctrine are sometimes referred to as *strict constructionists*.

original jurisdiction † The jurisdiction of a trial court, as distinguished from the jurisdiction of an appellate court.

origination clause Article I, § 7, clause 1, of the United States Constitution, which requires all revenue-raising bills to originate in the House of Representatives.

pardon † An act of grace by the chief executive of the government, ... relieving a person of the legal consequences of a crime of which he or she has been convicted. A pardon erases the conviction.

parens patriae † [Latin for] "the parent of the country."

pendent jurisdiction † The rule that, even though there is no diversity of citizenship, a federal court has the right to exercise jurisdiction over a state matter if it arises out of the same transaction as a matter already before the federal court.

plain meaning rule † The rule that in interpreting a statute whose meaning is unclear, the courts will look to the "plain meaning" of its language to determine legislative intent. The plain meaning rule is in opposition to the majority view of statutory interpretation, which takes legislative history into account.

plenary † Full; complete.

pocket veto † The veto of a congressional bill by the president by retaining it until Congress is no longer in session, neither signing nor vetoing it. The effect of such inaction is to nullify the legislation without affirmatively vetoing it. The pocket veto is also available to governors under some state constitutions.

police power † 1. The power of government to make and enforce laws and regulations necessary to maintain and enhance the public welfare and to prevent individuals from violating the rights of others. 2. The sovereignty of each of the states of the United States that is not surrendered to the federal government under the Constitution.

political question † A nonjudicial issue. The political question doctrine states that, under the Constitution, certain questions belong to the nonjudicial branches of the federal government to resolve.

prayer † Portion of a bill in equity or a petition that asks for equitable relief and specifies the relief sought.

preemption † The doctrine that once Congress has enacted legislation in a given field, a state may not enact a law inconsistent with the federal statute. ... A similar doctrine also governs the relationship between the state government and local government.

preemption doctrine Doctrine that state laws that interfere with federal laws are invalid pursuant to the supremacy clause.

pretext principle A law that is enacted by Congress supposedly under one of its enumerated powers, when the law's true purpose is to regulate a subject belonging to the states, is invalid. Today, the affectation doctrine has made the pretext principle of little significance.

primacy An approach to constitutional interpretation that requires state judges to apply their state's constitution before turning to the federal Constitution.

pseudonym A fictitious name. A plaintiff may sometimes be permitted to file a case using a fictitious name, if the plaintiff has a legitimate interest in protecting his or her privacy, such as when the facts of the case are embarrassing or the plaintiff's life may be threatened.

public rights doctrine Rule providing that if a claim is public in nature and not private, Congress may delegate its adjudication to a non-Article III tribunal.

quasi-judicial † A term applied to the adjudicatory functions of an administrative agency, i.e., taking evidence and making findings of fact and findings of law.

quasi-legislative † A term applied to the legislative functions of an administrative agency, [such as] rulemaking.

remand [†] n. The return of a case by an appellate court to the trial court for further proceedings, for a new trial, or for entry of judgment in accordance with an order of the appellate court. v. To return or send back.

removal of case [†] [T]he transfer of a case from a state court to a federal court.

reprieve [†] The postponement of the carrying out of a sentence. A reprieve is not a commutation of sentence; it is merely a delay.

rule of four [†] An internal rule of the Supreme Court, which provides that a case will be reviewed by the Court if four justices wish it to be reviewed.

selective incorporation doctrine Under the Due Process Clause of the Fourteenth Amendment, those rights in the federal Bill of Rights that are fundamental and necessary to an ordered liberty are applied against the states. Other incorporation theories exist.

self-executing [†] Self-acting; going into effect without need of further action.

severability rule A rule of interpretation that allows a court to remove unconstitutional portions from a law and leave the remainder intact.

Shays' Rebellion Daniel Shays, a veteran of the American Revolutionary War, and a group of fellow farmers rebelled in protest of economic conditions. This incident was cited by many as justification for abandoning the Articles of Confederation, the theory being that a stronger national government could provide better economic conditions and that a national military would be most effective in defeating rebellions.

sovereign immunity [†] The principle that the government—specifically, the United States or any state of the United States—is immune from suit except when it consents to be sued.

special master [†] A person appointed by the court to assist with certain judicial functions in a specific case.

standing The legal capacity to bring and to maintain a lawsuit. A person is without standing to sue unless some interest of his or hers has been adversely affected or unless he or she has been injured by the defendant. The term "standing to sue" is often shortened simply to "standing."

stare decisis [†] [Latin for] "standing by the decision." Stare decisis is the doctrine that judicial decisions stand as precedents for cases arising in the future. It is a fundamental policy of our law that, except in unusual circumstances, a court's determination on a point of law will be followed by courts of the same or lower rank in later cases presenting the same legal issue, even though different parties are involved and many years have elapsed.

statute [†] A law enacted by a legislature; an act.

sub judice [†] Before the court for consideration and determination.

supremacy clause [†] The provision in Article VI of the Constitution that "this Constitution and the laws of the United States ... shall be the supreme law of the land, and the judges in every state shall be bound thereby."

use immunity [†] A guaranty given a person that if he or she testifies against others, his or her testimony will not be used against him or her if he or she is prosecuted for ... involvement in the crime.

voluntary cessation of illegal acts An exception to the mootness doctrine, which provides that if an alleged harm has been ceased in order to avoid review, and there is a reasonable likelihood that the harm will reoccur or be recommenced, then the case may be heard.

***Younger* doctrine** The doctrine, drawn from *Younger v. Harris*, that federal courts will abstain in most cases from interfering with state court proceedings, even if federal constitutional issues are present. Except in extreme cases, federal review of federal constitutional issues must wait until appeal or habeas corpus review.

INDEX

Note: Page numbers containing an "n" designation refer to notes.

Chicago & Southern Air Lines v. Waterman Steamship Corp., 165, 183
Chisholm v. Georgia, 66, 171, 226
Cipollone v. Liggett Group, Inc., 320, 349
Circuit courts. *See* United States Courts of Appeals
Citation, 369
Citizen, 239
Civil law, 44, 68
    congressional immunity and, 194
    discovery, 274
    federal court abstention, 170
    jury trial, 52n8
Civil rights, 16, 27, 28, 29, 44
    appeals, 132
    congressional enforcement of, 229
    defendants, 28
    judicial protection of, 87, 141
    overcoming, 255
    precedent and, 82
    source of, 342–43, 347
    state constitutions and, 339–40, 342–47
    treaty power and, 262
Civil Rights Acts, 25
Civil Rights Amendments, 229
Civil rights laws, 70, 173, 366
Civil service system, 250, 287
Civil War, 25, 212
Civil War Amendments, 37, 173, 229
Claiborne, Harry, 224
Claims, related, 126
Claims Court, 58, 63, 143
Class actions, 147
Classifications, suspect, 255
Clear and manifest intent, 320
Cleveland, Grover, 240
Clinton, William, 277
Codes, 188, 189
Codification, 188–89
Cohens v. Virginia, 162, 168
Coleman v. Miller, 159, 163
Collateral consequences, 149
Collective bargaining, 203
Colorado River Water Conservation District v. United States, 168, 184
Comity, 170, 176, 177, 336–37
Commerce

foreign, 213, 214
interstate. *See* Interstate commerce
intrastate, 26, 43, 201, 211
nationalization of, 42
state and federal powers re, 3
states as participants, 328–30
Commerce clause, 37, 200–11
    as civil rights mechanism, 229
    dormant, 41, 320–30
    Indian tribes, 228
    purpose of, 322
    regulation of states under, 331, 334
    scope of, 40, 297–300
Committees, 188, 215
Commodity Futures Exchange Commission, 302
Commodity Futures Trading Commission v. Schor, 301, 302, 314
Common law, 1, 79, 187, 254, 273
Common law courts, 177
Commonwealth v. Edmunds, 341, 344, 345–46
Commonwealth v. Ludwig, 343, 351
Commonwealth v. Sell, 341
Commonwealth v. Triplett, 342, 347, 351
Commonwealths, 227, 228
Commutation, 251–52
Compacts, 228, 261, 335–36
Compelling interest, 255, 326
Compensation, 157, 227
Complete Auto Transit v. Brady, 326
Comptroller of the Currency, 153, 156
Computer-assisted legal research (CALR), 380, 382–83
Concurrent jurisdiction, 126, 128, 177, 199, 366
Concurrent resolutions, 188
Concurring opinions, 39
Confederation Congress, 3
Confidentiality, 273–75
Confirmation process. *See* Nomination and confirmation process
Conflicts of interest, 192
Congress, 10

adjournment, 190
adjudicative powers, transfer of, 301
administrative agencies and, 286–87, 288–89, 297–300, 308–12
aides, 198
civil rights and, 229
commerce powers, 200–11
confirmation process. *See* Nomination and confirmation process
constitutional amendment initiation by, 20–21, 224–26
court creation by, 55, 56, 140, 227
defense and military powers, 338
emergency powers, 214–15
enforcement legislation, 25, 173, 229
executive agreements and, 264–65
federal officials' removal, 287–95
federal property and, 227
fiscal powers, 212–13, 247, 273
foreign affairs powers, 213–14
habeas corpus suspension, 255
impeachment powers, 217–24
internal rules, 189
investigatory powers, 215–16
judiciary and, 22, 227
jurisdiction, control over, 66, 120, 140–42, 153
membership, 190–99. *See also* Congress members
military and, 213–14
necessary and proper powers, 232
powers of, 10, 12, 36, 42, 199, 229, 231–32
presidential power limits by, 241, 266
role of, 48–49
structure and organization, 189–90
taxation power, 212
territorial powers, 227–28
treaty approval, 263
vacancies in, 198–99
war powers, 165, 168, 213–14